Industrial Relations & Conflict Management

Volume 3

D1739403

Series Editors
Martin Euwema, Faculty of Psychology and Educational Sciences,
University of Leuven, Leuven, Belgium
Lourdes Munduate, Faculty of Psychology, University of Seville, Seville, Spain

Disseminating cutting edge theories and empirical research in the field of industrial relations and conflict management, from an interdisciplinary approach, and firmly based in theories on human behaviour in relation to work and organizations. Formally the series will publish monographs and contributed or edited volumes from leading psychology scholars. Specifically, the series integrates theories and research from industrial relations (sociology, business, law and psychology), with those on conflict management, mediation and more generally well-being and productive behaviour in the workplace. Volumes in this series respond to the demands of policymakers and the public, remaining relevant and applicable for science, industry and society. Delivering relevant research and conclusions from local, regional, national and international perspectives. The aim of the series is to contribute to cooperative and constructive relations in organizations at three levels: organizational level, team level and interpersonal level. The series will contribute to the existing academic research and literature by providing an advanced publication platform for improving the science of understanding industrial relations and conflict management. Publishing volumes which deliver valuable contributions from the range of developing perspectives on this subject.

More information about this series at http://www.springer.com/series/13458

Katalien Bollen • Martin Euwema
Lourdes Munduate
Editors

Advancing Workplace Mediation Through Integration of Theory and Practice

 Springer

Editors
Katalien Bollen
Department of Educational Research
    and Development
Maastricht University
Maastricht, The Netherlands

Martin Euwema
Department of Psychology
University of Leuven
Leuven, Belgium

Lourdes Munduate
Faculty of Psychology
University of Seville
Seville, Spain

ISSN 2199-4544   ISSN 2199-4552   (electronic)
Industrial Relations & Conflict Management
ISBN 978-3-319-82677-6   ISBN 978-3-319-42842-0   (eBook)
DOI 10.1007/978-3-319-42842-0

Printed on acid-free paper

This Springer imprint is published by Springer Nature
The registered company is Springer International Publishing AG Switzerland

Preface

In 2009, the United Nations expanded its services in managing workplace conflict by creating an expanded and geographically dispersed Office of Ombudsman and Mediation Services (UNOMS). Early on, at an occasion where the newly appointed regional ombudsmen were gathered, UN Secretary-General Ban Ki-Moon told us that "just as the United Nations addresses conflicts around the world, so must we also pay close attention to resolving and managing conflicts within the Organization." Shortly after, I arrived in Nairobi as part of the first cohort of regional ombudsmen embedded in seven different UN duty stations around the world.[1] The regional ombudsman role was designed to bring informal conflict resolution closer to UN operations outside of headquarters in New York. Since then, the role has evolved to not only provide direct conflict resolution services to staff but also to help build the competence of staff members to productively manage conflict.

Initially, the primary focus of the expanded UNOMS office was to offer mediation as a complement to the formal system of justice within the UN. From the beginning of my tenure in Nairobi, promoting mediation as a viable alternative to the formal challenge of administrative decisions by staff members has been an important part of my practice. Efforts to introduce mediation into the UN culture of dispute resolution, however, gained ground slowly.

With the direction of UNOMS leadership in New York, I, and the other UNOMS staff, began to explore new ways of promoting mediation by expanding along a fuller spectrum of informal conflict resolution services. Eventually, we added a focus on training designed not only to help participants develop the skills necessary to productively manage conflict but also to provide a nonthreatening forum for them to assess the degree of comfort they felt with us as conflict resolution professionals. As a result, I developed a training component to my practice designed to proactively help staff improve working relationships. Through this process, I discovered that the common denominator of aspects of my practice involves either acting as a bridge

---

[1] In addition to the UNOMS office in New York where the UN ombudsman is based, the seven United Nations duty stations that have a regional ombudsman are Santiago, Geneva, Vienna, Goma, Entebbe, Nairobi, and Bangkok.

between disparate perspectives or helping staff construct their own bridges between disparate perspectives. This bridge building not only resolves workplace conflicts and improves working relationships, but it also has begun to illustrate the connections that the secretary-general had referred to: the link between the UN's mandate and the way that we engage internally with one another as UN staff members.

My practice in this context provides an ever-constant reminder of the challenges that all human beings face in managing conflict in a positive and productive way. Being part of a peacemaking and peace-building institution does not immunize one to the corrosive effects of poorly managed conflict. The narrowing of perspectives during conflict, the activation of neural networks driven by fear and anger, and the sense of vulnerability invoked by uncertainty all exist within the UN workplace as well. In fact, the diversity of viewpoints, cultures, and backgrounds may also serve to amplify the misunderstandings often caused by these other factors. The process of making the implicit explicit, the shifting of frames, and the deepening of one's understanding of another's interests and narratives serve both micro- and macro-endeavors. It helps us engage more productively with the colleague down the hall or to help address global challenges.

The creation of the seven UNOMS regional offices and the establishment of a mediation division within UNOMS brought together a cadre of dispute resolution professionals that helped catalyze this insight. The rich interactive dynamics that result from such a critical mass of talent has sparked the group's learning, professional development, and innovation as part of the UN's efforts at workplace conflict resolution and beyond. These insights from our practice and interaction have led me to the following conclusion: as institutions and the relationships contained within them grow more complex, the systems designed to productively manage conflict must keep pace. The application of the knowledge gleaned from the scholarship and research involving workplace conflict, such as the ones presented in this book, becomes critical to keeping abreast with the rapid changes and ever-growing complexity of workplace relationships. We must increase the efficacy of workplace mediation by furthering new and more effective methods to leverage the tension inherent in productive conflict; to make the places where we work more innovative and collaborative through better dialogue; to deepen our understanding of the narratives, needs, and interests of our colleagues; to foster environments more robust in their collective decision-making; and to create a workplace that is not only more humane but, ultimately, more productive. When building bridges over increasingly wider differences, new bridge-building techniques become invaluable.

Regional Ombudsman, United Nations Ombudsman   Nicholas Theotocatos
and Mediation Services, Nairobi, Kenya

Contents

Chapter 1
Promoting Effective Workplace Mediation

Katalien Bollen, Martin Euwema, and Lourdes Munduate

Introduction

"Peace is not the absence of conflict but the ability to cope with it." – Dorothy Thompson

Since 1 year, Emma is manager at a pharmaceutical company with a team of ten analysts. Pedro is senior analyst, working more than 8 years in this team. He had hoped for Emma's position. During the past year, the relation between Pedro and Emma has become highly conflictive. Pedro is excellent in his work and in complex cases Emma needs his skills and specific professional knowledge. However, Pedro seems to give her the cold shoulder. He ignores her regularly and challenges her leadership over the team. What to do in order to solve this situation? Emma tried already several times to talk this over with Pedro, however this always ended in a severe discussion … Can she have Pedro replaced or fired? Are other team members siding with him? Can mediation be a way to find a solution? And if so, who could be the mediator and what approach and techniques should the mediator use best to help Emma and Pedro in finding an acceptable solution for their conflict?

K. Bollen (✉)
Department of Educational Research and Development, Maastricht University, Maastricht, The Netherlands
e-mail: k.bollen@maastrichtuniversity.nl

M. Euwema
Department of Psychology, University of Leuven, Leuven, Belgium
e-mail: martin.euwema@kuleuven.be

L. Munduate
Faculty of Psychology, University of Seville, Seville, Spain
e-mail: munduate@us.es

© Springer International Publishing Switzerland 2016
K. Bollen et al. (eds.), *Advancing Workplace Mediation Through Integration of Theory and Practice*, Industrial Relations & Conflict Management 3,
DOI 10.1007/978-3-319-42842-0_1

Conflict is part of organizational life at all levels. Between employees, teams, organizational units or divisions, tensions can arise. These conflicts occur both in lateral and hierarchical relations, from top team, till shop floor. Conflicts occur within the organization, as well as with suppliers, clients, governments and other stakeholders. Since conflicts often have destructive effects on both the organization and the people involved (De Dreu 2008; Giebels and Janssen 2005), the main challenge is to manage these conflicts in a constructive way (De Dreu and Van de Vliert 1997). Conflict management therefore is a core element of organizational practices, and particularly leaders and managers spend a large amount of time on the prevention of, and intervention in conflicts of all kind.

The way conflicts are prevented and managed reflects key elements of the organizational culture, referred to as the organizational conflict culture (Gelfand et al. 2012). Gelfand et al. (2012) distinguish collaborative, dominating, and avoidant conflict cultures. Their study shows that collaborative conflict cultures contribute to healthier, more productive and more innovative organizations. In such cultures, conflicts are recognized as inevitable and potentially constructive, and integrative problem solving is stimulated. The creative potential of these conflicts is optimally used, while the destructive effects of conflict are prevented (Katz and Flynn 2013; Raines 2012; Tjosvold 1991, 2008). Such cultures also offer a fertile soil for third party support in conflict, including mediation. Mediation is used in different types of conflicts: within the organization in both lateral and hierarchical relations, but also in conflicts with suppliers, clients, governments and other stakeholders. Consequently, workplace mediators may act in highly escalated collective confrontations between management and workers, but also in daily conflicts between two employees like Emma and Pedro. This book focuses on mediations in interpersonal conflicts between employees in the organization, often referred to as workplace mediation.

Workplace mediation is a process in which a third party facilitates constructive communication among disputants including decision-making, problem-solving and negotiation, in order to reach a mutually acceptable agreement (Goldman et al. 2008; Moore 2014). In this process, the mediator acts as a guardian of the process, while refraining from an evaluation of the case or directing parties to a particular settlement (Kressel 2014; Wall et al. 2001). The mediator's role is to help disputants to better understand each other's concerns and interests. In the mediation literature, there is an ongoing debate on the different types of mediation, especially to what extent mediators should also evaluate openly the case, give their opinions, or suggest solutions (Vindelov 2007). This is particularly true for workplace conflicts in which parties often have different hierarchical positions, related power and rights. Central questions in this respect are: Given the disbalance in power, can mediation be a fair procedure in these conflicts? Should the mediator strive for a power balance? And if so, how should the mediator do this? (Bollen 2014; Bollen and Euwema 2015).

Mediation as a form of Alternative Dispute Resolution (ADR) is increasingly used to solve different types of labor conflict in a non-judicial way (Kressel 2006). An important reason being the prevention of costly, lengthy and unsatisfying legal procedures (DePalo et al. 2011). Another important reason to use mediation is that it can limit or buffer the negative consequences of labor conflict in terms of wellbeing and productivity losses (Giebels and Janssen 2005). Although we mostly use the term workplace mediation in this book, one might find synonyms such as mediation in organizational conflict or labor mediation. Essentially, this all refers to mediation in conflicts within a work context between individual parties or teams.

In this volume, we focus on mediation in interpersonal conflicts between employees who occupy equal or different hierarchical positions. Often, mediations focus on two parties involved in the conflict. However, most people work in teams or small groups, and therefore both individuals and teams are impacted by conflict. Workplace mediation has to take into account this organizational setting. A related key question is: to what extent is the conflict taking place between two individuals, or are also other colleagues involved? Such team conflicts have specific dynamics compared to conflicts between two individuals, and therefore also ask for different ways of mediation (Walton 1969). In this handbook, we primarily focus on interpersonal conflicts, including hierarchical conflicts, while some of the contributions will address the team level as well. Collective labor conflicts, such as strikes organized by unions, are not addressed. Mediation in these conflicts is usually embedded in a broader institutional frame of social dialogue and contains other processes and structural features which receive separate attention (Euwema et al. 2015).

Mediation as a way to deal with conflicts constructively is an essential element in setting up a conflict management system in organizations or an organizational dispute system. Implementing mediation can help organizations to create effective and efficient procedures to deal with conflicts in a positive way that contributes to a healthy work climate (Bollen and Euwema 2015; Boxall and Macky 2014; De Dreu 2008; De Dreu and Weingart 2003; Dijkstra 2006; Elgoibar et al. 2016; European Commission 2002, 2004; Giebels and Janssen 2005). At the same time, mediation cannot be seen as panacea to all workplace conflicts between employees. There will be situations in which mediation is less suited, or a judicial procedure is the only option. For example, in case of workplace bullying or sexual harassment, mediation may not be in the interest of the victim, nor in the interest of organizational justice (Jenkins 2011; Olsen 2012). Therefore, workplace mediation should be part of a broader conflict management system in which conditions are stipulated for which mediation may work best or may be most effective. The recognition of this idea brought a surge in both researchers' and practitioners' interest to ponder on the question which mediator strategies should be used in different situations to be most effective (Bollen and Euwema 2013b; Coleman et al. 2014; Wall and Dunne 2012) and this calls for a contingency model to workplace mediation, as there is no one best approach, tactic or style to mediate workplace conflicts. With this handbook we aim to contribute to such a contingency approach. This in both a descriptive and prescriptive way: descriptive, to better understand differences in the use of workplace mediation and the conditions for its effectiveness; prescriptive, to offer decision rules for selecting mediation or other interventions in case of a conflict and more specific to offer rules to select specific mediation strategies and tactics.

The 3-R Model of Workplace Mediation: Regulations, Roles and Relations

Initial research on workplace mediation focused primarily on the question of its usefulness and effectiveness and which styles and tactics mediators should use to be successful (Bollen and Euwema 2013b; Kressel 2007; Mareschal 2005; Wall and Dunne 2012). These studies were searching for general rules for and applications of mediation. Soon however, it became clear that the context largely determines both the use of workplace mediation and its usefulness. Therefore, attention has shifted to the question which mediator strategies and tactics are most appropriate and effective given different specific mediation situations, and organizational circumstances (Bollen 2014; Bollen et al. 2014; Bollen and Euwema 2015; Coleman et al. 2014). Academics and practitioners realize that there is no one best approach, tactic or style to mediate, it all depends on the context of the conflict. This includes national and organizational culture, disputant characteristics, conflict characteristics, as well as mediator characteristics.

Therefore, it is essential to come to models that pay attention to the context that determines the roles of the different actors involved in mediation as well as their behavior since this will shape the mediation process. In response to this, we developed a heuristic model that can help mediators to get insight in the characteristics of the environment that affects the mediation process and that may help them in choosing the adequate mediation tactics. Inspired by Budd and Colvin's (2008) 'geometry of disputes resolution procedures', we developed the 3-R model of workplace mediation. This model refers to three different dimensions that are important to consider when deciding for mediation: Regulations, Roles and Relations. Together, these three dimensions determine the mediation features and the mediation outcomes at different levels (Fig. 1.1). The dimensions together create a three-dimensional pyramid that consists of different layers going from the broader context at the bottom, to specific tactics at the top.

At the bottom of the pyramid, we find more general characteristics of the context that determine the availability and use of mediation for a specific workplace conflict: (a) the wider context of conflict management and conflict in the sector and society, (b) the organizational conflict culture and (c) the availability of different types of third parties.

The top of the pyramid represents the actual mediation, including (d) mediation styles, (e) strategies and (f) tactics that result in a specific mediation outcome. *Mediation styles* refer to the different approaches in mediation -sometimes even 'schools' or ideologies- varying from evaluative and directive styles (Della Noce 2009), to transformative or narrative mediation (Folger 1996). The *mediator strategy* refers to a broad plan of action that may help to decide which specific or concrete actions are needed to achieve some objectives in particular conflict situations. As such, it refers to the mediator's general way of working in the mediation itself. An example could be the choice to rely solely on face-to-face meetings to mediate and/or to consider the integration of online tools in the mediation process. Evidently

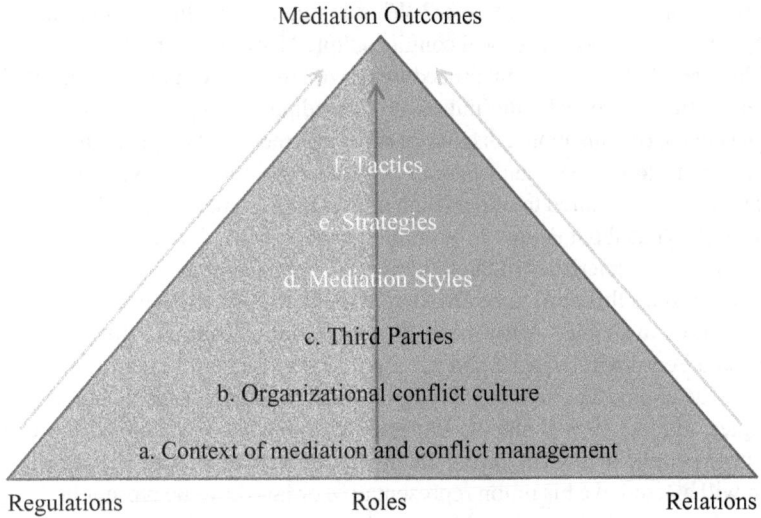

Fig. 1.1 The 3-R model of workplace mediation

the mediator strategy is highly influenced by the mediation style the mediator adheres to. *Mediation tactics*, refer to the most detailed level and thus the actual mediator behavior: the specific communication techniques and instruments used by the mediator in the pursuit of certain objectives. The tactics used are the behavioral specifics of the mediator strategy chosen by the mediator.

We explore the meaning and relevance of these three dimensions while referring to the case of Emma and Pedro.

Regulations

Emma and Pedro consider mediation. Recently, a new law has passed in the parliament of their country which makes mediation in escalated workplace conflicts mandatory before taking cases to court. Pedro is aware of the fact that under the new law, the company can no longer just fire him. Not before a serious attempt for mediation has been made. He also realizes that his legal position is strong, as he has an excellent and long performance record. Like Pedro, Emma is aware of the implications of the new law. She has been in contact with HR to let them know that she considers mediation, and they have sent her names of several external mediators. She has a preference for an experienced female mediator and proposes this to Pedro. Pedro rejects the suggested mediator.

The question whether mediation is an option for Emma and Pedro depends first of all on current regulations and procedures. In what *country* are Emma and Pedro working? Are there certain rules or laws regarding the use of workplace mediation or conflict management in this country? Is it legally possible for Emma to fire Pedro in case of conflict, and if so, at what costs? What regulations within *the organization* are there, reflecting the organizational conflict culture? How are workplace conflicts managed in general: through a legal procedure or with the help of union representatives or do parties themselves take the initiative? Is mediation integrated as a way to solve conflicts in the organizational dispute system? Are there certain procedures for Emma or Pedro to follow given their ongoing workplace conflict? In case Emma considers mediation, is she required to inform higher level management or can she hire a mediator herself? What about Pedro? Is he entitled to approach a third party? The next question refers to characteristics of the third party: Could this be an internal mediator (or a manager) or does this need to be an external mediator? Or are both internal and external mediators available? Answers to these questions determine the likelihood that Emma and Pedro will consider and use mediation to find a solution for their conflict.

Once the choice has been made to opt for mediation, the specific mediator styles, strategies and tactics will also be impacted by rules and regulations. For example: Can other people be present during the mediation, and if so, who? In some contexts, Pedro will ask to have his union representative or lawyer to be present in the mediation, and this might be acceptable. In other situations, this may not be possible. Another question relates to the payment of the mediation: Who will need to pay for the mediation? In some countries, the mediator is paid by the company, in other countries by the government, the union or an insurance company. Regulations on availability, time and payment impact the way the mediator acts in the mediation process. So, it might be that Emma and Pedro have to wait three months to meet with their external mediator, and that the mediator gets paid a standard fee for three sessions of one or two hours total.

In sum, the dimension *Regulations* refers to different regulatory frameworks towards workplace conflict at a societal, sectoral and organizational level. On a societal and sectoral level, this includes labor laws, as well as negotiated agreements on conflict management between social partners. On an organizational level, this refers to specific human resources policies which define conflict management including regulations for mediation, and for example the conditions under which external or internal mediators can be used. Currently, more and more organizations include mediation clauses in their collective and/or individual labor contracts to set the stage for mediation. These types of arrangements give rise to questions on how to deal with the voluntary character of mediation and which legal steps can be taken when mediation fails. Also, how the payment of the mediation is arranged, impacts the use and form of mediation. In this book, several chapters address how regulations on these different levels affect the implementation and growth of mediation (e.g., Deakin; Jordaan and De Wulf; Vilches Such, Verbeke and Menkel-Meadow).

Roles

Mediation might be an option for Emma and Pedro to find a way out of their conflict. The choice will depend on available roles and the expectations related to those roles. Emma as manager might believe she has to solve the conflict herself. She perceives bringing in a third party, and specially a mediator, as a proof of her failure as a manager or leader. Pedro might see the involvement of a mediator as a sign of weak leadership by Emma, and may for that reason promote the use of a mediator.

Emma's manager has suggested intervening himself. In fact, this manager has suggested to Emma firing Pedro. Emma is hesitant and contacts the HR officer who also offers to act as mediator. Emma is not convinced about the qualities of the HR officer as mediator, however proposes this to Pedro. Pedro responds furious, as he sees the HR officer as not impartial at all, always servicing Emma. Immediately Pedro contacts his union representative, and makes an appointment with the internal ombudsman to file a complaint on Emma's behavior. In the meantime, Emma starts to suffer also physically from the conflict: she is facing high blood pressure and visits her physician who advises her to take a few days sick leave. When getting to know the context of the conflict, the physician recommends the use of an external mediator to solve the situation as soon as possible.

The dimension *Roles* refers to the role expectations of the conflicting parties as well as to the roles of all persons potentially involved as third parties in the conflict. Conflicting parties have perceptions and expectations of their own and each other's roles, and the assistance of a mediator might not fit those role expectations: '*We should be able to manage this ourselves*' is often the standard, and also part of the organizational culture '*Professionals are able to solve their own conflict*'. Higher management might reinforce that norm, thereby making it difficult to bring in third parties in general and external third parties specifically.

The second element of this role dimension, explores all possible others who might intervene as third party in the conflict, or refer to mediation. In many organizations, managers or direct supervisors are expected to act as third party in conflict (Römer et al. 2012). This aligns with the idea that first line management should be able to handle daily conflict, with consultation of HR. However, when conflict escalates, we see that people occupying different types of functions are involved in conflict management as well as workplace mediation: human resource managers, legal counselors, shop stewards, union representatives, complaint officers, ombudsmen, as well as health and safety staff. In a study exploring the conflict management system in a bank with 15,000 employees in the Netherlands, 14 different functional roles, and 400 individual actors in these roles were identified as persons who could serve as a third party in workplace conflicts, line managers not included (Euwema 2008). Typical roles were health and safety officers, HRM, prevention officers and internal mediators. This is in line with the general observation that in most organizations, it is often not clear who will play what role in the process of managing conflict or more specifically mediation. Accordingly, both access and referral to mediation in workplace conflict is often poorly described, with an exception for specific categories of conflicts, such as discrimination or bullying (Deakin, this volume; Euwema 2008). This leaves many organizations confronted with the following questions: (a) Is there a conflict management protocol in case of a workplace conflict, or in case of an absence that is due to a conflict? (b) When to refer parties to mediation? (c) Who to turn to in case of conflict? Who to turn to in case of mediation? Are external or internal mediators used? Can parties freely choose a mediator? What is the role of colleagues who may assist disputants voluntarily? (d) What is the role of management in motivating employees to participate in mediation? Should managers be present during the mediation?

In this book these questions will be addressed throughout different chapters (Jones; Brinkert; Butts). While some chapters focus explicitly on mediation in the broader context of conflict management or organizational dispute systems, other chapters address the role of the manager as mediator and its relation to other parties.

Relations

Emma and Pedro have been working together now for 1 year and the conflict has put their relation under high pressure. Also, the relations in the team are impacted by their constant confrontations and irritations. Both are tired of each other, and don't see any future together. The team is divided; most team members have sided with either Emma or Pedro.

Emma is the manager of the team. As such, she has formal power and authority over Pedro. She considers using this. In her culture it is seen as weak leadership if she would not act strongly, and use her authority to correct Pedro or to remove him from the team, especially when he challenges her position.

Pedro derives power from his unique position as expert and his technical knowledge. He is convinced of the fact that he is needed for the good working of the company and believes that the organization recognizes the great value he adds. A manager like Emma in contrast, is easily replaceable.

In the company there are only a few female leaders, and the culture is rather macho. Talking about personal emotions and relations is something to do in a bar after work. Pedro has heard about mediation and believes this is something for softies, weak people. If it would come to mediation, the third party should be very knowledgeable and tell Emma what to do.

The last dimension refers to *Relations* and describes the characteristics of the relation between the conflicting parties, and their relation with the mediator. What are the formal and informal power structures that influence parties' interaction and as such the mediation process? What are the specific needs of the parties in relation to the conflict? Is the relationship to be terminated or will parties continue working together or at least stay in the same organisation? All this determines if and what types of mediation are suitable, or that other types of third party interventions like conflict coaching are more appropriate. These issues are explicitly addressed in the chapters by Butts and by Jones.

An ongoing debate both in academic and practitioner literature, is the use of mediation in a relation characterized by structural power differences, such as employer and employee, or manager and subordinate (Bollen 2014; Bollen et al. 2010, 2012; Bollen and Euwema 2015; Wiseman and Poitras 2002). It is important to analyze the structural qualities of the relation such as the formal power structure between parties and the legal rights they derive from this. To what extent are parties interdependent and how is the power balance? At the same time, it is important to take stock of the psycho-social qualities of the relationship given that most labor relations are more than just instrumental. How do parties perceive each other? What is their attitude: cooperative or competitive? To what extent do they perceive justice? Both structural and interpersonal characteristics will determine what type of mediator, strategy and tactics are used best to come to a mutually acceptable and satisfying solution.

The 3-R model of workplace mediation helps to analyze mediation in its context. First, it helps to understand the extent to which mediation is used, for what conflicts and how the process of entering the mediation is organized and functioning. Secondly, the model offers a framework to understand the choice for certain mediation styles, strategies and tactics based on the interplay of regulations, roles and relations. Finally, the 3-R model offers a tool to understand and explain specific outcomes of mediation based on the interplay between regulations, roles and relations.

In the concluding chapter of this handbook, we further elaborate on the dynamics between Regulations, Roles and Relations that result in a certain use of mediation and particular outcomes of workplace mediations. The central notion of this book is that mediation approaches, strategies and tactics used by mediators, should fit in the geometry of the conflict and the broader landscape of the organization as well as the society in which they are taking place.

Structure and Content of This Handbook

The 3-R model of workplace mediation is used to structure the chapters of the handbook. We focus on four main themes: (I) the mediation process, (II) the context of workplace mediation, (III) mediation and other third party roles and (IV) new developments. We start with the mediation process. This is the top of the 3-R pyramid and refers to mediator styles, strategies and tactics. The second part explores the foundations of the pyramid, the context and organizational settings in which the mediation is shaped. The third part focuses on the landscape of all possible parties involved as potential third parties in workplace conflict, and the relation between management and the role as mediator. Finally, we bring in new developments that take already place in the mediation landscape. More specifically we explore the role of technology as an important extra player in mediation, and we take stock in the final chapter.

Part I: The Mediation Process

Chapter 2: Getting Beyond Win-Lose and Win-Win: A Situated Model of Adaptive Mediation

Coleman, Kügler, and Mazzaro present in this chapter a model of adaptive mediation to identify appropriate mediator strategies and tactics. This innovative model, soundly based in research, identifies four fundamental dimensions of workplace conflict. Explicit attention is paid to constraints stemming from the context (*Regulations*), the conflict intensity, as well as the cooperative versus competitive nature of the relationship (*Relations*). The combination of these characteristics requires qualitatively different types of mediation and drives the strategic choices for mediation outcomes and relatedly mediator strategies and tactics. This new model prescribes the mediator to read relevant changes in situations and to respond flexibly by using strategies and tactics that fit with the particular situation at hand. This research adds to our understanding of the main antecedents of different mediation strategies and tactics that influence the course of the mediation.

Chapter 3: Workplace Mediation: Searching for Underlying Motives and Interests

In this chapter Kals, Thiel and Freund argue that successful mediations are the result of a careful analysis of the underlying structure of the conflict. This deep structure is formed by unfulfilled motives, needs and wishes in which the experience of injustice plays a crucial role. The challenge for the mediator is to make sure that the subjective perspectives of all conflict partners are mutually understood, and to guide disputants to a solution that is regarded as fair by all conflict parties.

Chapter 4: A Psychological Toolbox for Mediators: From Theory and Research to Best Practices

Harnack makes a selection of most relevant psychological theories and translates these into tools for mediation. All tools are designed to support the mediator in his strive to make the issues more comprehensible to parties and to fit the disputants' cognitive states. In contrast to more general tools that focus on procedures and techniques that a mediator may use, these tools focus on the mental processes that underlie the way people perceive, frame and process information, and how they construct their own (conflict) reality. The tools help the mediator to recognize heuristics and cognitive biases that drift parties away from constructive conflict management.

Chapter 5: Workplace Mediation: Lessons from Negotiation Theory

In this chapter Höhne, Loschelder, Gutenbrunner and Majer bridge the gap between negotiation theory and workplace mediation. Mediation is often defined as assisting parties in their negotiations, and therefore new insights from negotiation theory are highly relevant for mediators. The authors review influential negotiation theories, models, and concepts, and illustrate how these can help to better understand the pitfalls of (mediating) workplace conflicts. Capitalizing on these insights may alter parties' willingness to concede, their ability to discover hidden resources as well as integrative potential, and add to their problem-solving behavior.

Part II: Context of Workplace Mediation

In this part, four chapters explore how the broader context of conflict management systems impact the use of mediation in workplace conflict, as well as the mandatory or voluntary character of mediation. This is illustrated by examples stemming from the USA, UK and South Africa.

Chapter 6: Mediation and Conflict Coaching in Organizational Dispute Systems

Jones focuses on how to build best organizational dispute resolution systems that integrate various ADR components, so that this system covers the breadth of organizational conflicts. Special attention is paid to the role of conflict coaching as a rapidly growing ADR process in organizational settings, its role in organizational dispute system design, and the potential integration with workplace mediation or arbitration. Jones shows the importance of conflict coaching, both as proactive measure, and as follow up of workplace mediation. Systems should be designed in such a way that disagreements are recognized and dealt with in an early stage so that they contribute to constructive and productive employment relations.

Chapter 7: HRM Practices and Mediation: Lessons Learnt from the UK

Deakin elaborates the use of workplace mediation in the UK and identifies a number of challenges for further development. As in many countries, the UK has been promoting workplace mediation, however the use of workplace mediation is relatively limited. Deakin argues this is due to tensions between the positioning of mediation in formal dispute resolution and strategic conflict management. Main challenges are (a) a lack of understanding and precision over what mediation is and how it can be used, (b) difficulties in achieving a cultural shift away from a reliance on formal methods, towards a more flexible and informal approach and (c) the changing role of line managers and the HR function and the difficult positioning of them in workplace mediation.

Chapter 8: Towards an Integrated Workplace Mediation System: Reflections on the South African Experience

In this chapter, Jordaan and De Wulf describe in short the dispute resolution system in South Africa and provide the reader with good practices from the Office of Mediation of the World Bank Group. They show that two systems to solve workplace-related conflicts – one formalized in legislation (a statutory system) and another driven by the private sector-, can co-exist and even augment one another. Jordaan and De Wulf discuss principles that should underpin the introduction of a workplace mediation system and how to overcome the limits of workplace mediation. In addition, they describe the use and interplay of internal and external mediators. Finally, they argue that the effectiveness of workplace mediation is highly increased when it is integrated in an organizational conflict resolution system and not merely applied on an ad hoc basis.

Chapter 9: Mandatory Workplace Mediation

Although many scholars claim that mediation should be a process in which parties are involved voluntarily, workplace mediation is in many countries also mandatory. In their contribution, Vilches, Verbeke and Menkel-Meadow consider the impact of the legal system on workplace mediation, the role of mandatory mediation and the position of mediation in providing access to justice.

Part III: Mediation and Other Third Party Roles in the Organization

In this section, three chapters address how mediation differs from other types of conflict management like conflict coaching and what particularly managers can do as third party to solve workplace conflicts.

Chapter 10: An Appreciative Approach to Conflict: Mediation and Conflict Coaching

Conflict coaching developed in direct relationship to mediation. In this chapter, Brinkert explores the relation between conflict coaching and mediation. Propositions, priority actions, and ongoing cautions are identified which are important when linking workplace mediation and conflict coaching. Values and practices from appreciative inquiry, and the narrative approach to communication are used to coordinate and integrate workplace mediation and conflict coaching.

Chapter 11: The Manager as Mediator: Attitude, Technique, and Process in Constructive Conflict Resolution in the Workplace

Managers often agree with the concept of constructive conflict management and are willing to put this into action, however remain mystified when it comes to how to put these things into practice. In this chapter, Butts shows how to encourage and support managers in the implementation of transformative conflict management. Using three sample cases, Butts sets out a cost analysis of different scenarios of conflict management. She shows that subtle differences in manager's choice of strategies of handling the conflict can have a profound effect on the parties as well as the workplace environment. A series of mediator efficient tools, interventions and roles are presented. Butts ends with the message that the implementation of mediation needs the buy-in of management, as well as from employees, trade unions and employee representatives.

Chapter 12: Conflict-Positive Organizations: Applying Mediation and Conflict Management Research

In this chapter, Tjosvold, Wan and Tang elaborate on how to promote cooperative and constructive relations at various levels: between managers and employees, as well as within and between teams, departments and organizations. The aim of this chapter is to help organizations prepare and empower members to mediate and manage their conflicts constructively even without outside intervention. In order to do this, employees need leadership that encourages them to voice their opinions and that invests in strengthening relationships between employees. Disputants can use cooperative conflict management knowledge so that they can discuss their conflict open mindedly and constructively.

Part IV: New Developments

Choosing the right mediation forum or tools to mediate workplace conflicts is one of the challenges for designers of conflict management systems and mediators. Next to the mediator, a fourth party is playing more and more a central role in the process, that is technology in all sorts of media and communications (Bollen et al. 2014;

Bollen and Euwema 2013a). E-mediation and forms of hybrid mediation are developing at high pace. Therefore, in this part we explore this domain.

Chapter 13: Looking Back to Leap Forward: The Potential for E-mediation at Work

Parlamis, Ebner and Mitchell provide an overview of the broad field of Online Dispute Resolution (ODR) in order to illustrate the context in which e-mediation has developed and grown. It also sets the stage for a more nuanced discussion of how e-mediation might contribute to dispute resolution mechanisms in the workplace. Providing the reader with an overview of the ODR field and provoking new and promising areas of expansion for e-mediation in general and the workplace specifically, are the primary aims of this chapter. Based on relevant research, practical suggestions are made for the application of e-mediation to online and on-ground workplace disputes.

Chapter 14: It Takes Three to Tango: The Geometry of Workplace Mediation

In the final chapter of this handbook, Munduate, Bollen and Euwema take stock of research and good practices in the field of workplace mediation and the innovative trends presented in this handbook. We argue that the 3-R model for workplace mediation offers a comprehensive framework to understand the use of mediation and helps mediators to choose appropriate and effective strategies as well as tactics given a specific context. This determines the geometry of workplace conflict, characterized by certain procedures, structures and culture. In short, the use and effectiveness of workplace mediation should always be understood in the context of regulations, roles and relations. The chapter concludes with suggestions for a research agenda to further develop workplace mediation.

Conclusion

With this book, we aspire to provide a synthesis from multiple disciplines and arenas in which workplace mediation has been addressed over the years. Therefore, we bring together the knowledge from both leading scholars worldwide (USA, Europe, Africa, Asia) stemming from different disciplines such as organizational behavior, psychology, management, and law, as well as highly experienced scholar-practitioners. They present a multitude of ideas on what they see as crucial to the way forward in meeting the challenges posed by current mediation research and practice.

By combining cutting-edge theory, real cases and practice, this handbook offers a unique source of knowledge. Scholars in the fields of mediation and conflict management are provided with theoretical frameworks that may enhance our knowledge about the application, process and effects of workplace mediation. Managers, employees, mediators and human resource professionals, find critical knowledge and practical tools to deal constructively with conflicts. This handbook also responds to the demands of policymakers to make workplace conflict and mediation more debatable, manageable and to make parties responsible for their conflict and its resolution.

References

Bollen, K., & Euwema, M. (2013a). The role of hierarchy in face-to-face and e-supported mediations: The use of an online intake to balance the influence of hierarchy. *Negotiation and Conflict Management Research, 6*(4), 305–319.

Bollen, K., & Euwema, M. (2013b). Workplace mediation: An underdeveloped research area. *Negotiation Journal, 29*(3), 329–353.

Bollen, K., & Euwema, M. (2015). Angry at your boss: Who cares? Anger recognition and mediation effectiveness. *European Journal of Work and Organizational Psychology, 24*(2), 256–266.

Bollen, K., Euwema, M., & Müller, P. (2010). Why are subordinates less satisfied with mediation? The role of uncertainty. *Negotiation Journal, 26*(4), 417–433.

Bollen, K., Ittner, H., & Euwema, M. (2012). Mediating hierarchical labor conflicts: Procedural justice makes a difference − For subordinates. *Group Decision and Negotiation, 21*(5), 621–636.

Bollen, K., Verbeke, A., & Euwema, M. (2014). Computers work for women: Gender differences in e-supported divorce mediation. *Computers in Human Behavior, 30*, 230–237.

Boxall, P., & Macky, K. (2014). High-involvement work processes, work intensification and employee well-being. *Work Employment & Society, 28*(6), 963–984.

Budd, J. W., & Colvin, A. J. S. (2008). Improved metrics for workplace dispute resolution procedures: Efficiency, equity, and voice. *Industrial Relations, 47*(3), 460–479.

Coleman, P. T., Kugler, K., Gozzi, C., Mazzaro, K., El Zokm, N., & Kressel, K. (2014). Putting the peaces together: Introducing a situated model of mediation. *International Journal of Conflict Management, 26*(2), 145–171.

De Dreu, C. K. W. (2008). The virtue and vice of workplace conflict: Food for (pessimistic) thought. *Journal of Organizational Behavior, 29*(1), 5–18.

De Dreu, C. K. W., & Van de Vliert, E. (Eds.). (1997). *Using conflict in organizations*. London: Sage.

De Dreu, C. K. W., & Weingart, L. R. (2003). Task versus relationship conflict, team performance, and team member satisfaction: A meta-analysis. *Journal of Applied Psychology, 88*(4), 741–749.

De Palo, G., Feasley, A., & Orecchini, F. (2011). Quantifying the cost of not using mediation – A data analysis. *Report to the European Parliament (Directorate-General for Internal Policies)* http://www.europarl.europa.eu/committees/en/studiesdownload.html?languageDocument=EN &file=40771). Brussels: European Parliament.

Della Noce, D. J. (2009). Evaluative mediation: In search for practice competences. *Conflict Resolution Quarterly, 27*(2), 193–214.

Dijkstra, M. T. M. (2006). *Workplace conflict and individual well-being*. Amsterdam: Kurt Lewin Institute.

Elgoibar, P., Munduate, L., & Euwema, M. C. (Eds.). (2016). *Building trust and constructive conflict management in organisations*. Dordrecht: Springer Verlag.

European Commission. (2002). *Green paper on alternative dispute resolution in civil and commercial law* (COM (2002) 196 final). Brussels: European Commission.

European Commission. (2004). *Proposal for a directive of the European parliament and of the council on certain aspects of mediation in civil and commercial matters* (COM(2004) 718 final). Brussels: European Commission.

Euwema, M. C. (2008). Conflict management in organisaties. *Forum voor Conflictmanagement, 1*, 28–31.

Euwema, M. C., Munduate, L., Elgoibar, P., Pender, E., & Garcia, A. B. (2015). *Promoting social dialogue in European organizations: Human resources management and constructive conflict management*. Dordrecht: Springer International Publishing.

Folger, J. P. (1996). Transformative mediation and third party intervention: Ten hallmarks of a transformative approach to practice. *Mediation Quarterly, 13*(4), 263–278.

Gelfand, M. J., Leslie, L. M., Keller, K., & De Dreu, C. (2012). Conflict cultures in organizations: How leaders shape conflict cultures and their organizational-level consequences. *Journal of Applied Psychology, 97*(6), 1131–1147.

Giebels, E., & Janssen, O. (2005). Conflict stress and reduced wellbeing at work: The buffering effect of third-party help. *European Journal of Work and Organizational Psychology, 14*(2), 137–155.

Goldman, B. M., Cropanzano, R., Stein, J., & Benson, L., III. (2008). The role of third parties/ mediation in managing conflict in organizations. In C. K. W. De Dreu & M. J. Gelfand (Eds.), *The psychology of conflict and conflict management in organizations* (pp. 291–319). New York: Lawrence Erlbaum.

Jenkins, M. (2011). Practice note: Is mediation suitable for complaints of workplace bullying? *Conflict Resolution Quarterly, 1*, 25–38.

Katz, N. H., & Flynn, L. T. (2013). Understanding conflict management systems and strategies in the workplace: A pilot study. *Conflict Resolution Quarterly, 30*(4), 393–410.

Kressel, K. (2006). Mediation revisited. In M. Deutsch, P. T. Coleman, & E. C. Marcus (Eds.), *The handbook of conflict resolution: Theory and practice* (2nd ed., pp. 726–756). San Francisco: Jossey-Bass.

Kressel, K. (2007). The strategic style in mediation. *Conflict Resolution Quarterly, 24*, 251–283.

Kressel, K. (2014). The mediation of conflict: Context, cognition and practice. In P. Coleman, M. Deutsch, & E. Marcus (Eds.), *The handbook of conflict resolution: Theory and practice* (3rd ed., pp. 817–848). San Francisco: Jossey-Bass.

Mareschal, P. M. (2005). What makes mediation work? Mediators' perspectives on resolving disputes. *Industrial Relations: A Journal of Economy and Society, 44*(3), 509–517.

Moore, C. W. (2014). *The mediation process: Practical strategies for resolving conflict* (4th ed.). San Franscisco: Jossey-Bass.

Olsen, H. (2012). *Mediation is not the way to deal cases of workplace bullying*. Accessed on workplaces against violence in employment website www.wave.org.nz.

Raines, S. S. (2012). *Conflict management for managers: Resolving workplace, client, and policy disputes*. Chichester: Wiley.

Römer, M., Rispens, S., Giebels, E., & Euwema, M. (2012). A helping hand? The moderating role of leaders' conflict management behavior on the conflict-stress relationship of employees. *Negotiation Journal, 28*(3), 253–277.

Tjosvold, D. (1991). *The conflict positive organization: Stimulate diversity and create unity*. Reading: Addison-Wesley.

Tjosvold, D. (2008). The conflict-positive organization: It depends upon us. *Journal of Organizational Behavior, 29*, 19–28.

Vindelov, V. (2007). *Reflexive mediation: With a sustainable perspective.* Kopenhagen: Djof Publishing.

Wall, J. A., & Dunne, T. C. (2012). Mediation research: A current review. *Negotiation Journal, 28*(2), 217–244.

Wall, J. A., Stark, J. B., & Standifer, R. L. (2001). Mediation: A current review and theory development. *The Journal of Conflict Resolution, 45*(3), 370–391.

Walton, R. E. (1969). *Interpersonal peacemaking: Confrontations and third party consultation.* Reading: Addison Wesley.

Wiseman, V., & Poitras, J. (2002). Mediation within a hierarchical structure: How can it be done successfully? *Conflict Resolution Quarterly, 20*(1), 51–65.

Part I
The Mediation Process

Chapter 2
Getting Beyond Win-Lose and Win-Win: A Situated Model of Adaptive Mediation

Peter T. Coleman, Katharina G. Kugler, and Kyong Mazzaro

The good news for mediators and the field of mediation is that today there are over 100 different intervention techniques and tactics to choose from when attempting to help shepherd disputants to "yes" (Wall and Dunne 2012). This bounty of approaches allows for a great deal of flexibility and artistry when mediating disputes over disparate issues in dissimilar settings with varied, idiosyncratic disputants. For that reason, some compare mediating with playing jazz music, as both mediators and jazz musicians need to improvise in the moment, responding flexibly to advance the process by drawing from a repertoire of tactics in a way that fits the idiosyncratic ensemble in a situation (Bellman 2006). This often entails employing tactics from both distributive, win-lose and integrative, win-win strategies as needed (Van De Vliert et al. 1995).

However, this eclecticism also presents a considerable challenge to the scientific advancement of mediation. As Wall and Dunne suggest in their 2012 review of mediation research: "…Faced with such a complex set of categories, scholars have not been able to grapple with the two fundamental questions for mediation: What are the major causes/antecedents of mediators' strategies? That is, what causes mediators to use the strategies they do? And what are the major impacts of the mediators' use of particular strategies?" (p. 227).

Consequently, most models of mediation practice today are largely removed from evidence-based research, with one of the most glaring gaps being our

---

The authors wish to thank Christianna Gozzi, Nora El Zohm, Kenneth Kressel, Karen LaRose, Deanna Kowal and Ljubica Chatman for their contributions to this research.

P.T. Coleman (✉) • K. Mazzaro
Morton Deutsch International Center for Cooperation and Conflict Resolution Teachers College, Columbia University, New York, NY, USA
e-mail: pc84@tc.columbia.edu

K.G. Kugler
Ludwig-Maximilians-Universitaet Muenchen, Munich, Germany

© Springer International Publishing Switzerland 2016
K. Bollen et al. (eds.), *Advancing Workplace Mediation Through Integration of Theory and Practice*, Industrial Relations & Conflict Management 3,
DOI 10.1007/978-3-319-42842-0_2

understanding of the main antecedents of different mediation strategies and tactics that ultimately influence the course of the mediation (Coleman 2011; Coleman et al. 2015; Pruitt and Kugler 2014; Wall and Dunne 2012). In other words, which different strategies should mediators use in different types of mediation situations to be most effective?

In this chapter we describe a project that aims to answer this question. Over the past several years, our research team at the *Morton Deutsch International Center for Cooperation and Conflict Resolution* at Columbia University has embarked on a program of research to identify and model the most fundamental aspects of mediation situations that drive different strategic choices in mediator behaviors and mediation outcomes. Here, we summarize the findings from our research to date, outline our current understanding of our situated model of adaptive mediation, and then discuss the next steps and implications of the model for practice and training in mediation. Ultimately, we hope to offer a theoretical framework for the field that advances research and can be used in a new era of adaptive, evidence-based mediation practice.

Mediation: A Method in Search of an Evidence-Based Model

The frequency and popularity of using mediation as a primary dispute resolution process has been increasing in a variety of institutional settings over the past three decades including schools, nonprofit organizations, businesses, communities and multinational organizations like the United Nations and the World Bank (Kressel 2014; Wall and Dunne 2012). This increase in the usage and status of mediation has put pressure on our field to more closely link its practice with evidence-based research and measureable outcome assessment (Kressel 2014; United Nations Report of the Secretary-General 2012).

However, a close examination of the current state of mediation research reveals a piecemeal and incoherent understanding of what constitutes "effective mediation" and how to achieve it (Coleman et al. 2015; Wall and Lynn 1993; Wall et al. 2001; Wall and Dunne 2012). Studies are typically focused either at the individual level of the mediator (e.g. mediator styles and preferences; see Beardsley et al. 2006; Charkoudian 2012; Kressel 2007; McDermott 2012; Poitras et al. 2015; Riskin 1996; Wall and Kressel 2012) and therefore decontextualized from the broader system of conflict management in which mediators operate, or at the macro level examining case comparisons (see Bercovitch and Lee 2003; Wissler 1995) or data on mediation trends (see Greig 2001; Moordian and Druckman 1999) and therefore removed from the role of mediator decisions and actions. This incoherence contributes to the increasing gap between science and practice in mediation (Coleman 2011; Honeyman et al. 2009; United Nations 2012), and results in a proliferation of approaches to mediation that are informed by the experience of their proponents but effectively divorced from evidence-based research.

Although the field of mediation has made great strides over the past few decades, it has much to gain from an approach to mediation that moves beyond descriptive models and frameworks of practice and employs the scientific method and evidence-based management (Pfeffer and Sutton 2006; Rousseau 2006) by systematically building on comprehensive empirical findings. Such approach can generate and refine a conceptual model of mediation that can predict when different approaches to mediation are likely to be more and less effective (Pruitt and Kugler 2014; Wall and Dunne 2012).

In response to this, in 2011 our team launched a multi-year science-practice project on mediation in order to identify and develop an evidence-based model of mediation that could offer valid, predictive insights into effective practice under different mediation conditions. To meet this goal several steps were required:

1. Identify the fundamental situational dimensions that determine mediators' choice of different strategies in mediation.
2. Conceptualize how the basic dimensions combine to create distinct types of mediation situations.
3. Validate the conceptual model, and identify which mediation strategies and tactics are most commonly and effectively employed in each situation-type.

Thus, our team set out to empirically map the fundamental dimensions of mediation situations in order to theorize and thus develop a better understanding of the most basic situational differences mediators face in their work. We suspect, and will attempt to test the idea, that mediators tend to employ distinct clusters of strategies and tactics when facing each of these different mediation situations. Furthermore, we propose that mediators who develop the capacities to identify and respond to these situational differences with mediation strategies that "fit" each situation type – a competency we call *adaptivity* – will tend to be more effective in their practice.

The resulting situated model of adaptive mediation offers the potential to provide a framework for: (a) assessing mediators' abilities to adaptively use the most appropriate behavioral strategies and tactics in a given situation-type; (b) analyzing situations and providing recommendations for mediators about how to respond effectively to different types of mediation situations, and; (c) making clear predictions about the effectiveness of different mediator tactics in distinct situations to be tested in future research.

Toward a Situated Model of Adaptive Mediation

One of the forefathers of social psychology, Kurt Lewin, famously proposed that $Bf(P \times E)$ – that human behavior (B) is a function of aspects of the person (P; personality, mood, preferences, skills, etc.) as they interact with aspects of the social environment (E; norms, incentives, temperature, etc.; Lewin 1936). In other words, mediators' behaviors are determined by some combination of their own tendencies – *as they interact with* aspects of the specific situations they face. For example, a facilitative mediator may behave more forcefully under some conditions (like extreme time pressure) than others.

One of Lewin's most notable students, Morton Deutsch, agreed with Lewin's formula, but pushed the question further to ask, "What are the most *fundamental* dimensions of social situations that affect human behavior?" (Wish et al. 1976). Deutsch's subsequent theorizing and research moved social psychology toward the construction of conceptual models that situate individual decisions and behavior in the context of specific social and cultural forces (see Jost and Kruglanski 2002 for a summary). Our approach to model building in mediation follows this tradition and so began by asking, "What are the most fundamental aspects of mediation situations that drive differences in mediator behavior?"

Step 1: Identifying the Fundamental Dimensions of Mediation Situations

To begin to answer this question we first surveyed the empirical literature on mediation published over the last 25 years (see Coleman et al. 2015). Overall, the literature search revealed a broad list of different factors that were found to influence mediators' behavior in mediations, including characteristics of the mediators themselves, characteristics of the disputants, the disputant's perceptions, aspects of the conflicts, and elements of the mediation context:

Characteristics of Mediators: mediators' experience and skill base (Arnold 2007; Mareschal 2005; Poitras 2009), mediators' ties, knowledge and bias toward the parties (Savun 2008; Svensson 2009), mediator's emotional intelligence (Boland and Ross 2010), the clarity of the mediator's role and their role-conception (Grima and Trépo 2009; Van Gramberg 2006), power position of the mediator (Svensson 2007) and mediator's style (Alberts et al. 2005; Asal et al. 2002; Baitar et al. 2012a, b; Beardsley et al. 2006; Goldberg 2005; Jameson et al. 2010; Martinez-Pecino et al. 2008; Quinn et al. 2006; Wall et al. 2011; Wilkenfeld et al. 2003; Yiu et al. 2006).

Characteristics of Disputants: gender (Herrman et al. 2003) and relationship hostility (Mareschal 2005).

Disputants' perceptions: trust between mediator and parties (Stimec and Poitras 2009), perceived mediator credibility (Maoz and Terris 2006), perceived mediator's acceptability (Mareschal 2005), parties' perceptions of fair conduct (Goldman et al. 2008), perceptions of procedural justice (Bollen et al. 2012), perceived mediator's partiality and bias (Poitras 2009; Jehn et al. 2006), perceived mediator's warmth and consideration, as well as chemistry with parties (Poitras 2009).

Aspects of the Conflicts: conflict intensity and resolution status (Alberts et al. 2005; Baitar et al. 2012b; Bercovitch and Gartner 2006; Pinkley et al. 1995), as well as integrative potential (Maoz and Terris 2006; Terris and Maoz 2005).

Aspects of the Mediation Context: culture (Callister and Wall 2004), individual differences within cultures (Davidheiser 2006), the number of parties in multi-party mediation (Böhmelt 2011), a highly conflictual context (Grima and Trépo 2009), time pressure (Grima and Trépo 2009; Pinkley et al. 1995), shifts and changes in conflict dynamics (Vukovic 2012) and past mediation outcomes (Bercovitch and Gartner 2006).

As Wall and Dunne (2012) suggest, this multitude of factors presents an embarrassment of riches which makes it nearly impossible to deduce the major causes/antecedents of mediators' choices of strategies or to offer practical recommendations for mediators regarding which strategies might be most promising in a given type of mediation situation. Therefore, our next step was to reduce this multitude of factors by empirically identifying the most fundamental dimensions underlying the factors that we found in the literature.

We next conducted a survey study with 149 experienced mediators, asking them to describe and then characterize their last case of mediation along bipolar dimensions based on the list of different factors identified in the literature (such as "much common ground to no common ground", "high intensity to low intensity", and "no time pressure to high time pressure"; see Coleman et al. 2015). An exploratory factor analysis of the survey responses revealed that most of the factors could be collapsed meaningfully to four basic underlying dimensions of mediation situations (see Fig. 2.1). In other words, of all the various aspects of mediation that researchers had been investigating over the last 30 years, four aspects stood out as most determining of mediator behaviors:

1. The nature of the conflict itself and especially its level of intensity, destructiveness, emotionality and intransigence;
2. The degree of constraints or limitations placed on the mediation by the context or environment in which it takes place, including legal constraints, time limitations, constituent pressure, and so on;
3. The relationship between the parties in terms of their type of cooperative and competitive interdependence, closeness, and similarity; and
4. The overt versus covert nature of the issues and processes in the mediation, including the implicit versus explicit nature of the issues at stake and the degree to which hidden processes and agendas were operating in the conflict

To summarize, results from the survey study indicated that of the many aspects of mediation that have been studied, four factors emerge as most fundamental to mediation situations, characterizing differences in qualities of (1) the conflict, (2) the immediate context, (3) the disputant relationships, and (4) the nature of the issues and processes. These four dimensions were found to be largely unrelated to

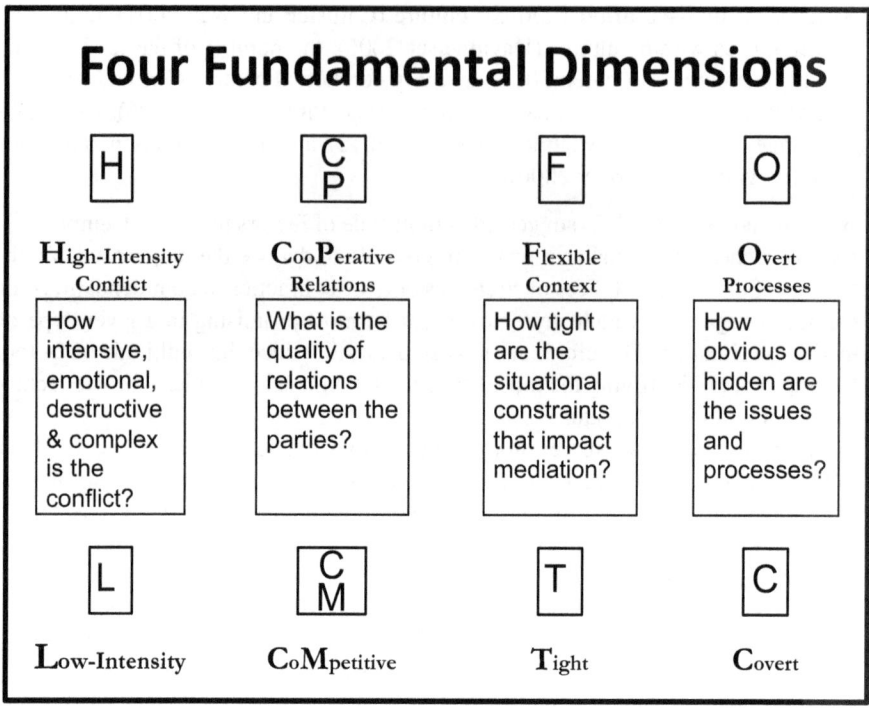

Fig. 2.1 The four fundamental dimensions of mediation

each other. Furthermore, these four basic aspects of mediation situations were found to be independently and distinctively related to differences in mediator's behavior and mediation processes and outcomes, even when controlling for factors such as mediator sex, experience, style preferences and goals (for details see Coleman et al. 2015). Specifically, we found that: (1) the higher the intensity of the conflict, the more unfriendly and disrespectful the behavior between the parties; (2) the higher the constraints on the mediation situation, the higher the degree of pre-mediation preparation needed and the higher the degree of settlement-orientation of the mediators; (3) the higher the level of similarity and common ground of parties, the more likely the mediation resulted in an agreement; and (4) the more explicit the issues, the higher the perception of procedural justice in mediation, the more often an agreement was reached and the more likely it was that the mediator focused on settlement of the agreement.

Step 2: Conceptualize How the Basic Dimensions Might Combine to Create Distinct Types of Mediation Situations

The four fundamental dimensions of mediation situations identified by the survey study with expert mediators constitute the core of our situated model of adaptive mediation, which provides a sense of the most basic types of contexts in which mediators address conflict (Coleman et al. 2015). Of course the four dimensions of the model rarely operate independently of one another, but are likely to interact in important ways. Therefore, our next task was to conceptualize how different values of the four dimensions might *combine* to promote qualitatively different situation-types, which in turn might afford different tactics used by mediators and ultimately lead to different mediation trajectories and outcomes.

As high and low degrees of each of the four dimensions of the situated model may logically interact with each of the other dimensions, we arrived at a preliminary conceptual matrix of 16 different types of mediation situations. In other words, if we take the most extreme cases of high vs. low intensity conflict, highly constrained versus highly unconstrained contexts, highly cooperative vs. highly competitive relations, and highly overt vs. highly covert issues and processes, then we arrive at a $2 \times 2 \times 2 \times 2 = 16$ cell matrix, representing 16 distinct types of mediation situations. Each of these different situation-types would be likely to induce different types of roles, areas of focus and strategies from mediators. In Table 2.1 we visualize the 16 cells and attribute labels that we think describe the qualitatively different types of situations. The labels provide a basic characterization of how mediators might experience the different situation types and act accordingly.

For instance, conflict situations of high-intensity conflicts with unconstrained contexts and competitive relations over covert issues (see Table 2.1) might be characterized as "crisis" conditions, and elicit a sort of ER Doctor role where the mediator shows high levels of attentiveness and sense of urgency, attempts to control damage, unearth what is hidden and identify the most effective forms of compromise. This type of mediation environment would likely elicit a strategy characterized by high pre-mediation preparation, a settlement-orientation, and evaluative, directive and pressing tactics. In contrast, situations presenting a low-intensity conflict in an unconstrained context over overt issues within cooperative relations (see Table 2.1) could be characterized as "paint-by-numbers" situations, and elicit more of an "Observer" role with less preparation and a more relationally-focused, non-directive, facilitative approach from mediators. Of course this initial matrix was conceptual and speculative and so needed to be validated and revised based on empirical data. This was the focus of the next phase of the project.

Table 2.1 Preliminary conceptual matrix of 16 types of mediation situations

		Conflict: low-intensity		Conflict: high-intensity	
		Relations: cooperative	Relations: competitive	Relations: cooperative	Relations: competitive
Context: unconstrained	Issues & Processes: covert	**Situation:** Mystery	**Situation:** Puzzle	**Situation:** Family Strife	**Situation:** Crisis
		Role: "Friend"	**Role:** "Colleague"	**Role:** "Therapist"	**Role:** "ER Doctor"
		Mediator focus: low concern; unearthing what is hidden, emphasizing common-ground and managing relations.	**Mediator focus:** Low concern; unearthing what is hidden and identifying the most effective compromise	**Mediator focus:** High concern; unearthing what is hidden, emphasizing common-ground and salvaging/ enhancing relations	**Mediator focus:** High concern; controlling damage; unearthing what is hidden and identifying the most effective compromise & implementation.
		Strategy: little preparation required; neutral-to-relationally-oriented and clarifying; facilitative, not pressing.	**Strategy:** Little preparation required; settlement-oriented and clarifying; evaluative but not pressing.	**Strategy:** Moderate preparation required; relationally-transformationally-oriented and clarifying; directive and pressing.	**Strategy:** High preparation required; settlement-oriented and analytic; evaluative, directive and pressing; urgent.
	Issues & Processes: overt	**Situation:** Free Ride	**Situation:** Splitting Hairs	**Situation:** Family Business	**Situation:** Brawl
		Role: "Laissez faire"	**Role:** "Moderator"	**Role:** "Process Consultant"	**Role:** "Police"
		Mediator focus: Low concern, emphasizing common-ground and enhancing relations.	**Mediator focus:** Low concern; identifying the most effective compromise.	**Mediator focus:** High concern; emphasizing common-ground and salvaging/ enhancing relations.	**Mediator focus:** High concern; controlling damage; identifying the most effective compromise & implementation.
		Strategy: Little preparation required; neutral-to-relationally-oriented and analytic; facilitative, not pressing, procedurally balanced and unbiased.	**Strategy:** Little preparation required; settlement-oriented and analytic; evaluative but not pressing; procedurally balanced and unbiased.	**Strategy:** Moderate preparation required; relationally-transformationally-oriented and analytic; directive and pressing; procedurally balanced and unbiased.	**Strategy:** High preparation required; settlement-oriented and analytic; evaluative, directive and pressing; urgent; procedurally balanced and unbiased.

Context: constrained	Issues & Processes	Situation: The Maze	Situation: Game	Situation: Business Dysfunction	Situation: Corporate Battle
	covert	Role: "Explorer"	Role: "Manager"	Role: "Investigator"	Role: "Lawyer"
		Mediator focus: Low concern; Unearthing what is hidden, identifying common-ground and managing relations.	**Mediator focus:** Low concern; unearthing what is hidden, clarifying the rules and identifying the most effective compromise.	**Mediator focus:** High concern; unearthing what is hidden, emphasizing common-ground and salvaging/enhancing relations.	**Mediator focus:** High concern; controlling damage; unearthing what is hidden, clarifying rules and identifying the most effective compromise and implementation.
		Strategy: Moderate preparation required: neutral-to-relationally-oriented and clarifying; rule-bound; facilitative, not pressing.	**Strategy:** Moderate preparation required; settlement-oriented but clarifying; rule-bound; evaluative but not pressing.	**Strategy:** High preparation required; rule-bound but relationally-transformationally-oriented and clarifying; facilitative, but directive and pressing.	**Strategy:** High preparation required; settlement-oriented but clarifying; rule-bound; evaluative, directive and pressing; urgent.
	Issues & Processes	Situation: Paint-By-Numbers	Situation: Chess Match	Situation: Child-Custody	Situation: The Divorce
	overt	Role: "Observer"	Role: "Referee"	Role: "Shepherd"	Role: "Judge"
		Mediator focus: Low concern, identifying common-ground and managing relations.	**Mediator focus:** Low concern; Clarifying the rules & identifying the most effective compromise.	**Mediator focus:** High concern; unearthing what is hidden, emphasizing common-ground and salvaging/enhancing relations.	**Mediator focus:** High concern; controlling damage; clarifying the rules and identifying the most effective compromise.
		Strategy: Little preparation required; rule-bound; neutral-to-relationally-oriented and analytic; facilitative, not pressing; procedurally balanced and unbiased.	**Strategy:** Moderate preparation required; settlement-oriented and clarifying; rule-bound; evaluative but not pressing; procedurally balanced and unbiased.	**Strategy:** Moderate preparation required; rule-bound but relationally-transformationally-oriented and analytic; directive and pressing; procedurally balanced and unbiased.	**Strategy:** High preparation required; settlement-oriented and analytic; rule-bound; evaluative, directive and pressing; urgent; procedurally balanced and unbiased.

Step 3: Validate the Conceptual Model and Identify Which Mediation Strategies and Tactics Are Most Commonly and Effectively Employed in Each Situation-Type

Next, we conducted a series of focus groups with experienced mediators (see Coleman et al. 2015; for more detail on these studies). Our team ran six focus groups with a total of 27 mediators who worked in various domestic mediation settings, including community, family and divorce, commercial, labor and workplace, government, and criminal court.[1] Mediation experience of the participants ranged from 1 to 24 years, with an average of 9.1 years. We were particularly interested in addressing three questions:

1. *Are some of the basic dimensions of the model weighted more heavily than others in determining mediator's strategies and tactics?*
2. *What specific behavioral strategies and tactics do mediators tend to employ when facing each of the mediation situation-types predicted by the model* (in terms of the four fundamental dimensions)? Here, we wanted to test the accuracy of our speculative 16-cell matrix of mediation situation-type/ behavioral-strategies.

Analysis of the data from the six focus groups revealed that although other situational differences do matter in mediation (power imbalances, cultural differences, etc.), the four conditions previously identified in our research were seen as the most fundamental to mediator decision choice. In addition, the focus groups agreed that the most primary and important of the four dimensions was the quality of the conflict (whether it is highly intense/intractable or less intense/tractable). In other words, if conflicts are or become highly intense in mediation this needs to be addressed first with a sense of urgency and priority if the mediation is to continue. Under these conditions, the high-intensity mediation strategy is likely to be employed regardless of the levels of the other three dimensions (constraints, competitiveness and covert processes). One mediator captured this during a focus group when stating: "… the high intensity is just the most obvious. It's like if someone is hit by a car … and if they're gushing blood; … they have many things that need to be addressed, but [first] you've gotta stop the gushing blood" (Quote by one of the participants, Coleman et al. 2015).

Beyond this, we learned that different situation types are associated with distinct and coherent mediation strategies. The mediation strategies are especially concise for constrained situations, high competitiveness and clear covert processes. More flexibility, cooperativeness, and overt issues and processes generally showed more moderation in behavior.

---

[1] At this stage of the research, we began to work separately with groups of domestic versus international mediators, as the behavioral tactics are considerably different from one setting to the next. The results described here focus on domestic mediation.

In sum, the results of the survey and the focus groups suggest a framework for characterizing mediation situations along the four dimensions (see Fig. 2.1) and inferring behavioral strategies that fit the situation. Choosing behavioral strategies that are aligned with the situational demands is what we call "adaptive mediation". As the mediation situation changes over time within one mediation, or as the mediator encounters different mediation situations across multiple mediations, the mediators are well served to adapt their behavioral tactics accordingly. The resulting model of adaptive mediation suggests that mediators respond to changes in mediation situations with a logical series of considerations: (1) How intense is the conflict?, (2) How constrained is the mediation context?, (3) How competitive or cooperative is the relationship of the disputants?, and (4) how overt versus covert are the issues and processes?

The flow of the questions necessary to address the fundamental aspects of a given situation and the respective behavioral tactics are outlined in the flow chart on adaptive mediation processes and described below (see Fig. 2.2).

As outlined above, the intensity of the conflict needs to be considered first. If the conflict is highly intense, the intensity requires full attention and ultimately should be decreased.

High Intensity Conflict Situations: The Medic The general strategy that emerged from the discussions for high intensity conflicts was one of *attempting to manage or lessen the intensity level of the conflict in a manner that would allow a constructive mediation process to continue.* If this becomes impossible, mediators recommended ending the mediation and referring the parties to alternative processes or authorities. This strategy is highly attuned to social-emotional issues, highly assertive, and suggests focusing on issues of high importance. Therefore, we labeled this role of the mediator in high-intensity situations *The Medic* – someone trained in the role of emergency medical responder, who must triage the problem and stabilize the situation sufficiently before moving onto other courses of treatment. This strategy included the following actions: the mediator is present, active, directive and enforces guidelines. Parties might vent or require time while the mediator reframes, rethinks, and reflects. It was noted in the focus groups that the mediator's self-awareness is critical in these situations. If the conflict shows lower levels of intensity the mediator can take on the role of the facilitator of the processes.

Low Intensity Conflict (Overall): The Facilitator Even though conflicts with lower levels of intensity can be very different, the general role of the mediator can be described as facilitator in the process towards conflict resolution. Strategies might vary, but are generally less active than in high intensity conflicts to the point where the mediator "disappears" and the parties own the process. A specific strategy can only be deduced when considering other situational aspects. When facing a low intensity conflict other aspects of the situation become important for the mediator's choice of the appropriate tactics. According to our model the mediator might consider the quality of the context (tight versus flexible contexts), the quality of the relationship (cooperative versus competitive relation-

Adaptive Mediation

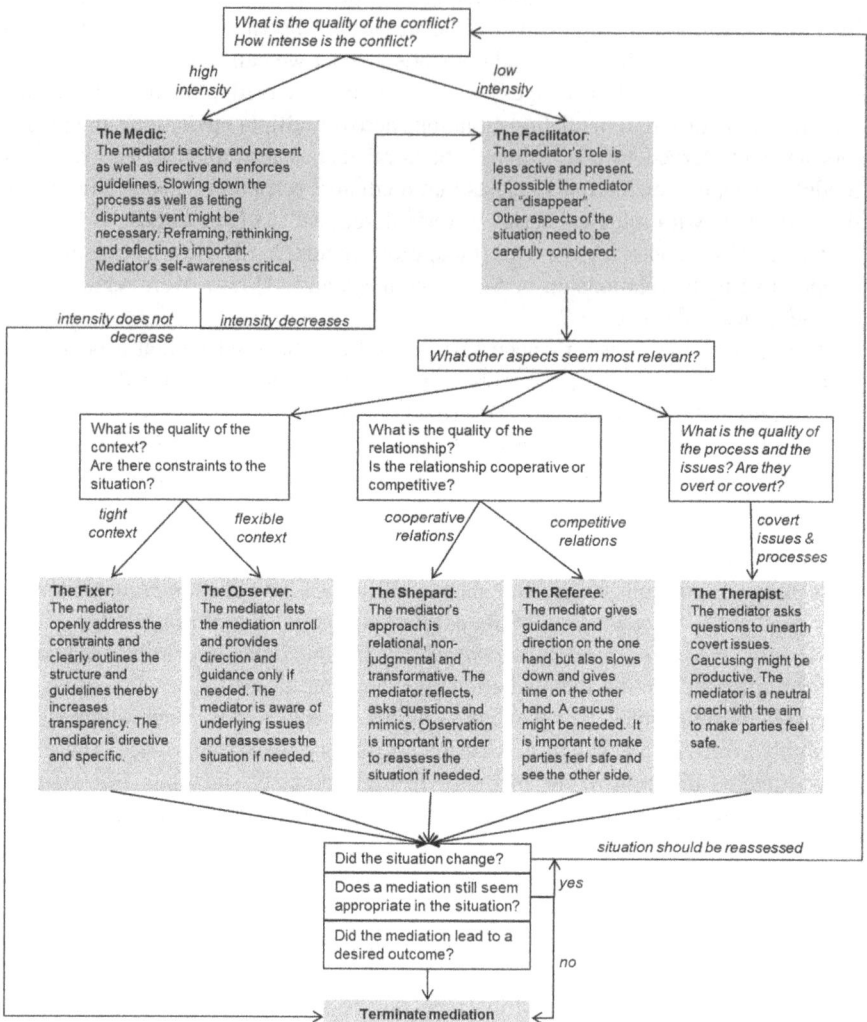

Fig. 2.2 A flow chart on adaptive mediation process

ships), and the quality of the issues and processes (over versus covert issues and processes), depending on what is most relevant in a given situation. As a situation changes a reassessment is necessary.

High Constraint (and Low Intensity) Mediation Situations: The Fixer Under these conditions, the general strategy as expressed by mediators was to *increase control and efficiency to work within the present constraints – or address and lessen the constraints*. This strategy is more task or problem-oriented than social-emotional, is directive, assertive, and focuses on prioritizing important issues and/or lowering aspirations of the disputants. Accordingly, we think of this role as *The Fixer* – such as Harvey Keitel in *Pulp Fiction* or a Mafia fixer that gets things done or, let's just say, adjusts expectations. The actions associated with this role include: Constraints are openly discussed and the structure and guidelines are clearly stated. The process is transparent and the mediator directive and specific.

Low Constraint (and Low Intensity) Mediation Situations: The Observer If the constraints and intensity are low and no other aspects of the situation seem relevant, the mediator can let the mediation unroll and observe. Some guidance and direction is provided to facilitate the conflict resolution process. However, the mediator ought to be attentive to changes in the situation. If other aspects seem relevant, for example, if covert issues emerge, the situation needs to be reassessed.

High Competition (and Low Intensity) Mediation Situations: The Referee Under highly competitive mediation conditions, the general strategy identified by the mediators was to try to *encourage the disputants to bargain fairly and settle efficiently, with more of a task-outcome focus than relational*. We refer to this mediator role as: *The Referee*. Some of the actions employed in this role included: Caucusing to help the parties prepare to bargain effectively, provide guidance and direction on fair distributive procedures, slow down and provide sufficient time for the negotiation to unfold, and help the disputants feel safe and understand the positions of the other side.

High Cooperation (and Low Intensity) Mediation Situations: The Shepard When highly cooperative conditions and relations display themselves in low-intensity mediation, the general strategy recommended by the mediators was what we consider *a more standard or default approach to mediation, one which utilizes more open, facilitative forms of dialogue and problem-solving, which are less directive and more relationally-focused*. We characterize this role as: *The Shepherd*. These are the strategies and tactics most mediators are trained to implement. Recommended actions include: Withholding judgment and applying more transformative approaches. This includes reflecting, asking questions, observing, and mimicking. Nevertheless the mediator should be alert to changes in the situation and to reassess the situation if needed (e.g., when the relationship becomes more competitive).

Highly Covert Issues/Processes (and Low Intensity) Mediation Situations: The Therapist Finally, when the mediator begins to suspect that there are important covert issues or processes at play that affect the mediation, they reported tending to shift their strategy to one where they are able to *probe more deeply and carefully into the hidden or underlying issues*. We call this role: *The Therapist*. It often involves: caucusing, inquiring and probing directly to unearth covert issues, being a neutral coach to help parties equally in exploring their underlying concerns, and ensuring safety.

These findings suggest that instead of 16 distinct mediation situation-types (as shown in Table 2.1), a more likely model of basic situational differences in mediation may be reflected by a simpler model of five basic (more extreme) situation-types: high-intensity, highly-constrained, highly-competitive, highly-cooperative and those entailing important covert issues and processes (see Fig. 2.2). The findings from the focus groups also suggest that mediators tend to alter their strategies based on the different types of situations they face across different mediations or in an ongoing mediation where circumstances change. Together our findings suggest that mediators would do well to consider the shifting tides of the four basic dimensions of mediations and adjust their strategies.

Ultimately, we posit that mediators ought to have the capacity to *adapt* in order to be effective (Coleman et al. 2010, 2012, 2013; Coleman and Kugler 2014; Van De Vliert et al. 1995). This may be a challenge to most mediators as prior research has shown that mediators often hold strong chronic preferences for how they approach mediations and find it difficult when situations require a different approach (Beardsley et al. 2006; Kressel 2007, 2014; Riskin 2005). However, the nature and value of adaptivity in mediation settings has yet to be specified sufficiently or empirically tested.

Next Steps in the Program of Research

We recently conducted a second survey study of experienced mediators to empirically validate and better specify the situation-type/behavioral strategy relationships (Coleman et al. 2015). Preliminary findings suggest further support for the situated model of adaptive mediation, and provide more detail on the nature of the different strategies and tactics associated with the distinct types of situations.

Based on the next iteration of the situated model, our team plans to develop an assessment instrument to (a) measure mediator's most dominant or commonly employed strategies as well as (b) assess their *adaptivity* or capacity to read important changes in mediation situations and to respond to them with strategies and tactics that are more "fitting" and thus more effective in those situations. This will allow us to begin to empirically test the implications of mediator adaptivity for effectiveness in mediation and sustainability of agreements. In time, we plan to develop new basic and advanced mediation trainings based on the situated model and on the concomitant strategies and meta-competencies associated with adaptive mediation.

Conclusion

The practice of mediation, with its ancient roots and intuitive win-win appeal, has recently gained a new level of attention. Yet much work remains to be done to refine and advance the practical utility of the method through systematic research. This chapter outlines a new theoretical approach to mediation that offers great promise for using evidence-based research to move the mediation field forward. The situated model of adaptive mediation provides an integrative platform for better conceptualizing basic differences in mediations situations, which allows us to begin to better understand which of the 100 plus tactics we might use in different mediation situations to best effect. As such, we can begin to understand the general contingencies associated with more and less directive, non-directive, facilitative, evaluative, integrative, and distributive approaches to mediation.

References

Alberts, J. K., Heisterkamp, B. L., & McPhee, R. M. (2005). Disputant perceptions of and satisfaction with a community mediation program. *International Journal of Conflict Management, 16*(3), 218–244.

Arnold, J. A. (2007). Influence of third party expertise on disputants' reactions to mediation. *Psychological Reports, 101*(2), 407–418.

Asal, V., Wilkenfeld, J., Young, K., Quinn, D., Pate, A., & Beardsley, K. (2002). *Mediating ripeness: The impact of mediation on negotiators' zones of agreement.* Paper presented at the Annual Meeting of American Political Science Association, Boston.

Baitar, R. B., Buysse, A., Brondeel, R., De Mol, J., & Rober, P. (2012a). Post-divorce wellbeing in Flanders: Facilitative professionals and quality of arrangements matter. *Journal of Family Studies, 18*(1), 62–75.

Baitar, R., Buysse, A., Brondeel, R., De Mol, J., & Rober, P. (2012b). Toward high-quality divorce agreements: The influence of facilitative professionals. *Negotiation Journal, 28*(4), 453–473.

Beardsley, K. C., Quinn, D. M., Biswas, B., & Wilkenfeld, J. (2006). Mediation style and crisis outcomes. *Journal of Conflict Resolution, 50*(1), 58–86.

Bellman, H. (2006). Improvisation, mediation, and all that jazz. *Negotiation Journal, 22*, 325–330.

Bercovitch, J., & Gartner, S. S. (2006). Is there method in the madness of mediation? Some lessons for mediators from quantitative studies of mediation. *International Interactions, 32*(4), 329–354.

Bercovitch, J., & Lee, S. (2003). Exploring the relevance and effectiveness of directive strategies in mediation. *International Journal of Peace Sciences, 8*(1), 1–19.

Böhmelt, T. (2011). *International mediation interaction: Synergy, conflict, effectiveness.* Wiesbaden: Springer.

Boland, M. J., & Ross, W. H. (2010). Emotional intelligence and dispute mediation in escalating and de-escalating situations. *Journal of Applied Social Psychology, 40*(12), 3059–3105.

Bollen, K., Ittner, H., & Euwema, M. (2012). Mediating hierarchical labor conflicts: Procedural justice makes a difference – for subordinates. *Group Decision and Negotiation, 21*(5), 621–636.

Callister, R. R., & Wall, J. A. (2004). Thai and US community mediation. *Journal of Conflict Resolution, 48*(4), 573–598.

Charkoudian, L. (2012). Just my style: The practical, ethical, and empirical dangers of the lack of consensus about definitions of mediation styles. *Negotiation and Conflict Management Research, 5*(4), 367–383.

Coleman, P. T. (2011). *The five percent: Finding solutions to seemingly impossible conflicts.* New York: Public Affairs.

Coleman, P. T., & Kugler, K. G. (2014). Tracking managerial conflict adaptivity: Introducing a dynamic measure of adaptive conflict management in organizations. *Journal of Organizational Behavior, 35*(7), 945–968.

Coleman, P. T., Kugler, K. G., Mitchinson, A., Chung, C., & Musallam, N. (2010). The view from above and below: The effects of power and interdependence asymmetries on conflict dynamics and outcomes in organizations. *Negotiation and Conflict Management Research, 3*(4), 283–311.

Coleman, P. T., Kugler, K. G., Bui-Wrzosinska, L., Nowak, A., & Vallacher, R. (2012). Getting down to basics: A situated model of conflict in social relations. *Negotiation Journal, 28*(1), 7–43.

Coleman, P. T., Kugler, K. G., Mitchinson, A., & Foster, C. (2013). Navigating power and conflict at work: The effects of power asymmetries and interdependence on conflict in organizations. *Journal of Applied Social Psychology, 43*, 1963–1983.

Coleman, P. T., Kugler, K., Gozzi, C., Mazzaro, K., El Zokm, N., & Kressel, K. (2015). Putting the peaces together: Introducing a situated model of mediation. *International Journal of Conflict Management, 26*(2), 145–171. Munich: Ludwig-Maximilians-Universitaet Muenchen. Germany

Davidheiser, M. (2006). Harmony, peacemaking, and power: Controlling processes and African mediation. *Conflict Resolution Quarterly, 23*(3), 281–299.

Goldberg, S. B. (2005). The secrets of successful mediators. *Negotiation Journal, 21*(3), 365–376.

Goldman, B. M., Cropanzano, R., Stein, J. H., Shapiro, D. L., Thatcher, S., & Ko, J. (2008). The role of ideology in mediated disputes at work: A justice perspective. *International Journal of Conflict Management, 19*(3), 210–233.

Greig, J. M. (2001). Moments of opportunity: Recognizing conditions of ripeness for international mediation between enduring rivals. *Journal of Conflict Resolution, 45*(6), 691–718.

Grima, F., & Trépo, G. (2009). Knowledge, action and public concern: The logic underlying mediators' actions in French labour conflicts. *The International Journal of Human Resource Management, 20*(5), 1172–1190.

Herrman, M. S., Hollett, N. L., Eaker, D. G., & Gale, J. (2003). Mediator reflections on practice: Connecting select demographics and preferred orientations. *Conflict Resolution Quarterly, 20*(4), 403–427.

Honeyman, C., Coben, J., & De Palo, G. (2009). Introduction: Negotiation teaching 2.0. *Negotiation Journal, 25*, 141–146.

Jameson, J. K., Bodtker, A. M., & Linker, T. (2010). Facilitating conflict transformation: Mediator strategies for eliciting emotional communication in a workplace conflict. *Negotiation Journal, 26*(1), 25–48.

Jehn, K. A., Rupert, J., & Nauta, A. (2006). The effects of conflict asymmetry on mediation outcomes: Satisfaction, work motivation and absenteeism. *International Journal of Conflict Management, 17*(2), 96–109.

Jost, J. T., & Kruglanski, A. W. (2002). The estrangement of social constructionism and experimental social psychology: History of the rift and prospects for reconciliation. *Personality and Social Psychology Review, 6*(3), 168–187.

Kressel, K. (2007). The strategic style in mediation. *Conflict Resolution Quarterly, 24*, 251–283.

Kressel, K. (2014). The mediation of conflict: Context, cognition, and practice. In M. Deutsch, P. T. Coleman, & E. Marcus (Eds.), *The handbook of conflict resolution: Theory and practice* (3rd ed., pp. 817–848). San Francisco: Josey-Bass.

Lewin, K. (1936). *Principles of topological psychology*. New York: McGraw-Hill.

Maoz, Z., & Terris, L. G. (2006). Credibility and strategy in international mediation. *International Interactions, 32*(4), 409–440.

Mareschal, P. M. (2005). What makes mediation work? Mediators' perspectives on resolving disputes. *Industrial Relations: A Journal of Economy and Society, 44*(3), 509–517.

Martinez-Pecino, R., Munduate, L., Medina, F. J., & Euwema, M. C. (2008). Effectiveness of mediation strategies in collective bargaining. *Industrial Relations: A Journal of Economy and Society, 47*(3), 480–495.

McDermott, E. P. (2012). Discovering the importance of mediator style – An interdisciplinary challenge. *Negotiation and Conflict Management Research, 5*(4), 340–353.

Moordian, M., & Druckman, D. (1999). Hurting stalemate or mediation? The conflict over Nagorno-Karabakh, 1990–95. *Journal of Peace Research, 36*(6), 709–727.

Pfeffer, J., & Sutton, R. I. (2006). Hard facts, dangerous half-truths, and total nonsense: Profiting from evidence-based management. *Harvard Business Review, 84*, 62–74.

Pinkley, R. L., Brittain, J., Neale, M. A., & Northcraft, G. B. (1995). Managerial third-party dispute intervention: An inductive analysis of intervenor strategy selection. *Journal of Applied Psychology, 80*(3), 386–402.

Poitras, J. (2009). What makes parties trust mediators? *Negotiation Journal, 25*(3), 307–325.

Poitras, J., Hill, K., Hamel, V., & Pelletier, F. (2015). Managerial mediation competency: A mixed-method study. *Negotiation Journal, 31*(2), 105–129.

Pruitt, D., & Kugler, K. G. (2014). Some research frontiers in the study of conflict and its resolution. In M. Deutsch, P. T. Coleman, & E. C. Marcus (Eds.), *The handbook of conflict resolution: Theory and practice* (3rd ed.). San Franscisco: Jossey-Bass.

Quinn, D., Wilkenfeld, J., Smarick, K., & Asal, V. (2006). Power play: Mediation in symmetric and asymmetric international crises. *International Interactions, 32*(4), 441–470.

Rousseau, D. M. (2006). Is there such a thing as "evidence-based management"? *Academy of Management Review, 31*, 256–269.

Riskin, L. L. (1996). Mediator orientations, strategies, and techniques: A grid for the perplexed. *Harvard Negotiation Law Review, 1*(7), 7–51.

Riskin, L. L. (2005). Replacing the mediator orientation grids, again: The new new grid system. *Alternatives to the High Cost of Litigation, 29*, 127–132.

Savun, B. (2008). Information, bias, and mediation success. *International Studies Quarterly, 52*(1), 25–47.

Stimec, A., & Poitras, J. (2009). Building trust with parties: Are mediators overdoing it? *Conflict Resolution Quarterly, 26*(3), 317–331.

Svensson, I. (2007). Mediation with muscles or minds? Exploring power mediators and pure mediators in civil war. *International Negotiation, 12*(2), 229–248.

Svensson, I. (2009). Who brings which peace? Neutral versus biased mediation and institutional peace arrangements in civil wars. *Journal of Conflict Resolution, 53*(3), 446–469.

Terris, L. G., & Maoz, Z. (2005). Rational mediation: A theory and a test. *Journal of Peace Research, 42*(5), 563–583.

United Nations. (2012). Strengthening the role of mediation in the peaceful settlement of disputes, conflict prevention and resolution. *Report of the Secretary-General*, 66th session, agenda item 34 (a), prevention of armed conflict. Retrieved from peacemaker.un.org/sites/peacemaker. un.org/files/SGReport_StrenghteningtheRoleofMediation_A66811.pdf.

Van De Vliert, E., Euwema, M. C., & Huismans, S. E. (1995). Managing conflict with a subordinate or a superior: Effectiveness of conglomerated behavior. *Journal of Applied Psychology, 80*, 271–281.

Van Gramberg, B. (2006). *Managing workplace conflict: Alternative dispute resolution in Australia*. Annandale: Federation Press.

Vukovic, S. (2012). Coping with complexity: Analyzing cooperation and coordination in multi-party mediation processes. *International Negotiation, 17*(2), 265–293.

Wall, J. A., & Dunne, T. C. (2012). Mediation research: A current review. *Negotiation Journal, 28*(2), 217–244.

Wall, J. A., & Kressel, K. (2012). Research on mediator style: A summary and some research suggestions. *Negotiation and Conflict Management Research, 5*(4), 403–421.

Wall, J. A., & Lynn, A. (1993). Mediation: A current review. *Journal of Conflict Resolution, 37*(1), 160–194.

Wall, J. A., Stark, J. B., & Standifer, R. L. (2001). Mediation: A current review and theory development. *Journal of Conflict Resolution, 45*, 370–391.

Wall, J. A., Dunne, T. C., & Chan-Serafin, S. (2011). The effects of neutral, evaluative, and pressing mediator strategies. *Conflict Resolution Quarterly, 29*(2), 127–150.

Wilkenfeld, J., Young, K., Asal, V., & Quinn, D. (2003). Mediating international crises cross-national and experimental perspectives. *Journal of Conflict Resolution, 47*(3), 279–301.

Wish, M., Deutsch, M., & Kaplan, S. J. (1976). Perceived dimensions of interpersonal relations. *Journal of Personality and Social Psychology, 33*(4), 409–420.

Wissler, R. L. (1995). Mediation and adjudication in the Small Claims Court: The effects of process and case characteristics. *Law and Society Review, 29*(2), 323–358.

Yiu, T. W., Cheung, S. O., & Mok, F. M. (2006). Logistic likelihood analysis of mediation outcomes. *Journal of Construction Engineering and Management, 132*(10), 1026–1036.

Chapter 3
Workplace Mediation: Searching for Underlying Motives and Interests

Elisabeth Kals, Kathrin Thiel, and Susanne Freund

Social Conflicts in Organisations

The conflicts to which we refer to in this chapter, so called social conflicts, are defined by the following four criteria: (1) Incompatibilities exist concerning the interests and positions of two or more parties. These incompatibilities prevent as many as one, possibly more of the conflict parties, to achieve their target state. (2) At least one of the conflict parties feels affected by the incompatibilities and often experiences injustice. (3) Conflict partners blame the other party to be responsible for interfering with its/their target state. (4) While the other party knows that others are impaired, it shows no willingness to change the own position (Montada and Kals 2013; Pruitt and Kim 2004). In contrast, intra-psychic conflicts, e.g., on personal career decisions, would be a typical example for non-social conflicts since they do not fulfill the four criteria, instead they only affect one person and his/her inner struggle between various positions (De Dreu and Van de Vliert 1997; Montada and Kals 2013; Pruitt and Carnevale 2003).

A sustainable solution of the above defined kind of workplace conflicts, that are restricted to inner organizational conflicts in this chapter, is essential for many reasons (Bollen and Euwema 2013; Jahn 2014; KPMG 2009). The results of an international study reveal that on average employees spend 2.1 h per week dealing with conflicts (CPP Inc. 2008). These conflicts add to the deterioration of the climate in the whole department and cause anxiety, anger, and indignation, an increase in sick leaves as well as the rise of the turnover rate (De Dreu 2008). To get an idea about the financial costs of workplace conflicts, a survey among 111 German companies shows expenses quantified in more than 50.000 Euros per company (KPMG 2009). The mentioned expenses relate to fines because of delays in delivery, loss of working

E. Kals (✉) • K. Thiel • S. Freund
Catholic University of Eichstätt-Ingolstadt, Eichstätt, Germany
e-mail: elisabeth.kals@ku.de

© Springer International Publishing Switzerland 2016
K. Bollen et al. (eds.), *Advancing Workplace Mediation Through Integration
of Theory and Practice*, Industrial Relations & Conflict Management 3,
DOI 10.1007/978-3-319-42842-0_3

hours, introduction costs for new staff members and costs due to poor performances (KPMG 2009). Euwema et al. (2007) found that on average a workplace conflict costs about 27.000 Euros per company per case in the Netherlands.

Therefore, it is of high practical relevance to sustainably resolve workplace conflicts. Considering that, mediation as an alternative extrajudicial process of conflict management executed by an impartial third party proves to be helpful (Bollen and Euwema 2013). On an economical level, studies show an increase in productivity (3–20 %) as well as a reduction of the amount of time employees are absent from work (30–70 %) within 1 year after the mediation (Müller-Wolf 1994). On a non-monetary level, anxiety declines and job satisfaction increases when workplace conflicts are mediated (McKenzie 2015).

Sustainable Solutions for Workplace Conflicts

The mediation approach presented in this chapter is an eclectic one, inspired by practical needs (Goldberg et al. 2007). Based on a psychological foundation it refers to different models and theories, e.g., on emotions, motives, behavior, decision-making, conflict and justice (Montada and Kals 2013). It follows the transformative mediation approach regarding the ambitious aim that the conflict should be solved sustainably. This can be achieved when the mediation process helps to identify opportunities for empowerment and to recognize the perspective of the conflict partners (Bush and Folger 2005; Bush and Pope 2002).

The solution should be regarded as fair by all partners and it thereby leaves the opportunity to the conflict partners to cooperate in the future, cooperation often based on a better relationship than before the conflict. To achieve such a solution level, we assume that the motives and interests that lie behind the positions have to be brought forward and fully understood (Kals and Ittner 2008; Montada and Kals 2013). Only in this case, the social conflict can be solved in a sustainable way. Otherwise, injured and unfulfilled motives and past experiences may lead to new disagreements over different topics and issues. That is in line with the distinction of interests and positions, made by the Harvard negotiation model (Fisher and Ury 2011).

For a long time, the prototypical case for conflicts was assumed to be colliding self-interests (see for example Kressel and Pruitt 1989). However, empirical research on the underlying motives of behavior during conflicts shows that the impact of self-interest tends to be overestimated (Baron 1988; De Dreu and Van de Vliert 1997; Miller and Ratner 1996) and that other-oriented motives also come into play (Pruitt and Kim 2004). The underlying motives of the conflict partners in workplace conflicts are mostly pluralistic in the way that there is a mix of several relevant motives. This is also due to the fact that one's work has to fulfill various core values. Examples can be struggle for career, income, self-esteem, and acceptance but also the fulfillment of interest of others, e.g. the working-unit or the company as a whole (Baron 1988; De Dreu and Van de Vliert 1997).

Perceived Injustice as Root Cause in Workplace Conflict

Within this mix of important motives, appraisals of justice play an important, yet often underestimated role (Deutsch 2006; Kals and Maes 2012; Mikula and Wenzel 2000; Montada 2003). In this respect, many social conflicts result from subjectively perceived injustice and can therefore be seen as justice conflicts. This means that normative justice judgments are injured or threatened (Deutsch 2006; Montada 2003). To lose a fair competition might be a problem, still it is not necessarily a social conflict. The latter is only the case when norms, like the rules of fair competitions, are injured, for example by illegal price fixing (Montada and Kals 2013). Distributive, procedural, and interactional justices are of special significance in the area of the workplace (Greenberg and Folger 1983; Nabatchi et al. 2007): What goods and burdens are allocated to whom? Is the allocation seen as fair, and what principle does it follow? How is the distribution process designed, and to what extent does it fulfill the conditions and rules of a fair process (Lind and Tyler 1988)? Consequently, whenever the experience of injustice occurs, conflicts tend to escalate fast. Social conflicts become "hot conflicts" when perceived injustice comes into play, e.g., when staff members are promoted due to sympathy rather than performance. Thus, the aggression and hostilities that the conflict parties display are oftentimes the consequence of the experience that one is treated unfairly.

The violated justice motive can be supplemented by a long list of potential other motives (illustrated in the following exemplifying questions) that might be either of relevance independently of justice judgments or as part of the content of the justice considerations. Such as:

- **Financial interests**: Who will get which bonus when extra payments are distributed? Who will be promoted next to the higher working position? The significant role of work for the fulfillment of material needs and motives becomes especially obvious when the employment is interrupted or terminated: What if I lose my job? What about the living of my family, the payment of my house?
- **Interests of self-esteem**: Work is an elementary source of satisfaction (Clark and Oswald 1994; Jandackova and Jackowska 2015; Winkelmann 2009): To what extent is my effort at work recognized and valued?
- **Formal and informal power**: Who gets to decide on the timing schedule to prepare and conduct meetings?
- **Autonomy**: To what level is there freedom to decide on working processes, working time, or working outcomes?
- **Responsibility**: Who is responsible for what processes and decisions?
- **Social proximity to and familiarity with the boss**: Who gets what kind of information first and has what kind of influence on the decisions of the boss?
- **Respect and social acceptance**: Who is to what extent respected by the various people and groups one has to interact with during the work process?

These motives are accompanied by corresponding emotions: Indignation as the key emotion of experienced injustice always indicates that the justice motive is of relevance (Haidt 2003). Frequently, indignation is supplemented by feelings of anger that are often not experienced as distinguished from indignation by the subject. However, all categories of emotions can be experienced during workplace conflicts, such as rage, disappointment about infringed claims or the loss of confidence, pride of already successfully taken responsibilities and being socially accepted (Kals and Kärcher 2001; Kannheiser 1992).

Mediating a Leadership Conflict: A Case Study

In the following, we will look at how the motives interplay and manifest themselves in behavior, which will be illustrated by a case study on a leadership conflict.

A midsized company started a restructuring process. Within this process, various departments were combined and new teams formed. This also implied that Mrs. Brown and Mr. Clark needed to run a department together, whereas they had management responsibility for their own departments before. Recently, several employees of this newly formed team expressed dissatisfaction and complaints concerning the internal cooperation within the department, since the occurance of disagreements between the two leaders starts to affect the members of the team as well. Mr. Rader, an experienced boss, situated on a level higher in the hierarchy than Mrs. Brown and Mr. Clark, contacts an external mediator due to what has happened at a presentation. During this presentation where Mrs. Brown and Mr. Clark, as well as the order partner were present, it was obvious that the two of them did not agree about the concept they presented and did not work together well.

Because of this weak performance, the company did not get the contract they aimed at. Mr. Rader told the mediator that he himself had tried to solve the situation without success since both of the conflict parties kept blaming the other person to be responsible. To him it is very important that this conflict gets solved since both of the staff members are highly estimated employees.

In order to give both of the conflict parties the opportunity to express their perspective on the conflict, the mediator asks them in the first mediation session to describe the situation from their point of view one after the other while the other party was asked to listen without interrupting. From this first talk with the parties, the mediator gets the following information:

Mr. Clark is a long-standing and committed employee of the company, close to retirement age. He and Mr. Rader have known each other since they started working in the company together several years ago. Over the years, a deep friendship has developed between the two of them. Mr. Clark complains about the fact that Mrs. Brown often makes decisions without informing him. According to him this was also true for this case: On their way to the presentation room, Mrs. Brown informed him that she had slightly changed the initial concept the evening before, in order to improve it. So, during the presentation it was the first time that he got to see the revised concept. Consequently, when the order partner asked questions about it, Mr. Clark was not fully able to answer as he was not totally updated regarding the new concept presented by Mrs. Brown. Very furiously he goes on to tell that whenever he answered a question, Mrs. Brown would either interrupt him or address the audience after he had finished explaining everything in another way. This made him look stupid and incompetent in front of his boss and the representatives of the partner company as well. Mr. Clark accuses Mrs. Brown of having restructured the presentation the night before on purpose in order to put him in a bad light in front of the team members, their boss and the external partner. Mr. Clark continues by referring to the fact that often she would work till late at night and overregulate the work of their team members by making agreements on many details without giving him the chance to intercede. His speaking rate as well as the tone of his voice indicate that this really upsets him. Mr. Clark feels overlooked by Mrs. Brown and has the feeling that it is her aim to belittle him in front of their boss by setting a high pace of work he cannot keep up with as well as by putting him in situations like the one described. He also expresses his concern that team members he worked with for a long time start to respect Mrs. Brown more than him, which worries him. While Mr. Clark describes the situation from his point of view it is obviously hard for Mrs. Brown to listen and not to interrupt him. At several points in time, she suddenly jumps off her chair and starts to approach him in a loud and sharp tone. The mediator has to remind her to just listen to Mr. Clark's report for now, as she will be given the chance to express her point of view later on.

Mrs. Brown can be described as a qualified and high-performing young woman who has high aspirations and wants to pursue her career. She has now been working for the company for 6 years, successfully leading her own team before the restructuring process. Concerning the described situation, she explains that the last night before the meeting she had read over the concept and realized that it contained several weak points which she felt important to improve. Because the meeting would take place at 10 am and Mr. Clark would only arrive at the office shortly before the meeting and would probably not have read the email she sent him at 11 pm the evening before, there was only little or no time left for her to tell him about the revised presentation. This is why he did not know about the changes she made. Mrs. Brown goes on to defend herself that this would not have happened if Mr. Clark, whom she considers to be lazy, would have arrived at the office earlier that morning. Regarding the restructuring process, Mrs. Brown complains that the newly formed department consists mostly of members of Mr. Clark's old team. While Mr. Clark was allowed to take most of his staff, her team workers were allocated to other departments, which was never justified. That is why Mrs. Brown does not only feel treated unfairly but also has the impression that Mr. Clark and Mr. Rader, good friends, are plotting against her. Concerning Mr. Clark's remark that she would overregulate the team, she explains in a rather aggressive tone that this is simply her way of leading people. She goes on to explain that in contrast to Mr. Clark's laissez fair style of leadership, she agrees on clear targets with their subordinates and supports them to reach these objectives for the good of the whole department. Outraged by the accusation of Mr. Clark that she would work late hours in order to run him down, she defends herself that it is necessary for her to work hard in order to get on with her career which is what she focuses on.

Let us recall what we know about the situation so far: the reason why Mr. Rader, the boss, contacted the mediator was to try to reconcile Mr. Clark and Mrs. Brown as their interactions started to affect the department in a negative way. From the perceptions of Mr. Clark and Mrs. Brown on the situation as presented in the first mediation session, it becomes clear that many issues have to be taken into account. The most important ones are:

- **Expectations regarding the communication between Mrs. Brown and Mr. Clark**: Mrs. Brown restructured the presentation and hoped to get Mr. Clark informed before the presentation took place. In Mr. Clark's perspective she should not have restructured the presentation they had agreed on the evening before, especially not without giving him the opportunity to approve the changes.
- **Ideas related to working hours and accessibility**: Mr. Clark accuses Mrs. Brown to work late hours in order to run him down, whereas Mrs. Brown declares that she wants to develop her career and to conduct the work as good as possible which includes high accessibility. With regard to the conflict situation she expected Mr. Clark to come earlier that very morning to have a last look at the presentation.
- **Composition of the working group**: The new working group consists mostly of members of Mr. Clark's old team.
- **Social proximity with Mr. Rader, related to (in)formal power**: Mr. Rader regards himself as a friend of Mr. Clark which may grant him informal power. Mrs. Brown on the other hand has the feeling that she has less power over Mr. Rader and that the two are plotting against her.
- **Styles of leadership**: The dual leadership is based on two different uncoordinated styles of leading. Whereas Mr. Clark displays a laissez faire style of leadership, Mrs. Brown exercises the leadership style of management by objectives.

At the beginning, the parties tend to be very emotional and to interrupt each other. It is important to comprehend their detailed emotions and to understand the motives, wishes and interests which underlie the various perceptions and statements of the two colleagues. In order to understand the motives and the related "deep structure" of the conflict, the mediator agrees on individual sessions with both Mr. Clark and Mrs. Brown, before getting both parties on the table again (Caucus).

From these individual sessions with each conflict party, the following becomes clear: Mr. Clark points out that, for health reasons, he has not enough strength left to work late hours like Mrs. Brown does. He is willing to work hard but it is also important for him to have freedom to do his work in a way that is consistent with his view on work and leadership based on a relationship of trust and loyalty within his team. He is afraid to lose the respect and good reputation among his team members if he would change his way of leading and managing the team. In addition, he stresses several times that Mrs. Brown does not seem to respect his experience, instead she seems to expect him to retire earlier rather than (too) late. Another issue that it is important to him is to maintain the good relationship with Mr. Rader and not to lose this friendship. Within this individual session he also affirms that Mrs.

Brown is a very talented woman who produces work of high-quality, has innovative ideas and that he values her for her professionalism.

During her individual session, Mrs. Brown tells the mediator that she is convinced that neither Mr. Clark nor Mr. Rader recognize her hard work or her potential to perform well. When she talks about her aspired goal to get on in her job, she recounts a story that took place in the past. Some time before the restructuring process, an interesting in-house vacancy for head of department at a subsidiary in the Middle East was advertised. Mr. Rader, who had promised to assist her to develop her career, was one of the persons with primary responsibility in the selection process. Because of her gathered know-how in the company as well as various experiences within the eastern culture, she considered herself to be well qualified for this job. Thus, she expected Mr. Rader to promote her for this position. But instead of her, a, in her eyes, less experienced external applicant got chosen for the job. She felt treated very unfairly by Mr. Rader as he had promised her to help foster her career and she felt qualified for the job. Furthermore, she accuses him that he did not even care to explain the situation to her afterwards. Instead of the job in the Middle East, she got a deplacement and needed to share the responsibility for a department with Mr. Clark. She experiences this situation as a step back. In addition, she has the feeling that Mr. Clark drives a wedge between her and the team members when he questions the agreements she makes with them and does not accept her leadership style. Mrs. Brown expresses that she feels lonely in her striving to do a good job for the company. To make things even worse, instead of being thankful that she takes a big part of responsibility, Mr. Clark accuses her of working too much. When she starts to talk about her way of leading the department, it becomes clear that her perception of leadership is very different than the one of Mr. Clark which she considers to be inefficient. At the same time, she assures that she respects him for his experience and hopes that they will find a way to work together for the benefit of their department as well as the company.

Based on these individual sessions, we get a deeper understanding of the conflict. The underlying motives of the conflict parties' behaviors become clearer and give an answer to the crucial question why Mr. Clark and Mrs. Brown act the way they do.

- **Expectations regarding communication**: For both Mr. Clark and Mrs. Brown, a good and efficient flow of information between them is important. However, the exchange of information is often blocked due to their way of how they talk to each other, as for both of them it is difficult to give information in a simple and informal way. Following the square of information by Schulz von Thun (2008), the objective of the messages is often overloaded or even blocked by the relationship content.
- **Ideas related to working hours and accessibility**: Communication problems have also to do with the different priorities concerning the work-life-balance of Mr. Clark and Mrs. Brown. As Mr. Clark is also restricted by the responsibility to take care of his health he cannot stay in the office as many hours as Mrs. Brown does.

- **Composition of the working group**: Although the composition of the newly formed working group was the responsibility of Mr. Rader and Mr. Clark was not involved in this decision, it affects the relationship of Mrs. Brown and Mr. Clark since it is still hard for her to accept.
- **Social proximity and informal power**: Mr. Clark as well as Mrs. Brown knew about the different extent of social proximity with their boss. However, Mr. Clark has not considered the related question of informal power before. He never intended to plot against Mrs. Brown but simply enjoyed his friendship with Mr. Rader.
- **Leadership style**: the different styles derive from different values and convictions, but at the same time both of them are struggling for the best outcome. While Mrs. Brown's style of leadership can be described as goal-oriented, Mr. Clark displays a relationship-oriented style.

Discussing these different topics, it becomes clear to the mediator as well as the conflict partners that on a deeper level of analysis, different values come into play: For Mr. Clark, in line with his need for a good work-life-balance, social relationships and social acceptance are very important values. In the same way as he is anxious to lose the friendship with Mr. Rader, he is afraid to lose the respect of his team as well as the relationship of trust within the working group if he would follow, for example, a stricter leadership style. At the same time, he also suffers from the perceived lack of acceptance by Mrs. Brown. Contrary to Mr. Clark, Mrs. Brown is more independent of other people's opinions and her social acceptance. For her, further career steps are of fundamental importance, especially since she felt treated unfairly when she did not get the job in the Middle East. Whereas Mr. Clark struggles for stability in his social relationships and workplace conditions, Mrs. Brown is aiming for development and improvement. However, both share the value of personal freedom and want to decide for themselves about their working and leadership style.

Reflections on the Mediation Case

Overlooking this case study on a leadership conflict, it becomes clear that emotions and accusations are caused by a broad range of motives that are lying beneath the topics that seem to play a role at a first glance. As in many social conflicts, the perception of injustice also plays a significant role in the case study (Deutsch 2006; Kals and Maes 2012; Mikula and Wenzel 2000; Montada 2003; Nabatchi et al. 2007). Mrs. Brown feels she has been unfairly treated by Mr. Rader since in her perception he decided not to promote her for the job abroad (level of distributive justice). The fact that he did not give her any reasons for this decision, nor informed her about the decision-making process (level of procedural justice) makes the situation worse. It is not only the outcome that bothers Mrs. Brown but especially the fact that the whole decision process remains unclear, which injures procedural justice (Bollen et al. 2012). This is also the case for the decision to not be allowed to also take some of her well-known staff members to the new team.

In agreement with Mrs. Brown, her perception of this situation is shared with Mr. Rader, since he is involved in this aspect of the conflict and therefore should be included in the mediation for the further understanding of the decisions as well as for the resolution of this part of the conflict. For this purpose, a session where all three of them are present is conducted. During this process Mr. Rader apologizes for not informing Mrs. Brown and tries to explain to her the decision-making in retrospect. It is especially this honest apology that opens the way to solve the conflict (Nebsit et al. 2012). This may also allow Mrs. Brown to see that there is no plotting against her. Following a cognitive theory of emotion (Lazarus et al. 1970), it also reduces Mrs. Brown's feelings of indignation that accompany her judgments of injustice (Haidt 2003; Weiner 2006). This shows *the importance of a look at the past in order to understand the present* (Montada and Kals 2013).

The justice motive also comes into play when Mr. Rader "distributes" social proximity between the two colleagues. This aspect was also reflected with all conflict partners so that they all become aware that the private friendship between Mr. Rader und Mr. Clark influences the work atmosphere. Furthermore, it also creates the impression that it affects decisions at work, like to give Mr. Clark an advantage by including most of his old staff in the new working unit. Nevertheless, by talking about this issue Mr. Clark's awareness grows that this composition implies problems for equally shared leadership and he starts to understand that their friendship might have been (miss)understood as plotting.

Moreover, most of the other conflict issues also touch upon justice. Both sides share the conviction that they themselves do a good job yet they do not feel recognized which is the case for different reasons. In Mrs. Brown's opinion, her social norm that hard work should be valued and appreciated by fostering her career is injured. This results in judgments of unfair treatment and feelings of indignation. In this regard, the justice motive seems to be on a higher, more inclusive level, compared to other motives. This is in line with the fact that the justice motive is an important motivational source for human behavior and experience which empirically cannot be reduced to hidden self-interest, but exists as an independent motive (Maes and Schmitt 2004; Mikula and Wenzel 2000; Montada 1998), also in conflict situations (Ohbuchi and Tedeschi 1997).

Also the conflict concerning the work-life-balance of Mr. Clark got clarified in the light of justice: The decision of Mr. Clark to work fewer hours than Mrs. Brown is among other things due to his responsibility for his health. If he would not take care of himself, he would not be able to perform well in the long run. He felt treated unfairly by Mrs. Brown, who seems to ignore this and made him feel guilty. They discussed this matter and agreed on fixed working hours. Mrs. Brown was able to accept Mr. Clark's need for freedom to decide on working hours within the prescribed range as it feels all right for him.

Based on this deeper understanding of the underlying motives and the history of the current conflict, it may become possible to find a sustainable solution (Montada and Kals 2013; Nabatchi et al. 2007). In the case study, both conflict partners got to know that their work is mutually valued which especially fulfills their need for appreciation. Their cooperation became more effective by means of (a) a clear agreement system, e.g., a regularly scheduled meeting (Jour Fixe) with the three of them as well as with the team to make arrangements, and (b) the implementation of rules on communication, e.g., to address aspects of disagreements as quickly as possible. It was made sure that the regular meetings are scheduled in a way that would grant Mr. Clark sufficient freedom. With the help of the mediator, they also came to an agreement about how concrete the targets should be for the team members. Moreover, the mediator helped to clarify the role confusion of Mr. Rader as both supervisor and friend of Mr. Clark in the way that the friendship was not given up but more awareness was given to avoid that this friendship subconsciously influences workplace decisions. This was very important for Mrs. Brown and significantly diminished her feelings of indignation. Mr. Rader also fixed with her future development lines and further possible career steps. Also Mr. Clark and Mrs. Brown mutually understood their needs and explanations for the displayed behavior.

Accordingly, the process as well as the solution of the mediation were successfully evaluated. The formative evaluation included a short evaluation after each session; the summative evaluation, the evaluation of the implementation of the solution and its functioning some weeks after the end of the mediation as well as 6 months later, as a longitudinal measure (follow-up). It was shown that the cooperation between the two colleagues was mostly conflict-free and in case smaller conflicts came up, Mrs. Brown and Mr. Clark were able to talk about it and explain their point of views at the very beginning of the conflict process so that there was no possibility of escalation. In the meantime Mrs. Brown's next career steps were fixed.

Such complex solution package would never have been found without understanding the "real" motives hidden behind the expressed positions of the conflict partners (Montada and Kals 2013). Instead, a quick solution would have been solely focused on an improved information transfer. The difficulty in taking into account the underlying motives is that most people are not aware of their motives and thus cannot provide information about them when they are directly asked about it. There are, however, many tools for the mediator to discover the underlying motives which shall be demonstrated by a look at the case study.

Strategies to Achieve Sustainable Solutions

Thinking and acting in pluralistic dimensions is a helpful strategy in order to understand one's own underlying needs, wishes and motives as well as those of the other party (Kals and Ittner 2008; Montada and Kals 2013). Initially, one might have thought that Mrs. Brown and Mr. Clark experience themselves as competitors: Who is able to show more competence during the presentation and is therefore earning to be promoted for further career steps? Such questions of direct competition, however, proved to be not significant. For Mrs. Brown the question of career and self-interest is of high relevance but for Mr. Clark social acceptance and freedom of choice are the dominant motives. Indeed, the explanatory hypothesis on the behavior of the conflict partners that comes to mind first often proves to be wrong. Therefore, the mediator should be open-minded to develop many alternative explanation hypotheses, based on theoretical knowledge, experience, and intuition (McKenzie 2015; Rooney 2007).

To gather these hypotheses, *a trained look at the manifest behavior and communication pattern of the conflict partners* is helpful (Bush and Pope 2002; Hoskins and Stoltz 2003; Schulz von Thun 2008). In our case study, the verbal but especially the non- and paraverbal patterns of communication of the conflict partners show their specific distress with one another. They displayed the same communication pattern both in the presentation situation as well as in the mediation sessions: Whenever Mr. Clark answered a question Mrs. Brown either interrupted him or, if present, addressed Mr. Rader. Subsequently, Mr. Clark started to raise his voice and stare to Mr. Rader. Furthermore, Mrs. Brown was polite but very clear and strict in her argumentation lines while she turned her body off from Mr. Clark and never gave him a smile.

In such an atmosphere of mutual tensions the first aim of a mediator is to equally *build trust* in a fair procedure, the effectiveness of the mediation process, and in his personal competence. For this purpose, the mediator should make explicit the procedure and rules of the mediation process and recall these rules whenever necessary, e.g., when the two colleagues interrupt each other instead of actively listening to each other. These rules *follow the paradigm of procedural justice* (Greenberg and Folger 1983), e.g., to give the same amount of talking time to all conflict partners or to be explicit about information that is of relevance. When the mediator establishes such rules and manages to stepwise promote direct communication between the conflict partners, the experience of justice and trust can grow, which is in line with the empirical foundation of the theory of disputant-disputant interpersonal justice (Nebsit et al. 2012).

Carl Rogers' *non-directive approach to communication* (2003) is one of the basic skills that can help to understand hidden motives and interests of the conflict partners. The nonviolent communication model of Marshall Rosenberg (2003), following the footpath of Carl Rogers, explicitly assumes that aggressions in conflicts are expressions of unfulfilled motives. These emotional expressions are not only of high diagnostic value but it is also important to resolve them for the mediation process to continue. As long as emotional expressions play an important role, the need of both colleagues to be recognized by the other person for his/her work, remains unfulfilled. Only when the colleagues come to know their mutual acceptance, their willingness to understand the other perspective instantly grows. This can be considered the turning point within the conflict resolution (Hoskins and Stoltz 2003).

It is important that the mediator displays an *authentic and empathic way of communication*, in which he acts as a role model (Rogers 2003). Other communication techniques and strategies need to supplement this approach: summarizing, structuring, the method of the controlled dialogue, posing open questions that promote (self)reflections, the usage of meta-communication techniques, and most notably reframing attacks and accusations into wishes, aims, interests, and needs that stand behind these attacks (Montada and Kals 2013; Rosenberg 2003; Schulz von Thun 2008). On a nonverbal level the mediator establishes rapport with the conflict partner who is currently speaking This is a helpful tool, taken from the methodology of neuro-linguistic programming (Bandler and Grinder 1975) and helps to get into contact with the conflict partner's views.

Often in conflict situations, all conflict partners regard their personal view as the only correct one on the situation. It is therefore important to sharpen the question of "How real is real?" (Watzlawick et al. 2014) into "How real is real in conflict situations?". In conflicts individual perspectives are stabilized by systematic distortions (Bless et al. 2004). Expressions of understanding and cooperation are overheard, whereas expressions of rejection are sensitively noticed. Both conflict partners fail to recognize that their efforts, experience and work are mutually appreciated. Instead, single words or gestures evoke connotations of, for example, negative feelings or past experiences, like when Mr. Clark turns to Mr. Rader, Mrs. Brown interprets it as a gesture of plotting against her. Such biases in the perception of the conflict partner's behavior promote self-fulfilling prophecies and vicious circles (e.g., Mrs. Brown reflects her impression by neither smiling at him nor having a talk with him about anything that does not affect work, which in return worsens their relationship). It has been shown empirically that to become aware of such vicious circles and self-serving biases in one's own perception, is an important way to overcome them (Kals et al. 2002). Such awareness can be achieved by the use of cognitive approaches which are of great importance in order to question the other parties' social perceptions, to reconstruct the understanding of the conflict, as well as to modify the experienced emotions (Bless et al. 2004; Bush and Pope 2002). *Questions to rethink one's perception and reconstruct the current conflict situation* can help to broaden the individual perspective, e.g.: How does the situation look like from an outside or future perspective? How might another person perceive the behavior of your colleague?

Often, *positive motivators are helpful* to strengthen the willingness for and success of perspective taking. In our case this was the insight that both parties share responsibility for the department as well as the well-being of the staff. A view to the future concerning the aspired result might further foster this motivation, e.g.: How would you recognize that you cooperate instead of working against each other? How would cooperation feel like? What would be the rewards for you personally? Despite of these positive motivators, negative motivators should be used very carefully and mainly in individual sessions, like the elaboration of the "worst alternative to a negotiated agreement" (WATNA). The impact and side-effects of the application of such techniques could be the reducing of internal motivation and the experience of pressure and tension that reduce creative thinking and problem solving (Montada and Kals 2013).

This shows that the whole portfolio of psychological methods and mediation techniques can be useful (Wall and Dunne 2012). The specific use of a method should be applied to the situation and context conditions by taking into account side-effects, as demonstrated by the WATNA-test. Furthermore, the basis for their application has to be the multipartiality of the mediator and his respect towards the conflict parties (Bush and Folger 2005). This is particularly important with regard to the growth of confidence in a fair mediation process and the awareness for the deep structure of the conflict to arise.

The practical aim of such a scientific mediation approach is to find a mutually experienced win-win-solution which is regarded as fair by all conflict parties (Zartman et al. 1996). Such a solution can arise when the deep structure of the conflict and the subjective perspectives of the conflict partners are mutually understood. At a first glance, such a mediation approach might be rejected because it seems too intense concerning time and effort. However, at a second glance, it may imply many advantages, especially in those cases where continued contact between the disputants is required. Examples for these advantages are the sustainability of the solution found, the possibility to gather knowledge about oneself, the improvement of being able to take different perspectives, the acquisition of new competences and wisdom even if the mediation might fail. Beyond, it reduces financial costs for the employers (Kals and Ittner 2008). In relation to the costs of workplace conflicts mentioned at the beginning of this chapter, the costs for conflict mediation are rather small (e.g., approx. 100–300 Euros per hour for an external mediator who preferable should cooperate with an internal mediator, who knows in-house rules and norms). In this respect, workplace mediation is still an underdeveloped research area (Bollen and Euwema 2013) but has a lot to contribute to the aim to deal fairly and efficiently with workplace conflicts.

References

Bandler, R., & Grinder, J. (1975). *The structure of magic: A book about language and therapy*. Palo Alto: Science and Behavior Books.

Baron, R. A. (1988). Attributions and organizational conflict: The mediating role of apparent sincerity. *Organizational Behavior and Human Decision Processes, 41*, 111–127.

Bless, H., Fiedler, K., & Strack, F. (2004). *Social cognition. How individuals construct social reality*. Hove: Psychology Press.

Bollen, K., & Euwema, M. (2013). Workplace mediation: An underdeveloped research area. *Negotiation Journal, 29*(3), 329–353.

Bollen, K., Ittner, H., & Euwema, M. (2012). Mediating hierarchical labor conflicts: Procedural justice makes a difference – for subordinates. *Group Decision & Negotiation, 21*(5), 621–636.

Bush, R. A. B., & Folger, J. P. (2005). *The promise of mediation*. San Francisco: Jossey-Bass.

Bush, R. A. B., & Pope, S. G. (2002). Changing the quality of conflict interaction: The principles and practice of transformative mediation. *Pepperdine Dispute Resolution Law Journal, 3*(1), 67–96.

Clark, A. E., & Oswald, A. J. (1994). Unhappiness and unemployment. *The Economic Journal, 104*(424), 648.

CPP Inc. (2008). *Workplace conflict and how businesses can harness it to thrive*. Mountain View.

De Dreu, C. K. W. (2008). The virtue and vice of workplace conflict: Food for (pessimistic) thought. *Journal of Organizational Behavior, 29*(1), 5–18.

De Dreu, C., & Van de Vliert, E. (Eds.). (1997). *Using conflict for organization*. London: Sage.

Deutsch, M. (2006). Justice and conflict. In M. Deutsch, P. T. Coleman, & E. C. Marcus (Eds.), *Handbook of conflict resolution* (pp. 43–68). San Francisco: Jossey Bass.

Euwema, M., Beetz, J., Driessen, S., & Menke, R. (2007). Wat kost een arbeidsconflict? *Forum voor conflictmanagement, 30*(6), 7–12.

Fisher, R., & Ury, W. (2011). *Getting to yes: Negotiating agreement without giving in.* New York: Penguin.

Goldberg, S. B., Sander, F. E. A., Rogers, N. H., & Cole, S. R. (2007). *Dispute resolution.* New York: Aspen.

Greenberg, J., & Folger, R. (1983). Procedural justice, participation, and the fair process effect in groups and organizations. In P. Paulus (Ed.), *Basic group processes* (pp. 235–256). New York: Springer.

Haidt, J. (2003). The moral emotions. In R. J. Davidson, K. R. Scherer, & H. H. Goldsmith (Eds.), *Handbook of affective sciences* (pp. 852–870). Oxford: Oxford University Press.

Hoskins, M. L., & Stoltz, J. M. (2003). Balancing on words: Human change processes in mediation. *Conflict Resolution Quarterly, 20*(3), 331–349.

Jahn, M. (2014). Konfliktkosten im Rahmen von BGM und BGF. In S. Hahnzog (Ed.), *Betriebliche Gesundheitsförderung* (pp. 75–82). Wiesbaden: Springer Fachmedien Wiesbaden.

Jandackova, V. K., & Jackowska, M. (2015). Low heart rate variability in unemployed men: The possible mediating effects of life satisfaction. *Psychology, Health & Medicine, 20*(5), 530–540.

Kals, E., & Ittner, H. (2008). *Wirtschaftsmediation.* Göttingen: Hogrefe.

Kals, E., & Kärcher, J. (2001). Mythen in der Wirtschaftsmediation. *Wirtschaftspsychologie, 2,* 17–27.

Kals, E., & Maes, J. (Eds.). (2012). *Justice and conflicts. Theoretical and empirical contributions.* Berlin: Springer.

Kals, E., Müller, M., & Maes, J. (2002). Aufklärung hilft! – Mediation kommunalpolitischer Konflikte. *Psychologie in Österreich, 5,* 227–232.

Kannheiser, W. (1992). *Arbeit und Emotion.* München: Quintessenz.

KPMG AG Wirtschaftsprüfungsgesellschaft. (2009). *Konfliktkostenstudie: Die Kosten von Reibungsverlusten in Industrieunternehmen.* Frankfurt a.M.

Kressel, K., & Pruitt, D. G. (Eds.). (1989). *Mediation research: The process and effectiveness of third-party intervention.* San Francisco: Jossey-Bass.

Lazarus, R. S., Averill, J. R., & Opton, E. M., Jr. (1970). Toward a cognitive theory of emotion. In M. B. Arnold (Ed.), *Feelings and emotions* (pp. 207–232). New York: Academic.

Lind, E. A., & Tyler, T. R. (1988). *The social psychology of procedural justice.* New York: Plenum Press.

Maes, J., & Schmitt, M. (2004). Gerechtigkeit und Gerechtigkeitspsychologie. In G. Sommer & A. Fuchs (Eds.), *Krieg und Frieden. Handbuch der Konflikt- und Friedenspsychologie* (pp. 182–194). Beltz: Weinheim.

McKenzie, D. M. (2015). The role of mediation in resolving workplace relationship conflict. *International Journal of Law and Psychiatry, 39,* 52–59.

Mikula, G., & Wenzel, M. (2000). Justice and social conflicts. *International Journal of Psychology, 35*(2), 126–135.

Miller, D. T., & Ratner, R. K. (1996). The power of the myth of self-interest. In L. Montada & M. J. Lerner (Eds.), *Current societal concerns about justice* (pp. 25–48). New York: Plenum Press.

Montada, L. (1998). Justice: Just a rational choice? *Social Justice Research, 11*(2), 81–101.

Montada, L. (2003). Justice, equity, and fairness in human relations. In J. Weiner (Ed.), *Handbook of psychology, Vol. 5* (Volume Editors: Th. Millon, & M. J. Lerner) (pp. 537–568). Hoboken: Wiley.

Montada, L., & Kals, E. (2013). *Mediation. Psychologische Grundlagen und Perspektiven.* Weinheim: Beltz.

Müller-Wolf, H.-M. (1994). Mediation von Konflikten und kritischen Prozessen in der beruflichen Praxis. *Gruppendynamik, 25*(3), 253–272.

Nabatchi, T., Bingham, L., & Good, D. H. (2007). Organizational justice and workplace mediation: A six factor model. *International Journal of Conflict Management, 18*(2), 148–174.

Nebsit, B., Nabatchi, T., & Bingham, L. B. (2012). Employees, supervisors, and workplace mediation: Experiences of justice and settlement. *Review of Public Personnel Administration, 32*(3),
260–287.

Ohbuchi, K. I., & Tedeschi, J. T. (1997). Multiple goals and tactical behaviors in social conflicts.
Journal of Applied Social Psychology, 27(24), 2177–2199.

Pruitt, D. G., & Carnevale, P. J. (2003). *Negotiation in social conflict.* Maidenhead: Open University
Press.

Pruitt, D. G., & Kim, S. H. (2004). *Social conflict.* New York: McGraw-Hill.

Rogers, C. R. (2003). *Client-centered therapy: Its current practice, implications and theory.*
London: Constable.

Rooney, G. (2007). The use of intuition in mediation. *Conflict Resolution Quarterly, 25*(2),
239–253.

Rosenberg, M. B. (2003). *Nonviolent communication: A language of life.* Encinitas: PuddleDancer.

Schulz von Thun, T. (2008). *Six tools for clear communication.* Hamburg: Institut für
Kommunikation.

Wall, A., & Dunne, T. C. (2012). Mediation research: A current review. *Negotiation Journal, 28*(2),
217–244.

Watzlawick, P., Bavelas, J. B., & Jackson, D. D. (2014). *Pragmatics of human communication: A
study of interactional patterns, pathologies, and paradoxes.* New York: Norton.

Weiner, B. (2006). *Social motivation, justice, and the moral emotions: An attributional approach.*
Mahwah: Erlbaum.

Winkelmann, R. (2009). Unemployment, social capital, and subjective well-being. *Journal of
Happiness Studies, 10*(4), 421–430.

Zartman, I. W., Druckman, D., Jensen, L., Pruitt, D. G., & Young, P. (1996). Negotiation as a
search for justice. *International Negotiation, 1*, 79–98.

Chapter 4
A Psychological Toolbox for Mediators: From Theory and Research to Best Practices

Klaus Harnack

"If you only have a hammer, you tend to see every problem as a nail."- Abraham Maslow (1966)

Maslow's law of the instrument describes the common phenomenon that once we discover a way to solve a problem, we tend to use this solution over and over again regardless the specific situation at hand. Especially when the cognitive and emotional load is high, we are more likely to rely on available heuristics (Gigerenzer and Todd 1999). Considering that conflict situations are often cognitively and emotionally loaded, the disputants tend to use available heuristics, for instance the fixed pie assumption (Harinck et al. 2000): the tendency to share divisible goods in a 50-50 manner without considering the underlying interests. As the mediator facilitates the process of conflict resolution, it is the task of the mediator to be aware of these tendencies and to make sure that parties do not fall prey to these heuristics, and instead make parties focus on the underlying interests.

The present chapter selects, illustrates, and transforms psychological theories and empirical findings into applicable tools to furnish the psychological toolbox of practitioners in the field of mediation whether it be full time mediators, or managers in the role of mediators. More specifically, the intended use of these tools is to facilitate and enhance the mediator's capability to sound out and recognize the possible resources that parties can offer to the process. Furthermore, all tools are designed to support the mediator in his strive to make issues more comprehensible to the parties and to fit their cognitive states (e.g. adjusting the level of detail for the cognitive needs of the parties). All tools require the mediator to take a very active stance.

Setting up an efficient personalized toolbox is a life-task. Once we discover a new tool and start using it, the tool broadens how we view a conflict and enriches our skills to form conflict related hypotheses and to uncover individual motivational stances and underlying interests (De Dreu and Carnevale 2003) as well as the psychological obstacles parties face in conflict (De Dreu et al. 2009). Suddenly, all

K. Harnack (✉)
Institut für Psychologie, Westfälische Wilhelms-Universität Münster, Münster, Germany
e-mail: klaus.harnack@uni-muenster.de

© Springer International Publishing Switzerland 2016
K. Bollen et al. (eds.), *Advancing Workplace Mediation Through Integration of Theory and Practice*, Industrial Relations & Conflict Management 3,
DOI 10.1007/978-3-319-42842-0_4

55

these prior nails turn into screws, clamps, and rivets, thereby enabling the mediator to become a better craftsman in his profession as a conflict analyst and catalyst.

A good mediator constantly adds new tools to his toolbox and with time, some tools emerge as more applicable than others do. This stresses the notion that the appropriate use of tools in mediation is a dynamic and flexible activity, which requires the mediator to act as a craftsman. At the same time however, some psychological tools and insights belong to the standard configuration of the mediator's toolbox due to their wide adaptability. The present set of tools aims to be such a basic configuration. All selected tools presented in this chapter are based on research related to social, motivational, and organizational psychology with a focus on the individual and have shown their practical relevance. Compared to more general tools, psychological tools focus on the mental processes that underlie the construction of the conflict – for example the way disputants perceive, frame and weight information (e.g. Stuhlmacher and Champagne 2000), how they construct their reality and view the elements of the conflict (e.g. Orr and Guthrie 2005).

In order to enhance the applicability of these mental processes, the present chapter is divided into two sections:

The first section ("Intra-individual differences") focuses on general intra-individual aspects: tools that play a role in each individual regardless of their personal characteristics or inter-individual differences. Specifically, we have a look at (1) the concept of psychological distance (Trope and Liberman 2010), (2) the idea of framing (Tversky and Kahneman 1981) and (3) the notion of utility, a concept to represent perceived value as defined by the prospect theory (Kahneman and Tversky 1979).

The second section ("Inter-individual differences") focuses on inter-individual differences in approaching a conflict (e.g. the perception of the conflict) and solving it. For this set of tools, the mediator needs to take into account parties' individual characteristics in order to apply tools successfully. In this section, we focus on (1) the concept of cognitive closure (Webster and Kruglanski 1994) (2) the importance of trust (Rousseau et al. 1998), and (3) the regulatory focus theory (Higgins 1997) or in other words parties' motivational bases towards the main issues of the conflict. The main selection criteria of all presented theories and empirical findings is the degree of their scientific approval and their practicability in the framework of mediation.

Intra-individual Differences

The configuration of the psychological toolbox begins with a set of tools applicable to all people in a wide range of conflict and mediation settings: face-to-face, online, or shuttle mediation (which is a series of one-to-one interviews conducted by the mediator without direct interaction of the disputants). Knowledge about the use of these tools is always relevant since they refer to intra-individual mental processes that take place (automatically) in many people, independent from their character or individual characteristics. Therefore, no individual assessment or evaluation is necessary.

Psychological Distance

Imagine there will be a company outing or team building event one year from now. Depending on the amicability of your colleagues, you might envision this as a nice or a horrifying picture. Research shows that thinking about the same event in different temporal distances (short versus long term), changes the level of detail in which you imagine the situation to be (Liberman et al. 2002): while considering the team building event in a distant future will depict an abstract, broad, and general picture (e.g. fun, inspiring versus boring), thinking about the same event in the near future (e.g. tomorrow), will increase the sharpness of the mental picture. You might think of how to get there (car, public transport, colleagues), the modest jokes of your colleague, or the boredom of the first team building activity.

The example reflects the construal level theory as developed by Trope and Liberman (2010). This theory assumes that the psychological distance between an entity and us shapes the level of detail of the mental resolution and that our default reference-point is the self, anchored in the present. It targets the questions: What is important to me now and what do I need to do now? Everything that adds distance to this reference-point automatically increases the level of abstraction. The notion of psychological distance is not limited to the temporal distance (time), but extends to spatial or physical distance (e.g. something that happens in your street versus to something which happens on the other side of the world), social and interpersonal distance (e.g. is it about your best friend versus it is about an unacquainted person), and hypothetical distance (e.g. something that will happen for sure versus something that is highly unlikely). For a meta-analysis see Soderberg et al. (2015), for a review see Liberman and Trope (2014).

A central part of the mediation process is to guide the parties towards their real underlying interests (Fisher and William 1991) and to disengage them from prior positions and issues which are most of the time more superficial. According to the construal level theory (Trope and Liberman 2011), the mediator needs to create a greater psychological distance and make sure that parties move away from the now and here in order to be able to focus on the bigger picture. A higher-level construal is one key element to help parties to find integrative solutions (Henderson and Trope 2009) since it broadens parties vision on the situation and directs attention towards primary features of the situation (e.g. the underlying interests – high construal) rather than towards secondary features like superficial issues (low construal) (Giacomantonio et al. 2010).

Henderson (2011) replicated this main effect by manipulating spatial distances: In this study, individuals negotiated with another person via a computer interface. In the first condition, participants believed that the counterpart was somewhere across town (physically faraway). In the second condition, participants believed that the counterpart was seated in front of a computer just next door (physically nearby). Results show that participants in the faraway condition (high construal) generated more integrative negotiation outcomes than the participants in the nearby condition (low construal).

The positive effects of creating psychological distance (high construal) can serve as a helpful tool to tackle deadlock situations in which parties have no apparent room to negotiate. It can help parties to discover new common grounds, as parties tend to focus on the essential and less on the superficial. The mediator can support parties by transferring the conflict issue to a higher construal level by referring to the distant future, assuming a more distant social constellation or if appropriate, by changing the likelihood of an event (hypothetical assuming a lower likelihood). In order to gain a better understanding of the tool, consider a mediation between a supplier and buyer of certain goods: One potential problem could be the exact timing of the delivery. Whereas discussing this issue for the next load, which involves high levels of details (the current status of employee's sickness, the ongoing road works, or the problems with the trucks loading ramps), could a discussion about a load in 1 year from now generate potential solutions like switching from truck to train delivery, using intermediate depots, or the change from large scale orders to frequent small orders. This broader picture helps the parties to explore their real underling interests, rather than focusing on current obstacles.

Framing

Think about the following anecdote about Nasreddin, a popular protagonist of short narratives in the Islamic cultural sphere, mostly subtle in humor and witty in nature.

Nasreddin used to take a donkey with its panniers loaded with straw across a frontier every day. When he trudged home every night, he admitted to be a smuggler at the frontier. As such, guards searched him over and over again: they searched his person, searched through the straw, steeped it in water, and even burned it from time to time. One of the customs officers met him years later. "You can tell me now, Nasreddin," What was it that you were smuggling?" "Donkeys," said Nasreddin.

The simple story points to the phenomenon called functional fixedness, the tendency to perceive objects and procedures in their traditional use (Duncker and Lees 1945). In the example, the donkey fulfills the transport function, as such the customs officers do not include it in their search for declared goods. A common example of functional fixedness in the context of conflict situations is money. People tend to focus solely on the monetary value of money and neglect its function related to social status, acceptance, power, security, self-confidence and symbol of love, etc. The mediator should try to bring parties' attention towards these other functions of money. Consider an in-house mediation in a large company between two department managers about their assigned budget. A possible working hypothesis for the mediator could be: The size of the budget represents the perceived importance in the company. It signals the future intent of the executive suite. Hence, the conflict might not be solely about the budget, but rather about guaranteeing the future of the department.

A superordinate category that includes functional fixedness is the concept of framing (Tversky and Kahneman 1981) which refers to the way people use information in order to construct reality and may change the motivational tendency to act. Is the glass half empty or half full? Is selling goods, a loss of those goods or a gain of money? These differently framed questions change the motivational stance and parties' valuing process. One of the most prominent examples is the Asian Disease Problem (Tversky and Kahneman 1981). In this hypothetical choice paradigm, participants were asked to imagine that the U.S. is preparing for the outbreak of an unusual Asian disease which is expected to kill 600 U.S. citizens. Two alternative programs to combat the disease have been proposed: "Assume that the exact scientific estimate of the consequences of the programs are as follows: In a first condition, the following consequences are presented: If Program A is adopted, 200 people will be saved. If program B is adopted there is a 1/3 probability that 600 people will be saved, and a 2/3 probability that no people will be saved." A second group of participants was presented with the same cover story, but with a different formulation of the consequences of the alternative actions: "If Program C is adopted 400 people will die. If Program D is adopted there is a 1/3 probability that nobody will die, and 2/3 probability that 600 people will die." Although programs A and C are identical as well as programs B and D, the average response changes dramatically due to the way the information is presented. In the first scenario, 72 % chose Program A (framing the consequences in terms of gains and lives saved), whereas in the second scenario 78 % chose Program D (framing the consequences in terms of expected deaths). This clearly illustrates our tendency to become risk-averse when we think in terms of gains (choosing the safe bet) and risk-seeking when we face a losing frame (choosing the gamble).

The knowledge that the presentation and documentation of information strongly influences the cognitive processing of information should be actively used by the mediator. More specifically, a mediator should stimulate parties to see the mediation process in terms of gains rather than losses, which leads to better agreements (Carnevale 2008). People in a gain frame usually have lower demands, make larger concessions, and are more likely to settle, compared to people in a loss frame (De Dreu et al. 1994). Particular attention should therefore be paid towards the gain-orientated presentation of information. For mediation practice, two suitable techniques are easily applicable: the first way is to reframe issues into a gain frame when parties' issues are recapitulated and the second way is to use a gain frame of stated issues and interests during the documentation of the mediation process, e.g. on a flip chart. For instance, the mediator could reframe the sentence "So I would be willing to give away X in order to get Y" into "So you will receive Y in exchange of X".

Utility

Classic economic theory assumes that each monetary unit compared to itself should have the same value, independent of the amount of the unit. This implies that an additional euro gained after a lottery win of 1 million euros, would have the same perceived value (utility) for the owner compared to an additional euro gained after a win of only 10 euros. In this case, the function between the utility and the monetary unit forms a straight line. The prospect theory in contrast, developed by Kahneman and Tversky (1979), denies this linear relationship and claims that value changes in respect to a reference point and with respect to gains and losses – so that an S-shaped function emerges. The S-shaped function results from a greater perceived value close to the reference point and decreasing utility with increasing of monetary value, e.g. the additional euro after a lottery win of 1 million euro is perceived as having less utility or value.

Additionally, the utility function predicts that the perceived value differs most around the reference point, with initial losses hurting more than gains in the same magnitude feel good. For example, imagine you bought stock for 100 euros. The day after you check the stock exchange prices in the newspaper and notice that the initial price has changed. The magnitude of your disappointment would be worse if the stock were at 99 euros, compared to the magnitude you would feel happy if the stock were at 101 euros (see Fig. 4.1).

The mediator can utilize this asymmetry in perceived value. Consider the following case: Imagine a car dealer and a potential buyer that almost settled their price negotiation over a car: 8400 euros. Once the negotiation parties reach this point, the car dealer has two options to finish the deal: (a) to further reduce the price by for instance 100 euros or (b) to offer the customer some extra gadgets, like car mats or a fancy key chain amounting to less than 50 euros. Taking the rational perspective of the buyer, the reduction of 100 euros is of course the economically better option, but in terms of perceived value, the second option is perceived as the better one since it represents a gain. According to the utility function, the value gained by the buyer in a reduction of 100 euros is smaller than the value gained by the additional gadgets for 50 euros, since the utility function flattens with an increase along the monetary axis. Therefore the experienced value-plus gained from a price reduction from 8400 euros to 8300 euros is smaller than the value-plus gained by an additional gain dimension, namely the additional offer of some car mats and the key chain. This utility frame can be used across a wide range of conflict issues.

The mediator should try to split domains that imply possible gains into as many domains as possible in order to achieve a higher value in their summation compared to the perceived value of this domain along just one axis (one dimension). Hence, instead of presenting a potential package containing X, Y, Z, present a solution composed of X plus Y plus Z. The reverse holds true for domains that imply potential losses. In this case, the mediator should try to integrate these domains into a single loss issue in order to minimize the perceived negative value. For instance, if a party is willing to concede in one dimension in which previous concession were

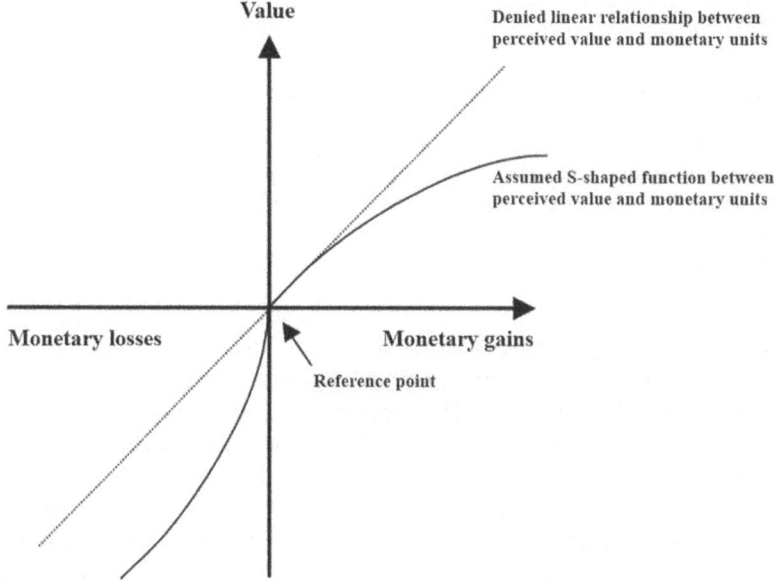

Fig. 4.1 The value function

made, the mediator should support this concession. This is better for the overall utility than making small additional concessions in a domain in which no previous concession were made.

This tool is also useful during the negotiation phase. Usually, people try to force the counterpart to make little concessions on several issues, rather than a large concession on a single issue. According to the value-function, it is more sensible to make additional concessions in one domain, rather than making several small concessions in different domains that were untouched before. In many cases, better integrative results can be obtained by maxing out one dimension than adding up small concessions on different dimensions.

Inter-individual Differences

In contrast to the first set of tools, these tools focus on inter-individual differences and parties' psychological nature. It requires the mediator to assess parties' psychological configuration prior to the application of tools in order to assess, which tools would work best for the party at hand.

Need for Closure

To what extent do you agree with the following statements?[1]

- *"I hate to change my plans at the last minute."*
- *"I enjoy having a clear and structured mode of life."*
- *"In most social conflicts, I can easily see which side is right and which one is wrong."*
- *"I dislike questions which could be answered in many different ways."*

If you agree rather than disagree with these sample items (Webster and Kruglanski 1994), you are likely to have a rather high need for cognitive closure which is defined as the individual's desire for a firm answer as compared to an ambiguous or open answer (Kruglanski 2013). The concept of cognitive closure is composed of five subcategories: (a) the desire for predictability, (b) preference for order and structure, (c) discomfort with ambiguity, (d) decisiveness, and (e) close-mindedness. The individual differences referring to these five subcategories are important indicators for the mediator on how to guide the parties throughout the mediation process. Research by De Dreu et al. (1999) shows that people with a high need for closure tend to seize and freeze on information and expose less flexibility in negotiations. This implies for instance that these people are more susceptible to *stereotypical information. In this case, it is the duty of the mediator to work actively against these tendencies because these biases hinder the conflict resolution process and hinder potential settlements.*

For people with a high need for cognitive closure, it is especially important to ensure a clear and transparent mediation process in order to maintain their full support, since a conflict situation itself inheres high levels of ambiguity and confusion. Although the need for cognitive closure is a stable personal trait, the mediator should be aware of the fact that external factors like time pressure can induce higher levels in the need for closure (De Dreu 2003). The main purpose of this tool is to create a mediation procedure that is personalized in terms of clarity, level of documentation, and structure.

Trust

Trust is a psychological state comprising the intention to accept vulnerability based upon positive expectations of the intentions or behavior of another (Rousseau et al. 1998, p395). The concept of trust refers back to the previous section, because one major factor that drives trust propensity is the individual need for cognitive closure. A recent study by Acar-Burkay et al. (2014) demonstrates that a higher need for cognitive closure is related with lower trust in distant others and higher trust in

---

[1] Sample Items – Need for closure scale (Webster and Kruglanski 1994)

socially closer individuals. These results support the empirical findings of an earlier study by Sorrentino et al. (1995) showing that certainty-oriented persons (high need for cognitive closure) either display high or low trust for their partners and spouses, whereas uncertainty-oriented persons typically attain only a moderate level of trust. This need for closure is an important indicator to the mediator, because it is related to trust, and a minimum level of trust between the parties is required in order to successfully conduct a mediation (moderate levels of trust towards the mediator is a mandatory condition before starting the mediation). If a minimum level of trust between the parties is not present in a mediation, misunderstandings and misinterpretations are likely to occur (Nadler and Liviatan 2006).

Since trust has positive effects on negotiations and conflict interactions (for a recent meta-analysis see Kong et al. (2014), it is a central task of the mediator to establish as much trust as possible between the conflict parties, especially in the early phase of a mediation process. One commonly used and effective strategy to build a minimum level of trust among the disputants is to establish a shared group identity (Tajfel 1982), which highlights shared norms, values, or simply sameness. One prominent example that stresses the simplicity of sameness is the name-letter-effect (Nuttin 1985): the tendency to prefer the letters of our own name over other letters. "What is similar to me must be good, hence I trust in it".

Further techniques to establish trust between the parties is to create a humorous atmosphere by the mediator (Kurtzberg et al. 2009) or the nudge by the mediator to exchange personal information (Thompson and Nadler 2002), especially when similarities can be distinguished. For example, the mediator could emphasize that two merchants share the same daily problems of selling, dealing with clients, and their belonging to the same professional category.

Regulatory Focus

There are two main approaches when entering mediation: either a person is motivated to win something versus not to lose something. According to the regulatory focus theory (Higgins 1997) promotion characterized by eagerness relates to the motivation to win, while prevention characterized by vigilance relates to the motivation not to lose something. For a person with a promotion focus, it is important to gain something even though it might involve drawbacks and failures, whereas for a person with a prevention focus, the suspension of possible failures is of essence. Two main insights for the mediator can be obtained out of the theory: (a) There should be a fit between the regulatory focus of the individual and the orientation of the negotiation (Appelt et al. 2009) and (b) a promotion focus results in more generous offers and more integrative settlements (Galinsky et al. 2005). For example if a conflict is about a price of goods, the buyer is usually in a prevention focus since he does not want to lose his money, while the seller is in a promotion focus as he wants to gain money. The mediator needs to make sure that the regulatory need of each party is respected. Consequently, a regulatory fit can be achieved, if the mediator emphasizes a potential gain (for the person in promotion focus) and a prevention of a loss (for the person in a prevention focus).

Conclusion

The central theme permeating the present chapter is that all tools are directed at the individuals' perception of the conflict. Analog to one of the major duties of the mediator, which is to reveal the underling interests of the stated positions of the parties, is the approach to reveal the actual individual perception of the conflict-related issues. Knowing the psychological consequences of inter- and intra-individual differences in perception, the mediator is enabled to conduct a more effective mediation. In a sense, all presented psychological tools are designed to overcome a spoken word or a presented picture and instead identify the perceived message or the perceived scenery. The toolbox should enable the mediator to work with the value of things instead of monetary units, to extend the pie instead of sharing the pie, and to fit the mediation process for the individual needs instead of following the default rules of conduct.

Although the present set of tools is by far not exploited by the present collection, it constitutes a starting point for an individual assortment of tools. When adding new tools to the toolbox, try to prefer simple to more complex tools, because simple tools are more adoptable and universal in nature. Consider a bent wire of an old coat hanger with a small hook that ends up as the most valuable tool in the laymen's toolbox, since it serves as the best mean to fetch back the children's socks out of the wastewater drain of the washing machine.

References

Acar-Burkay, S., Fennis, B. M., & Warlop, L. (2014). Trusting others: The polarization effect of need for closure. *Journal of Personality and Social Psychology, 107,* 719–735.

Appelt, K. C., Zou, X., Arora, P., & Higgins, E. T. (2009). Regulatory fit in negotiation: Effects of "prevention-buyer" and "promotion-seller" fit. *Social Cognition, 27,* 365–384.

Carnevale, P. J. (2008). Positive affect and decision frame in negotiation. *Group Decision and Negotiation, 17,* 51–63.

De Dreu, C. K. W. (2003). Time pressure and closing of the mind in negotiation. *Organizational Behavior and Human Decision Processes, 91,* 280–295.

De Dreu, C. K. W., & Carnevale, P. J. (2003). Motivational bases of information processing and strategy in conflict and negotiation. *Advances in Experimental Social Psychology, 35,* 235–291.

De Dreu, C. K. W., Carnevale, P. J., Emans, B. J., & Van De Vliert, E. (1994). Effects of gain-loss frames in negotiation: Loss aversion, mismatching, and frame adoption. *Organizational Behavior and Human Decision Processes, 60,* 90–107.

De Dreu, C. K. W., Koole, S. L., & Oldersma, F. L. (1999). On the seizing and freezing of negotiator inferences: Need for cognitive closure moderates the use of heuristics in negotiation. *Personality and Social Psychology Bulletin, 25,* 348–362.

De Dreu, C. K. W., Giacomantonio, M., Shalvi, S., & Sligte, D. (2009). Getting stuck or stepping back: Effects of obstacles and construal level in the negotiation of creative solutions. *Journal of Experimental Social Psychology, 45*, 542–548.

Duncker, K., & Lees, L. S. (1945). On problem-solving. *Psychological Monographs, 58*(5, Serial No. 270).

Fisher, R., & William, L. (1991). *Getting to yes*. New York: Penguin Group.

Galinsky, A. D., Leonardelli, G. J., Okhuysen, G. A., & Mussweiler, T. (2005). Regulatory focus at the bargaining table: Promoting distributive and integrative success. *Personality and Social Psychology Bulletin, 31*, 1087–1098.

Giacomantonio, M., De Dreu, C. K. W., & Mannetti, L. (2010). Now you see it, now you don't: Interests, issues, and psychological distance in integrative negotiation. *Journal of Personality and Social Psychology, 98*, 761–774.

Gigerenzer, G., & Todd, P. M. (1999). Fast and frugal heuristics: The adaptive toolbox. In G. Gigerenzer, P. Todd, & the ABC Group (Eds.), *Simple heuristics that make us smart* (pp. 3–34). New York: Oxford University Press.

Harinck, F., De Dreu, C. K., & Van Vianen, A. E. (2000). The impact of conflict issues on fixed-pie perceptions, problem solving, and integrative outcomes in negotiation. *Organizational Behavior and Human Decision Processes, 81*, 329–358.

Henderson, M. D. (2011). Mere physical distance and integrative agreements: When more space improves negotiation outcomes. *Journal of Experimental Social Psychology, 47*, 7–15.

Henderson, M. D., & Trope, Y. (2009). The effects of abstraction on integrative agreements: When seeing the forest helps avoid getting tangled in the trees. *Social Cognition, 27*, 402–417.

Higgins, E. T. (1997). Beyond pleasure and pain. *American Psychologist, 52*, 1280–1300.

Kahneman, D., & Tversky, A. (1979). Prospect theory: An analysis of decision under risk. *Econometrica: J Econ Soc, 47*, 263–291.

Kong, D. T., Dirks, K. T., & Ferrin, D. L. (2014). Interpersonal trust within negotiations: Meta-analytic evidence, critical contingencies, and directions for future research. *Academy of Management Journal, 57*, 1235–1255.

Kruglanski, A. W. (2013). *The psychology of closed mindedness*. New York: Psychology Press.

Kurtzberg, T. R., Naquin, C. E., & Belkin, L. Y. (2009). Humor as a relationship-building tool in online negotiations. *International Journal of Conflict Management, 20*, 377–397.

Liberman, N., & Trope, Y. (2014). Traversing psychological distance. *Trends in Cognitive Sciences, 18*, 364–369.

Liberman, N., Sagristano, M. D., & Trope, Y. (2002). The effect of temporal distance on level of mental construal. *Journal of Experimental Social Psychology, 38*, 523–534.

Nadler, A., & Liviatan, I. (2006). Intergroup reconciliation: Effects of adversary's expressions of empathy, responsibility, and recipients' trust. *Personality and Social Psychology Bulletin, 32*, 459–470.

Nuttin, J. M. (1985). Narcissism beyond gestalt and awareness: The name letter effect. *European Journal of Social Psychology, 15*, 353–361.

Orr, D., & Guthrie, C. (2005). Anchoring, information, expertise, and negotiation: New insights from meta-analysis. *Ohio State J Disput Resolut, 21*, 597–628.

Rousseau, D. M., Sitkin, S. B., Burt, R. S., & Camerer, C. (1998). Not so different after all: A cross-discipline view of trust. *Academy of Management Review, 23*, 393–404.

Soderberg, C. K., Callahan, S. P., Kochersberger, A. O., Amit, E., & Ledgerwood, A. (2015). The effects of psychological distance on abstraction: Two meta-analyses. *Psychological Bulletin, 141*, 525–548.

Sorrentino, R. M., Holmes, J. G., Hanna, S. E., & Sharp, A. (1995). Uncertainty orientation and trust in close relationships: Individual differences in cognitive styles. *Journal of Personality and Social Psychology, 68*, 314–327.

Stuhlmacher, A. F., & Champagne, M. V. (2000). The impact of time pressure and information on negotiation process and decisions. *Group Decision and Negotiation, 9*, 471–491.

Tajfel, H. (1982). Social psychology of intergroup relations. *Annual Review of Psychology, 33*, 1–39.

Thompson, L., & Nadler, J. (2002). Negotiating via information technology: Theory and application. *Journal of Social Issues, 58,* 109–124.

Trope, Y., & Liberman, N. (2010). Construal-level theory of psychological distance. *Psychological Review, 117,* 440–463.

Trope, Y., & Liberman, N. (2011). Construal level theory. *Handb Theor Soc Psychol, 1,* 118–134.

Tversky, A., & Kahneman, D. (1981). The framing of decisions and the psychology of choice. *Science, 211,* 453–458.

Webster, D. M., & Kruglanski, A. W. (1994). Individual differences in need for cognitive closure. *Journal of Personality and Social Psychology, 67,* 1049–1062.

Chapter 5
Workplace Mediation: Lessons from Negotiation Theory

Benjamin P. Höhne, David D. Loschelder, Lisa Gutenbrunner, Johann M. Majer, and Roman Trötschel

To avoid impasses and to reach mutually beneficial agreements in negotiation and mediation, parties need to overcome a multitude of pitfalls—both of psychological and structural nature. En route to facilitating beneficial agreements, mediators can build on negotiation theory, which provides a number of key insights into the psychological and structural backdrop of conflicts. Capitalizing on these insights may alter parties' willingness to concede, their problem-solving behavior, and their ability to discover hidden resources. In this chapter, we review some influential theories, models, and concepts from the field of negotiation research and illustrate how these can help to better understand the pitfalls of workplace conflicts. We furthermore discuss a number of implications that negotiation theory has for successful mediation in the workplace.

In the present chapter, we would like to encourage researchers and practitioners alike to zoom in on negotiation issues, their characteristics, and how these characteristics can help to explore new routes towards agreement. We begin this chapter with an illustrative example, which we revert to in the ongoing chapter. We then illustrate a number of influential negotiation theories and concepts, such as social and epistemic motivation, procedural framing, outcome framing, social identities,

B.P. Höhne (✉)
Institute for Distance Learning, Beuth University of Applied Sciences, Berlin, Germany
e-mail: bhoehne@beuth-hochschule.de

D.D. Loschelder
Department of Business Psychology and Experimental Methods, Leuphana University, Lüneburg, Germany

L. Gutenbrunner
Department of Psychology, Philipps-University of Marburg, Marburg, Germany

J.M. Majer • R. Trötschel
Department of Social and Organizational Psychology, Leuphana University, Lüneburg, Germany

© Springer International Publishing Switzerland 2016   67
K. Bollen et al. (eds.), *Advancing Workplace Mediation Through Integration of Theory and Practice*, Industrial Relations & Conflict Management 3,
DOI 10.1007/978-3-319-42842-0_5

and how resource characteristics can foster agreement. Finally, we review empirical research efforts in the field of workplace mediation. Here, we focus on the validation of negotiation principles within mediation as well as the summative evaluation of workplace mediation in general.

Emily and Frank in conflict

Imagine a conflict between two employees of a company, let us name them Frank and Emily. Both have worked in the same team for some time and share responsibilities for certain tasks. Frank was installed as the team leader a year ago and is also in charge of distributing the pending work. Recently, Frank also became a father and since then he has been ill and leaving work more frequently than usual. Naturally, this setup can lead to a number of workplace conflicts—many of them will depend on Frank's and Emily's personalities (e.g., social motives), on situational factors (e.g., interpersonal vs. intergroup interactions), as well as the interaction of personality and situation. We subsequently review several psychological theories and concepts that have profound implications for negotiations and conflict mediation and return to this introductory example throughout the chapter for illustrative purposes.

Lessons from Negotiation Theory

Social Motivation in Negotiations

Negotiations are mixed-motive situations (Lax and Sebenius 1986)—meaning that negotiators feel the need to stand up for their own interests and to compete with their counterpart for the best possible outcome. At the same time, it is paramount for negotiators to cooperate with the counterpart and to concede in order to reach any agreement at all. Hence, negotiators are faced with a motivational dilemma between *pro-self* and *pro-social* motives. Consequently, the influence of social motives has been an important topic of research for decades (Deutsch 1973; MacCrimmon and Messick 1976; Messick and McClintock 1968). Social motivation is defined as the extent to which parties strive to maximize primarily their own (*pro-self motivation*) or both their own *and* the counterpart's interests (*pro-social motivation*; e.g., De Dreu et al. 2000a).

A plethora of research in this field has led to one of the most prominent models in negotiations: The *Dual-Concern-Model* (Pruitt and Rubin 1986). Building on the insights of leadership models (i.e., *managerial grid*; Blake and Mouton 1964) and the influence of social motives on behavior (Deutsch 1973), Pruitt and Rubin propose that dominant strategies in negotiation can be predicted from two dimensions: (1) *self-concern* and (2) *other-concern*. First, self-concern entails parties' resistance to concede (Druckman 1994; Kelley et al. 1967) and their general toughness in conflict (Bartos 1974). Parties high in self-concern have ambitious, inflexible aspirations, whereas those low in self-concern have lower and more flexible

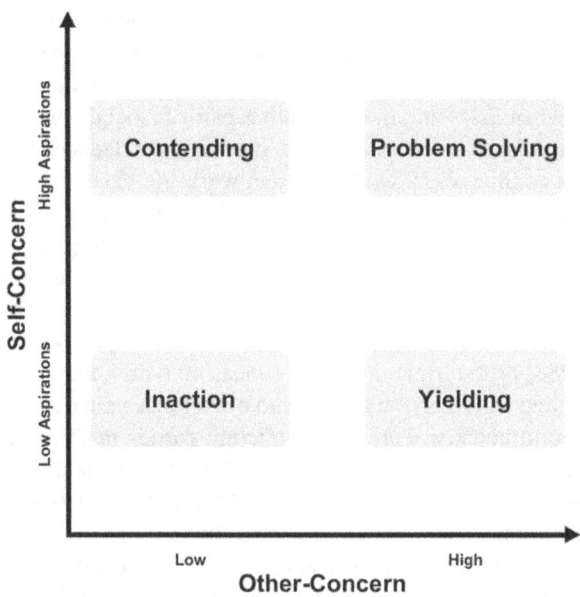

Fig. 5.1 The dual-concern-model (Adapted from Pruitt 1998; Pruitt and Carnevale 1993)

aspirations (Pruitt 1998). *Other-concern*, on the other hand, reflects parties' social motivation ranging from a pro-social motivation on one end of the continuum (*high other-concern*) to a pro-self motivation on the other end (*low other-concern*; Pruitt 1998). Pruitt and Rubin (1986; Pruitt 1998; Pruitt and Carnevale 1993) propose that high self-concern paired with high other-concern should facilitate problem solving strategies. Numerous studies revealed that a high resistance to concede paired with a pro-social motivation helps negotiators to find integrative win-win solutions (for a review see De Dreu et al. 2000a). Looking at other possible combinations Pruitt and Rubin (1986) predicted the following dominant strategies as a function of self- and other-concern as depicted in Fig. 5.1.

Returning to our introductory example, we would like to illustrate the difficulties and opportunities that mediators encounter when considering disputants' social motives. Especially in work-related settings, conflicts often appear between different levels of hierarchy, for example between a team member like Emily and a team leader like Frank (e.g., Bollen et al. 2012). The mediation of such conflicts is associated with specific difficulties on part of the team members (not leaders), who often show a lack of expressed self-concern due to their financial and work-related dependence (Bollen et al. 2010; Wing 2009). Specifically, employees might be hesitant to open up in conflict, let alone oppose their superiors. When faced with such uneven pairs of negotiators, with one yielding (pro-social) and one contending (pro-self) party, it might be wise for the mediator to support the subordinate party in establishing and voicing their interests. In order to do that the mediator has to first assess which social motives are predominant in a certain situation. As individuals usually have a dominant social motive in terms of a dispositional trait (Van Lange et al. 1997) as well as a situationally induced tendency to act in a pro-self or pro-social manner (Liberman et al. 2004), the mediator should look at both factors (disposition and situation) when assessing the conflicting parties' social value orientation. For the situational influence in the example the mediator can deduce at least two things: (1) In general a conflict about work-load and work-life balance is likely guided by a pro-self orientation. (2) Lower hierarchy in the workplace will likely impair the genuine expression of a pro-self orientation. Emily may strategically express a pro-social motivation in order to avoid any anticipated negative repercussions by her superior Frank. When looking at ways to find out about dispositional motivations, mediators can rely on a set of established tools like the ring measure (Liebrand and McClintock 1988) or the triple dominance measure (van Lange et al. 1997) which are easy to use and can likely be adjusted to a workplace environment.[1] Both tools allow mediators to quickly score the conflicting parties in three broad categories (cooperators, individualists, and competitors) based on their decisions in a profit distribution task (e.g. Option A: 480 for you, 80 for other; Option B: 540 for you, 280 for other; Option C: 480 for you, 480 for other).

By supporting underrepresented orientations (self or social), a mediator can foster negotiation styles that provide beneficial solutions for both conflicting parties (i.e. problem solving strategies). Several mediation strategies are available to meet this end. (1) The most basic strategy is asking specific questions aiming at the underrepresented orientations (e.g., "What is it *you* need in the situation?" focusing the pro-self-orientation). (2) Another promising technique is the *paradoxical intervention* (Benjamin 1995). By asking negotiators what the situation must look like to make it even worse and to escalate the conflict, the problem can be analyzed within a hypothetical scenario and can be described without risking to openly criticize a superior. In our example, the risk that Emily is strategically withholding her pro-self positions to avoid harming the relationship with her superior Frank is reduced. When all relevant information on how to aggravate the work situation is on the table, it can be reversed to deduce solutions on how to improve the situation instead. Within hierarchically structured work conflicts like our example, conflicting parties may not be able to speak openly; but the mediator can develop guidelines based on the results of a paradoxical intervention as means to resolve the conflict. Such recommendations can often be accepted more easily when offered by a neutral outsider (e.g., Harth and Shnabel 2015). With the help of paradoxical interventions, negotiators do not risk their relationship by excessive critique or demands because it is in the very nature of the task to generate exacerbating factors; yet the mediator can built on these proposals and make fully informed propositions to disputants. (3) As a third strategy, mediators can use perspective taking techniques, such as *controlled dialogue* or *role reversal* to support the pro-social orientation (e.g., Gutenbrunner and Wagner in press). On a cognitive level, perspective taking was shown to encour-

---

[1] Nowadays, variations of these measures can also be found online which provides a simple and quick way of testing social orientations. See for example http://vlab.ethz.ch/svo/index-normal.html.

age better coordination, problem solving, concession making, and integrative agreements (e.g., Galinsky et al. 2005, 2008; Richardson et al. 1994; Trötschel et al. 2011). Perspective taking may also support a pro-social orientation on an emotional level by encouraging empathy for the other side (e.g., Batson 1991; Gutenbrunner and Wagner in press).

Epistemic Motivation in Negotiations

The Dual-Concern-Model has been an influential and inspirational theory for researchers and practitioners alike; but it has also been criticized for its sole focus on motivational factors. To address this concern, De Dreu and Carnevale (2003) introduced a *Motivated Information Processing Model* (MIPM), which seeks to bridge the gap between motivational and cognitive approaches. The authors introduce epistemic motivation, which is defined as the extent to which a person feels the need to systematically collect and process information. People high (vs. low) in epistemic motivation approach cognitively challenging tasks willingly, regularly and on their own account. According to De Dreu and Carnevale (2003) the roots of epistemic motivation can be traced back to two concepts from persuasion research: (1) *Need for Cognition* (NC; Petty and Cacioppo 1986) which determines a person's need to intrinsically approach cognitively demanding tasks and (2) the *Need for Cognitive Closure* (NFCC; Kruglanski 1989; Kruglanski and Ajzen 1983). People with a high NFCC tend to have a low tolerance for ambiguity; they prefer to make decisions fast rather than prudently. In the realm of negotiations, a low epistemic motivation has been shown to lead to more cognitive fallacies, more heuristic processing, and negotiation outcomes of lower quality (i.e., compromises or lose-lose agreements; De Dreu et al. 1999, 2000; Harinck and De Dreu 2004). As a useful simplification of the model the authors elaborate four archetypes of negotiators as a function of social (pro-self vs. pro-social) and epistemic motivation (low vs. high; De Dreu and Carnevale 2003; De Dreu et al. 2006): (1) The *selfish miser*[2] relies on competitive heuristics (e.g., "your gain = my loss") and uses ethically questionable negotiation tactics such as lying, deceiving, threatening and bluffing. It is hard work for negotiators and mediators alike to gain a selfish miser's trust; concessions will often not be reciprocated. (2) The *pro-social miser* on the other hand is quick to cooperate and will be easily persuaded to concede. Nevertheless, a pro-social miser is less likely to intensively explore win-win solutions. Instead they prefer to settle quickly for an easy compromise. Thus, if you are looking for a sustainable and high-quality agreement a pro-social miser raises challenges. (3) The *selfish thinker* is high in epistemic motivation paired with pro-self motives. Selfish thinkers are able to systematically and efficiently process information gained in the process of a negotiation. Much like selfish misers they will also try to persuade, deceive or

---

[2] The term "miser" relates to Fiske and Taylor's (1991) concept of the *cognitive miser*, for a person who thinks heuristically.

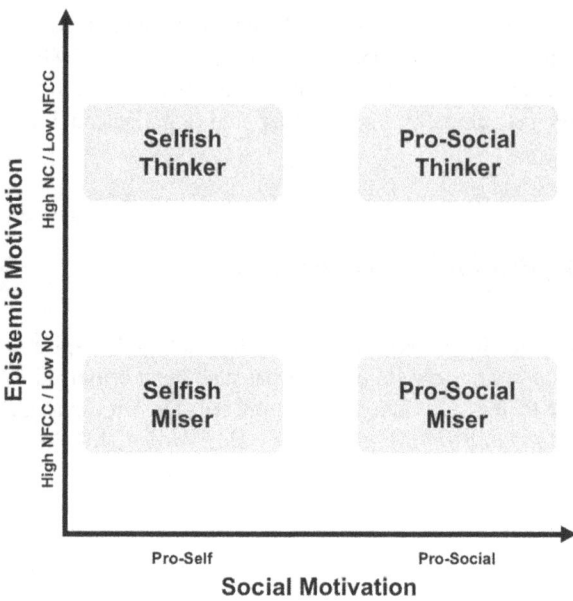

Fig. 5.2 The motivated information processing model and its four archetypes of negotiators (De Dreu and Carnevale 2003)

misrepresent information to further their cause, but are able to do this with more vigor and skill. One should be cautious when negotiating with selfish thinkers, as they will be quick to recognize and exploit information to further their goal of "winning" the negotiation (see also Loschelder et al. 2014, 2015). (4) Finally, the *pro-social thinker* searches and processes information systematically which helps the negotiation process. In contrast to the selfish thinker, the pro-social thinker uses this information to craft mutually beneficial outcomes, to make systematic trade-offs, and to detect hidden options. Pro-social thinkers are trusting and trustworthy partners in negotiation and conflict; they inquire and willingly provide information about preferences and priorities, which might help foster sustainable agreements. The four archetypes as a function of social and epistemic motivation are depicted in Fig. 5.2.

In the previous section, we talked about assessing social motives considering dispositional as well as situational factors. The same should be done for epistemic motivation in order to attain a first impression of parties' archetypical way of approaching a conflict. Depending on the mediator's impression of the conflicting parties, he or she can either assess parties' need for cognition with a short questionnaire (Cacioppo et al. 1984) or assess their tendency to approach problems heuristically (need for closure scale; see for example Roets and Van Hiel 2011).[3] Naturally,

---

[3] Again, there are also online tools for assessing NC and NFC which can for example be used in preparation for a face-to-face session.

if time or situation do not allow for a systematic, psychologically sound assessment of social and epistemic motivation, mediators can always rely on simple ground-laying questions to gain a general understanding of a parties' motivation (e.g. "Would you rather prefer a quick solution to this conflict or would you like to put in additional time and resources to find the best solution").

Considering ways of resolving detrimental orientations towards a conflict, especially in negotiations with parties low in epistemic motivation, a mediator can take remedial action. By guiding the communication, for instance through Socratic questioning, a mediator can reveal weaknesses of a negotiated solution (Cooley 2006). Several authors describe the critical questioning of early agreements (e.g., Are these agreements appropriate, fair, and efficient?) as a central responsibility of the mediator (Susskind and Cruikshank 1987; Fisher et al. 2011). The mediator can furthermore uncover resources for integrative solutions by using creativity techniques like brainstorming (Fisher et al. 2011). By asking to generate as many possible and impossible solutions as possible, negotiators' creativity is stimulated. Out of this large pool of solutions, negotiators can pick those which meet the criteria mentioned above. The probability that some of the generated solutions are more complete and accurate in covering parties' interests compared to the early agreement suggested by selfish or pro-social *misers* is very high. The mediator as an advocate for a sustainable and high-quality agreement should be active and focus more on the problem than on the relation of the negotiators (see for example Alexander 2008, for different mediation styles).

The selfish thinker on the other hand, is at least an equally large challenge to the mediator. Negotiators who use their profound understanding of the conflict to further their own advantage (at the expense of the counterpart), are unlikely to generate mutually beneficial solutions for both sides. Again, the production of many creative solutions might illustrate the integrative potential of a conflict situation and pave the way for a win-win solution. As mentioned above, perspective taking can also create an emotional basis for compromise. Finally, caucuses can be used to explore the potential for integrative solutions in a save space, without forcing the parties to "show weakness" or willingness to compromise in front of each other (e.g., Stulberg and Love 2009).

Procedural Framing

Recent research has attempted to zoom in on the issues and resources of a negotiation (Trötschel et al. 2015). To return to the introductory example, imagine that at some point during a mediation Frank and Emily discuss new ways of organizing their task responsibilities. Frank might *offer* to do more administrative work in exchange for Emily attending more late meetings. Reversely, he could *request* from Emily to attend the late meetings in exchange for him covering more administrative work. The two proposals are qualitatively identical; but they are framed differently—this framing has been coined *procedural framing* (Larrick and Blount 1997).

Whereas the *offer* framing puts a relatively stronger emphasis on what Frank is willing to give (i.e., the resource *administrative work* rather than the *late meetings*), the *request* framing places a stronger emphasis on meetings than on administrative work. This focus on certain resources that are to be exchanged in a negotiation or conflict has fundamental implications for parties' perceptions, their behavior and ultimately the negotiation outcomes (Trötschel et al. 2015). The party whose resource is placed into the limelight anticipates stronger losses, it is more averse to concede, and frequently ends up with higher individual outcomes than parties who focus on the resource they are about to gain. Importantly, when both parties focus on their own resources—which they ought to part with—the likelihood for hurtful non-agreements or stalemates increases exponentially (Loschelder et al. 2015).

To link the prior section on social motivation to this procedural-framing reasoning, a pro-self motivation seems to (1) maximize parties' propensity to frame proposals as requests rather than offers, (2) leads parties to evaluate requests more negatively than identical offers (far more so than pro-social parties), and (3) makes parties perceive particularly strong losses from requests (Loschelder et al. 2015; see also Bechara et al. 1997). As a consequence, the likelihood for negotiations and conflict to end up in a stalemate, a hurtful non-agreement, is exacerbated when two pro-self opponents exchange demands rather than requests. Thus, mediators should pay special attention to constellations with two or more pro-self oriented parties. As mentioned above it can be wise for the mediator to reinforce pro-social orientations in such situations. One way of achieving this is by asking the parties to reframe their proposals as offers instead of demands to establish a cooperative exchange setting. The focus on offers rather than requests can also be part of the communication rules mediators establish in the beginning. Well-aimed questions by the mediator (e.g., "What could you offer the other party/one another?") can support favorable procedural frames in the mediation process. For mixed-motivated conflict parties, mediators should make a conscious effort to extract offers from the pro-self disputant and to encourage pro-socials to utter their requests. Emily might need encouragement from the mediator to ask Frank for support in the administrative work, Frank might significantly improve his relationship with Emily by re-framing some of his requests into equivalent offers.

Apart from social motivation, procedural frames can also arise from the setup of the negotiation. Specifically, the setup of negotiations can be distinguished in three basic types of settings: (1) transaction negotiations (e.g., Emily and Frank negotiate the transaction of administrative tasks in exchange for the attendance to late meetings), (2) distribution negotiations (e.g., Frank and Emily negotiate the distribution of bonuses after a big contract), and (3) contribution negotiations (e.g., Emily and Frank negotiate how much work each of them puts into acquiring a new client). Whereas the role of procedural frames in *transaction* negotiations has been described above, the framing of proposals is also affected by the two other types of settings (Höhne 2015; Höhne et al. 2016).

In *distribution* negotiations, parties tend to request resources for themselves rather than to offer joint resources to the counterpart. Hence, both parties perceive distributions as a setting allowing for gains (mutual gain focus). In contrast, parties in *contribution* negotiations (e.g., the contribution of work hours to acquire a new client) tend to offer own resources rather than to request resources from the counterpart. Hence, both parties commonly perceive contribution negotiations as involving losses (mutual loss focus). As a consequence, parties in distribution settings are more successful in crafting win-win agreements than parties in contribution settings (Höhne et al. 2016). Mediators should be wary of negotiation settings that might induce a mutual loss focus (e.g., contribution negotiations) and try to point to potential gains in such settings. In general, situations that require parties to contribute mutually are often followed by situations in which resources are distributed (mutual gain focus). Mediators can use such setups to establish a more balanced negotiation by discussing contributions and future distributions simultaneously. In our example this would mean that Frank and Emily should not only discuss how many hours they are willing to put in to acquire a new client but also how they will distribute future bonuses if the customer were to be acquired.

To conclude with a central implication for workplace mediation, it seems paramount for mediators to ensure that parties frame proposals so that they place an emphasis on resources that each party is going to gain from an agreement (rather than the losses parties have to forego). Accordingly many textbooks on mediation training recommend paraphrasing and summarizing techniques to reframe statements as described above (e.g., Boulle et al. 2008; Moore 2003; Stulberg and Love 2009). If loss frames cannot be avoided due to the circumstances (e.g. employee layoffs), mediators can try to work out silver linings with the weaker party or attempt to change parties' perspectives to a more positive future outlook. Note that these situations may pose a challenge because the mediator has to switch into the role of a coach for the weaker party rather than a neutral third party.

Outcome Framing

The far more prominent form of framing, which has received a large amount of attention in negotiation research, is *outcome framing*. Outcome frames emerge when parties compare a potential agreement with an alternative outcome that serves as a reference point. If the reference outcome is worse than the potential agreement, the potential agreement is perceived as a gain. If the reference outcome is better than the potential agreement, the potential agreement is perceived as a loss. In contrast to procedural frames, outcome frames do not emerge based on how the social interaction itself is framed ("my X for your Y" versus "your Y for my X"); instead, they emerge from the comparison to a predefined reference outcome (Bottom 1998; De Dreu et al. 1995; Neale and Bazerman 1992). To exemplify, Emily's reference outcome for the distribution of tasks might be set to the time before Frank became team leader and father. Hence, she is likely to perceive the recent changes in their work agreement as a loss. By contrast, if Frank were to compare the current arrangement to his parental leave, he likely expects Emily to perceive a gain and to see the many hours he is putting in for the team.

Framing possible outcomes as losses rather than gains has a strong impact on negotiators' behavior and performance. Research shows that loss-framed negotiators act more self-servingly and concede less (Bazerman et al. 1985). Dyads of two loss-averse negotiators tend to find fewer win-win solutions in integrative negotiations (Bazerman et al. 1985), they end up with significantly more impasses (Trötschel and Gollwitzer 2007), and often apply less cooperative and more competitive strategies (De Dreu et al. 1994) than gain-framed negotiators.

While procedural framing can be easily influenced by mediators (e.g., by paraphrasing), outcome framing seems less flexible. Mediators can nonetheless try to change a negotiator's salient reference outcome or stable sensitivity to losses. If this fails, it is advisable to invite other stakeholders into the negotiation process. In our example, a mediator could invite Frank's and Emily's superior to frame a negotiation outcome in a relatively positive way to attenuate further conflict and dissatisfaction in the team. In addition to the change in perspective on the current state of negotiations, inviting a new positive stakeholder to the mediation can also introduce new resources to the negotiation which might help to pave the way to agreement. For instance, Frank's and Emily's superior could facilitate a switch of certain responsibilities not only between Frank and Emily, but also between other members of the team.

Intergroup Negotiations and the Social Identity Approach

Most negotiation studies focus on an *interpersonal* negotiation context (e.g., buyer-seller negotiations; Galinsky and Mussweiler 2001). Studies investigating *intergroup* processes in negotiations either studied the behaviors and outcomes of negotiation teams (e.g., Thompson et al. 1996), of group representatives (e.g., Ben-Yoav and Pruitt 1984; Steinel et al. 2009), or the impact of social identity processes in intergroup negotiations (e.g., Van Kleef et al. 2007; Trötschel et al. 2010).

Studies on team negotiations are characterized by parties' competitive perceptions and expectations (Morgan and Tindale 2002; Polzer 1996). Interestingly, the increased level of competition does not automatically translate into deteriorated outcomes (Morgan and Tindale 2002; Thompson et al. 1996). Contrariwise, negotiation teams can achieve better outcomes as compared to interpersonal negotiators. It appears that three or more heads within a negotiation team are more successful in detecting win-win agreements than solo negotiators who are possibly more limited in their cognitive capacities (Cohen and Thompson 2011). Still, the detection of win-win agreements does not inevitably translate into a reduced level of competition, nor does it improve social relationships between the negotiation teams (Morgan and Tindale 2002).

Looking at representative negotiations, however, a different picture unfolds: In his influential *boundary-role model* of group representation, Adams (1976) assumes that representatives in negotiations, who negotiate on behalf of a group constituency, must take on a specialized boundary role to deal with the members of both the outgroup and the ingroup. This boundary role may lead to an increased level of competition, which in turn may result in deteriorated outcomes. For instance, if Emily entered the mediation not only to find a solution for her personal conflict with Frank but also to represent the other team members, she would possibly feel the need to take a tougher stance in order to save face in front of her colleagues. Empirical studies on group representatives corroborate theses assumptions (e.g., Ben-Yoav and Pruitt 1984; Benton and Druckman 1974; Loschelder and Trötschel 2010; O'Connor 1997; Trötschel et al. 2010): Representative negotiations are marked by an increased level of competition similar to the one that has been found in team negotiation studies. The level of competition may even increase when representatives negotiate with a group mandate of a *selfish constituency* (Steinel et al. 2009), or when representatives have a *peripheral status* within their group (Van Kleef et al. 2007; Steinel et al. 2009). As solo negotiators in representative negotiations may not compensate detrimental intergroup effects by means of an increased number of problem solvers, they commonly end up with lower negotiation outcomes than solo negotiators in an interpersonal setting (Trötschel et al. 2010).

Having received an explicit group mandate may not be the only reason for an increased level of competition in intergroup negotiations. Competition can also function as a means to establish ingroup distinctiveness (Mummendey and Otten 1998). This notion is based on the theoretical assumptions of the social identity theory (Tajfel 1982; Tajfel and Turner 1979) and the self-categorization theory (Turner et al. 1987), which together comprise the social identity approach. At the heart of this social identity approach lies the idea that people categorize their social world into *ingroups* (groups to which one belongs) and *outgroups* (groups to which one does not belong). In a second step, individuals can then identify as unique individuals (i.e., personal identity) or instead on the basis of salient group memberships (i.e., social identity). The latter *social identities* are defined as the "(…) part of an individual's self-concept which derives from his knowledge of his membership of a social group (or groups) together with the value and emotional significance attached to that membership" (Tajfel 1978, p.63). Whereas a social identity implies perceptions of interchangeable group members ("We" vs. "Them"), personal identities place the individual's uniqueness into the limelight ("I" or "Me" vs. "You"). Importantly, people compare their ingroup with relevant outgroups and strive to achieve a positive social identity (Turner et al. 1987), which in turn exacerbates conflict.

In terms of our introductory example, Frank's and Emily's interpersonal conflict is transformed into an intergroup conflict, once either identifies with an important ingroup—that is, they do no longer negotiate for their individual good but as accountable group representatives (Benton and Druckman 1973; Druckman 1994; O'Connor 1997). These representative negotiations (see Steinel et al. 2009; Van Kleef et al. 2007) with activated social identities are more competitive, conflict-laden, and more likely to result in impasses than interpersonal negotiations between two individuals (Loschelder and Trötschel 2010; Trötschel et al. 2010).

To sum up, negotiators in an intergroup context act more competitively and run a higher risk to end with deteriorated outcomes. The increased level of competition can be rooted in the boundary role of group representatives (Adams 1976; Van Kleef et al. 2007) or in salient social identities (Turner et al. 1987; Trötschel et al. 2010). Ignoring social identification processes that may linger on a level below the conflict issues may prevent successful conflict resolution. Put differently, it seems paramount to examine a tool that allows mediators to successfully alleviate conflict-laden situations between groups and group representatives.

A Remedy: The Common Ingroup Identity Model

Building on the social identity approach, Gaertner and his colleagues have proposed the *Common Ingroup Identity Model* (CIIM; Gaertner and Dovidio 2000; Gaertner et al. 1993, 1989). The model also builds on Brewer's (1979) analysis of intergroup bias and suggests that social categories are hierarchically organized. Higher-level categories (e.g., a company) are more inclusive of lower level categories (e.g., company departments; different work teams). Intergroup conflict can be reduced by altering the level of category inclusiveness, shifting it from lower level subgroups to higher level, more inclusive superordinate categories (Gaertner and Dovidio 2000). Group members' cognitive representations are altered from belonging to different (sub-)groups to belonging to one overarching group (Gaertner et al. 1989). In other words, individuals who were formerly categorized as outgroup members are subsequently included in a shared, common ingroup on a superordinate level (Gaertner et al. 1994).

Returning to the introductory example, let us assume that Emily has entered the mediation process as an employee representative, whereas Frank has been asked to find a better general agreement on behalf of the company's team leaders. This intergroup setup is doomed to clash with excessive demands, elevated levels of conflict, and a high likelihood for impasses. A mediator might pre-empt the social identification threat by fostering a shared identification between Frank and Emily on a superordinate level. Mediators should ask the parties to switch their perspectives to a higher level category when stating their problems (e.g., "Try to think of the bigger strategy, from your company's point of view, how would you describe this problem?; Which solutions would someone suggest for this conflict who mainly had the best interests of the entire company at heart?; How can your group contribute to the company's success?"). What previously appeared as a conflict between *us* versus *them* is transformed into a superordinate conflict between *all of us* (as members of the same company).

Importantly, this change of identification process does not require group members to forsake their respective sub-group identities (see Haslam 2004; Haslam et al. 2003). Instead, group members can maintain a *dual representation*, in which they identify simultaneously with both the original (sub)group and the superordinate group (Gaertner and Dovidio 2000; Gaertner et al. 1993; Hewstone and Brown 1986; Hornsey and Hogg 2000; see Fig. 5.3).

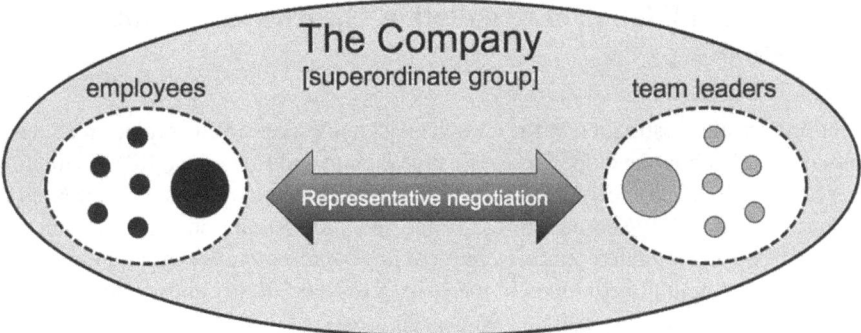

Fig. 5.3 Relevant social identities of an intergroup conflict. The large *black* and *grey circles* indicate the two representatives for the opposing subgroups of employees versus team leaders. A recategorization on a superordinate level—the company—integrates these subgroups on a higher identity level (See Gaertner and Dovidio 2000)

Previous research suggests that the Common Ingroup Identity Model is particularly applicable to representative negotiations. Sub-group identities are highly salient as negotiations revolve around divergent interests of the opposing groups. By means of integrating sub-group identities within a shared superordinate identity (Fig. 5.3), a mediator acknowledges for the underlying social structure of negotiations, and alleviates the impairments that stem from negotiators' competing identities. Psychological research from both the lab and the field suggests that, indeed, identity-based mediation is an effective tool to reduce conflict between opposing parties, to avoid non-agreements, and to foster more subjective satisfaction with an agreement compared to other forms of third-party intervention (see *common ingroup mediation;* Loschelder et al. 2016b).

Importantly, there appears to be a boundary condition, under which mediators should refrain from inducing an inclusive, shared identity: Groups might differ in terms of their relative *prototypicality* for the superordinate group—that is, the extent to which the own, lower-level group is more (or less) typical for the superordinate category. In our example, the over-arching company might have resulted from a recent merging process. While Frank is an employee of the new main corporation, Emily has entered the company during the merger and might still feel more related to her original company. In that sense, Frank would seem to be the more prototypical member of the superordinate group (i.e. the company). Under these conditions, mediators should refrain from fostering a shared identity on the higher company-level as research suggests that identity-based mediation backfires here; it fuels the conflict further rather than alleviating it (Loschelder et al. 2016b).

Empirical Validation of Negotiation Theories in Workplace Mediation

The empirical investigation of the effectiveness and process of workplace mediation is a relatively underdeveloped research area (Bollen and Euwema 2013). Evaluation research on mediation can broadly be divided into two approaches: (1) Research in controlled laboratory settings, investigating specific assumptions about the mediation process in simulated conflicts, and (2) large-scale surveys that monitor agreement rates of actual mediations in the field (Cross and Rosenthal 1999; Esser and Marriott 1995; Gutenbrunner and Wagner in press).

Workplace mediation is offered within organizations, meaning in interpersonal and intergroup conflicts between colleagues, teams, or between two hierarchical levels (organizational conflicts), as well as in collective bargaining processes between union and management (labor conflicts). Mediation in organizational conflicts is evaluated mainly in field studies.

In their literature review of mediation in organizational conflicts, Bollen and Euwema (2013) found evidence for mediation success (e.g., satisfactory agreements, perceived procedural justice). With a few exceptions (e.g., Loschelder et al. 2016b) most of the aforementioned principals of negotiation research were never systematically tested in the field of mediation and the generally scarce research often lacks control groups and follow-up evaluations.

In labor conflict, mediation has a longstanding history and was institutionalized as early as 1913 with the United Sates Conciliation Service (Rose 1952). Its success is documented in large field surveys, reporting agreement rates of about 70 % (e.g., Goldberg 1982; Medina et al. 2014; Miller 2001; for a review see Gutenbrunner and Wagner 2016). Yet again, these surveys often lack control groups and long-term evaluations. In contrast to organizational conflict, labor mediation is also examined in laboratory research. Especially in the 1970s and 1980s several studies were conducted to investigate mediation in simulated labor conflicts (e.g., Bartunek et al.1975; Bigoness 1976; Brookmire and Sistrunk 1980; Hiltrop and Rubin 1982; Johnson and Pruitt 1972; Johnson and Tullar 1972; Ross et al. 1990).

Although these studies did not explicitly investigate the theories described earlier, some of their results can be interpreted in light of negotiation research. Johnson and Pruitt (1972) as well as Johnson and Tullar (1972) found that anticipated arbitration leads to more concession making than anticipated mediation (see also Loschelder and Trötschel 2010). A looming arbitration might be especially threatening for parties with high self-concern (see *Dual-Concern-Model* above) due to the anticipated loss of decision control. In contrast, mediation can be a valuable tool to compensate a lack of *epistemic motivation.* Hiltrop and Rubin (1982) were able to show that parties benefited most from mediator's suggestions in highly complex conflicts (e.g., with multiple conflict issues), where negotiators struggle to process all relevant information. This result is further supported by Bartunek and colleagues (1975), who found mediators to be more effective when focusing on the content of the conflict, rather than the relation of the parties. The inferior effect of a relational orientation can be explained by unfavorable *procedural framing*. In the relation condition, the mediator taught the negotiators to paraphrase, meaning to "repeat back to the original speaker, in your own words, what you think he said" (Bartunek et al. 1975, p. 543). This paraphrasing does *not* constitute a favorable reframing (such as re-formulating proposals as offers rather than requests). By accounting for the findings from negotiation research, this relational mediation technique might have been more successful.

Conclusion

Negotiation theory offers a number of valuable insights into the psychological processes that fuel workplace conflict. These insights provide mediators with practical tools en route to helping parties resolve their conflict and finding a mutually beneficial agreement. Finally, the insights function as valuable analytical instruments, which help to interpret empirical findings of workplace mediation research. Among the most informative frameworks from negotiation theory, we elaborated on social and epistemic motivation, procedural and outcome framing, as well as social identification processes.

Our review of the literature on workplace mediation reveals that negotiation theory is only rarely discussed in the field. More research on the effectiveness of workplace mediation seems needed, especially with a focus on implications from negotiation theory and their practical implications for workplace mediation. If so, Frank and Emily may not live "happily ever after", yet we have high hopes that they will receive highly professional and effective mediation support that resolves many of their conflicts in the not so distant future.

References

Adams, J. S. (1976). The structure and dynamics of behavior in organizational boundary roles. In *Handbook of industrial and organizational psychology* (pp. 1175–1199). Chicago: Rand McNally.

Alexander, N. (2008). The mediation metamodel: Understanding practice. *Conflict Resolution Quarterly, 26*(1), 97–123.

Bartos, O. J. (1974). *Process and outcome in negotiation.* New York: Columbia University Free Press.

Bartunek, J. M., Benton, A. A., & Keys, C. B. (1975). Third party intervention and the bargaining behavior of group representatives. *Journal of Conflict Resolution, 19*(3), 532–557.

Batson, C. D. (1991). *The altruism question: Toward a social psychological answer.* Hillsdale: L. Erlbaum, Associates.

Bazerman, M. H., Magliozzi, T., & Neale, M. A. (1985). Integrative bargaining in a competitive market. *Organizational Behavior and Human Decision Processes, 35*(3), 294–313.

Bechara, A., Damasio, H., Tranel, D., & Damasio, A. R. (1997). Deciding advantageously before knowing the advantageous strategy. *Science, 275*, 1293–1295.

Benjamin, R. D. (1995). The constructive uses of deception: Skills, strategies, and techniques of the folkloric trickster figure and their application by mediators. *Mediation Quarterly, 13*(1), 3–18.

Benton, A. A., & Druckman, D. (1973). Salient solutions and the bargaining behavior of representatives and nonrepresentatives. *International Journal of Group Tensions, 3*(1–2), 28–39.

Benton, A. A., & Druckman, D. (1974). Constituent's bargaining orientation and intergroup negotiations. *Journal of Applied Social Psychology, 4*(2), 141–150.

Ben-Yoav, O., & Pruitt, D. G. (1984). Resistance to yielding and the expectation of cooperative future interaction in negotiation. *Journal of Experimental Social Psychology, 20*(4), 323–335.

Bigoness, W. J. (1976). The impact of initial bargaining position and alternative modes of third party intervention in resolving bargaining impasses. *Organizational Behavior and Human Performance, 17*(1), 185–198.

Blake, R. R., & Mouton, J. S. (1964). *The managerial grid: The key to leadership excellence.* Houston: Gulf Publishing.

Bollen, K., & Euwema, M. (2013). Workplace mediation: An underdeveloped research area. *Negotiation Journal, 29*(3), 329–353.

Bollen, K., Euwema, M., & Müller, P. (2010). Why are subordinates less satisfied with mediation? The role of uncertainty. *Negotiation Journal, 26*(4), 417–433.

Bollen, K., Ittner, H., & Euwema, M. C. (2012). Mediating hierarchical labor conflicts: Procedural justice makes a difference—for subordinates. *Group Decision and Negotiation, 21*(5), 621–636.

Bottom, W. P. (1998). Negotiator risk: Sources of uncertainty and the impact of reference points on negotiated agreements. *Organizational Behavior and Human Decision Processes, 76*(2), 89–112.

Boulle, L., Goldblatt, V., & Green, P. (2008). *Mediation: Principles, process, practice* (2nd New Zealand ed). Wellington: LexisNexis.

Brewer, M. B. (1979). In-group bias in the minimal intergroup situation: A cognitive-motivational analysis. *Psychological Bulletin, 86*(2), 307–324.

Brookmire, D. A., & Sistrunk, F. (1980). The effects of perceived ability and impartiality of mediators and time pressure on negotiation. *Journal of Conflict Resolution, 24*(2), 311–327.

Cacioppo, J. T., Petty, R. E., & Feng Kao, C. (1984). The efficient assessment of need for cognition. *Journal of Personality Assessment, 48*(3), 306–307.

Cohen, T. R., & Thompson, L. (2011). When are teams an asset in negotiations and when are they a liability? In E. A. Mannix, M. A. Neale, & J. R. Overbeck (Eds.), *Research on managing groups and teams: Negotiation and groups* (Vol. 14, pp. 3–34). Bingley: Emerald Group Publishing.

Cooley, J. W. (2006). *The mediator's handbook: Advanced practice guide for civil litigation* (2nd ed.). South Bend: National Institute for Trial Advocacy.

Cross, S., & Rosenthal, R. (1999). Three models of conflict resolution: Effects on intergroup expectancies and attitudes. *Journal of Social Issues, 55*(3), 561–580.

De Dreu, C. K. W., & Carnevale, P. J. (2003). Motivational bases of information processing and strategy in conflict and negotiation. *Advances in Experimental Social Psychology, 35*, 235–291.

De Dreu, C. K. W., Carnevale, P. J. D., Emans, B. J. M., & van de Vliert, E. (1994). Effects of gain-loss frames in negotiation: Loss aversion, mismatching, and frame adoption. *Organizational Behavior and Human Decision Processes, 60*(1), 90–107.

De Dreu, C. K. W., Carnevale, P. J., Emans, B. J., & van de Vliert, E. (1995). Outcome frames in bilateral negotiation: Resistance to concession making and frame adoption. *European Review of Social Psychology, 6*, 97–125.

De Dreu, C. K. W., Koole, L., & Oldersma, L. (1999). On the seizing and freezing of negotiator inferences: Need for cognitive closure moderates the use of heuristics in negotiation. *Personality and Social Psychology Bulletin, 25*(3), 348–362.

De Dreu, C. K., Weingart, L. R., & Kwon, S. (2000a). Influence of social motives on integrative negotiation: A meta-analytic review and test of two theories. *Journal of Personality and Social Psychology, 78*(5), 889–905.

De Dreu, C. K. W., Koole, S. L., & Steinel, W. (2000b). Unfixing the fixed pie: A motivated information-processing approach to integrative negotiation. *Journal of Personality and Social Psychology, 79*(6), 975–987.

De Dreu, C. K. W., Beersma, B., Stroebe, K., & Euwema, M. C. (2006). Motivated information processing, strategic choice, and the quality of negotiated agreement. *Journal of Personality and Social Psychology, 90*(6), 927–943.

Deutsch, M. (1973). *The resolution of conflict: Constructive and destructive processes.* New Haven: Yale University Press.

Druckman, D. (1994). Determinants of compromising behavior in negotiation: A meta-analysis. *Journal of Conflict Resolution, 38*(3), 507–556.

Esser, J. K., & Marriott, R. G. (1995). Mediation tactics: A comparison of field and laboratory research. *Journal of Applied Social Psychology, 25*(17), 1530–1546.

Fisher, R., Ury, W., & Patton, B. (2011). *Getting to yes: Negotiating agreement without giving in.* New York: Penguin.

Fiske, S. T., & Taylor, S. E. (1991). *Social cognition.* New York: McGraw-Hill.

Gaertner, S. L., & Dovidio, J. F. (2000). *Reducing intergroup bias: The common ingroup identity model.* Philadelphia: Psychology Press.

Gaertner, S. L., Mann, J., Murrell, A., & Dovidio, J. F. (1989). Reducing intergroup bias: The benefits of recategorization. *Journal of Personality and Social Psychology, 57*(2), 239–249.

Gaertner, S. L., Dovidio, J. F., Anastasio, P. A., Bachman, B. A., & Rust, M. C. (1993). The common ingroup identity model: Recategorization and the reduction of intergroup bias. *European Review of Social Psychology, 4*(1), 1–26.

Gaertner, S. L., Rust, M. C., Dovidio, J. F., Bachman, B. A., & Anastasio, P. A. (1994). The contact hypothesis the role of a common ingroup identity on reducing intergroup bias. *Small Group Research, 25*(2), 224–249.

Galinsky, A. D., & Mussweiler, T. (2001). First offers as anchors: The role of perspective-taking and negotiator focus. *Journal of Personality and Social Psychology, 81*(4), 657–669.

Galinsky, A. D., Ku, G., & Wang, C. S. (2005). Perspective-taking and self-other overlap: Fostering social bonds and facilitating social coordination. *Group Processes and Intergroup Relations, 8*(2), 109–124.

Galinsky, A. D., Wang, C. S., & Ku, G. (2008). Perspective-takers behave more stereotypically. *Journal of Personality and Social Psychology, 95*(2), 404–419.

Goldberg, S. B. (1982). Grievance mediation: A step towards peace in the bituminous coal industry. *West Virginia Law Review, 85*, 777–782.

Gutenbrunner, L., & Wagner, U. (in press). *Perspective taking techniques in the mediation of intergroup conflict.* Peace and Conflict: Journal of Peace Psychology.

Gutenbrunner, L., & Wagner, U. (2016). *Effectiveness of intergroup mediation: A comprehensive review.* Manuscript in preparation.

Harinck, F., & De Dreu, C. K. W. (2004). Negotiating interests or values and reaching integrative agreements: The importance of time pressure and temporary impasses. *European Journal of Social Psychology, 34*(5), 595–611.

Harth, N. S., & Shnabel, N. (2015). Third-party intervention in intergroup reconciliation: The role of neutrality and common identity with the other conflict party. *Group Processes and Intergroup Relations, 18*(5), 676–695.

Haslam, S. A. (2004). *Psychology in organizations: The social identity approach.* Thousand Oaks: Sage Publications.

Haslam, S. A., Eggins, R. A., & Reynolds, K. J. (2003). The ASPIRe model: Actualizing social and personal identity resources to enhance organizational outcomes. *Journal of Occupational and Organizational Psychology, 76*(1), 83–114.

Hewstone, M., & Brown, R. (1986). *Social psychology and society: Contact and conflict in intergroup encounters* (p. Xiii, 231-). Cambridge, MA: Basil Blackwell.

Hiltrop, J. M., & Rubin, J. Z. (1982). Effects of intervention mode and conflict of interest on dispute resolution. *Journal of Personality and Social Psychology, 42*(4), 665–672.

Höhne, B. P. (2015). It's called joint *venture* for a reason. Allocation context and resource valence as determinants of agreement quality in shared resource negotiations. Doctoral dissertation. Retrieved from http://katalog.leuphana.gbv.de.

Höhne, B. P., Loschelder, D. D., & Trötschel, R. (2016). *Keep your eyes on the prize when jointly venturing*. Allocation context and resource valence as determinants of agreement quality in shared resource negotiations. Manuscript in preparation.

Hornsey, M. J., & Hogg, M. A. (2000). Subgroup relations: A comparison of mutual intergroup differentiation and common ingroup identity models of prejudice reduction. *Personality and Social Psychology Bulletin, 26*(2), 242–256.

Johnson, D. F., & Pruitt, D. G. (1972). Preintervention effects of mediation versus arbitration. *Journal of Applied Psychology, 56*(1), 1–10.

Johnson, D. F., & Tullar, W. L. (1972). Style of third party intervention, face-saving and bargaining behavior. *Journal of Experimental Social Psychology, 8*(4), 319–330.

Kelley, H. H., Beckman, L. L., & Fischer, C. S. (1967). Negotiating the division of a reward under incomplete information. *Journal of Experimental Social Psychology, 3*(4), 361–398.

Kleef, G. A., Steinel, W., Knippenberg, D., Hogg, M. A., & Svensson, A. (2007). Group member prototypicality and intergroup negotiation: How one's standing in the group affects negotiation behaviour. *British Journal of Social Psychology, 46*(1), 129–152.

Kruglanski, A. W. (1989). The psychology of being "right": The problem of accuracy in social perception and cognition. *Psychological Bulletin, 106*(3), 395–409.

Kruglanski, A. W., & Ajzen, I. (1983). Bias and error in human judgment. *European Journal of Social Psychology, 13*(1), 1–44.

Larrick, R. P., & Blount, S. (1997). The claiming effect: Why players are more generous in social dilemmas than in ultimatum games. *Journal of Personality and Social Psychology, 72*(4), 810–825.

Lax, A. D., & Sebenius, K. J. (1986). *The manager as negotiator*. New York: Free Press.

Liberman, V., Samuels, S. M., & Ross, L. (2004). The name of the game: Predictive power of reputations versus situational labels in determining prisoner's dilemma game moves. *Personality and Social Psychology Bulletin, 30*(9), 1175–1185.

Liebrand, W. B., & McClintock, C. G. (1988). The ring measure of social values: A computerized procedure for assessing individual differences in information processing and social value orientation. *European Journal of Personality, 2*(3), 217–230.

Loschelder, D. D., & Trötschel, R. (2010). Overcoming the competitiveness of an intergroup context: Third-Party intervention in intergroup negotiations. *Group Processes and Intergroup Relations, 13*(6), 795–815.

Loschelder, D. D., Swaab, R. I., Trötschel, R., & Galinsky, A. D. (2014). The first-mover disadvantage: The folly of revealing compatible preferences. *Psychological Science*. doi:10.1177/095679761352016.

Loschelder, D. D., Friese, M., & Trötschel, R. (2015). *Strategic offers for egoistic reasons: The interplay of social motivation and procedural framing at the bargaining table*. Manuscript in revision.

Loschelder, D. D., Trötschel, R., Swaab, R. I., Friese, M. & Galinsky, A. D. (2016a). The information-anchoring model of first offers: When and why first offers help vs. hurt negotiators. *Journal of Applied Psychology, 101*(7).

Loschelder, D. D., Trötschel, R., Swaab, R. I., Höhne, B. P., & Gaertner, S. L. (2016b). *Common identity mediation in representative negotiations: Economic and psychological benefits of a shared identity*. Manuscript in revision.

MacCrimmon, K. R., & Messick, D. M. (1976). A framework for social motives. *Behavioral Science, 21*(2), 86–100.

Medina, F. J., Vilches, V., Otero, M., & Munduate, L. (2014). How negotiators are transformed into mediators. Labor conflict mediation in Andalusia. *Revista de Psicología del Trabajo y de las Organizaciones, 30*(3), 133–140.

Messick, D. M., & McClintock, C. G. (1968). Motivational bases of choice in experimental games. *Journal of Experimental Social Psychology, 4*(1), 1–25.

Miller, P. S. (2001). A just alternative or just an alternative? Mediation and the Americans with Disabilities Act. *Ohio State Law Journal, 62*, 11–29.

Moore, C. W. (2003). *The mediation process: Practical strategies for resolving conflict* (3rd ed.). San Francisco: Jossey-Bass.

Morgan, P. M., & Tindale, R. (2002). Group vs individual performance in mixed-motive situations: Exploring an inconsistency. *Organizational Behavior and Human Decision Processes, 87*(1), 44–65.

Mummendey, A., & Otten, S. (1998). Positive–negative asymmetry in social discrimination. *European Review of Social Psychology, 9*(1), 107–143.

Neale, M. A., & Bazerman, M. H. (1992). Negotiating rationally: The power and impact of the negotiator's frame. *Academy of Management Executive, 6*(3), 42–51.

O'Connor, K. M. (1997). Motives and cognitions in negotiation: A theoretical integration and an empirical test. *The International Journal of Conflict Management, 8*(2), 114–131.

Petty, R. E., & Cacioppo, J. T. (1986). The elaboration likelihood model of persuasion. In L. Berkowitz (Ed.), *Advances in experimental social psychology* (Vol. 19, pp. 123–205). New York: Academic.

Polzer, T. (1996). Intergroup negotiations: The effects of negotiating teams. *Journal of Conflict Resolution, 40*(4), 678–698.

Pruitt, D. G. (1998). Social conflict. In D. Gilbert, S. T. Fiske, & G. Lindzey (Eds.), *Handbook of social psychology* (4th ed., Vol. 2, pp. 89–150). New York: McGraw-Hill.

Pruitt, D. G., & Carnevale, P. J. (1993). *Negotiation in social conflict*. Pacific Grove: Brooks-Cole.

Pruitt, D. G., & Rubin, J. Z. (1986). *Social conflict: Escalation, stalemate, and settlement*. New York: Random House.

Richardson, D. R., Hammock, G. S., Smith, S. M., Gardner, W., & Signo, M. (1994). Empathy as a cognitive inhibitor of interpersonal aggression. *Aggressive Behavior, 20*(4), 275–289.

Roets, A., & Van Hiel, A. (2011). Item selection and validation of a brief, 15-item version of the need for closure scale. *Personality and Individual Differences, 50*(1), 90–94.

Rose, A. M. (1952). Needed research on the mediation of labor disputes. *Personnel Psychology, 5*(3), 187–200.

Ross, W. H., Conlon, D. E., & Lind, E. A. (1990). The mediator as leader: Effects of behavioral style and deadline certainty on negotiator behavior. *Group and Organization Management, 15*(1), 105–124.

Steinel, W., De Dreu, C. K., Ouwehand, E., & Ramírez-Marín, J. Y. (2009). When constituencies speak in multiple tongues: The relative persuasiveness of hawkish minorities in representative negotiation. *Organizational Behavior and Human Decision Processes, 109*(1), 67–78.

Stulberg, J. B., & Love, L. P. (2009). *The middle voice: Mediating conflict successfully*. Durham: Carolina Academic Press.

Susskind, L., & Cruikshank, J. L. (1987). *Breaking the impasse: Consensual approaches to resolving public disputes*. New York: Basic Books.

Tajfel, H. E. (1978). *Differentiation between social groups: Studies in the social psychology of intergroup relations*. London: Academic.

Tajfel, H. (1982). Social psychology of intergroup relations. *Annual Review of Psychology, 33*(1), 1–39.

Tajfel, H., & Turner, J. C. (1979). An integrative theory of intergroup conflict. In W. G. Austin & S. Worchel (Eds.), *The social psychology of intergroup relations* (pp. 33–47). Brooks-Cole: Monterey.

Thompson, L., Peterson, E., & Brodt, S. E. (1996). Team negotiation: An examination of integrative and distributive bargaining. *Journal of Personality and Social Psychology, 70*(1), 66–78.

Trötschel, R., & Gollwitzer, P. M. (2007). Implementation intentions and the willful pursuit of prosocial goals in negotiations. *Journal of Experimental Social Psychology, 43*(4), 579–598.

Trötschel, R., Hüffmeier, J., & Loschelder, D. D. (2010). When yielding pieces of the pie is not a piece of cake: Identity-based intergroup effects in negotiations. *Group Processes and Intergroup Relations, 13*(6), 741–763.

Trötschel, R., Hüffmeier, J., Loschelder, D. D., Schwartz, K., & Gollwitzer, P. M. (2011). Perspective taking as a means to overcome motivational barriers in negotiations: When putting oneself into the opponent's shoes helps to walk toward agreements. *Journal of Personality and Social Psychology, 101*(4), 771–790.

Trötschel, R., Loschelder, D. D., Höhne, B. P., & Majer, J. M. (2015). Procedural frames in negotiations: How offering my resources versus requesting yours impacts perception, behavior, and outcomes. *Journal of Personality and Social Psychology, 108*(3), 417–435.

Turner, J. C., Hogg, M. A., Oakes, P. J., Reicher, S. D., & Wetherell, M. S. (1987). *Rediscovering the social group: A self-categorization theory* (p. 239). Cambridge, MA: Basil Blackwell.

Van Lange, P. A. M., Otten, W., De Bruin, E. M. N., & Joireman, J. A. (1997). Development of prosocial, individualistic, and competitive orientations: Theory and preliminary evidence. *Journal of Personality and Social Psychology, 73*(4), 733–746.

Wing, L. (2009). Mediation and inequality reconsidered: Bringing the discussion to the table. *Conflict Resolution Quarterly, 26*(4), 383–404. doi:10.1002/crq.240.

Part II
The Context of Workplace Mediation

Chapter 6
Mediation and Conflict Coaching in Organizational Dispute Systems

Tricia S. Jones

As new Alternative Dispute Resolution (ADR) processes are developed, it becomes imperative to refine how best to build organizational dispute resolution systems that effectively integrate the various ADR components (e.g., mediation, conflict coaching, facilitation) so that the total system affords coverage of the breadth of the organization's conflicts. In this case, integration also means allowing conflicts to proceed from one ADR component to another, enabling a disputant to loopback to ADR components not initially utilized, and affording disputants the opportunity to use more than one ADR option simultaneously to support optimal conflict management.

ADR and Organizational Dispute System (ODS) courses are common in business (Bowen 2012a, b) and law schools (Rogers 2010). Stephens et al. (2012, 2013) found that ADR course offerings in MBA programs and undergraduate business programs increased 68 % since their previous surveys 8-years earlier. Along the same line, in the United States, there have been impressive increases in the use of ADR in businesses (Stephens et al. 2012, pp. 24–25) with around 90 % of business using mediation and 80 % using arbitration rather than litigation to resolve disputes. Moreover, the use of ADR and ODS in a variety of workplaces is growing internationally, with strong initiatives in the UK, Australia, the United States as well as Asia (Ridley-Duff and Bennett 2011; Roche and Teague 2012).

Conflict coaching is a relatively new and rapidly growing ADR process in the public and private sectors (Brubaker et al. 2014); one that offers the opportunity for inclusion as an element in intelligent and sophisticated organizational dispute system [ODS] design. This chapter suggests ways that conflict coaching can optimize and be optimized in ODS, particularly but not exclusively, in terms of its integration with workplace mediation.

T.S. Jones (✉)
School of Media and Communication, Temple University, Philadelphia, PA, USA
e-mail: tsjones@temple.edu

© Springer International Publishing Switzerland 2016   89
K. Bollen et al. (eds.), *Advancing Workplace Mediation Through Integration of Theory and Practice*, Industrial Relations & Conflict Management 3,
DOI 10.1007/978-3-319-42842-0_6

The argument in this chapter is that time is ripe to uncover assumptions and implementation practices that currently limit the utility of conflict coaching and ODS in order to set an agenda for how conflict coaching can best serve ODS for the future. This argument is presented in the following discussions: (1) an overview of conflict coaching and assumptions limiting its use, (2) an overview of ODS in private and federal sectors and assumptions limiting its use, and (3) identification of areas for potential optimization of conflict coaching and ODS. In the last section I'll suggest how the more innovative applications of conflict coaching could be used for maximum effect in three different conflict scenarios.

An Overview of Conflict Coaching

An overview of conflict coaching as a dispute resolution process is presented in the chapter by Ross Brinkert (see Chap. 10 in this volume) and in other resources that have introduced conflict coaching to the ADR community (Jones and Brinkert 2008). Since the initiation of conflict coaching in the mid-1990s, we have learned about various models, applications, and best-fits with organizational contexts including higher education, health care, private sector, and government (Mazur 2013).

Conflict coaching is a one-on-one process in which an internal or external conflict coach works with a party involved in conflict to accomplish three goals: (1) conflict analysis that provides the party with a coherent understanding of the conflict issues and drivers for the party and others central to the conflict; (2) identification of a future preferred direction for strategic action, and (3) skills development to enable the party to implement the preferred strategic action with a strong likelihood of success in managing or resolving the conflict (Jones and Brinkert 2008). Conflict coaching is a dispute resolution process, with the emphasis on conflict analysis and intervention rather than a general or executive coaching purpose (Bacon and Spear 2003). As such, it is critical that conflict coaches are knowledgeable about conflict dynamics and a variety of dispute resolution interventions. The best coaching is performed by conflict experts who respect party's self-determination and who use a non-directive, transparent, voluntary, flexible process to efficiently address the conflict at hand (Jones and Brinkert 2008).

Here, it is helpful to consider similarities and differences between conflict coaching and mediation. Both are interest-based processes involving a third-party neutral, in which the conflict party retains decision-making control: the party decides whether to take action or resolve the conflict and no third party can dictate that decision or the nature of the resolution. In both conflict coaching and mediation the third party does not have a vested interest in the party's(ies') resolution, but helps parties to analyze the conflict and to consider options for action. Both are informal and flexible in terms of the procedures and the nature of the information allowed in the discussion. However, unlike conflict coaching which involves only one conflict party in the process, mediation is facilitated negotiation between two or more parties to a conflict and the mediator's role is to help the parties engage in constructive interaction to come to a mutually acceptable agreement. Another important difference is that conflict coaching allows the third party to provide more direct skills instruction to the party – to help the party understand how to better enact behaviors that will promote desired outcomes (for example, helping a party develop and practice negotiation skills to be used in conversation with the other party outside of coaching) (Jones and Brinkert 2008). Some mediators see caucus as an opportunity to "educate" a party about strategy and tactics in the mediation; but conflict coaching has skills development as a central goal that dominates a significant part of the coaching process (Jones 2014).

Conflict coaching has been traditionally linked with mediation programs in workplace, community, or educational settings (Jones and Brinkert 2008). The initial motivation for development of conflict coaching was to provide service to parties who needed help but were not able to get other parties involved in the conflict to attend mediation (Tidwell 1997). Understandably, conflict coaching was initially understood as a supplement to a mediation program. Eventually, conflict coaching became recognized as a stand-alone dispute resolution mechanism effective for a variety of workplace disputes, especially identity-based conflicts like affirmative-action and equal employment opportunity claims (Northrup 1989). And, increasingly, conflict coaching is seen as a leadership development tool, especially when a leader's conflict "incompetence" negatively impacts his or her career trajectory. A leader may have technical competence that merits promotion to higher levels, but may be refused promotion because s/he cannot intervene to create constructive conflict climates (Jones and Ingersoll 2012). In such cases, conflict coaching becomes a means of "training for one" that prepares leaders for advancement (Brubaker et al. 2014).

The current thinking about conflict coaching focuses on three general questions: (1) When is conflict coaching effective and appropriate?, (2) Who is most suited to act as a conflict coach?, and (3) How can a conflict coaching program be sustained? These questions guide the foundation of a conflict coaching program for the workplace. The first question raises concerns about utility, about the nature of workplace conflicts and/or parties that are best referred to conflict coaching. The second question pertains to qualifications necessary for a good coach; for example, do managers make good conflict coaches for their direct reports? And the third question assumes that a conflict coaching program is developed and functioning, and the challenge is now how to maintain it and grow it.

When Is Conflict Coaching Effective and Appropriate?

When one analyzes the appropriate utility of conflict coaching, it is critical to answer the following:

(a) *For what type of disputes?* (e.g., Are discrimination disputes deemed inappropriate for coaching?; Are superior/subordinate conflicts considered to benefit from conflict coaching?; Are multi-party disputes too complex for conflict coaching?)

(b) *For what parties*? (e.g., Can anyone in the workplace use conflict coaching or are some organizational members restricted from the process?)

(c) *At what point in the conflict* is the use of conflict coaching most likely to prevent and/or reverse conflict escalation?

(d) *What conflict coaching model* should be used? (e.g., Using a narrative model like Jones and Brinkert (2008) or a problem-solving model like Tidwell (1997)?)

(e) *What interventions/skills building* will be provided by the conflict coach? (e.g., helping parties improve their feedback skills, or their negotiation skills, or their apology skills)

(f) *What will be the learning transfer?* (e.g., Determining when and how the party will use the skills that have been developed – when and how to negotiate as planned)?

(g) *What is the estimated effectiveness?* (e.g., What will count as success for the party(ies) and how will the party be able to measure it and benchmark it?)

(h) *What is the relationship to larger frames* of coaching or leadership development? (Is conflict coaching used only to resolve an episode or is it focused on helping the leader develop core competencies that are helpful in future positions?)

Who Is Best Qualified to Be a Conflict Coach?

(a) Who should be a conflict coach? (Are managers and supervisors able to serve as conflict coaches or is this role reserved for ADR specialists or HR specialists?)

(b) How should they be trained? (What form of training and apprenticeship is necessary to develop conflict coaching excellence?)

(c) How should conflict coaches be used? (Should conflict coaches be full time positions or, as many federal agencies do, are conflict coaches personnel who have full time jobs but serve as conflict coaches or mediators as a collateral duty function – in addition to their regular duties?)

(d) Where should conflict coaches come from? (Is it better to develop and use conflict coaches internal to the organization or to hire external contractors to serve as conflict coaches?)

How Can a Conflict Coaching Program Be Sustained Once It Is Initiated?

(a) How should conflict coaching programs be marketed? (What is the best way to publicize the program to let organizational members know it exists, why it may be useful and how they can access it?)

(b) What professional "home" or responsibility should house/provide conflict coaching? (Should the conflict coaching program, and larger ODS, be housed in Human Resources, aligned with an Ombuds office, or in a separate office for Alternative Dispute Resolution?)

These are excellent questions, and continued exploration of the best answers is important – but not enough.

Three Limiting Assumptions of Current Thinking on Conflict Coaching

The current thinking about conflict coaching limits its potential. The following three assumptions about the use of conflict coaching encourage its underutilization:

1. *Framing conflict as dyadic and episodic.* Conflict coaching tends to be seen only or primarily as something to help one party in a two-party conflict. This emphasis is reinforced in workplace conflicts that are somewhat telescoped as between superior/subordinate, peer/peer, etc. Effective conflict coaches should help a party appreciate the impact of the larger system on the conflict (Jones and Brinkert 2008). Often, the conflict itself is usually defined as a function of a dyadic relationship "gone bad" rather than complex multiple relationships created from systems operations and pressures. In many workplaces, coaching and workplace mediation are targeted to Affirmative Action/EEO cases and this underscores the dyadic frame of discrimination by an "other" rather than discrimination as a function of hegemony or oppressive systems (Miller 2014; Mumby 1988).

2. *Presenting conflict coaching as an alternative to other ADR processes – especially as an alternative to mediation.* There is a growing tendency to integrate coaching and workplace mediation; still, the majority of organizations treat these as alternatives – that one substitutes for the other. Internal structures and policies may direct certain disputes to various offices that are associated with coaching versus mediation. For example, in higher education conflict coaching is usually conducted by an ombudsperson while AA/EEO complaints are channeled to an internal mediation process. These distinct pathways of processing are functionally and structurally reinforced rather than intentionally segregated. While these pathways of processing can be changed over time, users of the ODS start assuming that they have to choose between conflict coaching and mediation, and the potential for synergy is lost.

3. *Using conflict coaching PRIOR to other ADR process.* When conflict coaching and workplace mediation are used together coaching is almost always used as preparatory to mediation (Jones 2015). Conflict coaching can be aligned with mediation at various stages of mediation implementation, as is advocated later in this chapter, but programs rarely allow for or explore that combination. And even

more rarely is conflict coaching used or understood as a process in conjunction with other ADR components like early neutral evaluation, facilitation, or arbitration.

Ironically, limitations in the current application of conflict coaching stem partially from underlying assumptions in most ODS models. This next section surfaces these assumptions as prelude to considering how different approaches can liberate conflict coaching application in ODS.

Current Thinking About ODS

In this section the focus is on ADR in the most advanced ODS systems in the US: federal agency ADR systems. Since the passage of ADRA (Alternative Dispute Resolution Act) in 1996, federal agency ADR systems incorporate conflict coaching and workplace mediation more consistently than any other workplace context. And, in terms of sophistication, federal agencies have enacted the most complex and sustainable systems, often reaching the potential discussed in the ODS literature (Costantino and Merchant 1998; Lipsky et al. 2003; Slaiku and Hasson 1998; Ury et al. 1988).

A Brief Overview of ODS in the United States Government

The foundational models of ODS share characteristics that are uniformly considered best practices of ODS (Smith and Martinez 2009, p. 128):

- Multiple process options for parties, including rights-based and interest-based processes
- Ability for parties to "loop back" and "loop forward" between rights-based and interest-based options
- Substantial stakeholder involvement in the system's design
- Participation that is voluntary, confidential and assisted by impartial third-party neutrals
- System transparency and accountability
- Education and training of stakeholders on the use of the available process options

Smith and Hernandez (2009) add that these models are generally silent on core questions that they argue should be more central.

1. *"What are the goals that motivate the system?"*

    Whether a system is designed to reduce litigation and related expenses, or to increase organizational loyalty and commitment through positive climate, or both, will impact which conflict components are included and how they are resourced.

2. *"What is the system's structure in terms of its process options and incentives for use?"*

As ODS theorists suggest (Costantino and Merchant 1998), system structure defines which component is accessed and in which order, with clear effects on whether the system is accessible and easy to use.

3. *"Who are the stakeholders of the system?"*

Is the ODS designed primarily to address the needs of management and administration, external constituencies, or non-managerial employees? Stakeholders determine the desired outcomes of the ODS but are also involved in design and implementation.

4. *"How is the system supported in terms of financial and personnel resources?"*

System designers may build a wonderful system that simply is too expensive to operate or depends on collateral duty personnel who cannot take the necessary time away from their regular work to perform the ADR functions.

5. *"How successful and accountable is the system?"*

Success is often defined as reduction of litigation or formal grievances and the costs associated with those. Accountability is usually in terms of whether stakeholder groups feel their interests have been met by the ODS.

These questions suggest that more attention is needed on the purpose than on the construction of ODS – an argument that will be echoed in the last section of this chapter.

The gold standard of ODS, at least in the United States, is the federal agency ADR systems that have resulted from the implementation of the Alternative Dispute Resolution Act [ADRA] (for a thorough history of the development of the federal agency systems see McCabe 2012). As Lisa Blomgren Bingham and her colleagues (2009) summarize, before the 1990s there was little use of ADR in the federal sector. Threats of litigation resulted in congressional action that incorporated ADR in all three branches of the government, with the greatest impact in administrative agencies and federal courts. This momentum resulted in the passage of ADRA (first in 1990 and then reauthorized in 1996) which requires every federal agency to (a) adopt an ADR policy; (b) designate a senior official to be a dispute resolution specialist; (c) provide regular training on ADR; and (d) review all contracting, granting, and negotiated agreements processed, to explore inclusion of ADR.

The outcome indicators for federal ADR systems are good: cost savings, more speedy resolution of disputes than achieved through litigation, and more "intangible" advantages including increased senses of well-being (Mazur 2013). Moreover, the direction of these systems in terms of more emphasis on conflict coaching makes them a critical target system for the optimization recommended in this chapter.

Until recently, the primary emphasis in federal ADR systems was on the use of mediation for AA/EEO cases. For example, when this author began working with the Veterans Administration (VA) to design and implement their conflict coaching programs from 2008 to 2011, the initial challenge was to build support for applications of mediation and conflict coaching in other dispute areas within the VA as well as adding conflict coaching as a component of AA/EEO dispute resolution work.

The trend now is clearly to have ADR processes available for a wide range of work-place disputes including but not limited to AA/EEO (Mazur 2013).

Elsewhere (McKinney and Bagnell 2012), Mazur notes a very important trend – the declining use of mediation in the federal government. Her analysis is that conflict coaching is rapidly replacing workplace mediation as the ADR tool of choice in the federal sector. Although it is difficult to say for certain, likely reasons for the increasing reliance on conflict coaching are the flexibility of the process, the privacy of the process, and the fact that conflict coaching can go forward without securing agreement to participate from anyone other than the party. And there is growing evidence of that trend since conflict coaching has recently been added to the Equal Employment Opportunity Commission's Management Directive 110 (MD-110) that requires all federal agencies to offer ADR for EEO complaints (Nabatchi and Stanger 2013). The inclusion of conflict coaching in the MD-110 is proof positive that the federal sector has endorsed conflict coaching as a critical ADR tool.

Limiting Assumptions of Current Thinking on ODS

Having complex organizations like federal agencies embrace the concept of ODS lends gravitas and resources that support implementation and maintenance of ODS. Yet, the price of admission is also dealing with large, uber-bureaucratic, and sometimes impenetrable systems that can inhibit experimentation and refinement. Even private sector or non-governmental public organizations that are large enough to initiate ODS (e.g., higher education institutions, health care systems, Fortune 100 companies) are "systems" heavy and labor to match the reality of ODS implementation with the first principle of ODS – to insure fast, easy, and accessible dispute resolution (Costantino and Merchant 1998).

Avgar's (2009) research on ODS implementation in health care industries, reminds us that often the emphasis is on a decision to implement an ADR program rather than attention to how to maintain and maximize it, which may evoke dissensus among levels of management and workers about how seriously to take the ADR effort.

It is also noteworthy that few ODS systems outside of federal agencies have been in existence for the long-term (Brubaker et al. 2014). At the federal level, ODS is 20 years old with many systems expanding beyond the use of mediation only in the last decade. The maturity of the intervention is a function of its youth, and the learning curve for improvement is similarly ripening: "Conflict management systems are difficult for managers and employees to understand. Different managers often feel naturally attuned to one or another option in the system, but various disputants may be drawn to other options. Added to this confusion is the fact that most employees and managers do not understand all the relevant policies and procedures – let alone how each option in the system actually works. "(Rowe 2009, pp. 235–236).

Limitations of ODS, more in terms of practice than true possibility, further constrain the use of conflict coaching. These limitations reinforce four separatist, sequential and simplistic assumptions about what conflict coaching offers and how it can be used.

1. *ODS "Technique" Based and Siloed.* Colvin (2012) has argued that the field of ADR focuses on single techniques or components (e.g., mediation vs. conflict coaching vs. facilitation) rather than on combinations of components. This tendency stems from reliance on single-tool programs (instituting only workplace mediation rather than a true ODS) and is reinforced by difficulty of assessing the effectiveness of more than one tool or component simultaneously. ODS models that have emphasized a "quadrant-based" design (like Slaikeu and Hasson 1998) have been interpreted (or perhaps misinterpreted) to separate components artificially. As is discussed in the next section, conflict coaching should be seen as a tool that can function as a stand-alone or in combination with other components.

2. *Insufficient Analysis of Fit of Conflict to Selected Component.* Often, the decision for a certain conflict management option, is left to the preference of the disputant or intake officer who may suggest the "appropriate" route for conflict management. Coupled with the "either/or" mentality discussed above, there is no guarantee that the right process is initially or ever accessed. This is reminiscent of a common complaint in federal EEO/AA systems – that if the only route to mediation available in an agency is a discrimination complaint, every conflict "becomes" a discrimination complaint to gain access to the system.

3. *Bias Toward Interest-Based Processes.* Ever since the groundbreaking arguments about benefits of interest-based approaches to dispute resolution, and the need to privilege interest-based processes while also providing rights-based and power-based processes (Ury et al. 1988), ODS has given much more attention to encouraging ODS components to be used as interest-based. Roche and Teague (2012) present a compelling critique of ODS from this perspective, arguing that even in "integrated conflict management systems" the interest-based practices take precedence over rights-based fallback procedures, such as formal grievance processes. In many federal agencies it is seen as a failure if an interest-based procedure leads to or is followed by the use of a rights-based or power-based strategy.

4. *ODS Focuses on Individual/Interpersonal Conflicts Rather than Group Conflicts.* Most ODS systems do not provide a strong stable of services to address multi-party, inter-group or intra-group conflicts. Other than facilitation or dialogue processes, which are relatively rare even in federal sector ODS, there are very

few options if the conflict is not dyadic. Very recently some agencies, like the Environmental Protection Agency's ADR offices, have been looking at the potential for using conflict coaching as a tool for multi-party disputes to add more components to their systems for this need (Jones 2015).

Case of Nurse Lisa and Dr. Gray

Lisa James has 11 years of nursing experience as an emergency room nurse. Recently her work situation changed when Dr. Michael Gary joined the hospital as a senior operating room physician. Dr. Gary has a reputation for surgical excellence, but also for abusive behavior toward nurses he perceives as questioning his judgment in the operating room. In the last months, Lisa's been on the receiving end of this behavior during operations – all for helpful, patient-centered suggestions she delivered in a reasonable tone of voice. Lisa's nurse manager is the head nurse of the ER, Sharon Sparks. Lisa has not talked with Sharon about the climate and workplace civility concerns because she assumes Sharon is disinterested and/or unwilling to address Dr. Gary's behavior. Lisa has observed two of her colleagues bringing the issue of Dr. Gary's behavior to Sharon her attention and has not seen evidence that Sharon intervened on the nurses' behalf.

The case of Lisa James can be used to explain how some of the current thinking on conflict coaching and workplace mediation may affect how Lisa can deal with this conflict. In many ODS programs it is likely that this conflict may be seen as an interpersonal conflict between Lisa James and Dr. Gary. But, it could also be seen as a conflict including Sharon and/or as a conflict that involves the entire emergency room unit. Current thinking about conflict coaching and ODS may encourage Lisa to see this as an interest-based conflict rather than exploring the strong possibility that it is a rights-based conflict (for example, workplace bullying) that would suggest different approaches for management. Further, even if both conflict coaching and workplace mediation were used, chances are that in mediation the parties to mediation would be limited to Lisa and Dr. Gary – or Lisa and Sharon, but probably not all three or the unit supervisor. And in many organizations, if the conflict were framed as rights-based Lisa's choices for conflict management may be presented as "either-or" – choosing an interest-based emphasis through coaching or mediation, or pursuing a more rights-based process like arbitration. The goal is to help move us beyond the limitations of our current thinking to more sophisticated ways to use conflict coaching and mediation in ODS.

Optimizing Conflict Coaching in ODS

This section concentrates on four suggestions that are currently feasible in order to optimize the use of conflict coaching. These suggestions are doable and require little more than a change of attitude about how to use conflict coaching. At the end of each suggestion area, a brief list of questions for potential research or evaluation is presented.

Using Conflict Coaching as "Coaching-Plus" Wrap-Around Support for Workplace Mediation and Other ADR Processes

A previously discussed, a limitation is that conflict coaching is often seen as a process that disputants use instead of other ADR processes, or before the party proceeds to mediation. A more integrated model is advocated with ADR components being used together sequentially or concomitantly and with interests-based, rights-based and power-based strategies available together. The interaction of ADR processes in ODS was studied by Bendersky (2007) using her "complementarities model" that examines how interests-based and rights-based ADR processes work in concert and what impact this has on the success of the ODS. She tested the complementarities model with quasi-experimental field design in a Canadian government agency with three conditions: (a) a rights-based grievance procedure alone, (b) a rights-based grievance procedure and an interest-based training, and (c) both components plus an interest-based conflict coach. She found that the third condition was superior in producing positive conflict- related employee attitudes and behavior than the other conditions. Therefore, understanding how to combine coaching and other ADR processes may yield greater benefits for the organization and the individual.

As Fig. 6.1 suggests, conflict coaching can provide a wrap-around service to support any other ADR process, but most commonly mediation or arbitration. Conflict coaching can be used as a singular, stand-alone process as well.

Case of Pat and Randy

Pat and Randy are trainers employed by a federal agency to design and deliver a conflict and communication skills program for agency workers in benefits claims offices. The agency Human Resources department has had a number of complaints from claims specialists about dysfunctional conflict between peers. In response, the HR department hired Pat and Randy to co-develop and co-deliver the conflict skills training program. The relationship between the co-trainers did not begin well, with each assuming that s/he was to "head" the training project. The conflict has escalated. The co-trainers are barely communicating with each other during training or between trainings. Neither demonstrates a willingness to share materials or helps the other with set up. Both trainers openly "correct" and "criticize" the other during training sessions which makes the training participants feel confused and uncomfortable. Further, both Pat and Chris complain about the other to the training program director. The training program director has not taken any formal action but has let it be known that he is unimpressed with both parties and expects them to work it out on their own.

Fig. 6.1 Conflict coaching as a wrap around service

Either Pat or Randy could choose to use conflict coaching as a **stand-alone process**. If Pat so chose, a conflict coach in the ADR program could help him analyze the conflict from multiple perspectives, select preferred strategic action and work on skills to put that plan into action. The conflict coaching process would be confidential and no one else would necessarily know that the coaching process occurred (other than basic scheduling records if the coaching occurred during Pat's work hours).

Conflict coaching could be used **prior to mediation** to help Pat prepare for mediation. For example, Pat may use the coaching process to better understand Randy and to consider how to best share Pat's story during mediation. Coaching can help Pat generate potential options for solution and evaluate whether there is a better alternative to mediation or negotiated agreement. Or, Pat may come to understand that he would rather engage in arbitration or adjudication and work with his coach to prepare for those processes.

Pat could also choose to engage a conflict coach **during mediation**. This would not have to be with the knowledge of the mediator or the other party. Perhaps Pat wants conflict coaching to reflect on information and options presented during mediation. In some mediation programs a party has the right to call a caucus during mediation or ask for an interruption of the mediation process in order to consider new information and reschedule a continuation. In either of these cases the party can access a conflict coach during the interlude, either from internal programs or external coaching services.

Finally, conflict coaching can be used **post-mediation (or post-ADR process)** to help Pat with the implementation and maintenance of the agreement, if any, reached in mediation. Or, post-mediation can help Pat work through issues that arose during mediation that he wants to deal with more intensely. Post-mediation coaching is very helpful if the mediation did not yield an agreement or if the agreement falls through. If Pat were a supervisor in this situation, post-mediation conflict coaching could provide "training for one" in better ways to interact with subordinates.

Research questions for this suggestion include:

What kinds of conflicts are best handled through stand-alone coaching compared to "coaching-plus" processes (combination of coaching with another ADR process)? It may be that discrimination or identity-based conflicts benefit more than distributive resource conflicts from this wrap-around process. That information would be very valuable for the design and upgrade of current AA/EEO processes. As conflict coaching expands to multiparty disputes it is quite likely that conflict coaching used before and during multi-party mediation greatly increases the quality of mediation outcome and participants' satisfaction with the process.

How do "coaching-plus" processes impact the achievement of resolution and the quality and maintenance of resolution? Agreement rates and avoidance of litigation are common success metrics in ODS, but quality of agreement and maintenance of agreement are rarely examined. The logical expectation is that wrap-around processes would provide more conflict analysis, solution generation and solution evaluation which should increase decision quality and agreement maintenance.

How do "coaching-plus" processes help inform ADR/ODS system reform and redesign? In earlier discussion, pathways of processing were identified as underutilized in many ODS. "Coaching-Plus" processes provide new pathways and may indicate where new components should be added to the ODS. For example, facilitation and dialogue processes or early neutral evaluation are generally underutilized in ODS but experience with "coaching-plus" could indicate new complementarities as Bendersky (2007) suggests that redefine the ODS.

Appreciating Conflict Coaching as a Tool to Prepare for Other ADR Processes

An important use of conflict coaching is to "leverage other ADR processes" (Jones and Brinkert 2008). We articulated six ways a conflict coach can help a party understand and use ADR options, as explained in Table 6.1. Many ADR professionals realize that ODS may not be well-used because parties simply do not understand what the ADR components are; or if the parties do understand mediation or other processes, they don't feel prepared to actually take part in that process. Conflict coaching can explain processes like mediation, arbitration, facilitation and fact-finding to a party trying to determine where s/he wants to pursue resolution.

Table 6.1 Six ways to leverage ADR processes in conflict coaching

Coach and party process option	Description
Investigation	The coach helps the party to learn about the existing organizational dispute system.
Explanation	The coach helps the party understand the differences between different dispute resolution processes (e.g., mediation versus facilitation).
Preparation	The coach helps the party strategize about how to use a dispute resolution process to best advantage (e.g., preparing for mediation with an opening statement, development of interests for both parties, brainstorming and consideration of different possible solutions).
Selection and timing of system access	The coach can support the party in determining the best level of intervention, when and whether the party should consider other dispute processes, and how best to coordinate involvement in the dispute system.
Reflection and analysis	The coach can help the party to reflect on the success of their choices and what they have learned.
Future planning	The coach can help the party to plan next steps.

Sometimes the party doesn't understand the ADR resources that are available inside the organization or outside in the larger community. Conflict coaches can help the party investigate options and weigh advantages of options. If an ADR process like arbitration is chosen, conflict coaches can help a party learn more about what will actually happen in that process and how s/he can prepare presentation, evidence, and external support to get the most out of it.

Collateral duty mediators and coaches may not have the depth of knowledge that is appropriate for this type of coaching.

Research questions for this suggestion include: To what extent does conflict coaching result in the following: (a) Party satisfaction with the ADR process selected? (b) Party utilization of the ADR process selected? (c) Success of conflict management through the selected ADR process? It is beneficial to examine how well leveraging ADR through conflict coaching increases the general awareness of the ODS and how it can link with external ADR resources in the broader community. The latter is particularly important for smaller organizations that may depend on access to external ADR resources.

Using Conflict Coaching to Support Online Dispute Resolution Processes

Online dispute resolution (ODR) is a vibrant alternative to conventional face-to-face interaction. Initially designed to address ADR with geographically dispersed parties (Breaux 2015), e-mediation, e-arbitration, and e-coaching are now standard practices (Fernandez and Masson 2014; Liyanage 2012). Rabinovich-Einy and Katsh (2012) argue that ODR should be explored as an adjunct to any ADR system.

Conflict coaching using online access or communication technology is a natural extension of ODS, especially for large organizations with disputants in various locations. For example, geographically dispersed teams in conflict can use online conflict coaching even if members are a world away from the coach or each other.

Research questions for this suggestion include: Does online coaching differ from face-to-face coaching in terms of: (a) Party satisfaction with the process? (b) Coach's ability to effectively conduct coaching conversations? (c) Party willingness to engage in conflict coaching? and/or (d) Number of conflict coaching sessions required?

As online dispute resolution research suggests (Fernandez and Masson 2014), the adequacy of online versions of ADR processes is research-proven. However, there is a strong need for more comparative research focusing on the kinds of questions raised here. If such research demonstrates no significant advantage for face-to-face conflict coaching or workplace mediation versus online versions, this could result in increased use of the ODS and lower costs for conducting sessions.

Using Conflict Coaching and "Meta-Coaching" to Address Change Related Conflict for Leaders

ODS and ADR literature contains little about how these systems can be used to improve organizational development and organizational change (Hubbell 2013). This omission is more striking given calls for attention to ADR, and especially conflict coaching processes, as integral to leadership development (Brubaker et al. 2014; Kuttner 2011) and the need to manage change-related conflicts and build participative structures during change (Bloch and Erbe 2010).

Conflict coaching, or more specifically a "meta-coaching approach" (Jones 2014), is suggested to prepare leaders to handle change-related conflicts for themselves and for their subordinates. A meta-coaching approach means "coaching about coaching" or helping to develop a leader's ability to coach his/her direct reports in dyadic or group conflicts.

Case of Merging Universities
The State University System has recently been notified that legislative action will result in a merger of several universities in the 20-member system due to severe financial shortfalls for the current and projected fiscal years. Southern State University and Southeastern College have been identified for consolidation that will require the merging of similar disciplinary programs. The departments of history in both institutions have masters and undergraduate programs, while Southern State University has a doctoral program. The department chair of Southern State University, Professor Martin will be chair of the consolidated department and knows she faces a great deal of conflict with this merger. She would like to create constructive conflict conversations between the members of the merging departments before and after the actual merger.

Meta-coaching fits the *State University System* scenario. Professor Martin may benefit from learning how to coach members of the departments prior to engaging in the actual merger process. Professor Martin may also benefit from understanding how she may be seen as a party to the conflict with individual faculty or members of the administration. The fact is that, as in many merger and change situations (Miller 2014), the leaders in charge of change must exercise conflict competence on multiple levels at once – as witnesses to conflicts, as parties to conflicts, and as leaders guiding unit members through the conflicts.

In Table 6.2, a set of abbreviated questions is presented that compares three levels of intervention that relate to these types of conflict processing. Each of these levels may be conducted independently, but as in the case of Southern State University and Professor Martin, they are likely to occur as stages of an unfolding dynamic. The Levels can be defined as follows: (1) Level 1 – Individual conflict coaching to help the leader consider how s/he can personally better manage conflict as a party to the conflict (this level includes basic questions following the standard conflict coaching process developed by Jones and Brinkert (2008)), (2) Level 2 – Leader-Group conflict (this level focuses on conflicts expected between the leader and the group(s) because of the change process), and (3) Level 3 – the Meta-coaching level (this level focuses on coaching the leader to be able to coach members of the groups in order to reduce dysfunctional conflicts that impede change). Applied to the Southern State University case, Professor Martin could be coached in terms of the conflicts she is experiencing with the change (Level 1); and/or the conflicts she expects to have between herself and the groups (Level 2); and/or how to act as an informal conflict coach to facilitate the merger process between the groups (Level 3).

For example, it is quite possible that Professor Martin is experiencing her own conflict with the mergers of institutions – her own reactions to losing the identity of her home institution and home department – a conflict that would fit a Level 1 process. Professor Martin could engage with a conflict coach to analyze her own conflict(s) and to determine her own needs in moving forward.

Even under the best circumstances, merging groups or departments creates tensions between group members and the group leader – this may ask for a Level 2 conflict coaching intervention. In Level 2 the concentration would be on using conflict coaching to help alleviate conflicts between Professor Martin and either individuals in the new group, individuals in the old group, or between Professor Martin and either group. Again, in Level 2, the recipient of conflict coaching is a party to a conflict with members engaged in his/her sphere of influence during the change.

Finally, Level 3 assumes that Professor Martin has developed the ability to serve as an informal conflict coach in leading discussions with members of the faculty experiencing change-related conflict in the newly merged unit. Level 3 work, asks the leader to become more of a hybrid coach/facilitator in this larger change effort.

Table 6.2 Meta-coaching questions for the stages 1 to 3 of the comprehensive conflict coaching model process

	Questions for level 1	Questions for level 2	Questions for level 3
Stage	Individual conflict coaching	Coaching leader-group conflict	Coaching leader to facilitate group coaching
Preparation	Do you understand the nature and purpose of conflict coaching?	Would it be helpful to offer coaching to other members of the group as well?	Who should participate in this process?
	Does this process suit your needs?		Can you explain the nature of coaching to the group you will be working with?
	Are you willing to take part in the process?		Do you have the authority/approval to facilitate these conversations with the group?
			Do you have the acceptance of the group to participate in coaching/facilitation?
Stage 1: Discovering the initial story	What is the conflict about?	Who are the members of the group?	Are there reasons to structure the group process or interaction in a certain way?
	What else might be important to the conflict?	Would group members define themselves as in conflict with you? With each other?	How might this structuring affect the way the conflict narrative is told?
	Would other people in the conflict tell a different story?	Does the conflict differ with different members of the group?	How might information from relevant external groups be obtained, and presented to the group?
		Which external groups/persons impact this conflict?	
		How does the organizational context affect this conflict?	

(continued)

Table 6.2 (continued)

Stage	Questions for level 1 Individual conflict coaching	Questions for level 2 Coaching leader-group conflict	Questions for level 3 Coaching leader to facilitate group coaching
Stage 2: Identity	How are you and the other person currently portrayed in this conflict?	What is the nature of the group identity?	How does your facilitation impact the group identity? Positively? Negatively?
	Who do you and the other person want to be?	How is the group identity affecting the conflict and conflict interactions?	Is the group identity impacted for all or most members?
	What are you doing to protect your identity?	How is the organizational culture or identity affecting the conflict?	How does the organization or system enhance or impede your facilitation?
	What are you doing that might affect the other person's identity?	Are there tensions between showing respect to some members of the group rather than others?	How does the facilitation affect your identity with the group? Within the system?
Stage 2: Emotion	What are you feeling in this situation?	Are there different emotions experienced within the group?	Are there issues of emotion that would affect your facilitation? (emotional contagion?)
	What is the other person feeling?	How common or consensual are their emotional experiences?	How might approaches to interaction be used to reduce negative emotional experience?
	How do you want to feel?	How are the group emotions affecting each other?	
	How does the other person want to feel?	How the is the "group" as other affecting your emotions (as contrasted with individual as "other")?	
	What could you do to feel better?		
	What could the other do to feel better?		

(continued)

Table 6.2 (continued)

	Questions for level 1	Questions for level 2	Questions for level 3
Stage	Individual conflict coaching	Coaching leader-group conflict	Coaching leader to facilitate group coaching
Stage 2: Power	How would you describe the power relationship you have with the other person?	What are the power dynamics within the group?	What power do you have in deciding the nature of the coaching/facilitation?
	What do you and the other person want to accomplish?	How do the power dynamics in the group affect your power relationship with the group?	Who else has power in making decisions on the nature of coaching/facilitation?
	What, if anything, do you need to accomplish your goals?	How does your power change by dealing with the group rather than the individuals?	
	What behaviors are most likely going to help you to meet your goals?	What power do you have in determining how to aggregate or divide when managing the conflict interactions?	
Stage 3: The best story	What is your vision of the best outcome?	Does your vision of the best outcome differ depending on specific members of the group?	How can you best build a collective vision if one is needed?
	What skills do you need to make the best outcome happen?	If so, how do these visions differ?	If not, how can you facilitate the conversations to allow for separate visions?

The questions in levels build on each other. Questions for Level 3 would include questions for Level 1 and 2

The meta-coaching process suggests the importance of locating epicenters of conflict(s) during change on multiple levels and using the same conflict coaching approach to prepare as a leader and to facilitate change readiness for members of a unit.

There are many possible research questions to ask about the meta-coaching processes. As a new development (Jones 2014) in the field, it raises issues about the implementation and impact of coaching as a meta-process. Some of those questions include the following:

– How well can leaders learn the meta-coaching process?
– What impact does conflict coaching and/or meta-coaching have on reducing dysfunctional conflict during organizational change?

- Are there counterproductive outcomes from using conflict coaching and meta-coaching in these ways?
- Are other ADR processes more effective at achieving the reduction of dysfunctional change-related conflict than conflict coaching?
- Are other organizational development processes more effective at achieving the reduction of dysfunctional change-related conflict than conflict coaching?

Conclusion

Conflict coaching is a powerful process that offers advantages for ADR and ODS. An overview of current thinking reveals how underlying assumptions about conflict coaching and ODS are limiting the full potential of conflict coaching and decreasing the power of ODS systems in turn. Several suggestions are offered about how conflict coaching can be expanded and how workplace conflict specialists can examine the benefits or drawbacks of those enhanced conflict coaching processes and applications.

The most important directions for future work are those that see the possible synergies between conflict coaching and workplace mediation. Several of those have been suggested here, such as the development of "coaching-plus" processes and using coaching and workplace mediation as wrap-around services. In the short term, that direction will build best upon available systems and resources. It also allows us to engage in badly needed research on the efficacy of conflict coaching and workplace mediation separately as well as together.

References

Avgar, A. C. (2009). Unexplored drivers for adopting employer ADR programs: The need for a stakeholder perspective. *Dispute Resolution Journal, 64*(4), 8–61.

Bacon, T. R., & Spear, K. (2003). *Adaptive coaching: The art and practice of client-centered approach to performance improvement*. Palo Alto: Davies-Black.

Bendersky, C. (2007). Complementarities in organizational dispute resolution systems: How system characteristics affect individuals' conflict experiences. *Industrial and Labor Relations Review, 60*, 204–224.

Bingham, L. B., Hallberlin, C. J., Walker, D. A., & Won-Tae, C. (2009). Dispute system design and justice in employment dispute resolution: Mediation at the workplace. *Harvard Negotiation Law Review, 14*, 1–50.

Bloch, B., & Erbe, N. (2010). The organizational ombudsman as change agent for organizational and social capital. *Journal of the International Ombudsman Association, 3*(2), 72–75.

Bowen, P. G. (2012a). Dispute resolution (ADR) as an undergraduate business subject. *Business Education Innovation Journal, 4*(2), 32–34.

Bowen, P. G. (2012b). Teaching ADR to undergraduate business students. *Dispute Resolution Journal, 67*(3), 78–82.

Breaux, P. W. (2015). Online dispute resolution: A modern alternative dispute resolution approach. *Computer & Internet Lawyer, 32*(5), 1–4.

Brubaker, D., Noble, C., Fincher, R., Park, S. K., & Press, S. (2014). Conflict resolution in the workplace: What will the future bring? *Conflict Resolution Quarterly, 31*, 357–386.

Colvin, A. J. (2012). American workplace dispute resolution in the individual rights era. *International Journal of Human Resource Management, 23*, 459–475.

Costantino, C. A., & Merchant, C. S. (1998). *Designing conflict management systems: A guide to creating productive and healthy organizations.* San Francisco: Jossey-Bass.

Fernandez, A. J., & Masson, M. E. (2014). Online mediations: Advantages and pitfalls of new and evolving technologies and why we should embrace them. *Defense Counsel Journal, 81*, 395–403.

Hubbell, L. D. (2013). The multiple roles of the organization development practitioner. *Journal of Multidisciplinary Research (1947–2900), 5*(2), 71–81.

Jones, T. S. (2014, February 23). *Meta-coaching: Helping coaches coach for change in organizations.* Association for Conflict Resolution, Teleseminar, Workplace Division.

Jones, T. S. (2015). *Conflict coaching as a tool for environmental and public policy conflict.* Washington, DC: Environmental Protection Agency. Presentation to the CPRC Office.

Jones, T. S., & Brinkert, R. (2008). *Conflict coaching: Conflict management strategies and skills for the individual.* Thousand Oaks: Sage Publications.

Jones, T. S., & Ingersoll, D. (2012). Creating constructive conflict cultures for strategic enrollment management. In B. Bontrager, R. Ingersoll, & D. Ingersoll (Eds.), *Strategic enrollment management* (pp. 71–93). New York: Education Systems.

Kuttner, R. (2011). Conflict specialists as leaders: Revisiting the role of the conflict specialist from a leadership perspective. *Conflict Resolution Quarterly, 29*, 103–126.

Lipsky, D. B., Seeber, R. L., & Fincher, R. (2003). *Emerging systems for managing workplace conflict: Lessons from American corporations for managers and dispute resolution professionals.* San Francisco: Wiley.

Liyanage, K. C. (2012). The regulation of online dispute resolution: Effectiveness of online consumer protection guidelines. *Deakin Law Review, 17*, 251–282.

Mazur, C. (2013). ADR: Faster, cheaper, better – And not just for EEO complaints. *Public Administration Review, 73*, 61–62.

McCabe, D. (2012). Dispute resolution in the federal sector: An analytical historiography. *Advances in Competitiveness Research, 20*(1/2), 29–36.

McKinney, B. C., & Bagnell, J. (2012). *Readings and case studies in mediation* (2nd ed.). Wilmington: Kendall Hunt.

Miller, K. (2014). *Organizational communication: Approaches and processes* (7th ed.). Boston: Cengage Learning.

Mumby, D. K. (1988). *Communication and power in organizations: Discourse, ideology and domination.* Norwood: Ablex.

Nabatchi, T., & Stanger, A. (2013). Faster? Cheaper? Better? Using ADR to resolve federal sector EEO complaints. *Public Administration Review, 73*, 50–61.

Northrup, T. (1989). The dynamic of identity in personal and social conflict. In L. Kreisberg, T. Northrup, & S. Thorson (Eds.), *Intractable conflicts and their transformation* (pp. 55–82). Syracuse: Syracuse University Press.

Rabinovich-Einy, O., & Katsh, E. (2012). Technology and the future of dispute systems design. *Harvard Negotiation Law Review, 17*, 151–199.

Ridley-Duff, R., & Bennett, A. (2011). Towards mediation: Developing a theoretical framework to understand alternative dispute resolution. *Industrial Relations Journal, 42*, 106–123.

Roche, W. K., & Teague, P. (2012). The growing importance of workplace ADR. *International Journal of Human Resource Management, 23*, 447–458.

Rogers, N. H. (2010). The next phase for dispute resolution in law schools: Less growth, more change. *Ohio State Journal on Dispute Resolution, 25*(1), 1–6.

Rowe, M. (2009). Organizational systems for dealing with conflict & learning from conflict: Introduction. *Harvard Negotiation Law Review, 14*, 233–237.

Slaiku, K., & Hasson, R. (1998). *Controlling the costs of conflict: How to design a system for your organization.* San Francisco: Jossey-Bass.

Smith, S., & Martinez, J. (2009). An analytic framework for dispute systems design. *Harvard Negotiation Law Review, 14*, 123–169.

Stephens, D. B., Stephens, R. D., & Kohl, J. P. (2012). U.S. business colleges still lag in teaching ADR. *Dispute Resolution Journal, 67*(2), 22–28.

Stephens, R. D., Stephens, D. B., & Kohl, J. P. (2013). Alternative dispute resolution in the MBA curriculum: Corporate practice, curriculum content, and the MBA curriculum reform movement. *Dispute Resolution Journal, 68*(4), 12–28.

Tidwell, A. (1997). Problem solving for one. *Mediation Quarterly, 14*, 309–317.

Ury, W., Brett, J., & Goldberg, S. (1988). *Getting disputes resolved: Designing systems to cut the costs of conflict*. San Francisco: Jossey-Bass.

Chapter 7
HRM Practices and Mediation: Lessons Learnt from the UK

Ria Deakin

Given that much of the research about the use of workplace mediation in the UK has been published in the last 5 years, you may be forgiven for thinking that the idea of workplace mediation is a relative newcomer to debates about how conflict should be dealt with in the workplace. This conclusion, however, would be inaccurate. Arguments for the greater use of workplace mediation as a way of improving workplace relations by moving to more informal approaches and tackling the numbers of employees who seek resolution through formal systems have been present in policy debates for decades. Despite this, just 7 % of workplaces indicated that they have experience with workplace mediation (in the 12 months prior to the survey) (van Wanrooy et al. 2013). This presents a confusing picture of the status of workplace mediation in the UK and it is to this confusion that this chapter seeks to speak.

Drawing on the limited amount of empirical research available, the discussion will concentrate on issues surrounding the use of workplace mediation in the UK[1] and, in so doing, will identify a number of key challenges influencing its progress. These challenges should be seen as interrelated and grounded in tensions between the positioning of mediation in both formal dispute resolution and strategic conflict management discourses. The first challenge relates to issues of clarity and a lack of understanding and precision over what mediation is and how it can be used. The second challenge focuses on the potential for cultural transformation and refers to difficulties in achieving a cultural shift away from a reliance on formal methods and towards a more flexible and informal approach. The final challenge relates to the changing role of line managers and the HR function and is concerned with the difficult positioning of the HR function and line managers within workplace mediation. The purpose of this chapter is, therefore, to consider how workplace mediation

---

[1] From the outset it is important to note that the majority of the research focuses on England.

R. Deakin (✉)
University of Huddersfield, Huddersfield, UK
e-mail: R.Deakin@hud.ac.uk

© Springer International Publishing Switzerland 2016
K. Bollen et al. (eds.), *Advancing Workplace Mediation Through Integration of Theory and Practice*, Industrial Relations & Conflict Management 3,
DOI 10.1007/978-3-319-42842-0_7

is positioned within conflict management and dispute resolution debates in the UK, with a view to exploring why, despite its presence in policy and practice for many years, its widespread use is yet to gain sufficient momentum. Having explored the issues surrounding these challenges the chapter will then conclude by identifying the lessons to be learnt from the UK experience.

The Influence of Law and Policy

When talking about the role of workplace mediation in the UK, one cannot divorce it from the legal and policy context since this shapes the environment in which organisations operate. How to deal best with disputes in the workplace has been the subject of a number of government consultations, with the most recent reviews being undertaken in 2007 (Gibbons), and again in 2011 by the Conservative-led coalition government (BIS 2011a, b). These reviews sought to identify how changes could be made to traditional systems and mechanisms for dealing with individual disputes.

The Traditional Approach and the Search for Alternatives

Formerly known as Industrial Tribunals when established in 1964, Employment Tribunals (ETs) were intended to provide an efficient and informal way of resolving legal disputes in the workplace. Until July 2013, there was no fee for pursuing a claim. ET panels can consist of a legally qualified employment judge and two lay members (one with an employer-focused perspective and the other with an employee-focused perspective); although for certain jurisdictions (e.g. breach of contract), the judge may sit alone. Legal representation is not required, although an increased formalization has meant that claimants who are not legally represented are frequently disadvantaged in the tribunal process (Morris 2012). Appeals from an ET can be made to the Employment Appeal Tribunal (EAT).

A claim to an ET (and possibly EAT) represent the final steps in what may be considered the traditional approach for dealing with individual workplace disputes. Prior to recourse to an ET, attempts should be taken to deal with the dispute through the use of a formal procedure such as those governing disciplinary and/or grievance matters. The traditional approach may thus be characterized by a reliance on formal, rigid procedures, a concern with investigations and evidence gathering, and the involvement of third party decision makers who judje and decide on the basis of the evidence presented.

Though an ET claim should be pursued as a last resort where other mechanisms have failed, a persistent concern about the number of claims being submitted to the ET system, together with the associated costs to employers and to the tax payer, has placed a focus on the perceived dominance of the legal route. This has meant that, as in many other countries, the UK discussion of Alternative Dispute Resolution (ADR) mechanisms has been driven by a desire to reduce the burden on the legal system and to tackle problems of inefficiency and dissatisfaction in the handling of disputes through the courts (Bennett 2014).

In addition to workplace mediation, examples of the ADR options available include the use of Acas[2] arbitration and judicial mediation. Uptake of the arbitration service has been extremely poor (Sanders 2009) and the success of judicial mediation has been questioned (Boon et al. 2011). The introduction in April 2014 of the mandatory need to consider Acas early conciliation, rather than the previously optional pre-claim conciliation, marks the first step to make engagement with an ADR process necessary in order to pursue a legal claim. However, unlike workplace mediation, these routes exist once a dispute reaches the stage at which an ET claim has been submitted, and therefore seem to sit nicely within discourses about dispute resolution grounded in a legal context.

Workplace Mediation: A Tool for Change?

Workplace mediation, on the other hand, may sit somewhat more uncomfortably with the arguments about stemming the number of disputes at an external, legal level. Rather than taking effect once an issue has escalated, workplace mediation is championed as an early intervention tool helping to deal with conflict at an early stage (Gibbons 2007). The idea is therefore, to prevent conflict escalating to the point at which an ET claim might be lodged.

Of course, internal mechanisms for attempting to deal with disputes at the workplace level are well established through the use of grievance, disciplinary and dignity at work procedures. Such procedures are widely found in UK workplaces, with 97 % of employees working in organizations with a disciplinary procedure and 97 % of employees being covered by a grievance procedure (van Wanrooy et al. 2013:27). These procedures are, however, elements of a formal dispute resolution process and are characteristic of a problematic adversarial and inefficient system. They are also reactive rather than proactive, and are not concerned with the early resolution that mediation is fated to provide. Formal procedures do provide a degree of familiarity, structure and potential protection against litigation (or fear of litigation) that the unfamiliar, informal methods do not (Harris et al. 2012). When considered in this way, it becomes apparent that encouraging a greater use of workplace mediation requires more than simply introducing it as an option: what is needed, is a change in attitude towards workplace conflict and the way that it is dealt with.

---

[2] The Advisory, Conciliation and Arbitration Service (Acas) is a non-departmental government organisation offering free and impartial advice to employers and employees. In addition to this, they also provide arbitration and mediation services for collective and individual disputes, deliver early conciliation, conduct research, and develop Codes of Practice which are utilised as tools for establishing best practice.

This need for a culture change is not absent from the policy discourse. While it was arguably more implicit and certainly second to the traditional 'docket-clearing' arguments in the 2007 Gibbons Review, the need for culture change and transformation towards a more cooperative, proactive and strategic attitude towards managing workplace conflict was explicit throughout the government response to the 2011 consultation: the coalition government saw mediation as a great potential to transform conflict cultures (BIS 2011a). This conclusion was, grounded more in the potential of mediation, rather than the direct experience of workplace mediation. What was needed was a long term commitment to increase the knowledge of, and access to workplace mediation. In light of this pivotal role, the recommendations offered in response to the 2011 consultation related to mediation seem somewhat lackluster, being limited to two regional pilot schemes to establish a network of mediators for SME employers and an encouragement to share practice in the retail sector. Evidence as to the success of either of these schemes is difficult to come by, and focus in the debates about workplace conflict have been dominated by other changes introduced, namely Acas early conciliation, and the introduction of ET fees.

The notion that the position of mediation in the UK is a confusing picture was introduced above, and is further illustrated by consideration of the legal and policy context. There is a desire to position conflict management at a strategic level and to replace the dominance of formal practices but, little clarity is provided as to where the boundaries between formal and informal practices should lie. A transformation in culture is therefore being sought but without adequately addressing how the necessary endurance, of the traditional approach is to be accommodated. Before discussing the evidence available to help understand how the relationship between the formal and informal aspects may fare in practice, it is important to first address the matter of what workplace mediation means in a UK context.

Issues of Clarity: Understanding Mediation in the UK

A Practical Agenda

Although a slight aside, it is useful to reiterate at this point that whilst there has been a growth in research activity around workplace mediation in the UK, the body of work is still relatively limited. Against the importance of the policy context and a desire to deliver cultural change, it is perhaps interesting to note that much of the research conducted so far has been funded by Acas and/or the Chartered Institute for Personnel and Development (CIPD) (e.g. Acas and CIPD (2013)) and has focused on establishing best practices (Bennett 2014). While some of the findings from these projects have been published in peer reviewed academic journals (e.g. Bennett (2013), Harris et al. (2012) and Saundry et al. (2013b)), much of the evidence about the use of workplace mediation and attitudes towards conflict management currently exist as research reports, available either on the Acas and/or the CIPD websites; this is interesting for a number of reasons.

The first is that this has left discussions about workplace mediation and dealing with conflict at work largely conceptually and theoretically underdeveloped. It has, however, provided easily accessible information and advice to those within organizations who may be interested in using workplace mediation. Secondly, it demonstrates how a practical agenda is driving knowledge and understanding of workplace mediation in the UK. Indeed, managing conflict at work was identified as one of Acas's workplace trends for 2015, helping to place it on the radar for good employers. Perhaps cynically, it is also interesting to note that, whilst Acas provides many of its services free of charge, its provision of workplace mediators and training is a private, paid for service, placing it in competition with many other providers of mediation. Acas is, therefore in an interesting position and given their role in setting standards of good practice, this potentially gives them power to influence the way mediation as a product develops.

The Dominance of Facilitative Mediation

The dominant model of mediation used in the UK is facilitative mediation (Latreille 2011). Facilitative mediation is a voluntary and confidential process, where two or more parties to a conflict seek a mutually agreeable solution to their situation. The process is informal but structured, and is facilitated by an impartial third party, the mediator. The role of the mediator is to help the parties to identify and express the issues involved and to help facilitate understanding between the parties. A facilitative mediator should treat all parties equally and should not make suggestions for possible solutions (Ridley-Duff and Bennett 2011). An impartial mediator is seen as crucial for managing power imbalances in the mediation process and helping to "level the playing field" between disputing parties (Bennett 2013). The outcome of a facilitative mediation is determined by the parties and is non-binding. The power and endurance of the outcome comes from the control the parties had over the decision (Ridley-Duff and Bennett 2011). The contents of a mediation and any agreement should be private and confidential, and any details shared with anyone other than the mediator and the parties involved, should be with the consent of the parties involved (Bennett 2014).

Consistent with the docket clearing arguments, mediation is positioned as a cheaper and more efficient way of dealing with issues in the workplace (CIPD 2015). Although often funded by the employer, facilitative mediation typically takes 1–2 days and is therefore much more efficient in terms of time, and minimizes costs associated with HR and management time involved in the pursuance of formal routes (Latreille and Saundry 2015). Mediated cases tend to focus on issues involving interpersonal issues e.g. relationship breakdowns and claims of bullying and harassment; it is seen as less suitable for claims of discrimination or disputes over conditions of employment (CIPD 2013; Latreille 2010).

Feedback from participants of mediation is usually positive, although not unanimously so. Parties have questioned the sufficiency of the shorter time period for addressing the problems and have felt that they had had to accept partial blame for the situation where they felt this was not warranted (Saundry et al. 2013a). Concern has also been expressed about the sustainability and longevity of initially positively rated outcomes (Saundry et al. 2013a).

Questioning the Integrity of Workplace Mediation

Mediation as a practice is not without its critics and some, such as Dolder (2004), have questioned the extent to which a mediator can remain impartial – especially when they are being paid by the employer. Questions also arise in respect of the suitability of mediation in certain types of disputes. In the UK, mediation is seen as being suitable for a wide range of disputes, often associated with grievances (Bennett 2013) including bullying and harassment (BIS 2011a). Research indicates that mediation is frequently used where allegations of bullying have been raised, although such allegations are often aligned with issues of performance management or communication breakdown (Latreille 2010). The prominence placed on mediation to deal with bullying and harassment is interesting and raises questions about the assumptions of power (im)balance in the mediation process and of accountability (Keashly and Nowell 2011).

The broad scope of potential cases for mediation, offers the opportunity for a greater use of workplace mediation, but the term mediation is subject to interpretation. Mediation may be used by some in a looser way, for example to refer to a conversation with two people, rather than to the structured process referred to here (Saundry and Wibberley 2012). At a time where it is important to increase understanding of the appropriate use and potential of workplace mediation, this imprecision and lack of clarity in the use of the term could be a hindrance. This may be particularly problematic since word of mouth is important for increasing the use of mediation, and prior experience of workplace mediation has been found to influence perceptions and its potential future use (Latreille et al. 2012). It is important to seek to understand more about the way in which mediation not only operates in practice, but also the way it is talked about and positioned. A lack of clarity and understanding over its meaning and appropriate use, may stall efforts to establish mediation as an important tool for changing conflict management cultures.

Current Practice, Exploring the Potential for Cultural Transformation

In seeking to argue that mediation is currently hindered by the need to straddle two, highly related discourses – dispute resolution and strategic conflict management – there is the risk of making imprecise assumptions about the way in which the boundaries may be drawn between the two. For present purposes, dispute resolution is used to refer to the traditional, adversarial, reactive and formal approaches to dealing with conflict, such as disciplinary and grievance procedures. This typifies the most common approach to dealing with conflict in the workplace in the UK (Wood et al. 2014) since this approach provides employers and managers with a clear, defined structure to follow.

A Familiarity in Formal Approaches

Though familiarity may play a role in the continued dominance of formal procedures, this is not necessarily tantamount to comfort and experience with such procedures. Rather, the familiarity may stem from a sense of security provided by the adversarial system, and for managers and employers particularly. Formal approaches provide the ability to point to consistent, clear and defined, principally objective procedures to help demonstrate, that they acted in the way a good, reasonable employer should (Wood et al. 2014). The trade union position on familiarity is perhaps more difficult to discern and will be considered below. The employee perspective has received relatively little attention, although there are indications that the control afforded by the mediation process is attractive (Fox 2005; Saundry et al. 2013a).

In 2004, a statutory three-step procedure for dealing with disciplinary and grievance complaints was introduced by the government. The procedure was intended to simplify the process of dealing with conflicts and make clear for all employers what was expected of them (Sanders 2009). Rather than simplifying the process, the statutory procedures proved to be an administrative burden for employers and for ETs, and following the 2007 Gibbons review were repealed in 2009 (Davey and Dix 2011). Instead of the statutory procedures, employers are directed to follow the Acas Code of Practice on Disciplinary and Grievance Procedures. Unreasonable failure to comply with the Codes carries the threat of a 25 % adjustment in the amount awarded, should a claim proceed (Davey and Dix 2011; Employment Act 2008).

In the context of the discussion about the role of workplace mediation in this formal process, it is of interest to note that the Gibbons review also saw a greatly increased role for workplace mediation. However, only tentative steps were made to reflect this, with reference to workplace mediation being included only in the foreword to the Code, rather than the body. This was seen as a wasted opportunity by some and did little to change practice in relation to workplace mediation (Wood et al. 2014). Of even greater interest is the fact that, even after the noticeably more strategically and transformational minded language of the 2011 consultation, a recently revised version of the Acas Code did not provide for a more prominent role for workplace mediation.

The Inhibiting Fear of Litigation

Fear of litigation has been found to be a barrier to the potential increased use of workplace mediation (Saundry and Wibberley 2014). This seems to especially be the case for small and medium enterprises (SMEs) (Harris et al. 2012). This is perhaps not surprising since such employers are known to lack access to adequate HR and legal advice, and are disproportionately represented as respondents in ET claims. There is a concern that mediation does not provide the protection of formal procedures, and therefore it remains something SMEs are wary of (Fox 2005).

For some employers, the inclusion of workplace mediation in the Acas Code of Practice-even in its limited form-, has had an opposite result and has encouraged them to try workplace mediation (Deakin 2014). The motive for these employers is not necessarily aligned with a conflict management strategy or a desire to seek early resolution, but rather is seen as a further means of demonstrating, that they have acted in the way a good employer should. Used in this way, it is not necessarily indicative of the desired cultural shift. Here the use of mediation may rather be considered as the accommodation of an informal method (i.e. mediation) into an otherwise formal procedure. This is reflected in the fact that employers largely seem to be using mediation as a last resort (Latreille and Saundry 2015).

The positioning of mediation within dispute resolution discourses therefore is not necessarily equivalent to its positioning in the strategic conflict management approach. Strategic conflict management is a minority, but nevertheless increasingly significant perspective in UK discussions about conflict at work, and is to be understood as representing the desired cultural shift. The perspective is characterized by a more proactive and cooperative form of dealing with conflict and the utilization of alternative methods such as workplace mediation as part of a coordinated and strategic plan to drive and facilitate cultural change (Latreille and Saundry 2015). Here, workplace mediation is seen as a part of a wider strategy to create an open and respectful culture where conflict can be stemmed at an early stage in a proactive, rather than simply reactive way. What strategic conflict management seeks to do, is to shift the focus away from the need for formal procedures and to establish mediation as an alternative, possibly prior, step. For strategic conflict management to be successful, a culture that is conducive to a change, is of vital importance.

Distinguishing Internal and External Workplace Mediation

It is at this point that it is perhaps pertinent to address an issue which is arguably given insufficient attention in UK debates: the need to distinguish between the potential of internal workplace mediation schemes compared with the potential of external workplace mediation. Although an employer may use both, internal mediation has been the dominant focus of much of the UK research and refers to the establishment of an internal capability and structure to deal with disputes through mediation.

In introducing an internal workplace mediation scheme, an organization identifies suitable existing employees to be trained and act as mediators. A coordinator who acts as gatekeeper to ensure only suitable cases proceed to mediation is appointed. Steps should also be taken to ensure that the scheme is sufficiently publicized and embedded. Establishing an internal mediation scheme requires an upfront investment of both time and money, as well as an ongoing effort to develop an enduring scheme (Latreille 2010). External mediation, on the other hand, refers to the use of mediators who are not direct employees of an organization and who are paid on a case-by-case basis.

If the desire is to create a culture where workplace mediation is seen as an established part of dealing with conflict across an organization, establishing an internal mediation scheme seems to offer much greater potential. However, research has shown that simply introducing an internal mediation scheme may have little impact on an organization. There have been some interesting findings about the relevance of size, sector, and the influence of trade unions in determining the degree to which the introduction of internal workplace mediation schemes may be seen as successful. These findings are discussed below.

Factors Influencing the Success of Internal Workplace Mediation

The attitude towards the use of mediation and SMEs has been outlined above, and in addition to fear of litigation, the potential cost has been identified as being prohibitive (Latreille et al. 2012). Further, smaller organizations may also lack the ability to identify a sufficiently impartial mediator from within the company and thus the use of internal mediation may not be suitable for SMEs (Latreille et al. 2012). Time will tell whether the establishment of networks such as those piloted by the government (see above) gain any ground in increasing the use of mediation in smaller organizations – although the lack of momentum following previous pilot schemes for SMEs does not instill much confidence (Fox 2005).

The use of internal mediation has been relatively prevalent in large, public sector organizations, for example in the higher education sector (Bennett 2014) and the National Health Service (NHS) (Latreille and Saundry 2015; Saundry et al. 2013b).

The use of mediation in the higher education sector provides an interesting example, and the study conducted by Bennett into the use of workplace mediation in 16 universities in the North of England found that different institutions had different experiences. Some universities experienced a great deal of demand for the service and experienced a reduction in the number of grievance complaints, but others saw little use and thus little impact at an organisational level. This mixed experience has a number of consequences.

One consequence is that the potential for transformation is limited. Return on investment may be seen as poor and therefore conflict management may not be seen as a viable or worthwhile subject at strategic level. Further it means that employees who received mediation training, may get little opportunity to utilize that training and develop their skills further. In order to counter the latter problem, a network of mediators has been established to facilitate the sharing of knowledge and experience across the universities. In respect of the first issue, it is to be acknowledged that any change in practice and change in attitude and/or culture can only occur over time. Therefore, a focus on short term returns is not helpful (BIS 2011a; Gibbons 2007). When there is a need to establish a business case for investment in such practices, difficulties in quantifying benefits, coupled with an operational focus on short-termism, may be problematic for growth in the use of workplace mediation.

The potential traction of an internal mediation scheme has also been linked to the degree of support afforded by trade unions within a workplace. In some instances, trade union representatives had been trained as mediators but in others, trade unions had expressed a concern that workplace mediation would be used as a way for problems to be "swept under the carpet" or to undermine the traditional role of trade unions in the workplace (Bennett 2014, 2013). Across the research, there is a clear indication that greater success was seen where trade unions had been actively consulted and involved throughout. Findings by Saundry and Wibberley (2014) also indicate that informal approaches may be more successful in organizations with pre-existing high levels of trust between management, employees and employee representatives/trade unions.

Mediation as One Potential Option

What is important about the emerging body of research into the use of mediation, and internal mediation specifically, is the importance of viewing the use of mediation as one tool in a tool box for dealing with conflict (Latreille and Saundry 2015). There is a role for formal procedures to play, for example in serious cases of bullying or misconduct, but there are situations where mediation may be more suitable (Bennett 2014). For establishing an informal culture for dealing with workplace conflict, mediation alone is not sufficient and strategies should involve other components such as training managers in how to deal with conflict (Latreille 2015; CIPD 2015).

It is particularly interesting that this recognition of mediation as an option within other options has brought with it a shift in focus away from mediation and the role it may play as a process towards a greater emphasis on the importance of training of employees in conflict management skills.

In recent research conducted by the CIPD, training managers in how to deal with difficult conversations, was found to be the third most common method for dealing with a dispute, after grievance and disciplinary action (CIPD 2015:11). This had been used by 47 % of employers surveyed, compared with 24 % for internal mediation and 9 % for external mediation (CIPD 2015:11). The significance of training line managers in conflict management skills was noted by Saundry and Wibberley (2014), who also suggested that the introduction of workplace mediation had had the greater impact in relation to attitudinal change towards dealing with conflict, not on the parties to the dispute, but rather on those who had received mediator training. This has potentially important consequences for arguments about the significance of workplace mediation in establishing a more informal conflict management culture. In the long term, if a culture where conflict can be dealt with in a strategic and pro-active way by identifying and dealing with sources at an early stage, it may be that it is not only disciplinary and grievance procedures which become increasingly rare but also the use of workplace mediation itself.

Such findings though encouraging, are perhaps overly optimistic. Underlying the potential for a shift in culture is a list of caveats and preconditions related to organizational characteristics and the availability of resources. There is little evidence to indicate a trend among employers towards a more informal approach (CIPD 2015; Wood et al. 2014). Arguments for a key role for workplace mediation in strategic conflict management are also strongly conditioned and grounded by the prior and dominant practices associated with the more formal approach, and with the danger or threat that a previously mediated case may escalate into an ET claim. Training, on the other hand, is less controversial to reconcile with the operation of formal practices.

Against such a backdrop, the current positioning and potential of workplace mediation is a little tricky to discern. In further seeking to understand how mediation may straddle the two discourses, it is important to understand the roles played by HR and line managers and it is to this that the discussion will now turn.

The Role of HR and Line Managers

A desire to move towards a more strategic approach for dealing with workplace conflict necessitates a changing role for HR practitioners and line managers. Seeking a more strategic role for HR is not a new endeavor, and evidence suggests that in relation to dispute handling, there has been an increasing devolution of responsibility away from HR to line managers (Saundry et al. 2015). Line managers, however, may not be confident or indeed competent to deal with disputes and this ability (or lack thereof) applies to both formal (Jones and Saundry 2012) and informal approaches (Saundry et al. 2015). Particularly in relation to the latter, line managers have expressed concerns about the lack of consistency and of potential protection involved in informal methods.

Aside from issues of capability and confidence, line managers may also lack the capacity to deal with conflict issues as operational issues are prioritized (Latreille and Saundry 2015). To address line manager hesitance, HR must concentrate on building the confidence and skills of line managers (Saundry and Wibberley 2014; Jones and Saundry 2012). This may take the form of training, for example in how to have difficult conversations or mediation skills, and/or by providing an advisory and support system. Both roles have been shown to have a positive impact on line managers and access to HR was found to be a key factor in developing a more informal approach toward conflict management (Saundry and Wibberley 2014).

This dynamic between HR and line managers also has important implications for mediation and raises the question of whose responsibility it is to promote its use. This again may come down to question of whether or not internal or external mediation is to be used. In both instances, the incorporation of workplace mediation into formal procedures should occur, and indeed, even though only 7 % of employers had used it, provision for mediation is included in 62 % of disciplinary procedures and 62 % of grievance procedures (van Wanrooy et al. 2013:27). Van Wanrooy et al. (2013) suggest this gap may be due to a perceived lack of need for mediation, or may be a reflection of the fact that mediation is not yet 'embedded in the culture of conflict handling' (:27). As noted above therefore, simple incorporation is not sufficient, promotion is also required.

Current evidence indicates that the responsibility for this promotion lies with a mediation coordinator and/or with HR (Bennett 2014, 2013). Promotion may be as simple as HR recommending mediation once complaints arise, but can be more sophisticated, for example the use of coordinated publicity campaigns across an organization. HR may be involved in organizing mediation and where mediation is contained within a complaint, for example a grievance, all other aspects of the associated formal procedure should be halted. If mediation is unsuccessful and there is a need to continue with the formal complaint, information disclosed in the mediation process should not be shared with HR or used to inform any subsequent decision. If mediation is successful, HR may be required to play a role in facilitating an agreed outcome.

The role to be played by HR within mediation itself is controversial and relates mostly to internal mediation. Conflicting opinions have been expressed about the propriety of HR personnel acting as internal mediators, with concerns focusing on whether or not such mediators could be perceived as sufficiently impartial (Bennett 2014). This criticism notwithstanding, the evidence collected in the UK indicates that internal mediators are frequently drawn from HR (see for example Latreille and Saundry 2015).

Lessons Learnt from the UK

The role of workplace mediation in the resolution of disputes in the UK is currently unsettled. From a comparative perspective, the UK approach is not necessarily unique, although the focus on facilitative "in-work" mediation rather than court-annexed approaches, distinguishes it from many other EU countries (Purcell 2010). Given the contextual background, one may perhaps have anticipated that it would move along a different trajectory. For example, despite the government-level interest in increasing its use, intervention at legislative level has not been forthcoming. Mediation – both at the workplace level and at the point where an ET claim has been lodged – remains entirely voluntary, with no mandatory requirement to even consider mediation and/or meet with a mediator; this means that there are no legal or clearly defined penalties for refusing mediation.

The lack of a state-led institution for providing free mediation services at any stage of a dispute necessitates a reliance on other, predominantly private, providers and/or internal mediators; this reflects the experience of Australia (Van Gramberg 2006). Although there are a number of professional bodies for mediators to join and a number of accredited qualifications available, unlike in countries like France or Spain, there are no minimum qualifying requirements for mediators (De Palo et al. 2014).

These features of the UK approach have led to concerns being expressed over the integrity and quality of mediation (Dolder 2004). There are also features which shape the barriers identified in this chapter, namely a lack of clarity over meaning, the tensions between formal and informal approaches, and questions over the nature of relationships between HR and line managers. If these are the challenges to be overcome, what lessons can be learnt from the UK experience to avoid or mitigate these?

The first lesson is to acknowledge the need for a more nuanced discussion over the meaning of mediation. If understanding of, and confidence in, the use of mediation is going to increase, greater care should be taken to distinguish between experiences of non-structured conversations labelled as "mediation" and those relating to the structured process of mediation. Confusion over the use of the term may erroneously attribute poor experiences to structured mediation and may serve to complicate arguments in favor of a move towards a greater use of mediation.

The first lesson leads to the second which is the need for clear direction on the positioning of mediation within existing structures, and on its relationship with formal procedures. This relates not only to timing and the need to suspend formal approaches for the duration of the mediation, but also greater clarification over how workplace mediation is viewed by ETs. This may help to reduce the perceived risk of using mediation and increase employer confidence in its value.

An important component of the first two lessons is the need for greater education – for both employers and employees. This may come in the form of more academic research into the use of mediation, and more research into the value of mediation across a range of disputes and contexts. It may also continue to come from Acas and the CIPD through research, freely available guides and training sessions. With a growth in supply of mediators, it may also increasingly come from mediation providers themselves. What should also be encouraged is collaboration between these actors.

Crucially, however, greater investment in education should come from the government. Whilst a mandatory engagement with mediation may be a step too far in compromising the significance of voluntary participation in facilitative mediation, putting resources into the provision of free access to mediation services (likely through Acas) akin to Acas early conciliation, may help to encourage a greater use of mediation as an early intervention tool and help to add substance to policy rhetoric around cultural transformation.

The final lesson is that mediation alone is not enough. Providing education around, and access to, mediation is insufficient. Where possible, employers should also invest in conflict management and/or mediation training for HR personnel and line managers.

As a closing comment, it is important to remember that there are reasons why formal procedures exist and more attention should be given to understanding how mediation can operate within existing structures before jumping ahead to see how it may operate in a desired alternative culture.

References

Advisory, Conciliation and Arbitration Service and the Chartered Institute of Personnel and Development. (2013). *Mediation: An approach to resolving workplace issues.* London: Acas Publications and CIPD Publications.

Bennett, T. (2013). Workplace mediation and the empowerment of disputants: Rhetoric or reality? *Industrial Relations Journal, 44*(2), 189–209.

Bennett, T. (2014). The role of workplace mediation: A critical assessment. *Personnel Review, 43*(5), 764–799.

Boon, A., Urwin, P., & Karuk, V. (2011). What difference does it make? Facilitative judicial mediation of discrimination cases in employment tribunals. *Industrial Law Journal, 40*(1), 45–81.

Chartered Institute of Personnel and Development. (2015). *Conflict management: A shift in direction*? Research Report.

Davey, B., & Dix, G. (2011) *The dispute resolution regulations two years on: The Acas experience.* Acas (Ref: 07/11).

De Palo, G., D'Urso, L., Trevor, M., Branon, B., Canessa, R., Cawyer, B., & Florence, R. (2014). *Rebooting the mediation directive: Assessing the limited impact of its implementation and proposing measures to increase the number of mediations in the EU.* Brussels: DG for Internal Policies.

Deakin, R. (2014). *A theoretical framework for exploring the feasibility and fairness of using mediation to address bullying and harassment in UK workplaces.* PhD thesis.

Department of Business, Innovation and Skills. (2011a). *Resolving workplace disputes: Government response to the consultation.* London: BIS.

Department of Business, Innovation and Skills. (2011b). *Resolving workplace disputes: A consultation.* London: BIS.

Dolder, C. (2004). The contribution of mediation to workplace justice. *Industrial Law Review, 33*(4), 320–342.

Fox, M. (2005). *Evaluation of the Acas pilot of mediation, appeals and employment law visit services to small firms* (Acas Paper 05/05). London: Acas Publications.

Gibbons, M. (2007). *Better dispute resolution: A review of employment dispute resolution in Great Britain*. London: Department of Trade and Industry.

Harris, L., Tuckman, A., & Snook, J. (2012). Supporting workplace dispute resolution in smaller businesses: Policy perspectives and operational realities. *International Journal of Human Resource Management, 23*(3), 607–623.

Jones, C., & Saundry, R. (2012). The practice of discipline: Evaluating the roles and relationship between managers and HR professionals. *Human Resource Management Journal, 22*(3), 252–266.

Keashly, L., & Nowell, B. (2011). Conflict, conflict resolution and bullying. In S. Einarsen, H. Hoel, D. Zapf, & C. Cooper (Eds.), *Bullying and harassment in the workplace: Developments in theory, research and practice* (2nd ed., pp. 423–446). Boca Raton: CRC Press, Taylor and Francis.

Latreille, P. (2010). *Mediation at work: Of success, failure and fragility* (Acas Paper 06/10). London: Acas Publications.

Latreille, P. (2011). *Mediation: A thematic review of Acas and CIPD evidence* (Acas Paper 13/11). London: Acas Publications.

Latreille, P., & Saundry, R. (2015). *Towards a system of conflict management? An evaluation of the impact of workplace mediation at Northumbria Healthcare NHS Foundation Trust* (Acas Paper 02/2015). London: Acas Publications.

Latreille, P., Buscha, F., & Conte, A. (2012). Are you experienced? SME use of and attitudes towards workplace mediation. *International Journal of Human Resource Management, 23*(3), 590–606.

Morris, G. (2012). The development of statutory employment rights in Britain and enforcement mechanisms. In L. Dickens (Ed.), *Making employment rights effective: Issues of enforcement and compliance* (pp. 7–28). Oxford: Hart Publishing.

Purcell, J. (2010). *Individual disputes at the workplace: Alternative disputes resolution*. Dublin: European Foundation for the Improvement of Living and Working Conditions. http://www.eurofound.europa.eu/sites/default/files/ef_files/docs/eiro/tn0910039s/tn0910039s.pdf

Ridley-Duff, R., & Bennett, A. (2011). Towards mediation: Developing a theoretical framework to understand alternative dispute resolution. *Industrial Relations Journal, 42*(2), 106–123.

Sanders, A. (2009). Part one of the employment Act 2008: 'Better' dispute resolution? *Industrial Law Journal, 38*(1), 30–49.

Saundry, R., & Wibberley, G. (2012). *Mediation and early resolution. A case study in conflict management* (Acas Paper 12/12). London: Acas Publications.

Saundry, R., & Wibberley, G. (2014) *Workplace dispute resolution and the management of individual conflict-A thematic analysis of five case studies*. Acas Research Paper, Ref: 06/14.

Saundry, R., McArdle, L., & Thomas, P. (2013a). Reframing workplace relations? Conflict resolution and mediation in a primary care trust. *Work, Employment and Society, 27*(2), 212–231.

Saundry, R., Bennett, T., & Wibberley, G. (2013b). *Workplace mediation: The participant experience* (Acas Paper 02/13). London: Acas Publications.

Saundry, R., Jones, C., & Wibberley, G. (2015). The challenge of managing informally. *Employee Relations, 37*(4), 428–441.

Van Gramberg, B. (2006). The rhetoric and reality of workplace alternative dispute resolution. *Journal of Industrial Relations, 48*(2), 175–191.

Van Wanrooy, B., Bewley, H., Bryson, A., Forth, J., Freeth, S., Stokes, L., & Wood, S. (2013). *The 2011 workplace employment relations study. First findings*. Palgrave Macmillan. https://www.gov.uk/government/uploads/system/uploads/attachment_data/file/336651/bis-14-1008-WERS-firstfindings-report-fourth-edition-july-2014.pdf

Wood, R., Saundry, R., & Latreille, P. (2014) *Analysis of the nature, extent and impact of grievance and disciplinary procedures and workplace mediation using WERS 2011*. Acas Research Paper, Ref: 10/14.

Chapter 8
Towards an Integrated Workplace Mediation System: Reflections on the South African Experience

Barney Jordaan and Greet De Wulf

Workplace mediation is more than merely a potentially useful process for conflict resolution and disputes in the workplace. Reuben (2005) argues that the new world of work – characterized by a breakdown of hierarchies, de-siloing of functions, flexible job descriptions, and greater employee mobility requires adherence to principles of democratic governance. In this regard, effective and constructive internal dispute resolution systems are a vital consideration for any organization. Workplace mediation, which allows for a large measure of party autonomy and self-determination (Reuben 2005), plays a critical role here by channeling inevitable tensions in the work environment into a constructive direction, supportive of broader organizational change.

In this contribution we focus on workplace disputes in a broad sense as involving any conflict or dispute arising in the work environment that involves employees' rights, interests or concerns, whether those arise from a grievance (against another employee or management), interpersonal conflict, complaints of unfair treatment, workplace bullying or alleged non-compliance by the employer with an employee's contract of employment or legitimate expectations. Our focus is therefore not on disputes arising out of or pertaining to collective bargaining, or that relate to the relationship between employer and trade union.

For this contribution, we draw not only on research but also on the combined experience of the authors as conflict and dispute resolution practitioners in South Africa. Both of us acted as neutrals in private practice as well as accredited members of mediation panels of private and public dispute resolution agencies. In addition, we have been involved in the development of workplace mediation systems in three tertiary institutions and two large corporates. This gave us some insight into the importance of establishing a supportive framework in organizations to optimize

B. Jordaan (✉) • G. De Wulf
Vlerick Business School, Gent, Belgium
e-mail: barney.jordaan@vlerick.com

© Springer International Publishing Switzerland 2016
K. Bollen et al. (eds.), *Advancing Workplace Mediation Through Integration of Theory and Practice*, Industrial Relations & Conflict Management 3,
DOI 10.1007/978-3-319-42842-0_8

the potential benefits of workplace mediation and its long term effectiveness. Especially the experience of one of the authors as external consultant to the Office of Mediation of the World Bank Group provided valuable insights into how the effectiveness of a workplace mediation system can be improved by tying it into a more comprehensive, integrated organizational conflict resolution system.

We address the following questions: (1) Is there a role for workplace mediation where a statutory system already caters for the resolution of workplace disputes? Our experience of, and involvement in the South African system suggests that co-existence is not only possible but probably also to be encouraged to broaden access to justice in the work context. (2) What are the limits of workplace mediation and how could these be remedied? While we strongly believe in the value and benefits of mediation in workplace conflicts, we are also very aware of its limits as a dispute or conflict resolution process. We highlight some of these limitations and suggest possible practical remedial measures to overcome, or at least minimize them. We also make the point that workplace mediation could be far more effective if it is not merely applied on an ad hoc basis but incorporated into a coherent workplace mediation system. (3) This raises the third question, i.e., what are some of the principles that should underpin the introduction of a workplace mediation system if it were to be consistent with the 'democratic character of the new workplace' (Reuben 2005:67). (4) Finally, we suggest that a workplace mediation system would be more sustainable in the long run if it were incorporated into a more comprehensive organizational conflict management system. We look at some of the key factors that need to be taken into account when implementing such a system.

Workplace Mediation and Its Assumed Benefits

Definitions of mediation abound (Boulle and Nesic 2001; Menkel-Meadow 1995; Moore 2003). For our purposes, workplace mediation can be defined as a flexible process conducted confidentially, in which a third person who is not directly involved in the matter (the mediator) assists parties in working towards a negotiated agreement of a labor dispute, with the parties in ultimate control of the decision to settle and the terms of resolution (Brand et al. 2012). The third party may be an external neutral appointed by the parties directly or by a dispute resolution agency, but could also be someone from inside the organization (e.g., a line or human resources manager).

Workplace mediation can be applied to a broad range of disputes and conflicts that arise in the workplace, e.g., to help parties communicate more effectively or to rebuild their relationship, but also to address grievances regarding employer practices or its non-compliance with an employee's terms of employment (Bollen and Euwema 2013a).

Various considerations support more widespread use of workplace mediation, ranging from benefits for the individual and the organization at large, to promoting access to justice and democratic values in the workplace (ACAS 2013; Reuben 2005). It can also restore relationships at work and assist with the development of workplace 'social capital'; prevent conflict escalating into disputes; save actual and associated costs such as management time; improve morale and productivity; help to retain valuable employees; reduce the number of formal grievances raised; assist in developing an organizational culture that focuses on managing and developing people; reduce absence due to sickness; and provide a model for effective conflict management skills and capabilities (Avgar 2010; CIPD 2011; Latreille 2012). The confidentiality of the process can also offer a breathing space that allows more open and honest discussions (ACAS 2013). The introduction of a mediation scheme was also found to have a transformative effect on the culture of conflict management in an organization (Saundry and Wibberley 2012; Saundry et al. 2013). Ridley-Duff and Bennett (2011) add that mediation can produce better substantive outcomes for the disputing parties with higher levels of satisfaction and consequently, a higher percentage of working relationships remaining intact in the aftermath of conflict.

One major potential benefit of workplace mediation which is sometimes over-looked, is its relationship with employee perceptions of fairness, justice and trust in the workplace (ACAS 2014; Reuben 2005). These are key in promoting employee engagement and workplace collaboration (Bollen et al. 2012; Saks 2006). As Colquitt (2001) has suggested, justice does not simply relate to the outcome of a decision (distributive justice) but critically to the way in which that decision was arrived at (procedural justice) and how this was dealt with by managers and/or colleagues (interactional justice). Accordingly, where decisions and actions are seen to be 'just', employees are more likely to co-operate and reciprocate with increased discretionary effort (Bollen and Euwema 2013a). Fuchs and Edwards (2012) make a very explicit link between employees' justice perception, their sense of unity or identification with the organization and their willingness to go the extra mile.

Workplace Mediation in Addition to a Statutory System

The South African experience shows that two systems to solve workplace-related disputes, one formalized in legislation and another driven by the private sector can co-exist comfortably and also augment one another.

The Statutory System

The South African statutory system provides for the creation and protection of certain fundamental employer and employee rights, and also for the resolution of individual and collective disputes arising between employer, employees or trade unions (Bendix 2010). While certain disputes must be heard by the Labour Court (e.g., involving alleged unfair discrimination) the key organ responsible for dispute resolution is the Commission for Conciliation Mediation and Arbitration (CCMA). The enabling statute essentially provides for three different dispute resolution processes, i.e. mediation, conciliation and arbitration. 'Conciliation' is an evaluative process, where the commissioner provides a non-binding opinion about the perceived merits of each party's case in the light of legal norms to procure a quick settlement. It differs from mediation in the sense that the mediator generally does not express a view on the merits of the parties' cases but rather tries to facilitate an agreed resolution to the dispute. It is up to the commissioner to decide which of the two processes to use in a particular dispute. In practice, conciliation tends to be the main process used for individual rights disputes whereas mediation is normally used for disputes arising from collective bargaining or large scale redundancies. Arbitration is a final and binding process where the presiding commissioner, after hearing evidence, makes a decision that ends the dispute.

Three things about the statutory system stand out. First, an attempt must first be made to resolve the matter through conciliation or mediation. In the case of disputes of right (e.g. over alleged unfair dismissal or unfair treatment), the dispute will be referred either by the aggrieved employee or a trade union acting on her behalf. Only if an attempt at conciliation or mediation fails, the dispute may be referred for arbitration or, in certain cases, adjudication by the Labour Court. Second, the CCMA's services are in most cases offered free of charge. The purpose behind its establishment in November 1996 was to provide 'social justice' in the employment arena. This is achieved through the accessible and expeditious conciliation and mediation of all employment disputes – both individual and collective – and the final adjudication of unresolved disputes of right through arbitration and in some instances by the Labour Court. Despite its budgetary limitations, it has played a very positive role in 'limiting social tensions and in creating and preserving a deliberative labour policy' (Benjamin 2013:46). Third, the statute does not express any preference for any particular mediation 'style' and provides broad powers to commissioners to determine not only what process to follow, but also to engage with the merits of a dispute in a highly evaluative non-binding way. It is, in short, a robust process aimed at resolving as many disputes as possible, as quickly as possible at the conciliation stage, with commissioners sometimes conciliating five or more disputes in a single day (Tokiso 2014:31).

Finally, the CCMA's jurisdiction is limited. While it may conciliate most disputes of right (e.g. involving unfair dismissal, unfair discrimination, breach of collective agreements, or unfair labour practices) as well as disputes arising from failed collective bargaining (disputes of interest), its arbitral jursidiction – which is activated when conciliation fails – is limited to specific rights disputes only, primarily disputes concerning unfair dismissal and unfair labour practices. Rights disputes are adjudicated by the Labour Court if conciliation by the CCMA has failed (Grogan 2014b). The CCMA has no jurisdiction to deal with interpersonal conflicts or general workplace grievances not involving the infringement of rights.

Private Dispute Resolution

In South Africa, employment rights may arise from contract, common law, collective agreement or statute (Grogan 2014a). Unless a party wants access to the arbitration services of the CCMA, or seeks access to the Labour Court to enforce certain statutory employment rights, there is no obligation to use formal dispute resolution processes of the CCMA to solve employment-related issues. They may instead opt by agreement to use private mediation or private arbitration by an external neutral. This third person might either be an independent provider of dispute resolution services, or someone assigned by a private sector dispute resolution agency at the request of the disputing parties (Grogan 2014b).

In South Africa, privatized dispute resolution in the employment field developed in the early 1980s, when Black workers were only beginning to be included in the protective framework of employment legislation. The statutory dispute resolution institution available at the time – the industrial court – lacked credibility among the emergent Black trade union movement (Bendix 2010). The establishment of the privately sponsored and managed Independent Mediation Services of South Africa (IMSSA) served to fill that void by providing mediation and arbitration services at relatively modest fees. IMSSA subsequently transformed into a new organization named Tokiso Dispute Settlement.

Today, private dispute resolution continues to fill a void, but this time for different reasons than before:

1. The first, relates to time available for CCMA commissioners to resolve disputes, especially disputes of right. The CCMA bears a heavy caseload. According to its 2013–2014 Annual Report, the CCMA receives more than 680 referrals per day. The huge caseload means that the time allocated for conciliation has been reduced over time. Currently, it takes 1 h per conciliation before the matter is marked as unresolved and ready to be processed to arbitration or referred to the Labour Court (Tokiso 2014).
2. A second reason relates to the relative inexperience of commissioners handling conciliations: while the most junior commissioners are allocated conciliations, the more experienced ones are allocated arbitrations (Tokiso 2014). As such, it is less likely that a junior commissioner will be able to understand properly the nature and characteristics of the dispute as well as parties' positions and interests in the limited time available in order to come to a solution. For more complex disputes, it is likely that parties will seek out private dispute resolution agencies (Tokiso 2014).
3. The third reason, is most relevant in the context of the current topic: many workplace conflicts are not 'justiciable' and therefore not capable of application of rights-based norms such as those applied in conciliation or arbitration. Examples of this type of conflict include communication breakdown, organizational change, personality clashes, intra-managerial rivalry including power struggles, disputes between and within teams as well as issues concerning management style. All of these could have an impact on employee well-being and performance

as well as workplace collaboration and trust (De Dreu et al. 2004). Workplace mediation provides a form of access to justice in such matters and in this way complements the narrower focus of the statutory dispute resolution system. It allows employees and the employer to get beneath the problem and to make changes to working practices that can benefit employees and the organization in the long term.

The main disadvantage of the private system is cost: unless the employer is prepared to foot the bill, private mediation is out of reach of most employees. This, together with the fact that the services of the CCMA are generally free, limits the number of instances where private mediation (through external neutrals) is being used.

Limits of Workplace Mediation

Workplace mediation is subject to a number of limitations.

Internal Versus External Mediators

Compared to internal mediators, the use of external mediators tends to be more costly, subject to time delays and associated with the formalization of the dispute (Latrielle 2010). The South African experience bears testimony to this. Latrielle (2010) in his review of UK workplace mediation, shows that resolution rates are lower when external mediators are used. One reason could be that external mediators only tend to become involved when conflicts have become more intractable (Latrielle 2010).

Where parties are either unable (because of jurisdictional constraints) or unwilling (e.g., because of cost considerations) to use external agencies for conflict or dispute resolution, using an internal mediator would be a sensible alternative. The use of an internal mediator might also provide some comfort to the parties involved, that the mediator is familiar with the organization's culture, context and history. Yet, when internal mediators are used, finding someone who is completely impartial may be difficult. This could affect users' perceptions of the fairness of the process in a negative way and affect parties' satisfaction with the mediation and their well-being (Latreille 2012). It may also be difficult for senior staff to have confidence and trust in someone who does not have sufficient organizational status (Latreille 2012).

Power Imbalance Between Disputants

Power relations between participants may shape the conduct and outcome of the process, irrespective of whether internal or external neutrals are used (Bollen et al. 2012; Bollen and Euwema 2013b; Sherman 2003). While mediators can maintain a degree of equality within the process, they cannot change the fundamental power relationships that exist between parties, nor can they protect the weaker party outside the mediation session itself (Sherman 2003). Consequently, the 'weaker' party may be too intimidated to contribute fully to the process (Wiseman and Poitras 2002). The power imbalance may not simply reside in the hierarchical relationship between the parties, but also in the degree to which they are able to articulate their views, their level of formal education, or extravertedness (Bollen and Euwema 2013b). This could provide a potential advantage to more senior, experienced and confident staff (Saundry et al. 2013).

Responsibility for the Conflict

There is a risk that mediation could be used to shift the responsibility for the conflict from the organization to the individual, with mediation as a pragmatic way for management to dispose of difficult issues (Bush and Folger 2005). Saundry et al. (2013) use the example of a case involving bullying, harassment or discrimination: an apparent settlement through mediation can mask the continuation of behaviors that are unacceptable and require more formal action in the organization. A recent UK study also suggests that line managers may be resistant to mediation, seeing it both as a threat to their authority and as a symbol of failure (Saundry and Wibberley 2012).

Timing of the Mediation Process

While common knowledge suggests that mediation would be more effective if it is used as early as possible in a dispute, Saundry et al. (2013) also found that parties experience the process as stressful and daunting and not something to be entered into unless absolutely necessary. This delays recourse to mediation, allowing the conflict to escalate.

Voluntarism in Mediation

Workplace mediation assumes that parties to mediation accept mutual responsibility for, and are willing and committed to seeking a resolution (Seargeant 2005). In the work environment, individuals may feel obliged to take part in mediation, fearing reputational damage or other ramifications if they refuse (Latreille 2012). This could be true for managers who might feel compelled to be seen to support organizational policies and values, but also for employees who might fear repercussions if they refuse to participate (Saundry et al. 2013). Some organizations may also prefer issues to be resolved quickly in order to avoid cost or image damage and may pressure employees into agreeing not only to mediation but also to settle (Coben 2000).

Confidentiality

Confidentiality may be difficult to maintain within a working environment and this may restrict the extent to which organizations can learn from disputes to review and improve workplace practices (Fox 2005; Saundry et al. 2013). It may also obscure serious and/or persistent misconduct by a manager, e.g. harassment of a staff member (Bush and Folger 2005; Saundry et al. 2013) or be used tactically by someone to try and obtain information that is not generally available.

Good Principles to Underpin the Introduction of Workplace Mediation

Ad hoc use of workplace mediation is unlikely to transform the culture of conflict management in organizations (ACAS 2014). This hinges instead on the development of, amongst others, (a) conflict skills for line managers, (b) structures of employee voice and representation and (c) the integration of mediation into a more comprehensive conflict management system (Lynch 2001; Reuben 2005).

In the section following, we make some suggestions about how this could be done. Here we first address the principles that we believe should guide the development and implementation of such a system before turning to the incorporation of mediation into a more comprehensive dispute resolution system.

It has been predicted that the 'new world of work' is likely to be far more democratic than the workplace of old. The latter reflects primarily the interests of the employer, whereas the new workplace calls for greater recognition of the needs, interests, and concerns of employees 'beyond mere economics' (Reuben 2005:20) and thus greater investment by employers in the development of social capital. Social capital is linked to, among others, retention of talent, staff motivation, trust and collaboration (Avgar 2010; Reuben 2005;) as well as the cultivation of 'pro-change behaviour' (Fuchs and Edwards 2012).

Reuben's analysis (2005) of the relationship between the nature of the new workplace, democratic values and dispute systems design, provides a useful framework for those who see workplace mediation as a means of promoting access to justice. The values that underpin this framework also provide antidotes to some of the limitations of workplace mediation that we touched on earlier. The core values are: transparency, self-determination and participation, equality, accountability of the mediator and rationality. These should be reflected in the design of workplace conflict resolution systems and processes (Avgar 2010; Reuben 2005; Wojkowska 2006).

Transparency: Balancing Access to Information with Confidentiality

The confidential nature of mediation poses a challenge to the need for transparency (Reuben 2005; Rubins 2009). This could generate suspicion and mistrust between the parties – if and when caucuses are used – and in the organization at large (ACAS 2013).

Caucuses, the use of one-to-one conversations with the parties separately, tend to shield information and therefore inhibit transparency. They also limit opportunities for the disputants to learn more about one another and from the mediation process itself. At the same time, a caucus can allow parties to openly and transparently air their views, feelings and concerns without the pressure of the other party. Caucuses could be used tactically, e.g., if a party is unwilling to share information face-to-face with the other party, the situation threatens to get out of hand, or the mediator believes that it might be the best option given the circumstances. The mediator can agree with parties to what extent information they will exchange privately, will be subject to disclosure to the other party.

As far as transparency towards others in the workplace is concerned, mediation is a fundamentally different process from arbitration or litigation. In the case of mediation, confidentiality is agreed upon. Therefore, the need for transparency diminishes (Rubins 2009: 48). However, where the outcome potentially impacts others or the workplace at large, the mediator could be given permission after consultation with the parties, to open the session to other parties or to assist the parties in developing joint communiqués to keep relevant stakeholders informed. This might be the situation, if the matter has received widespread attention in the organization.

Participation and Self-Determination: Promoting Voluntarism and Informed Decision-Making

Participation is about the extent to which employees can participate in the structural choices for the design of the process in which they will be participating (Reuben 2005). The most obvious application of this would be a choice in the selection of the mediator. Mediators can apply a variety of styles (Riskin 2003) that could impact on the course of the process and its outcome (Reuben 2005). We would therefore argue that parties to workplace mediation need to be given sufficient information not only to understand the purpose and nature of the process, but also the process options potentially available to the neutral in pursuit of a resolution of the conflict (Reuben 2005). In this manner, they would be enabled to help shape both the process and the mediator's role in it. Lurie's 'guided choice' approach could be useful in this regard (Lurie and Lack 2014).

Participation is also related to the question whether workplace mediation should be voluntary or compulsory, and to the issue of party autonomy or self-determination. Party self-determination is central to all models of mediation (Wolski 2015). The essential elements of self-determination are active and direct participation by the parties in the process; informed consent as to the identity of the mediator, the nature of the process and the outcome; information about the available alternatives to settlement; and the absence of coercion on the parties to accept a particular outcome (Reuben 2005; Wolski 2015).

We would agree with Sander's view that a via media is possible between a compulsory and voluntary system of mediation: there is a difference between 'coercion *into* mediation [and] coercion *in* mediation' (Sander 2000:8). The World Bank Group's Conflict Resolution System (discussed in more detail below) provides a good example: managers who are at the receiving end of a mediation request are compelled to attend the intake and first formal mediation session but may choose not to participate beyond that (Javits 2013).

Equality: Finding an Antidote for Power Imbalances

Equality means that the same rules should be applied 'in the same manner to all persons who are similarly situated' (Reuben 2005:32) irrespective of race, gender, age, or similar grounds. Equality also relates to power imbalances and how those are managed by the mediator (Reuben 2005). If a mediator is not able to manage power imbalances effectively, this could result in the autonomy of the less powerful party being undermined or, in worst cases, 'the direct or indirect coercion of that party's choices' (Reuben 2005:47). Possible remedies include allowing for a review of outcomes, or access to representation (e.g., by a fellow employee or trade union representative) (Dolder 2004). McDermott et al. (2000) found that employee participants with representation were more satisfied with the fairness of the process than those without. Agreement rates were also higher when parties are represented.

Accountability of the Mediator: Addressing Questions of Mediator Status and Impartiality

It could be argued that because mediators do not make decisions about the settlement of a dispute – leaving that to the parties – the issue of accountability does not arise. However, this does not cater for situations where mediators without the consent of the parties adopt a very evaluative or directive style (Riskin 2003) or where other pressures – e.g., the need for a quick resolution – result in the issues not being properly aired or a party is left feeling coerced into a solution (Reuben 2005). Even where mediators are subject to public or professional oversight, this does not extend to the mediator's role within the process, or the level of 'cajoling' or pressure to settle that a mediator might apply on a party.

Furthermore, unlike most agreements, the results of mediated settlements cannot generally be legally reviewed for substantive fairness. In most cases this might not be necessary, yet in the workplace context there is a real risk that factors such as mediator coercion, party incompetence, inequality or other circumstances suggesting a lack of meaningful autonomy, could come into play. The position becomes especially acute when internal mediators are used: not only is there a lack of oversight, but the mediator might be accountable internally, directly or indirectly, to a key decision-maker and potentially interested party in the organization.

Possible remedies include implementing a system of mediator certification, also for in-house mediators; commitment by mediators to a code of conduct; allowing parties a choice of mediators after having been provided with information about, e.g., the mediator's style and experience; and the option to incorporate a review process by an internal or external expert to assess the merits of the mediated settlement agreement (Reuben 2005).

Rationality

Reuben (2005) points out that while one of the strengths of mediation is the ability of parties to make decisions about the outcomes of their disputes according to values and standards that are uniquely important to them, this also makes the process more idiosyncratic. This concern is probably most acute where mediation is used to deal with disputes involving rights issues. A possible antidote could be to exclude rights-based disputes from the scope of workplace mediation, or to include a review process as suggested above. Another option might be a cooling-off period, allowing the parties to seek counsel over the proposed terms of any settlement (Welsh 2001), or for the mediator to play the 'devil's advocate', through reality testing or by painting 'what-if' scenarios.

Workplace Mediation as a Part of an Integrated Conflict Management System

As we suggested earlier, for mediation to have a potentially transformative effect on an organization's conflict management culture, managers have to be equipped with appropriate conflict management skills, employees need to be given voice and representation and mediation needs to be integrated into a comprehensive conflict management system (Lynch 2001; Reuben 2005). It is the latter aspect that we address here.

In most organizations, mediation is a novel and unknown concept. Skepticism from the side of managers about its impact on them (fear of the unknown) and concerns about its usefulness on the part of employees, make it important to be cautious when developing and implementing workplace mediation. A limited and evaluated pilot programme could serve to counteract this (Latreille 2012).

What is essential, is an integrated approach which locates conflict management as a central element of HR strategy (ACAS 2014; Latreille 2012; Lynch 2001). The overall purpose would be to address not only the symptoms of workplace conflict but also its underlying causes, which is essential to the success of the system (Ridley-Duff and Bennett 2001). Attention should also be paid to conflict prevention and development of a certain level of 'conflict consciousness' and competence in the organization and among employees (Lynch 2001).

Enabling Environment

The successful implementation of an integrated conflict management system is heavily dependent on an enabling environment within the organization (Lynch 2001). This includes, among others, leaders from all stakeholder groups acting as champions of the system; stakeholder buy-in and managerial support; institutionalized incentives that reward good conflict management practices and discourage poor ones; allocation of resources; structures that support implementation, institutionalization and trust in the conflict management system; capacity building; and system monitoring and evaluation (Latreille 2012; Lynch 2001). The existence of a generally positive employment relations climate greatly facilitates the introduction and acceptance of a workplace mediation system (Latreille 2012). An organization's responsiveness to mediation may be particularly affected if conflict is negatively viewed by management as an 'emotional' issue or a sign of failure, instead of them acknowledging the link between the existence of conflict, employee behaviour in conflict situations and work performance (Kenny 2014).

Organization Size

While the use of ad hoc workplace mediation is not dependent on company size (Latrielle 2010), size does matter when it comes to the implementation of comprehensive conflict management systems. While knowledge and experience of mediation can overcome preconceptions about the cost and efficiency of mediation in SMEs (Antcliff 2014), larger organizations are more likely to adopt formal systems than smaller ones for reasons of cost and capacity (Johnson 2008; Latrielle 2010; Seargeant 2005). We have found, when advising SME clients on employment workplace related matters, that they were often open to the idea of mediation and sometimes implemented it systematically to a limited degree as part of their disciplinary, performance management, harassment or grievance procedures.

Emphasis on Early Resolution

While formal procedures have an important role to play in the workplace, many disputes could potentially be settled without the need to pursue formal procedures (ACAS 2014). In our experience, once formal procedures have been triggered, the tendency is for differences to become more adversarial. Conflicts tend to escalate, positions to harden, coalitions form and it sometimes becomes very difficult to alter people's perceptions and to have an open discussion. Ultimately, the likelihood of a mutually acceptable outcome also decreases. Early intervention is therefore desirable (Zapf and Gross 2001). As stated earlier parties are often reluctant to initiate a mediation process and turn to mediation at a very late stage. Saundry et al. (2013) propose a two-speed mediation process to cater for this: a relatively 'light touch' informal discussion, facilitated by an individual with mediation skills and knowledge who could be deployed quickly to nip emerging disputes in the bud, while the more extended and formal mediation process could be reserved for more difficult and complex disputes.

In the next paragraph, we try to show how multiple entry points into mediation allow for a party to a conflict to receive advice and guidance about the availability of mediation and other appropriate resolution mechanisms.

Showcase: CRS of the World Bank Group

The Conflict Resolution System (CRS) of the World Bank Group provides a good example of a system that provides multiple entry points into mediation (Javits 2013). The CRS has an open door policy that gives staff direct access to its various services, offering them multiple points of entry into both informal and formal means of addressing staff complaints (Javits 2013). Formal systems are those that require a particular process to be followed to activate the relevant service, whereas no prescribed procedures exist for accessing informal processes.

Four organs are provided for, which may be accessed by any staff member in no particular sequence. They are (a) Ombuds Services, (b) so-called Respectful Workplace Advisors, (c) the Office of Mediation and (d) Peer Review Services (referred to below as 'CRS' organs).

(a) The *Ombuds Services* operate independently of the organization's formal structure and offer impartial and confidential assistance to staff with employment-related concerns. The office does not issue decisions, but may provide recommendations (e.g., that a matter should be referred for mediation). With a grievant's consent, the office may communicate with other staff at any level to assist dispute resolution and may also engage with management regarding systemic issues facing the organization. It may also, if requested by a grievant, become involved in trying to resolve issues in an informal way.

(b) *Respectful Workplace Advisors* are volunteer peers who offer confidential assistance to staff experiencing employment-related conflicts and concerns (Javits 2013). They do not formally participate in dispute resolution, but provide advice to fellow employees on how to resolve problems or engage the Group's other conflict resolution services, including mediation. Ombuds Services supervise the Respectful Workplace Advisors programme (Javits 2013).

(c) The *Office of Mediation* reports directly to the office of the Group's president and offers impartial conflict resolution services to staff. This includes mediation, group facilitation and training services. Once a formal request for mediation is received, the office contacts all participants to conduct an intake. The purpose of the intake is to ensure the participants' understanding of the process and to help the office determine whether the case is appropriate for mediation. The participants are required to sign an agreement to mediate and may rank their preference for the mediator from a list of internal and external mediators. After the first session, any participant is free to decide whether they want to continue with the process or withdraw from it. Agreements reached during mediation are captured in a memorandum of understanding that binds the parties (Javits 2013).

(d) *Peer Review Services* ('PRS') consist of panels of volunteer staff, drawn from managers and non-managers who may, upon request by an employee, review an employment-related matter to determine whether a manager's decision accords with relevant organizational rules and conditions of employment. A panel will typically review the submissions of the employee and management concerned, and submit its findings to the vice president of the manager responding in the case. The vice president, in consultation with the vice president for human resources, will determine any relief to be provided. If a matter has been referred to the PRS for a finding, it may recommend that the matter is referred for mediation to the Office of Mediation instead (Javits 2013).

Each CRS organ is able to direct a staff member to the most appropriate process if it is not able to assist in the resolution of the issue. The focus of all CRS organs is on amicable (i.e. non-adjudicative) resolution of disputes. The Conflict Resolution System is, integrated into a comprehensive Internal Justice System (IJS) that includes an adjudicatory organ (the Administrative Tribunal) which hears cases involving alleged non-compliance by managers with the terms of a staff member's contract or group policy.

In a private sector context, we generally recommend to employers to include mediation as an option in internal grievance procedures, both as a precursor to the filing of a formal grievance and as an option in the course of a formal grievance process.

Participant Evaluation and Continuous Improvement

Evaluating a mediation scheme from the disputants' perspective can be more sensitive than the evaluation of other company policies because of the confidential nature of the process (Lynch 2001). Yet, the success and continuous improvement of the system depends on accurate feedback about the experiences of participants in terms of, their level of satisfaction with the process and outcome; the quality of the scheme; and the impartiality and professionalism of the mediators (ACAS 2013). Latreille's study found that the absence of more formal and robust evaluation of mediation schemes was considered a weakness and also a potential threat to the efficacy of the system, as was the absence of attempts to measure the durability of resolutions effected through mediation (Latrielle 2012). Understanding participants' mediation experience is central to assess perceptions of mediation effectiveness but also to understand the role it plays within wider employer-employee relations, including a change in the conflict culture of the organization (Latrielle 2012).

Debriefing of Mediators

Mediating can be a lonely affair, even more so when as an internal mediator, since one is under constant scrutiny from peers. Therefore, where internal mediators are involved, it is advisable for them to have debriefing opportunities to ask for feedback, a second opinion or to deal with stress, frustration and concerns by sharing experiences with a mediation coordinator or co-mediator. We have found informal peer mediation groups in which mediators can share experiences to be very useful.

Conclusion

Workplace mediation holds many potential benefits for organizations, e.g., restoration of damaged relationships at work; an increase in 'social capital; preventing conflict escalation; reducing the costs of workplace conflict; improving morale and productivity; helping to retain valuable employees; and assisting in developing a more open organizational culture where conflicts are addressed sooner rather than later, or not at all.

Yet workplace mediation also presents particular challenges, including issues of confidentiality, power imbalances and mediator impartiality.

We tried to demonstrate that a system of informal workplace mediation can co-exist with formal, state-sponsored systems for resolution of employment-related disputes: either to cater for conflicts and disputes that are not 'justiciable' under the formal system, or to alleviate pressure on formal systems caused. We provided some suggestions about the principles that need to inform the introduction or implementation of a workplace mediation system.

If the process is integrated into an effective and constructive internal dispute resolution system, it can also play a vital role in the democratization of the modern workplace and the promotion of access to justice at the organizational level.

References

ACAS. (2013, February). *Mediation: An approach to resolving workplace issues* [online]. Available at http://www.cipd.co.uk/binaries/mediation-anapproach- to-resolving-workplace-issues_2013.pdf. Accessed on 6 July 2015.

ACAS. (2014, March). *Reframing resolution – Managing conflict and resolving individual employment disputes in the contemporary workplace* [online]. Acas Policy Discussion Papers. Available at http://www.acas.org.uk/media/pdf/6/9/reframing_policy_paper_FINAL.pdf. Accessed 15 Apr 2016.

Antcliff, V. (2014). Use of mediation by SMEs in Great Britain [online]. Available at http://www2. mmu.ac.uk/media/mmuacuk/content/documents/carpe/2013-conference/papers/social-innovation/ValerieAntcliff.pdf. Accessed on 3 Aug 2015.

Avgar, A. C. (2010). Negotiated capital: Conflict, its resolution, and workplace social capital. *International Journal of Conflict Management, 21*(3), 236–259.

Bendix, S. (2010). *Industrial relations in South Africa*. Cape Town: Juta.

Benjamin, P. (2013). Assessing South Africa's Commission for Conciliation, Mediation and Arbitration (CCMA). ILO Working Paper 47 [online]. Available at http://www.ilo.org/wcmsp5/groups/public/---ed_dialogue/---dialogue/documents/publication/wcms_210181.pdf. Accessed 2 July 2015.

Bollen, K., & Euwema, M. (2013a). State of the art: Workplace mediation – An underdeveloped research area. *Negotiation Journal, 29*(3), 329–353.

Bollen, K., & Euwema, M. (2013b). The role of hierarchy in face-to-face and E-supported mediations: The use of an online intake to balance the influence of hierarchy. *Negotiation and Conflict Management Research, 6*(4), 305–319.

Bollen, K., Ittner, H., & Euwema. (2012). Hierarchical labor conflicts: Procedural justice makes a difference – For subordinates. *Group Decision and Negotiation, 21*(4), 621–636.

Boulle, L., & Nesic, M. (2001). *Mediation: Principles process practice*. London: Bloomsbury Professional.

Brand, J., Steadman, F., & Todd, C. (2012). *Commercial mediation: A user's guide*. Cape Town: Juta.

Bush, R., & Folger, J. (2005). *The promise of mediation: Responding to conflict through empowerment and recognition*. San Francisco: Jossey Bass.

CCMA Annual Report 2013–2014 [online]. Available at: http://www.ccma.org.za/UploadedMedia/2013–14%20Annual%20Report.pdf. Accessed 2 July 2015.

CIPD. (2011). Conflict Management, London: Chartered Institute of Personnel and Development [online]. Available at http://www.cipd.co.uk/binaries/5461_Conflict_manage_SR_WEB.pdf. Accessed 2 July 2015.

Coben, J. (2000). Mediation's dirty little secret: Straight talk about mediator manipulation and deception. *Journal of Alternative Dispute Resolution in Employment, 2*(4), 4–7.

Colquitt, J. A. (2001). On the dimensionality of organizational justice: A construct validation of a measure. *Journal of Applied Psychology, 86*, 386–400. doi:10.1037/0021-9010.86.3.386.

De Dreu, C. K. W., van Dierendonck, D., & Dijkstra, M. T. M. (2004). Conflict at work and individual well-being. *International Journal of Conflict Management, 15*(1), 6–26.

Dolder, C. (2004). The contribution of mediation to workplace justice. *Industrial Law Journal, 33*(4), 320–342.

Fox, M. (2005). Evaluation of the ACAS pilot of mediation and employment law: Visits to small companies. ACAS Research Paper 05/05 [online]. Available at http://www.acas.org.uk/media/pdf/i/q/research-paper-05-05-accessible-version-July-2011.pdf. Accessed 20 June 2015.

Fuchs, S., & Edwards, M. R. (2012). Predicting pro-change behaviour: The role of perceived organisational justice and organisational identification. *Human Resource Management Journal, 22*(1), 39–59.

Grogan, J. (2014a). *Workplace law*. Cape Town: Juta.

Grogan, J. (2014b). *Labour litigation and dispute resolution*. Cape Town: Juta.

Javits, J. (2013). Internal Dispute Resolution at International Organizations [online]. Available at http://www.mediate.com/mobile/article.cfm?id=10468. Accessed 3 Aug 2015.

Johnson, T. (2008) Knowledge and use of mediation in SMEs [online]. Available at http://www.acas.org.uk/media/pdf/m/e/research-paper-02-08-SME-mediation-report-accessible-version-July-2011.pdf. Accessed 3 Aug 2015.

Kenny, T. (2014). Developing the conversation about workplace mediation. *Journal of Mediation & Applied Conflict Analysis* [online]. Available at http://eprints.maynoothuniversity.ie/4676/. Accessed 31 July 2015.

Latreille, P. (2010). *Mediation at work: Of success, failure and fragility* [online]. Available at: http://www.acas.org.uk/media/pdf/1/4/Mediation_at_work_of_success-failure_and_fragility-accessible-versionmay-2012.pdf. Accessed 15 Apr 2016.

Latreille, P. (2012). Mediation: A thematic review of the Acas/CIPD evidence [online]. Available at: http://www.acas.org.uk/media/pdf/h/m/1311_Thematic_review_of_workplace_mediation-accessible-version-Apr-2012.pdf. Accessed 6 July 2015.

Lurie, P. M. & Lack, J. (2014). Guided choice dispute resolution processes: reducing the time and expense to settlement [online]. Available at www.transnational-dispute-management.com/article.asp?key=2153. Accessed 30 July 2015.

Lynch, J. (2001). ADR and beyond: A systems approach to conflict management. *Negotiation Journal, 17*(3), 207–261.

McDermott, P., Obar, R., Jose, A., & Bowers, M. (2000). An evaluation of the equal employment opportunity commission mediation program, US equal employment opportunity commission [online]. Available at http://www.eeoc.gov/eeoc/mediation/report/chapter6.html#VI.B.1. Accessed 3 Aug 2015.

Menkel-Meadow, C. (1995). The many ways of mediation: The transformation of traditions, ideologies, paradigms and practices. *Negotiation Journal, 11*(3), 217–242.

Moore, C. W. (2003). *The mediation process: Practical strategies for resolving conflict.* San Francisco: Jossey-Bass.

Reuben, R. C. (2005). Democracy and dispute resolution: Systems design and the new workplace. *Harvard Negotiation Law Review, 10*(11), 11–68.

Ridley-Duff, R., & Bennett, A. (2011). Towards mediation: Developing a theoretical framework to understanding alternative dispute resolution. *Industrial Relations Journal, 42*(2), 106–123.

Riskin, L. L. (2003). Decision making in mediation: The new old grid and the new grid system. *Notre Dame Law Review, 79*(1), 1–53.

Rubins, N. (2009). Reconceptualising the mediation of investor-state disputes. *Rutgers Conflict Resolution Law Journal, 7*(1) [online]. Available at http://pegasus.rutgers.edu/~rcrlj/articlespdf/boralessafall09.pdf. Accessed 30 July 2015.

Saks, A. M. (2006). Antecedents and consequences of employee engagement. *Journal of Managerial Psychology, 21*(7), 600–619.

Sander, F. E. A. (2000). The future of ADR. *Journal of Dispute Resolution, 1,* 1–10.

Saundry, R., & Wibberley, G. (2012). Mediation and early resolution: A case study in conflict management [online]. Research paper, No 12/12. London: Acas. Available at: http://www.acas.org.uk/media/pdf/5/c/Mediation-and-Early-Resolution-A-Case-Study-in-Conflict-Management-accessible-version.pdf. Accessed 6 July 2015.

Saundry, R., Bennett, T., & Wibberley, G. (2013). Workplace mediation: The participant experience, research paper 2/13 [online]. Available at: http://www.acas.org.uk/media/pdf/t/j/Workplace-mediation-the-participant-experience.pdf. Accessed 8 July 2015.

Seargeant, J. (2005). The ACAS small firms mediation pilot: Research to explore parties' experiences and views on the value of mediation [online]. ACAS Research Paper 04/05. Available at http://www.acas.org.uk/media/pdf/d/l/Research_Paper_04_05-accessible-version-July-2011.pdf. Accessed 8 July 2015.

Sherman, M. (2003). Mediation, hype and hyperbole: How much should we believe? *Dispute Resolution Journal, 58*(3), 43–51.

Tokiso Dispute Settlement. (2014). *Dispute resolution digest.* Cape Town: Juta & Co.

Welsh, N. A. (2001). The thinning vision of self-determination in court-connected mediation: The inevitable price of institutionalization? *Harvard Negotiation Law Review, 6*(1), 85–91.

Wiseman, V., & Poitras, J. (2002). Mediation within a hierarchical structure: How can it be done successfully? *Conflict Resolution Quarterly, 20*(1), 51–65.

Wojkowska, E. (2006). Doing justice: How informal justice systems can contribute [online]. Available at http://ru.unrol.org/files/UNDP%20DoingJusticeEwaWojkowska130307.pdf. Accessed 15 July 2015.

Wolski, B. (2015). On mediation, legal representatives and advocates. *University of New South Wales Law Journal, 38*(1), 1–43.

Zapf, D., & Gross, C. (2001). Conflict escalation and coping with workplace bullying: A replication and extension. *European Journal of Work and Organizational Psychology, 10*(4), 497–522.

Chapter 9
Mandatory Workplace Mediation

Virginia Vilches Such, Alain Laurent Verbeke, and Carrie Menkel-Meadow

Introduction

Mediation has found an entrance in the agenda of policy makers and dispute system designers for several reasons, including its claim to improve access to justice. Yet, there are still many questions regarding the type of conflicts that is really suited to be mediated, and how to design mediation systems capable of delivering the benefits claimed. In fact, the perfect recipe to design an effective and satisfactory mediation system has not been found yet. The challenge is big: how can mediation deliver fairness and justice? For a comprehensive response, we need insights and perspectives from multiple disciplines. Currently, Dispute System Design arises as a new research area that studies conflict from a variety of perspectives (psychology, sociology, law, economics, etc.).

Despite all enthusiasm for mediation, the image of its real use and impact is scattered and in Europe, very modest. One of the suggested solutions to increase the use of mediation is simply to impose it. Hence, an urgent and important question for policy makers and dispute system designers is whether mandatory mediation may be the "secret ingredient" to make mediation really work.

V. Vilches Such
University of Seville, Seville, Spain
e-mail: virginiavsuch@gmail.com

A.L. Verbeke (✉)
Faculty of Law, University of Leuven, Leuven, Belgium
e-mail: alv@kuleuven.be

C. Menkel-Meadow
UC Irvine School of Law, Irvine, CA, USA

Georgetown Law, Washington DC, USA
e-mail: meadow@law.georgetown.edu; cmeadow@law.uci.edu

© Springer International Publishing Switzerland 2016
K. Bollen et al. (eds.), *Advancing Workplace Mediation Through Integration of Theory and Practice*, Industrial Relations & Conflict Management 3,
DOI 10.1007/978-3-319-42842-0_9

However, from a legal point of view, it is not clear whether mandatory mediation is compatible with the fundamental right of access to courts. And from a psychological perspective, making mediation mandatory may not only have important benefits (by sitting together parties might connect again and overcome some psychological barriers), but also undeniable drawbacks (letting go voluntariness as an essential key element of mediation.

In this chapter we briefly state the problem, and raise some of the relevant questions when considering mandatory mediation. We first explore how mediation could be embedded within the scope of the right of access to justice and as a complement to court.

In the section "Mediation and access to justice", we explore mediation and access to justice while considering workplace mediation. The United States (US) approach is linked to the access to justice frame, and the continental approach to collective bargaining. Two examples of different workplace mediation systems in Europe are explained; the cases of United Kingdom (UK) and Spain.

In the section "Workplace mediation and access to justice", we present the dilemma of mandatory as opposed to voluntary mediation as one of the most prominent questions that current policy makers face. By explaining the benefits and drawbacks of both alternatives, we encourage empirical studies on how mandatory mediation may affect parties' satisfaction. Such data are key information for policy makers to decide on whether mandatory mediation is appropriate.

In the section "Mandatory mediation: the "magic" ingredient for a successful future of mediation?", we explore two international court decisions on the relation between mandatory mediation and the fundamental right of access to justice. First, the European Court of Human Rights (ECrtHR) criteria in light of article 6 of the European Convention of Human Rights (ECHR) and second, a paradigmatic ruling of the European Court of Justice (ECJ). Finally, in the section "How to reconcile mandatory mediation with access to justice?", we will briefly present the main conclusions drawn from this chapter.

Mediation and Access to Justice

Traditionally, the right of access to justice is understood as the "right to an effective remedy by the competent national tribunals for acts violating the fundamental rights granted him by the constitution or by law" (Article 8 of the Universal Declaration of Human Rights),

> the right to a fair and public hearing by a competent, independent and impartial tribunal established by law (Article 14 of the International Covenant for Civil and Political Rights), or
> the right to a fair and public hearing within a reasonable time by an independent and impartial tribunal established by law (Article 6 of the European Convention of Human Rights).

Accordingly, justice systems have been based mainly on judicial proceedings.

However, in many jurisdictions, the current state of the administration of justice has proven to be unsatisfactory for users (Barendrecht et al. 2008). In its Green

Paper on Alternative Dispute Resolution (2002), the European Commission (EC) linked problems of administration of justice in the European Union (EU) with the increasing volume of disputes brought before courts, the longer duration and high costs of the procedures as well as the complexity and technical obscurity of legislation. Moreover, sociological research demonstrates how adversarial legal systems with formal complaints about wrongful acts, defenses and extensive fact-finding, do not fulfill disputants' needs and wishes of being heard or improving their relationship (Barendrecht et al. 2008).

Already many years ago, new formulas were sought to create a more effective system for access to justice that would better satisfy citizens' needs. It was clear from the outset that the solution would not be 'one size fits all'. Sander (1979) suggested the multi-door courthouse, designed as a dispute resolution center offering conciliation, mediation, arbitration, and ombudsmen in order to address different types of conflict (Sander 1979; Kessler and Finkelstein 1988).

Menkel-Meadow (2006) introduced the concept of process pluralism theory. This "comes from a belief that new processes of human engagement, including reason, principle, fair bargaining, passions, as well as moral and emotional empathy, are necessary to solve new (and old) human problems so we can live together in peace, with justice" (Menkel-Meadow 2015b). She found inspiration in the theory of "eumonics"; the science, theory or study of good order and workable arrangements developed by Fuller (1954) who differentiated ten different legal processes suited for different issues of human problem-solving and governance. He defined mediation as a process that tries to reorient parties towards each other in ongoing relationships (Fuller 1971).

Recent psychological theories on justice have constructed a new concept of justice that goes beyond the traditional "giving each his due" (distributive justice). In this context, we refer to restorative justice. Rather than punishing and looking backwards, this type of justice aims at repairing damage and healing pain, in a future oriented manner. It is a "process that brings together all the parties affected by an incident of wrongdoing to collectively decide how to deal with the aftermath of the incident and its implications for the future" (Marshall 1998; Roche 2004 in Menkel-Meadow 2007). Interpersonal justice refers to users' perception of a fair process, based on the way people treat each other during a process or procedure. Informational justice relates to the way people are informed during and about a process. Procedural justice refers to the process as being fair through consistency, bias suppression, accuracy, correctness and the possibility to decide over the content of the outcome (Tyler 2003).

The fundamental right of access to justice, has evolved into an obligation of the State to offer different models of conflict resolution in order to response to a variety of users' needs while reducing the administration to a minimum (Soleto 2011). Within such a context, mediation is one of the means proposed for improving the justice system. The EC encourages mediation because it offers an "untapped potential as a dispute resolution method and as a means of providing access to justice for individuals" (Dir. 2008/52/EC). Mediation may contribute to a better access to justice in two different ways, one being more quantitative and another more qualitative

(Menkel-Meadow 2015a). As a quantitative value, mediation may create a more efficient system of justice by diminishing the workload of courts, simplifying procedures, and solving problems in a quicker way. Literature on mediation claims that mediation has the potential to reduce economic costs, mitigate parties' stress, encourage empathy, reduce the length of the procedure and increase agreement fulfillment (Butt et al. 2005; De Palo and Canessa 2014). As a qualitative value, mediation contributes to improving human communication and establishing a different form of justice, with more party tailored solutions rather than court commanded resolutions (Menkel-Meadow 2015a). Psychological theories on justice seem to support the idea that mediation may increase people's perception of justice and fairness. This double set of very different mediation goals and expectations results in a wide variation of mediation processes. One question that can be asked is: How to balance the tension between individual party choice and the need for collective control of the process by the state? (Menkel-Meadow 2015a). This tension is illustrated by the following discussion on mandatory mediation (infra).

What remains uncontested, is the value of mediation as an appropriate way to improve access to justice. Although empirical studies on the effectiveness of mediation are limited (Bollen and Euwema 2013), there are some in the field of workplace conflicts. For instance, the REDRESS program, a mediation system based on the transformative model for the US Postal Services "is the most extensive field test of employment mediation" (Blomgren et al. 2009); REDRESS evaluation teaches us that properly structured conflict programs are capable of producing systemic outcomes that benefit both employees and employers. Other examples are the studies on mediation in hierarchical workplace disputes (Bollen et al. 2012), and the effectiveness of mediation strategies in rights conflicts and conflicts of interest (Martinez-Pecino et al. 2005).[1]

In spite of all the good news, mediation surely has its limits and drawbacks. First, it is only one approach out of many more, it does not fit all people's needs (Menkel-Meadow 2002). Hence, mediation cannot work for every kind of dispute. There are situations where parties may prefer to go to court rather than settling a case in mediation. Examples include situations, where all parties' interests are exclusive and they can only be satisfied by a complete victory; where a party wants to set precedent, create doctrine or establish a reputation that will deter future litigation; where parties use litigation for larger strategic or corporate ends, and when conflicts are so escalated that people cannot talk to each other anymore (Mnookin et al. 2000). Second, in a tradition of adversarial litigation, voluntary mediation may trigger some kind of "submission problem". The suggestion of one party for mediation may be distrusted by the other one (Barendrecht 2010). We know this phenomenon of "reactive devaluation" from negotiation theory, where a good offer may be rejected merely because it has been suggested by the other side (Mnookin et al. 2000). These outcomes support the idea that mediation may need the threat of a court procedure in order to be effective.

---

[1] For a literature review on the State of the Art of workplace mediaton up until 2013 see Bollen and Euwema (2013).

Workplace Mediation and Access to Justice: Voluntary or Mandatory Mediation?

In the working environment, we differentiate between employment (individual statutory claims) and labour (collective) issues. There are countries such as the US where both types of conflicts are linked to distinct legal concepts and very different legal processes (Menkel-Meadow 2011).

In the context of workplace mediation,[2] two main currents have triggered the integration of mediation within the justice system. The US approach on the one hand, with mediation as a means for access to justice and to mitigate the problems of the overburdened administration of justice. On the other hand, the continental approach with workplace mediation as an instrument to support collective bargaining (e.g. Spain).

The US Approach: Workplace Mediation for Improving Access to Justice

Improving access to justice and overcoming the limits of court proceedings, may be an important contribution of mediation. It may make the justice system more effective and increase user's satisfaction. The US offers a good illustration of the advancement of workplace mediation with such purpose.

In the US, the workforce may be divided in labour and employment, with the former united in Trade Unions (labourers) and the latter solely protected by statutory employment regulations. This distinction is "key to understanding the current separation of collective and individual rights consciousness in employees and in the law as well as processes that claim to protect those rights" (Menkel-Meadow 2011).

In general, the origins of mediation in the US, come from the industrial relations field first starting in labour mediation and then jumping to other fields such as civil issues and, employment issues. More than a century ago, the very first initiatives to introduce mediation for labour issues were at State level: Maryland, in 1878, followed by Pennsylvania (1883), New York (1886) and Massachusetts (1886). In general terms, these States established arbitration, mediation and investigation followed by public report (Barrett 1995). The earliest regulation at the Federal level, focused

---

[2] The concept of workplace mediation is studied more in depth in chapter _ of this book.

In a broad sense "the goal of workplace mediation is to settle interpersonal employee conflicts arising out of a continuing or terminated employment relationship" (Brim 2001; Dolder 2004; Doherty and Guyler 2008 in Bollen and Euwema 2013). Workplace mediation may seek to resolve disagreements over work conditions, conflicts between employees, the reintegration of employees after a leave of absence (Shaw et al. 2008), and disagreements about an employee's termination. It may also address complaints about sexual harassment (Bond 1997; Oser2004–2005), discrimination (McDermott and Ervin 2005), bullying (Doherty and Guyler 2008; Fox and Stallworth 2009), multiparty conflicts and/or business-to-business conflicts (Rome 2003).

on the railway industry given its importance to the economy. The Erdman Act of 1898 (at the federal level), authorized both mediation and arbitration in railroad disputes. Under this act, mediation had to be requested by one party and accepted by the other. The duty of mediation was an additional official duty upon the chairman of the interstate commerce commission and the commisioner of labor. Officers were not authorized to offer mediation on their own motion (McCabe 1917). Most cases were mediated since Unions eschewed arbitration (Barrett 1995), this leading to an unexpected success of mediation for labour conflict resolution. What finally led to the repeal of the Erdman Act and the substitution for it, the Newlands Act (1913), was the dissatisfaction of the railroads with its arbitration provisions (McCabe 1917). Since neither the Erdman Act, nor the Newlands Act satisfied the railroads, they created the Railway Labour Act (1926) and choose mediation over arbitration as a dispute system mechanism to solve collective bargaining disputes in railroads (Barrett 1995).

The success of mediation in railroad disputes under the Erdman Act, resulted in the establishment of the first permanent, governmental mediation within the U.S. Department of Labor with competences beyond the railroad industry. In 1913, the Department of Labor assigned the Secretary of Labor "the power to act as a mediator and to appoint commissioners of conciliation in labor disputes whenever the interests of industrial peace may require it to be done". Wilson, first Secretary of Labor, established the first mandatory agency in the Government to fully develop this task.

In the first years of the Department, the conciliation service had a limited role (only 33 cases in 1913–1914). But war times drastically increased labor disputes, making it necessary to establish a permanent conciliation staff. Thus, in 1917, the Congress created the United States Conciliation Service (USCS) as a division within the Department of Labor (Barrett 1995). The USCS's jurisdiction was limited by application of the interstate commerce standard and it acted only upon request (Barrett 2000).

Except during WWI (World War I), during the 1920s–1930s, unions had little power because they lacked a legal basis for engaging in negotiations and only few negotiations and even less conciliations occurred (Barrett 1995). In 1934, the Congress created the National Mediation Board in order to manage the RLA (Railway Labours Act).

In 1936, the Congress extended its scope to the airline industry as well, thus extending the competences of the National Mediation Board to both industries. Except for railroads and airlines, the jurisdiction of the USCS was limited by the application of the interstate commerce standard and, a policy requiring the disputing parties to request conciliation assistance (Barret 1995). In 1935, The National Labor Relations Act, also known as the Wagner Act, included the right to bargain collectively and set prohibitions against employer interference or unfair labor practices (NLRA, § 157). Under this scope, the National Labour Relations Board (NLRA) was created with the main mission of avoiding abuse of workers by employers and surveilling trade union elections (Macho 2014). These rights favoured a proper collective bargaining with more balance of power among workers and employers. This context became the natural scenario for mediation (Macho 2014).

WWII (World War II) raised the production needs considerably, so the priority was to maintain the efficiency of the production and to ensure that strikes and lock outs would not put productivity in danger. The USCS was still functioning but with the rise of conflicts it was not enough to ensure social peace. Thus, a new agency was created in 1941, the National Defense Mediation Board with the main mission of trying to solve those cases that were not resolved by the USCS. Still, soon it was evident that a new agency with more competences was needed (Macho 2014). Thus, in 1942, the National War Labour Board was created. It saw disputes not settled by the Service and referred to it for hearing and settlement recommendations (Barrett 1995). Once the war ended, the functions of these institutions were transferred to the Labor Department.

With the end of the war, cooperation among employers and trade unions ended and the level of conflict rised again, with the difference that now unions had gained more power than in previous periods. In this new context, a new reform of the industrial relations was needed, and the result was the Labour Management Relations Act of 1947. This act installed the Federal Mediation and Conciliation Service (FMCS) as an independent agency of the U. S. Government, with the mission of "preventing or minimizing the impact of labor-management disputes on the free flow of commerce by providing mediation, conciliation and voluntary arbitration" (Federal Mediation and Conciliation Service 2016). The social partners had to inform the FMCS if they wanted to modify or renew a collective agreement. Thanks to this provision, the FMCS was in direct contact with parties along the negotiation process and could act either under request or on its own motion (Macho 2014).

In 1978, the Congress extended the FMCS charter to mediate disputes beyond the private sector to the Federal government, and again in 1979 to the U.S. Postal Service. One year later, the Labor-Management Cooperation Act provided for FMCS to assist in the establishment and maintenance of labor-management committees at plant, area, and industry levels (Federal Mediation and Conciliation Service 2016).

As a result of all this, mediation consolidated as a dispute resolution mechanism for dealing with labour disputes, and labour mediation served as a prototype to extend mediation to other kind of issues (Macho 2014).

Likewise, the Civil Rights Act of 1964, created the Equal Employment Opportunity Commission (EEOC) which offers mediation upon request of the parties (EEOC 2016). The main objective of this Act was to end any kind of discrimination. Under Tittle VII, it includes employment discrimination based on race, colour, religion, sex, and national origin.

Finally, it is worth mentioning the National Employment Mediation Resolution Act (NEDRA). This congressional bill was proposed, eventually not passed, to the House on June 7, 2000, with the following objectives:

- encouraging the use of ADR, particularly mediation of EEO and other employment disputes as well as statutory-based diversity disputes;
- requiring converted federal and possibly state contractors to offer mediation to resolve EEO and other employment disputes at an early stage;

- promoting voluntary resolution of EEO and employment disputes using a legal concept similar to the "duty to bargain" facilitated by a third-party neutral (i.e. a mediator);
- encouraging the implementation of internal dispute resolution systems which are fair, regular, and cost-effective and recognize the traditional proximate relationship between employers and workers as well as the possible existence of an imbalance of power and finally diminishing workload in administrative agencies and courts" (Stallworth and Kaspar 2013).

The main pillar of the NEDRA is that it proposed "directed participation" in mediation after the exhaustion of certain internal procedures. The employee would have the option to submit the matter to mediation and any settlement would remain entirely voluntary (Stallworth and Kaspar 2013). Some authors defend that an appropriate strategy would be to enact the NEDRA, either as a Congressional Legislation or as a Presidential Executive Order, which would require federal contractors to implement internal conflict management systems, and provide EEO disputants early access to ADR, mediation, and voluntary arbitration as a matter or good public policy (Rogers and McEwen 1997).

The EU Approach: Workplace Mediation as an Instrument for Supporting Collective Bargaining

At the national level, the regulation of workplace disputes in EU Member States is very heterogeneous. As an illustration of this variety, we briefly describe two different cases: the UK and Spain.

The System in the UK

As trade unions' attempts for better wages and working conditions were often thwarted by the legislator and the judiciary, they demanded non-intervention of the Government, also known as voluntarism. This redefined the legislator's role as a mere facilitator of the labor relations subservient to the self-regulating powers of employers and workers. Voluntarism shaped the British industrial relations until 1960. Before that time, British industrial relations were primarily established through collective bargaining (De Roo and Jagtengbert 2003). In the 1940s and 1950s, employers, workers and the Government saw conciliation and arbitration as the more suitable mechanisms for preserving the voluntary system. However, in the 1960s, Great Britain experienced a falling in investment levels. In 1965, the Donovan Commission[3] concluded that the industry-wide bargaining structure was not so effective anymore, while the enterprise level had become more efficient to protect rights. The Commission recommended to give individual employees a minimum of

---

[3] A Royal Commission composed of Trade Unions and Employers' Associations created by the Labor Government of the Prime Minister Wilson.

legal rights with the objective of establishing social peace while maintaining the voluntary system to some extent. The Industrial Relations Act (1971) implemented the proposals of the Donovan Commission, restricting the principle of voluntarism (De Roo and Jagtengbert 2003).

Under the Industrial Training Act 1964, Employment Tribunals (ETs) were introduced. Employment Tribunals adjudicate in disputes arising from the imposition of levies on employers by Industrial Training Boards. ETs were expected to take into account the social policy intentions underlying the legislation as the regular courts had failed to do so. They were composed of lay-experts and a legally qualified chairperson. The input of laymen was supposed to bring more specific expertise, facilitate access to justice and overcome the distrust of trade unions towards the regular courts (De Roo and Jagtengbert 2003).

Once the ETs were fully implemented, a conciliation phase was inserted within the ET procedure with the objective of diminishing the excessive workloads of the ETs. The idea was that promoting amicable settlements would also preserve the voluntary system. As this was highly criticized for not being impartial, the Conciliation and Arbitration Service was established in 1974, renamed 1 year later as the Advisory Conciliation and Arbitration Service (ACAS) (De Roo and Jagtengbert 2003). In the UK, conciliation refers to the situation before a formal complaint is launched before the employment tribunals (ACAS 2015). Mediation refers to the attempts made to resolve disputes in the workplace with the help of a third person. In theory, conciliators should have a less pro-active role than mediators, who may offer recommendations to parties (ACAS 2016). ACAS offers early conciliation services for both employment and labor disputes (in the UK they are classified as individual and collective disputes) and collective mediation.

In case of an individual dispute, parties are legally required to contact ACAS before entering a court claim; neither party is obliged to take part in conciliation and can give up the process whenever they wish. The initiation of ACAS Early Conciliation suspends limitation periods for presenting a claim during 1 month, unless the conciliator decides to extend this period for 2 weeks more (ACAS 2015). This conciliation procedure is free of charge and ACAS involves an independent conciliator who discusses the issues with both parties in order to help them reach a better understanding of each other's position and underlying interests. Normally, these discussions are held by phone calls (ACAS 2015).

Additionally, there is the ACAS Collective Conciliation, ACAS helps to resolve disputes between groups of employees (usually via trade unions) and employers in order to prevent industrial action (ACAS 2016). Either party can contact ACAS independently to discuss the issue confidentially without any further obligation. ACAS conciliation is most commonly used in disputes over pay, terms and conditions, resourcing levels or long-term business restructuring (ACAS 2016).

Finally there is the ACAS Collective Mediation to help an organisation and its employees (usually represented by a trade union) to resolve a particular dispute (ACAS 2016). The parties agree on terms of reference, including that they will seriously consider ACAS recommendations. Collective mediation can be triggered at any stage; it is encouraged to turn to mediation before positions in a dispute become entrenched, or the working relationship starts to break down (ACAS 2016). This is a completely a voluntary process, so both sides must agree to take part and are allowed to stop the process at any stage (ACAS 2016).

The Spanish System

In Spain, Labor Law is an independent branch of law which has been recognized long before the twentieth century. It includes matters of collective and individual labor law (Olea and Rodríguez-Sañudo 2010). The dispute system for labour and employment issues is in hands of a specialized court system; the social jurisdiction (Jurisdicción Social), and Social Jurisdiction Act (Ley 36/2011, de 10 de octubre, Reguladora de la Jurisdicción Social).

Social Jurisdiction emerged as a critic to the Civil Law court system, as labor conflicts should not be in hands of the bourgeois civil jurisdiction (Rodriguez-Piñero 2003). According to the preamble of the Social Jurisdiction Act, the singular nature of the industrial relations and its specific necessities in procedural matters, explain and justify the existence of this social branch of the Law (Social Jurisdiction Act 2011). The long tradition of these specialized courts has culminated in a high efficiency and social prestige of the social jurisdiction (Cruz Villalón 2003).

During the Franco regime (1939–1878), courts were the only means for solving (and pacifying) disputes and protests. The role of courts was intensified as a means for compensating the lack of collective autonomy and private dispute resolution mechanisms. The Spanish Constitution of 1987 confirmed the role of the social jurisdiction, recognizing the fundamental right of effective judicial protection established in its Article 24. Later, Article 4, 2, (g) of the Employee's Statute (RD-L 2/15) (Rodriguez-Piñero 2003).

Today, things have changed and autonomy has gained relevance, leaving space for more autonomous mechanisms of conflict resolution such as mediation and arbitration (Rodriguez-Piñero 2003). Already in 1991, the Constitutional Court of Spain welcomed the use of Alternative Dispute Resolution (ADR) stating that the establishment of autonomous mechanisms of dispute resolution is beneficial for the parties because it allows them to solve their disputes according to their interests in a quicker and more comfortable way. It is also beneficial for the system because the use of these means lower the workload of the courts (STCo 217/1991, in Tascón López 2009).

The Social Jurisdiction Act establishes several options for using mediation in labor disputes. However the scope of action of the mechanisms available for mediation, is limited. The three possibilities for mediation in labor disputes in Spain are the following:

(a) *Mandatory Previous Conciliation.* This type of conciliation' is held before the Mediation, Arbitration and Conciliation Centers (CMACs) which are part of the labor administration. This is a necessary step that parties must follow before they can present a claim before Labor Courts. In practice, this has become a mere administrative step and conciliators usually dedicate few minutes to each case and their influence over the process is minimal.

(b) *Mechanisms created by social partners*. The mandatory previous conciliation can be substituted by mechanisms created by the social partners through sectorial collective agreements or Agreements on Conflict Resolution (Cruz Villalón 2003). The most representative trade unions and employer's organizations of Spain created the Interconferencial Service of Mediation and Arbitration (Servicio Interconferencial de Mediación y Arbitraje, SIMA). This institution offers mediation and arbitration services for collective conflicts whose scope exceeds the territory of one autonomous region. However, it excludes individual (employment) disputes. Moreover, each autonomous region has its own agreement on conflict resolution and has created its own system of dispute resolution. Many of the regions, exclude individual (employment) disputes. Yet, in some regions such as Andalusia, the success of the Extrajudicial Labor Dispute Resolution System of Andalusia (Extrajudicial de Resolución de Conflictos Laborales de Andalucía, SERCLA) encouraged social parties to extend its scope of action to certain matters in individual (employment) disputes.

(c) *Joint Committees*. The third possibility established by the LRJS is that social partners, in the framework of collective bargaining, create a joint committee. This body is composed of representatives of trade unions, employers and the labor administration. Its main function is to solve conflicts on the interpretation and application of collective agreements (Canvas Martínez 2007).

Mediation at the EU Level

In a comparative report by Valdés (2003) for the EC, two classifications of mediation systems in Western Europe are suggested.

In the first classification, there are three general categories of workplace mediation systems according to the responsible entity or organism: first, courts associated with the broader judicial system; second, administrative authorities related to labor ministries (i.e. labor inspectors); finally, autonomous mechanisms which in most cases involve the participation and/or management by social partners.

The second classification of mediation systems identifies two groups, based on the relationship between mediation and the judicial system. The first group with the mediation system in a subordinate role to the judicial system. Non-jurisdictional mechanisms are designed almost as auxiliary techniques falling under jurisdictional activity, as simple appendices to judicial protection. The second group embraces those systems that are functionally autonomous. They are not designed as procedures in chronological sequence. Submitting the dispute to the judiciary does not necessarily mean that mediation has ended.

According to Valdés (2003), ADR and mediation systems for workplace disputes are supporting and enhancing the process of collective bargaining. On the one hand, collective bargaining is the source of ADR in Labor Law and, on the other hand ADR contributes to legitimating the collective bargaining process as a means for managing and regulating industrial relations. This primary use as a means of supporting resolution of collective labor disputes, may influence the development of processes and institutions in charge of mediation services. Hence, workplace mediation may be known and used in unionized workplaces, much less in non unionized settings. This does not preclude its contribution to a more effective justice system or user satisfaction, nor its usefulness for conflicts in individual employment settings. There is no reason to exclude mediation as a means to settle higher end corporate employment issues. The perception that the role of mediation is limited to collective bargaining, may result in fewer interest in developing mediation in systems where collective bargaining is well established, and works efficiently (e.g. in Germany) (Valdés 2003).

At the EU level, the regulation of workplace mediation remains limited. Some argue that the EU Mediation Directive is not applicable in cross-border employment disputes and this for the following reasons: First, employment or workplace mediation is not specifically mentioned in the Directive, neither in the title nor within the text. And second, the Directive literally reads that it (mediation) should not apply to rights and obligations on which the parties are not free to decide themselves under the relevant and applicable law. Such rights and obligations are particularly frequent in family and employment law (Dir. 2008/52/EC). Others however consider that the Directive is to be applied to labor issues in those matters that are open for party negotiation (Arastey 2014). For instance, parties are free to mediate on issues like overtime as far as they respect mandatory legal restrictions (e.g. in Spain there is a limit of 80 h a year). Two main arguments support this idea. First, in some Member States such as in the Netherlands, labor regulation is included within the Civil Law regulation; labor disputes are solved by civil jurisdictional bodies. Second, labor issues are included in other regulatory instruments of the EU in civil and commercial matters.[4] Therefore, we believe that in the Directive, there is no generic exclusion of employment issues but only of those matters that are not open for negotiation by the parties or only within the mandatory limits of law.

Moreover, the EC has demonstrated its interest in setting up an international mediation system for cross-border employment disputes. In 2003, the EC ordered a comparative study on "Conciliation, Mediation and Arbitration in the States of the European Union" in the field of collective unionized labor disputes to assess the possibilities of establishing a new instrument for ADR for collective disputes at the European level. One of the main findings is the great differences among national labor law systems, and the wide range of mediation processes in each country to deal with collective workplace disputes (Valdés 2003).

We conclude that mediation has a long tradition as a complementary means to workplace disputes resolution. Moreover, the NEDRA proposal and the EU's

---

[4] E.g. Council Regulation (EC) No 44/2001 of 22 December 2000, on jurisdiction and the recognition and enforcement of judgments in civil and commercial matters; and the Council Regulation (EC) No 1348/2000 of 29 May 2000 on the service in the Member States of judicial and extrajudicial documents in civil and commercial matters.

attempts of establishing EU level mediation systems, prove the increasing interest for mediation in both labor and employment settings.

Mandatory Mediation: The "Magic" Ingredient for a Successful Future of Mediation?

The issue of mandatory mediation is a delicate one, even paradoxical, because of the inherent voluntary nature of mediation. However, some sort of mandatory requirement to start mediation seems in some cases the only way to get parties at the mediation table.

When mediation is mandatory, there is an obligation to come to start the mediation process. Once started, the principle of voluntariness demands that parties may at any time terminate the mediation (Verbeke 2009). Continuing participation in the process cannot be mandatory, although some legislators and courts have required 'good faith' participation (Menkel-Meadow 2011). The ILO (1998) agrees that the obligation to start mediation does not affect the autonomy of the parties nor modifies their position in the process. Even if attendance to the mediation meeting is compulsory, the voluntary nature of the process remains protected as long as parties are free to leave the process at any moment.

As to requiring parties to start mediation, there are several formulas with different degrees of enforceability: mandatory mediation ordered by law, mediation clauses in private contracts, and incentives or penalties for the use of mediation (Ginebra and Tarabal 2014).

The legislature may impose mediation, either as a procedural requirement (normative approach) or giving the judge the possibility to impose parties to turn to mediation (discretionary approach). An example of the normative approach is the case of Spain, where the Social Jurisdiction Act 2011 establishes mandatory mediation for any collective labor conflict before introducing the claim to the Social Courts.

Within the complexity of this question, we focus on two considerations. First, the benefits from the user's perspective of mandatory mediation and second, the possible legal implications of establishing mandatory mediation.

Benefits of Mandatory Mediation

The benefits but also drawbacks of mandatory mediation as opposed to voluntary mediation remain a hot and delicate topic among social scientists and scholars. Menkel-Meadow (2009) finds a serious baseline problem in empirical research analyzing dispute resolution processes, due to the multiple issues contested in mediation and the various forms and types of processes. She is therefore skeptical whether we can ever truly measure, with any degree of accuracy, whether one particular process is ever better or worse than another in a particular case".

Some people question the usefulness of establishing an obligation to enter mediation, given that mediation effectiveness depends on the will of the parties to collaborate (EC 2002). Moreover, forcing the parties to attend to mediation, would only make them persist in their views and positions (Valdés 2003). For some, it truly is a betrayal to the very essence and core values of mediation to make mediation obligatory (Nolan-Haley 2012).

At the same time, there is sufficient empirical and anecdotal evidence that directed participation in mediation (with only voluntary settlement outcomes) is effective, when using measures of satisfaction with the process and the outcome as indicators (Brett et al. 1996). Empirical research demonstrates that party perceptions of fairness as well as settlement rates are often comparable in both mandatory and voluntary mediation programs (Brett et al. 1996). Also Wissler (1997) found little differences between mandatory and voluntary mediation in terms of case outcome and participant evaluation.

Brett et al. (1996) suggest it is necessary to make a distinction between "compulsion to enter mediation" and "compulsion to settle mediation", as only the latter goes against the nature of mediation. The fact that mediation is required may also solve reactive devaluation issues when one party suggests mediation (see supra). Most importantly, being required to come to mediate makes mediation known to the parties and educates them about the process and what it can accomplish. Unknown is unloved. Through even one mediation session, parties may gain knowledge and experience about the process and culture of mediation. This information benefit or educational effects (Menkel-Meadow 2015a) are an important element to take into account for policy makers, as the lack of knowledge about mediation has been consistently identified as a barrier to the wider use of mediation (Department of Business, Innovation and Skills 2011). In this regard, Nabatchi and Bingham (2000) conclude that those who have more experience with mediation, value more the process and experience its benefits more. In their research, participants stated that experience with mediation affected their subsequent approaches to conflict.

Based on these arguments, some authors defend the use of law to increase and impose the use of mediation (Rogers and McEwen 1997). Stallworth and Kaspar (2013) defend the enactment of the NEDRA for integrating mediation for conflicts as well as employment related conflicts, arguing that economics are the precipitating and driving factor behind decisions implementing legitimate conflict management systems.

Legal Implications of Legal Mediation

As to the legal implications of mandatory mediation, there are certain key aspects to be taken into account:

1. the possibility of appealing to courts after the agreement; with a large variation in the comparative landscape although many countries do not allow appeal.
2. the effect on limitation periods of the judicial procedures;
3. the enforceability of the agreement and
4. the confidentiality of the information disclosed in the mediation.

Mandatory mediation should not diminish the guarantee of fully effective judicial protection (De Roo and Jagtenberg 1994). But what does that mean in practice? We see that this is addressed in different ways in different countries. Understanding these legal implications may help researchers to gain insight in the main questions that policy makers and dispute system designers face. In fact, the question whether there should be more mandatory mediation, has been put at the top of the agenda of the EU after the publication of the report "Rebooting the Mediation Directive: Assessing the limited impact of its implementation and proposing measures to increase the number of mediations in the EU" (EP 2014). This study aimed to analyze the so called "Paradox of Mediation in the European Union" that highlights that despite the multiple benefits claimed for mediation and the multiple efforts made by the EU, the EC and most of the National Governments, mediation has only been used in 1 % of the civil and commercial disputes in the EU (EP 2014). It has been pointed out that resistance to mediation may be explained by many different causes, culturally (both social and legal), historically, economically and "legalism or legality" (Menkel-Meadow 2015a).

One of the main conclusions of the study is that only a certain degree of compulsion to mediate (currently allowed but not required by EU law), can generate a significant number of mediations. In fact, all of the other pro-mediation regulatory features mentioned, such as strong confidentiality protection, frequent invitations by judges to mediate and a solid mediator accreditation system, have not generated any major effect on the occurrence of mediation (EP 2014).

In particular, the study asked about possible legislative and non-legislative proposals in the EU to promote the use of mediation. Respondents were asked to rank the likely impact of the following solutions and proposals in their country with a ranking scale from (1) extremely negative impact, to (5) an extremely positive impact. Where one measure could have both positive and negative effects, respondents were asked to mention both positive and negative aspects when ranking these proposals. For example, if mandatory mediation might have an extremely positive impact on the number of mediations but will also generate some resistance, instead of ranking that measure with 'Extremely Positive Impact', they were asked to rank it with positive impact. If the resistance would be significant, they should rank it with no significant impact or even negative impact. The legal solutions evaluated in the study are the following (EP 2014):

1. Require counsel to inform parties on mediation as an alternative to litigation, and enforce penalties for lawyers failing to do so;
2. Require mandatory mediation information sessions before litigation;
3. Make mediation mandatory for certain cases;

4. Make mediation mandatory in some cases with the ability to opt out at little or no cost during the first meeting;
5. Make mediation mandatory for the stronger party, defined as the party with greater bargaining or economic power. Require stronger parties who refuse to mediate participate in mediation to provide a written reason for this refusal;
6. Grant judges the power to order litigants to make use of mediation;
7. Require judges to explain why they did not refer a case to mediation;
8. Assess the productivity of judges partly based on the number of cases referred to mediation;
9. Impose sanctions for parties' refusals to attend mandatory mediation proceedings such as holding these parties liable for litigation costs, even if they prevail in the subsequent trial of the case;
10. Provide incentives for parties who choose to mediate, such as providing refunds of court fees or tax credits;
11. Require a third-party to review the settlement focusing on violations of law, public policy or unconscionable stipulations;
12. Require that legal assistance is made mandatory to parties in mediation;
13. Require each Member State to designate a minimum number of cases to be mediated each year in order to achieve the objective of 'ensuring a balanced relationship between mediation and judicial proceedings' set forth in Article 1 of the 2008 Mediation Directive;
14. Other;
15. Out of the list of legislative measures above, please identify the one solution that would have the single, most positive impact on the use of mediation in your country.

Out of this list, the six most effective legislative measures to increase mediation use, by number of references expressed are the following:

1. Make mediation mandatory for certain cases: 132 votes.
2. Require mandatory mediation information sessions before litigation: 110 votes.
3. Provide incentives for parties who choose to mediate, such as providing refunds of court fees or tax credits: 97 votes.
4. Require counsel to inform parties on mediation as an alternative to litigation: 72 votes.
5. Impose sanctions for parties' refusals to attend mandatory mediation: 59 votes.
6. Grant judges the power to order litigants to make use of mediation: 51 votes.

It is remarkable that the two most voted measures directly relate to compulsory actions. The second one may be linked to ethical codes or practices that require lawyers to fully inform their clients about a variety of options for disputes resolution (Menkel-Meadow 2015a).

EP (2014) concludes that unless the law introduces elements of mandatory mediation, mediation would not ever be revitalized, at least in the EU. It is important to notice that this study was made in the context of Civil and commercial matters[5], so we cannot automatically expand these conclusions to workplace disputes.

The plea for more mandatory mediation has received mixed support. In Israel, the President of the Israeli Supreme Court (Ahron Barak) encouraged the use of mediation as an attempt to change the legal culture toward a more conciliatory one. Despite the incentive structures established to encourage the use of mediation and the high amount of trainings, some noted that the use of mediation became too mechanistic and lost the true potential for conflict resolution (Menkel-Meadow 2015a).

Our belief is that the clear distinction between the requirement to go to the table and the requirement to reach an agreement, may solve the dilemma (Menkel-Meadow 2015a). As long as the latter remains entirely voluntary, mediation is by no means at risk.

How to Reconcile Mandatory Mediation with Access to Justice?

For mandatory mediation to comply with the access to justice standards, several elements of the institutional context are relevant. They include process access (How easy is it to get to mediation?); process efficiency (How long does the mediation process take?); and process information (Is the process clearly explained?) (McDermott et al. 2000). If mediation stops the limitation periods for claiming before the courts and the mediation takes too long, the process may be extended excessively making it difficult for people to get access to mediation. Consequently, a maximum period of time for the mediation process may be considered. It is also possible however that if mediation does not stop the statute of limitations, access to justice would be made impossible since a long mediation may prevent parties to seize courts as they have run out of time.

Needless to say that the fundamental right of access to justice and all guarantees of due process, put a heavy burden on legislators, decision makers and dispute system designers. However, as any fundamental right, also the principle of effective judicial protection is not absolute. It may be restricted to achieve objectives of general interest inasmuch as those restrictions do not constitute, with regard to the objectives pursued, a disproportionate and intolerable interference which infringes up the very substance of the rights guaranteed.[6] We would even claim that effective

---

[5] There are no data on the research on whether employment disputes were integrated under the research in those systems where civil and labor conflicts fall within the same procedural laws.

[6] See: Case C-28/05, Dokter and Others, [2006] ECR I-5431, para. 75; Case C-394/07, Gambazzi, [2009] ECR I-2563, paras 29–32, especially para. 29. In the same way, as to more dated decisions, see: Case C-62/90, Commission of the European Communities v Federal Republic of Germany, [1992] ECR I-2575, para. 23; Case C-44/94, Fishermen's Organisations and Others, [1995] ECR I-3115, para. 5.

judicial protection should be finetuned and reformulated in a way that it may include the obligation to at least start a mediation process. Access to justice should not necessarily include an unlimited and unconditional access to courts at any time.

Two important references in International Law – the Case Law of the European Court of Human Rights (ECrtHR) and a paradigmatic case ruled by the European Court of Justice (ECJ) – may serve as an illustration of the conditions and concerns that legislators and decision makers should bear in mind concerning compulsory mediation.

Mandatory Mediation and the ECrtHR

Article 6 of the European Convention of Human Rights reads as follows:

> In the determination of his civil rights and obligations [...] everyone is entitled to a fair and public hearing within a reasonable time by an independent and impartial tribunal established by law [...].[7]

Although the literal writing of the article only states "civil rights and obligations", the Court argues that Article 6 is applicable to disputes concerning social matters, including proceedings to an employee's dismissal by a private firm (ECrtHR 2013). The right of access to courts requires that litigants should have an effective judicial remedy enabling them to assert their civil rights. The right to a fair trial includes three elements: the right to a public hearing, the right to a trial within a reasonable time, and the right to independent and impartial tribunal established by law (Schiavetta 2004).

As explained, under certain circumstances some limitations are possible.

First, limitations may not restrict nor reduce the right of access for an individual in such a way that the very essence of the right is impaired. Any limitation should pursue a legitimate aim and there should be a reasonable relationship of proportionality between the means employed and the aim sought to be achieved. No violation of art. 6.1 can be found if the restriction is compatible with the principles established by the Court (ECrtHR 2013). Some examples of legitimate restrictions are the establishment of statutory limitation periods, security for costs orders, or a legal representation requirement.

Second, the ECrtHR already established, that a waiver of a person's right to have his or her case heard by a court or tribunal, is frequently encountered in civil matters, especially regarding arbitration clauses in contracts. Accordingly, the ECrtHR

---

[7] See Convention for the Protection of Human Rights and Fundamental Freedoms as amended by Protocol No. 11 and 14 and Supplemented by Protocols 1,4,6,7,12 and 13, http://www.echr.coe.int/Documents/Convention_ENG.pdf, accessed on 26 February 2016. Article 6 has a further two sections (6(2) and 6(3)), both of which relate primarily to the rights of individuals charged with a criminal offence, although they can serve as a point of reference in civil cases.

establishes that such waiver has undeniable advantages for both the parties and the administration of justice. Consequently, this does not violate the Convention. The Court added that this requires that the waiver is permissible and established freely as well as unequivocally. Indeed, in a democratic society, the right of access to court is too important to be forfeited merely because an individual is party to a settlement reached in the course of a procedure ancillary to court proceedings (ECrtHR 2013).

Further, the right of access to justice must be practical and effective which means that an individual must have a clear, practical opportunity to challenge an act that is in interference with his rights. Therefore, the laws, should not prevent litigants from using an available remedy (ECrtHR 2013). In practice, this means that the right to court may be impaired by (1) the high costs of the proceedings when taking into account the individual's financial capacity (i.e. excessive court fees),; (2) issues regarding time-limits (i.e. applicants were told that their action was statute-barred at such a late stage of the proceedings which , deprived them of any possibility to assert their right; (3) the existence of procedural bars preventing or limiting the possibilities of applying to a court (ECrtHR 2013). In this regard, there is a considerable difference between compulsory arbitration and compulsory mediation. In mediation, parties always have the option to leave the process and to come back to the judicial proceedings without getting an agreement. Once they have reached an agreement, legislators should make sure that the possibilities of implementing the agreement are also in line with the guarantees of article 6.

Bearing in mind all of these considerations, let us now turn to the debate in the UK regarding the possibilities for courts to impose penalties to parties who refused mediation. The first significant case that dealt with this question was Cowl versus Plymouth City Council (2001). It concerned a public law dispute over the rehousing of elderly residents in a nursing home run by the Plymouth City Council. The latter offered an alternative process to the residents with the aim of avoiding litigation, but residents declined. The Court of Appeal considered the Council's initiative as reasonable and criticized the refusal of the residents, and the fact that the case had progressed so far when an ADR process was made available.

Following Cowl, the courts strongly encouraged the use of mediation without imposing penalties for rejecting to use it. For the first time, judicial encouragement turned into quasi compulsion since the court made it possible to deprive the party that refused to mediate. This case triggered a debate whether, this ruling meant a requirement that all cases need to be mediated.

It remained unsure however whether courts could require parties to participate in mediation and, if not, whether a court could impose cost sanctions against successful litigants who had refused to mediate. The Court of Appeal held that truly and reasonably unwillingly parties should not be required to mediate since this would imply a violation of the litigant's fundamental rights to have access to the courts, as guaranteed by Article 6 of the European Convention on Human Rights.

The Court suggests a non-exhaustive list of six factors to take into consideration when deciding whether rejection to mediate was reasonable or not:

(a) The nature of the dispute;
(b) The merits of the case. The fact that a party unreasonably believes that his case is watertight, is no justification for refusing mediation. But the fact that a party reasonably believes that he has a watertight case, may be sufficient justification for a refusal to mediate;
(c) Other settlements methods that have been discussed;
(d) Costs of the mediation are disproportionately high, especially when the sums at stake in litigation are comparatively small,
(e) Possible delay in the court proceedings; and
(f) Unreasonable perspectives of success.

The Court stated that compulsory referral would achieve nothing except to add to the costs to be borne by the parties, and damage the perceived effectiveness of the ADR process". The Court ruled that its role was to encourage but not to compel parties to engage in ADR. Therefore, compulsory referral to mediation was not considered acceptable, although encouragement to use ADR could be "robust".

Two small comments. First, one should note that reasoning may have been different if mediation would be provided for free to parties. Second, there is an essential difference between mediation and arbitration as forms of ADR: arbitration ends in a final agreement established by the third neutral, which parties normally are compelled to follow whereas in mediation there is never a final binding decision imposed by a third party.

Mandatory ADR and the ECJ

The ECJ concluded that mandatory out-of-court settlement is acceptable under EU law and formulated under what conditions this obligation is to be accepted. There is an obligation to turn to mandatory out-of-court settlement for the resolution of consumer disputes arisen under the Directive 2002/22/CE of the European Parliament and of the Council of 7 March 2002 on Universal Service and users' rights relating to electronic communications networks and services (Universal Service Directive). Marzocco and Nino argue that the non-absolute nature of the principle of effective judicial protection allows it to affirm that the imposition of a compulsory mediation attempt does not necessarily contrast with the principle itself. So what are the necessary conditions for that contrast not to occur in practice?

Here the ECJ establishes two kind of requirements. First, a general requirement to achieve an objective of general interest. And second, specific requirements regarding the regulation of the mediation process.

The General Requirement of Pursuing and Achieving an Objective of General Interest

Within the legal framework of the European Union, the principle of effective judicial protection is a general principle of Community law, stemming from the constitutional traditions common to the Member States. It has been enshrined in Articles 6 and 13 of the European Convention on the Protection of Human Rights and Fundamental Freedoms, and in Article 47 of the Charter of Fundamental Rights of the EU (proclaimed in Nice on 7 December 2000). However, according to the ECJ, the right to effective judicial protection is not granted unconditionally and restrictions are possible. They must actually correspond to objectives in the general interest and must not be disproportionate with regard to the objective pursued in a way that infringes upon the very substance of the rights guaranteed.[8]

The Specific Requirements

Furthermore, the ECJ formulated the following specific requirements:

1. The procedure does not result in a decision which is binding for the parties.
2. Out-of-court settlements shall not cause a substantial delay for legal proceedings.
3. The opening of the out-of-court settlement shall suspend the period for the time-barring of claims;
4. Out-of-court settlement shall not give rise to costs for the parties, or only low costs.
5. Electronic means shall not be the only means by which the settlement procedure may be accessed. According to Kokott (2009) argues that if parties would rely solely on the Internet there would be a disproportionate infringement upon the right to judicial protection.
6. Interim measures are possible when the urgency of the case requires.

Kokott (2009) states that a mandatory dispute resolution procedure does not constitute a disproportionate infringement upon the right to effective judicial protection. Limitations mentioned in the main proceedings constitute a minor infringement upon the right to enforce by courts and is outweighed by the opportunity to end the dispute quickly and inexpensively".

---

[8] Case C-28/05 Dokter and Others [2006] ECR I-5431, paragraph 75, and Case C-394/07 Gambazzi [2009] ECR I?0000, paragraph 32.

Conclusions

Mediation is an appropriate means for resolving workplace disputes (in both labor and employment settings) and contributes to overcoming the current dissatisfaction with the administration of justice. Today, it is a State obligation to offer a justice system with a certain level of quality, capable of resolving conflicts that arise in a modern society. This modern justice system shall offer several dispute mechanisms appropriate to different types of conflict. In this context, mediation has evolved into a complementary method to traditional justice administration for both labor and employment disputes.

There are several approaches and purposes for establishing workplace mediation systems, either as a means to improve access to justice, or as an instrument to support collective bargaining. When designing mediation systems as dispute resolutions mechanisms, there are two key elements that need to be guaranteed: the right to effective access to justice and users' satisfaction.

The challenge for policy makers and dispute system designers is to encourage the creation and adaptation of mediation systems to users' needs, without putting at risk effective access to justice. This implies that the use of mediation should be spread, without giving in to the essential standards of access to justice.

The response on whether compulsory mediation is compatible with effective judicial protection, remains a delicate and contested matter.

In our view, mandatory mediation deserves support in labor and employment disputes, and in other disputes as well, as a means of forcing parties to attend at least one mediation meeting without giving in to the fundamental principle of voluntariness. Following Barrett (2014), we believe that given the creativity of ADR practitioners and scholars, ADR will continue to grow and expand to new areas of practice, and new ADR practice will emerge. We hope that our legal institutions, like all human institutions, will evolve to meet the changing demands of an ever-diversifying world of different values, and save perhaps one: a human universal to survive and flourish (Menkel-Meadow 2002).

References

ACAS. (2015). Conciliation explained. Available at: http://www.ACAS.org.uk/media/pdf/o/g/Conciliation-Explained-ACAS.pdf. Last accessed on 9 Mar 2016.

ACAS. (2016). Collective disputes. http://www.ACAS.org.uk/index.aspx?articleid=2012. Last accessed on 9 Mar 2016.

Arastey, M. L. (2014). La Mediación en las Relaciones Laborales: Reflexiones para un Futuro de Salud Laboral y Organizacional. In *Mediación es Justicia. El impacto de la Ley 5/2012 de Mediación Civil y Mercantil.* (1st ed., p. 463). Barcelona: Huygens Editorial.

Barendrecht, M. (2010). *Legal aid, accessible courts or legal information? Three access to justice strategies compared (November 10, 2010), 12.* TISCO Working Paper Series on Civil Law and Conflict Resolution Systems No. 010/2010; Tilburg Law School Research Paper No. 24/2010;

Global Jurist, Vol. 11, Issue 1, January 2011. Available at SSRN: http://ssrn.com/abstract=1706825

Barendrecht, M., Kamminga, P., & Verdonschot, J. H. (2008). *Priorities for the justice system: Responding to the most urgent legal problems of individuals (March 2008), 37.* TISCO Working Paper No. 001/2008; Tilburg University Legal Studies Working Paper No. 002/2008; TILEC Discussion Paper No. 2008–011. Available at SSRN: http://ssrn.com/abstract=1090885 or http://dx.doi.org/10.2139/ssrn.1090885

Barrett, J. (1995). The origin of mediation: The United States conciliation dervice in the U.S. Department of Labor. Retrieved from: http://mediationhistory.org/fmcs01/publication/the-origin-of-mediation-the-united-states-conciliation-service-inthe-u-s-department-of-labor/

Barret, J. (2000). *A brief history to the DOLs conciliation service.* Retrieved from: http://mediationhistory.org/fmcs01/wpcontent/uploads/2015/02/BriefHistoryofDOL.pdf.

Barrett, J. (2014). The future of alternative dispute resolution. Retrieved from: www.mediate.com/articles/BarrettFuture.cfm

Blomgren et al. (2009). Dispute system design and justice in employment dispute resolution: Mediation at the workplace. *Harvard Law Review, 14*(1), 1–50.

Bollen, K., & Euwema, M. (2013). Workplace mediation: An underdeveloped research area. *Negotiation Journal, 29*(3), 329–353. http://doi.org/10.1111/nejo.12028.

Bollen, K., Ittner, H., & Euwema, M. C. (2012). Mediating hierarchical labor conflicts: Procedural justice makes a difference-for subordinates. *Group Decision and Negotiation, 21*(5), 621–636. http://doi.org/10.1007/s10726-011-9230-1.

Bond, C. A. (1997). Shattering the myth: Mediating sexual harassment disputes in the workplace. *Fordham Law Review, 65*(6), 2489–2533.

Brett, J., Barsness, Z., & Goldberg, S. (1996). The effectiveness of mediation: An independent analysis of cases handled by four major service providers. *Negotiation Journal, 12*, 259–268.

Brim, R. (2001). *Talks replacing torts in workplace conflict; more businesses relying on mediation.* Lexington: Herald-Leader.

Butt. T., Munduate, L., Barón, M., & Medina, F. J. (2005). *Intervenciones en Mediación. En L. Munduate, y F.J. Medina (Coord.), Gestión del Conflicto, Negociación y Mediación* (pp. 265–303).

Canvas Martinez, F. (2007). Las Comisiones Paritarias y la solución de los conflictos laborales derivados de la interpretación y aplicación del convenio colectivo [Comisiones Paritarias and resolution of labor conflicts derived from the interpretation and application of the collective agreement]. *Revista del Ministerio de Trabajo y Asuntos Sociales,* Sevilla, 115–135, 91.

Cowl -v- Plymouth City Council. (2001). EWCA Civ 1935 (Eng.)

Cruz Villalón, J. (2003). Por el ensanchamiento de la mediación y el arbitraje en los conflictos laborales [On the spread of mediation and arbitration in labour conflicts]. *Revista Andaluza de Trabajo y Bienestar Social (12–19).*

Department of Business Innovation and Skills. (2011). *Resolving workplace disputes: Government response to the consultation* (United Kingdom). Retrieved from: http://www.bis.gov.uk/assets/biscore/employment-matters/docs/r/11-1365-resolving-workplace-disputes-government-response.pdf

De Palo, & Canessa. (2014). Sleeping? Comatose? Only mandatory consideration of mediation can awake the sleeping beauty in the European Union, Jed. D Melnik Annual Symposium. *Cardozo Journal of Conflict Resolution, 16*, 713–730.

De Roo, A., & Jagtenberg, R. (1994). *Settling labour disputes in Europe.* Deventer: Kluwer Law and Taxation Publishers.

De Roo, A., & Jagtengbert, R. (2003). *Settling labour disputes in Europe.* Netherlands: The Society for Personality and Social Psychology.

Dolder, C. (2004). The contribution of mediation to workplace justice. *Industrial Law Journal, 33*(4), 320–342.

EC. (2002). Green paper on alternative dispute resolution in civil and commercial law /*COM/2002/0196 final*. Retrieved from: http://eurlex.europa.eu/LexUriServ/LexUriServ. do?uri=CELEX:52002DC0196:EN:HTML

EP. (2014). *Rebooting the mediation directive: Assessing the limited impact of its implementation and proposing measures to increase the number of mediations in the EU*. Retrieved from: http://www. europarl.europa.eu/RegData/etudes/etudes/join/2014/493042/IPOL-JURI_ET(2014)493042_EN. pdf

Equal Employment Opportunity Commissión. EECO at 50. www.fmcs.gov/aboutus/our-history/. Last accessed at: 3 Mar 2016.

European Courts of Human Rights. (2013). Guide on article 6: Right to a fair trial. Acailable at: http://www.echr.coe.int/Documents/Guide_Art_6_ENG.pdf

Federal Mediation and Conciliation Service. www.fmcs.gov/aboutus/our-history/. Last accessed on: 3 Mar 2016.

Fox, S., & Stallworth, L. E. (2009). Building a framework for two internal organizational approaches to resolving and preventing workplace bullying: Alternative dispute resolution and training. *Consulting Psychology Journal: Practice and Research, 61*(3), 220–241.

Fuller, L. (1954). American legal philosophy at mid-century. *Journal of Legal Education, 6*, 457–477.

Fuller, L. (1971). Mediation. Its forms and functions. *South California Law Review, 44*, 305–309.

Ginebra, E. & Tarabal, J. (2014). Mediación Obligatoria e Inducción a la Mediación. In *Mediación es Justicia. El impacto de la Ley 5/2012 de Mediación Civil y Mercantil.* (1° ed., p. 463). Barcelona: Huygens Editorial.

ILO. (1998). *Manual de Mediación, Ginebra.* Retreived from, http://cemical.diba.cat/publica-cions/fitxers/manual_mediacion_OIT.PDF.

Kessler, G. & Finkelstein, L. J. (1988). The evolution of a multi-door courthouse. *Catholic University Law Review, 37*(3), 577–590.

Kokott, J. (2009). *Opinion of the advocate general Kokkot delivered on 10 November 2009.* Cases C-317/18 to C-320/08. Retrieved from: http://eur-lex.europa.eu/legal-content/EN/TXT/PDF/? uri=CELEX:62008CC0317&from=EN

Ley 36/2011 Reguladora de la jurisdicción social (Social Jurisdiction Act 36/2011) Spain, Boletín Oficial del Estado, 11.10.2011.

Macho, C. (2014). Origen y Evolución de la Mediación: el Nacimiento del Movimiento ADR en EEUU y su expansión por Europa. ADC, tomo LXvII, fasc. III. 931–996.

Marshall, T. F. (1998). *Restorative justice: An overview.* Minneapolis: Cent. Restorative Justice, Peacemaking.

Martinez-Pecino, R., Munduate, L., & Medina, F., (2005). Effectiveness of mediation strategies in rights conflicts and conflicts of interests. IACM 18th annual conference. Available at: http:// ssrn.com/abstract=735086

Marzocco, A. M., & Nino, M. (2012). The EU Directive on mediation in civil and commercial matters and the principle of effective judicial protection. *Lex et Scientia, XIX*(2), 105–127.

McCabe. D., (1917). Federal intervention in labour disputes under the Erdman, Newlands and Adamsom Acts. In *Proceedings of the Academy of Political Scienci in the City of New York* (vol 7). N° 1 Labor Disputes and Puclic Services Corporation. (94–107). Academy of Political Science. Retrieved from: http://www.jstor.org/stable/1171718

McDermott, E. P., & Ervin, D. (2005). The influence of procedural and distributive variables on settlement rates in employment discrimination mediation. *Journal of Dispute Resolution, 1*, 45–60.

Menkel-Meadow, C. (2002). When litigation is not the only way: Consensus building and media-tion as public interest lawyering. *Journal of Law & Policy, 10*, 37–61.

Menkel-Meadow, C. (2006). Peace and justice: Notes on the evolution and purposes of legal pro-cesses. *Georgetown Law Journal, 94*(2), 553–580.

Menkel-Meadow, C. (2007). Restorative justice: What is it and does it work? *Annual Review of Law and Social Science, 3*, 161–187.

Menkel-Meadow, C. (2009). Empirical studies of ADR: The Baseline problem of what ADR is and what it is compared to. In (Peter Cane and Herbert Kritzer, editors, forthcoming) *Oxford handbook of empirical legal studies.* Retrieved from: https://www.researchgate.net/publication/228139673_Empirical_Studies_of_ADR_The_Baseline_Problem_of_What_ADR_is_and_What_it_is_Compared_to?enrichId=rgreq-bd5a15259a2385c24185ab32d3d3d4ec-XXX &enrichSource=Y292ZXJQYWdlOzIyODEzOTY3MztBUzoyODk1NTc1NDQyMjY4MTlA MTQ0NjA0NzMwNjkxMQ%3D%3D&el=1_x_

Menkel-Meadow, C. (2011). The NRLA's legacy: Collective or individual dispute resolution or not? *Journal of the ABA Section of Labor & Employment Law, 26*(2), 249–266.

Menkel-Meadow, C. (2015a). Variations in the uptake of and resistance to mediation outside of the United States. In *Contemporary issues in international arbitration and mediation. The Fordham Papers 2014,* Leiden, Brill, 2015, 189–221.

Menkel-Meadow, C. (2015b). Process pluralism in transitional/restorative justice. *International Journal of Conflict Engagement and Resolution, 3*(1), 3–32.

Mnookin, R., Peppet, S., & Tulumello, A. (2000). *Beyond winning: Negotiating to create value in deals and disputes* (2nd ed.). Cambridge, MA: The Belknap Press of Harvard University Press.

Nabatchi, T., & Bingham, L. B. (2000). Transformative mediation in the USPS Redress Program:Observations of ADR specialistst. *Hofstra Labor & Employment Law Journal, 18,* 399–427.

Nolan-Haley, J. (2012). Is Europe heading down the primrose path with mandatory mediation? *Carolina Journal of International Law & Commercial Regulation, 37,* 981–1011.

Olea, M., & Rodríguez-Sañudo, F. (2010). Spain. En International encyclopaedia for labour law and industrial relations (47–112). The Netherlands: Kluwer Law International BV.

Oser, J. (2004–2005). The unguided use of internal ADR programs to resolve sexual harassment controversies in the workplace. *Cardozo Journal of Conflict Resolution, 6,* 283–312.

Real Decreto Legislativo 2/2015, de 23 de octubre, por el que se aprueba el texto refundido de la Ley del Estatuto de los Trabajadores. Boletín Oficial del Estado 255, sec 1; pag 100224–100308.

Rodríguez-Piñero, M. (2003). Indisponibilidad de los Derechos y Conciliación en las Relaciones Laborales (Non-disposability of rights and conciliation in labor relations), *Revista Andaluza de Trabajo y Bienestar Social, 25,* 23–42.

Rogers, N., & McEwen, C. (1997). Employing the law to increase the use of mediation and to encourage direct early negotiations. *Ohio State Journal on Dispute Resolution,* 831–864.

Rome, D. L. (2003). A guide to business-to-business mediation. *Dispute Resolution Journal, 57*(4), 51–59.

Sander, F. (1979). Varieties of dispute processing. In A. Levin & R. Wheeler (Eds.), *The pound conference: Perspectives on justice in the future.* West Publisher Group, Berkeley.

Shaw, W., Hong, Q.-N., Pransky, G., & Loisel, P. (2008). A literature review describing the role of return-to-work coordinators in trial programs and interventions designed to prevent workplace disability. *Journal of Occupational Rehabilitation, 18*(1), 2–15.

Soleto, H. (2011). La Mediación Vinculada a los Tribunales. In Mediación y Resolución de Conflictos: Técnicas y Ámbitos. (245–267). Madrid: Tecnos.

Schiavetta, S, (2004). The relationship between e-ADR and article 6 of the European Convention of Human Rights pursuant to the case law of the European Court of Human Rights. *Journal of Information Law and Technology, 1.* Retrieved from: https://www2.warwick.ac.uk/fac/soc/law/elj/jilt/2004_1/schiavetta/.

Stallworth, L., & Kaspar, D. (2013). Employing the law to provide "early access" to integrated conflict management systems and ADR processes: The proposed national employment dispute resolution Act (NEDRA). *Ohio State Journal on Dispute Resolution.* http://cemical.diba.cat/publicacions/fitxers/manual_mediacion_OIT.PDF

Tascón López, (2009). La solución extrajudicial de conflictos laborales en el modelo español: a medio camino entre el desiderándum legal y el ostracismo social (Extrajudicial conflict resolution for labor disputes in the Spanish Model). *Revista universitaria de ciencias del trabajo*, 209–226.

Tyler, B. (2003). A four-component model of procedural justice: Defining the meaning of a "fair" process. *Personality & Social Psychology Bulletin, 29*, 747–758.

Valdés, F. (2003). *Conciliación, Mediación y Arbitraje en los Países de la Unión Europea*. (S. G. de P. M. de T. y A. Sociales, Ed.) (1º ed.). Madrid: Subdireccion General de Publicaciones Ministerio de Trabajo y Asuntos Sociales.

Verbeke, A. (2009). Mediation. Faciliteren van onderhandelingen. In *Reflectie op mediation* (pp. 27–46). Maklu: Antwerp.

Wissler, R. (1997). The effects of mandatory mediation: Empirical research on the experience of small claims and common please courts. *Willmate Law Review,* 576–577.

Part III
Mediation and Other Third Party Roles in the Organization

Chapter 10
An Appreciative Approach to Conflict: Mediation and Conflict Coaching

Ross Brinkert

This chapter seeks to contribute to the 25-year effort to integrate complementary communication interventions like mediation and negotiation into a framework to provide individuals with numerous conflict management options and have options that address conflict at the lowest possible level (Costantino and Merchant 1996; Lipsky et al. 2003; Slaikeu and Hasson 1998; Ury et al. 1988). More specifically, it aims to build on connections made among conflict coaching and mediation in the workplace. Prior such connections have been made among conflict coaching and dialogue and facilitation (Brinkert 2013) and conflict coaching and processes associated with the organizational ombuds role (Brinkert 2010a), a role acknowledged as frequently incorporating conflict coaching (e.g., Levine-Finley 2014). However, research on conflict coaching developed in the alternative dispute resolution (ADR) field in direct relationship to mediation (Tidwell 1997), is lacking. Additional focused consideration of the relationship between conflict coaching and workplace mediation is highly justified given only one prior publication seems to have probed this area in detail (Winter 2005).

This chapter offers some basic definitions before providing present day overviews of workplace mediation and conflict coaching, respectively. The general intersection of workplace mediation and conflict coaching is then considered in terms of how it has been explored in previous writing. All of this content is then used to support the identification of propositions, priority actions, and ongoing cautions regarding the current and near future, linking together workplace mediation and conflict coaching. Finally, using concepts derived from Appreciative Inquiry (Cooperrider and Whitney 2005), a narrative approach to communication (Kellett and Dalton 2001), and work in positive organizations (Cameron and Dutton 2003), the chapter finishes with a broader view of what might be accomplished as workplace

R. Brinkert (✉)
Penn State Abington, Abington, PA, USA
e-mail: rsb20@psu.edu

© Springer International Publishing Switzerland 2016   173
K. Bollen et al. (eds.), *Advancing Workplace Mediation Through Integration of Theory and Practice*, Industrial Relations & Conflict Management 3, DOI 10.1007/978-3-319-42842-0_10

mediation and conflict coaching are further coordinated and situated, at least in some additional instances, to serve purposes beyond the conflict arena like having conflict scholars and practitioners advance gratitude communication (Brinkert 2016).

Some Basic Definitions

Workplace mediation typically involves a neutral or impartial third party intervening between two or more parties, primarily or solely from a process standpoint, to more effectively manage a conflict and work toward resolution.

Executive Coaching is a one-on-one leadership development process intended to assist the individual in meeting organizational goals (Stern 2004). Conflict is a specialty area from which an executive coach might need to draw given an individual's unique needs (Stern 2004).

Conflict Coaching typically involves a coach working one-on-one with a party in a conflict to support the individual in better understanding the nature of the conflict and possibly developing relevant strategies and tactics to use in addressing the conflict (Brinkert 2006).

Workplace Mediation Overview

One recent study of cross-sector workplace mediation found that cases typically involved relationship difficulties, poor communication, and issues of management style and practice (Bennett 2013). The use and nature of workplace mediation differs somewhat according to occupation and sector (Bennett 2013) with higher education, for instance, shown to be unique because of the sector's ethos, labor process, client base, and interest in networking within the sector (Bennett 2014).

Despite the fact workplace mediation has existed for a number of decades, it remains an underdeveloped research area with benefits not firmly established (Bollen and Euwema 2013). The need for more research stems, in part, from there being various approaches to mediation, including the facilitative, evaluative, and transformative style (McDermott 2012). This wide-ranging diversity in the field has as a consequence that the effectiveness of specific strategies remains unclear (Wall and Dunne 2012).

While workplace mediation research gaps persist, important insights have been established in recent years. The body of work by Bingham and colleagues (e.g., Bingham and Pitts 2002; Nabatchi et al. 2010) reporting on the use of transformative mediation in the United States Postal System is considerable. Another notable cluster of findings, previously explored by Bollen and Euwema (2012, 2016) and

Bollen et al. (2010) and drawn upon extensively in the following two paragraphs, includes subordinate and supervisor differences regarding mediation satisfaction and effectiveness, the importance of justice, and the need for greater efforts in offering preventative mediation.

Subordinates and supervisors assess mediation satisfaction differently. Although both subordinates and supervisors feel satisfied with the mediation, supervisors feel more satisfied than subordinates. More precisely, subordinates' satisfaction is more negatively affected by uncertainty than supervisors' satisfaction (Bollen et al. 2010). And for subordinates, perceptions of procedural justice add to their perception of mediation effectiveness while this is not the case for supervisors (Bollen et al. 2012). Therefore, the concept of justice deserves more attention.

Justice is, in various ways, an important factor in workplace mediation. Recent research demonstrated that it was crucial for subordinates to have their anger recognized by the mediator and this added to their perceptions of mediation effectiveness (Bollen and Euwema 2015). Justice-related communication such as disputant-disputant corroboration and apology have been shown to increase the likelihood of settlement (Nesbit et al. 2012). Fairness brings satisfaction even when an agreement is not reached (Jehn et al. 2010). Research indicating that lower power parties are more impacted by conflict (Van Kleef et al. 2006; Bollen et al. 2012), essentially an unfair burden on them, and the argument that the benefits of conflict are overstated (De Dreu 2008) have been used to support the call for broader use of preventative mediation and the use of one-on-one processes as part of it, including caucus and precaucus (Bollen and Euwema 2016).

Just as justice has emerged as an important concept in workplace mediation so has the role of trust. As with issues of justice, these trust-related findings are sometimes counterintuitive and relate to the issues of mediator effectiveness and party expectations. As summarized by Bollen and Euwema (2016), trust in the mediator is highly important, including making the parties feel more communicative and safe (Stimec and Poitras 2009). The mediator's abilities to promote understanding between the parties and to speak the language of the parties led to the parties trusting the mediator (Bollen and Euwema 2012 as in Bollen and Euwema 2016). Trust was related to party satisfaction but unrelated to reaching agreement (Bollen and Euwema 2012 as in Bollen and Euwema 2016). Other research determined that the mediator's ability to gain party confidence was more important than mediator skills in helping them reach agreement (Goldberg and Shaw 2007).

In addition to a need for more research on workplace mediation, the practice itself is challenged in some quarters. For example, its lack of visibility, lack of clarity around credentialing, and some people's aversion to it (Carter 2008), mean that other dispute resolution processes and other related and broader actions may need to be advanced.

Conflict Coaching Overview

As noted by Brinkert (2006), conflict coaching has its roots in two places, the alternative dispute resolution (ADR) field (Tidwell 1997) and the executive coaching field (Kilburg 2000; Stern 2004). Each of these fields is well-known for having contributors from a wide range of academic and professional disciplines. Conflict coaching has continued to develop in both of these fields and the models used are quite diverse. Conflict coaching models from a predominantly ADR standpoint include the narrative-based Comprehensive Conflict Coaching model by Brinkert (2006) and Jones and Brinkert (2008), and the executive coaching, ADR, and neuroscience-based CINERGY™ model by Noble (2011). These two models both emphasize situating conflict coaching within an integrated dispute systems framework and can be applied before, during, after, and in place of mediation. Conflict coaching has been carried out by trained internal or external neutrals, managers, and peers.

In the process of detailing a cognitive-behavioral approach to executive coaching, Ducharme (2004) noted the prior delineation of no less than eight other distinct executive coaching approaches with Kilburg's (1996, 2000, 2004) combined systems and psychodynamic model cited as the most common. Kilburg (1996, 2000, 2004) and Stern (2004) address conflict; however, the extent to which other executive coaching models address conflict, if at all, remains to be determined. Also, there can be considerable breadth to even one given approach to executive coaching. For instance, in making the case for a cognitive-behavior therapy approach, Ducharme (2004) described cognitive-behavioral therapy as a broad term, including practitioners predominantly using cognitive techniques to those predominantly using behavioral techniques. Professional plasticity was also documented in the case of a consulting psychologist, beginning work with a client as an executive coach and then shifting into complementary intergroup conflict management assignments, behavioral skills training, fact-finding assignments, and system-wide organizational development and change demonstrates the plasticity of a discipline and roles (Freedman and Perry 2010). Further complicating the landscape of executive coaching is the finding that the ethical code currently available for executive coaches is problematic because it is not relevant, has shortcomings, and is actually an ethical obstacle (Diochon and Nizet 2015). One proposed solution is to rewrite the code by involving different stakeholders (Diochon and Nizet 2015).

In the last 15 years, conflict coaching has been adopted by a considerable number of large government-related institutions, including the Department of Defence/Civilian Forces in Canada, the United States Transportation Security Administration, and the Department of Defence in Australia (Brubaker et al. 2014). There has also been general mention of conflict coaches working with workplace leaders in the private sector (Brubaker et al. 2014). As noted at the outset of this chapter, conflict coaching has been argued as theoretically applicable to the dialogue and facilitation area (Brinkert 2013) and the ombuds area (Brinkert 2010a). Its importance has also been outlined from a theoretical standpoint for government managers in the United

States (Brinkert 2009) and nurses (Brinkert 2011), the latter because of the documented frequency and costs associated with conflict in nursing (Brinkert 2010b). In terms of research on the conflict coaching process, one study reported on the application of conflict coaching by nurse managers in a Magnet health system in the United States (Brinkert 2011). One-on-one conflict coaching-type assistance has been widely adopted by some organizational ombuds and shared as case studies and theoretical models (Gadlin 2014; Levine-Finley 2014). Conflict coaching will likely continue to increase with ombuds leaders such as Gadlin (2014) calling for a more activist organizational ombuds office. While conflict coaching has earned respectability among ADR practitioners, additional research efforts are needed.

The General Intersection of Workplace Mediation and Conflict Coaching

Workplace mediation and conflict coaching differ in that conflict coaching interventions do not necessarily involve all parties in a conflict and conflict coaches may provide skill training while mediators work in a more purely facilitative capacity. However, it is valuable to point out the basic theoretical compatibility of workplace mediation and conflict coaching. Not only did conflict coaching grow out of efforts to support mediation (Tidwell 1997), but the emphasis on party/client empowerment, perspective-taking, and the availability of non-adversarial options for addressing conflict are generally evident in both. This is a larger issue than mediation and conflict coaching simply having much in common. Mediation and conflict coaching, at least as the latter grew out of the ADR tradition, both align with organizational dispute system design (ODSD) assumptions and have largely developed purposefully in accord with them. These assumptions were summarized by Jones and Brinkert (2008) and include the following: promotion of interest-based approaches, the creation of low cost rights-based and power-based options, the ability for parties to maintain control (Ury et al. 1988); the inclusion of preventative approaches, use of needs assessment to respect organizational culture (Constantino and Merchant 1996); possibly involve the use of internal and external systems, and consist of integrated critical subsystems, including evaluation (Slaikeu and Hasson 1998). In terms of narrower theoretical similarities between mediation and conflict coaching, Winter (2005) noted the importance of issues of neutrality or impartiality, a process emphasis, practitioner psychological competencies, and a future-orientation to the process.

There is also a practical fit between workplace mediation and conflict coaching. Jones and Brinkert's (2008) work in situating conflict coaching in relation to dispute systems can apply more narrowly to ways conflict coaching can advance workplace mediation through investigation of mediation, explanation of mediation, preparation for mediation, selection and timing of access to mediation, reflective analysis of mediation, and future planning for mediation. From a slightly different standpoint, and analogous to how conflict coaching can be applied in relation to dialogue and facilitation processes (Brinkert 2013), conflict coaching can be used in the pre-conflict period, the pre-mediation decision period, the mediation preparation period, the mediation period, and the post-mediation period.

Notwithstanding a high degree of theoretical and practical compatibility between workplace mediation and conflict coaching, some problematic issues have been previously identified. Winter (2005) provided a thorough examination of the intersection of mediation and coaching, raising many issues of theoretical and practical significance that remain very relevant. Issues identified as needing to be addressed include the following: definitions of the basic terms "mediation" and "coaching," the disordered marketplace of mediation and coaching vendors, the sometimes interchangeable usage of the terms "mediation" and "conflict coaching," how practitioners get trained, and what practitioner competencies are necessary (Winter 2005).

Propositions, Priority Actions, and Ongoing Cautions for the Integration of Workplace Mediation and Conflict Coaching

Consideration of the current state of workplace mediation and the current state of conflict coaching along with consideration of what has already been written on the intersection of the two areas supports the identification of the propositions below. In turn, these themes support the proposal of specific priority actions and ongoing cautions in the advancement of workplace mediation and conflict coaching. The ordering of the lists is not intended to imply order of importance or, where relevant, order of application. Similar numbering across the lists is insignificant. Finally, none of these lists is intended to be exhaustive.

Propositions

Proposition #1: Both mediation and conflict coaching can be characterized as extremely diverse in terms of current theory and practice. There is diversity in terms of theoretical justification for models of workplace mediation and conflict coaching. There is diversity in academic background, current disciplinary area, training, and environments of applied involvement of scholars and practitioners in the two areas. Even within specific communities, such as those scholars and coaches identifying with the executive coaching community as opposed to the ADR community, there is considerable diversity. Diversity in these respects seems to bring benefits and drawbacks. Some positive outcomes have been documented and other positive outcomes are apparent. These involve various practitioners, using various models, in various settings, with various parties/clients and various organizational sponsors. Diversity of theory and practice, including diversity among scholars and practitioners, has very possibly resulted in a certain degree of diffusion of practices that would not have occurred were the field more organized or controlled from the outset. However, there is a lack of clarity for those already involved and all those considering involvement. The lack of clarity is probably most challenging for those without a history of involvement, including would-be parties/clients, sponsors, practitioners, and scholars. This may affect the confidence of those considering leading or otherwise engaging these practices.

Proposition #2: More research is needed on workplace mediation and conflict coaching respectively, and, consequently, the intersection of the two also requires research, ideally within an ODSD framework. As noted above, there are some well-developed areas of workplace mediation research; however, much more research should be carried out, especially since mediation has been widely implemented in some workplace settings for 20 years or more. There is very little research on conflict coaching and yet, as with mediation, there are pockets of reasonably heavy applied activity. At least on the face of it, these are obvious places to begin. Research would be welcome from those involved with the practices themselves but thought should be given to how to recruit relative outsiders as researchers of these practices as well. Research funders may want to give special consideration to researchers unaligned with the practices under review. In the case of conflict coaching, both main practitioner groups of coaches need to be researched, those coming from a general executive coaching background and those coming from a general ADR background. It would be extremely valuable to have the integration of mediation and conflict coaching studied within organizations that are already using developed organizational dispute systems.

Proposition #3: The state of theory, research, and practice concerning workplace mediation and conflict coaching supports immediate advancement on integrating the two processes. Such efforts could independently strengthen each area and could also strengthen the combination. The dearth of research does not mean the development of practice should be halted until research catches up. Certain workplace mediation and conflict coaching advancements are theoretically supported, others are supported by past conflict coaching research, others are supported by research in allied fields, and others still are supported by those active with it in applied settings.

Priority Actions

Given the breadth of the propositions outlined immediately above and the rather small number of researchers and theoreticians and still relatively small number of individuals acting as sponsors or practitioners in the workplace mediation and conflict coaching arenas, it makes sense to more narrowly demarcate next steps related to the themes. Each of the following proposed priority actions relates to one or more of the propositions introduced above. Each priority action is put forth as a desirable action, or set of actions, for scholars, practitioners, and/or organizational sponsors of workplace mediation and conflict coaching in the midterm future (i.e., coming 2–5 years).

Priority Action #1: Any and all communities working at the intersection of workplace mediation and conflict coaching are encouraged to share more about their activities and accomplishments at the same time as they invite others, including relative outsiders, to study them too. It is difficult to overstate the need for more theoretical research, applied insights to be generated and made available. Presumably, the most efficient place to start is reporting on the workplace mediation and conflict coaching work already carried out and/or currently and/or soon to be carried out. There seems to be a considerable amount of applied work taking place in workplace mediation and conflict coaching around the world, at least in western cultures. More of this needs to be reported in scholarly and trade publications and, whenever possible, researched by individuals from various points of view, including those who are less involved or completely uninvolved with the advancement of particular models. This priority action reflects key theme #1 and key theme #2. It will help to create awareness and, hopefully, clarify the nature of the diversity of workplace mediation and conflict coaching, and it will build the body of research. Incidentally, a "community" could be a research collective, proponents of a given model, practitioners of a given model, parties/clients of a given model, organizational sponsor, or other tightly or loosely-coordinated partnership or grouping within the workplace mediation and conflict coaching area.

Priority Action #2: Conflict coaching should be used to respond to the call for greater development of preventative workplace mediation. The development and greater use of preventative mediation and, with that, increasing attention to the value and potential value of caucus and pre-caucus, is well-justified given power differentials between many parties, insights into what makes different parties satisfied with mediation, greater awareness of the negative effects of deep-seated conflict, and the potential to make a positive and proactive difference with the use of mediation. Conflict coaching could be used to structure the caucus or pre-caucus process. It could also be used to promote preventative mediation, especially in cases when coaches are getting accessed as executive coaches or de facto executive coaches and, thus, may be working with individuals who do not currently think of themselves as being in a mediation-worthy conflict but might do well to consider preventative mediation.

Priority Action #3: Other, often relatively narrower, peer-reviewed theory, research, and practice insights should receive serious consideration for incorporation into revised models of workplace mediation and/or conflict coaching. The fact that much more research is needed does not mean that important research and theoretical contributions have not been made. There have been important developments and these may immediately impact workplace mediation and conflict coaching practice. Some of these breakthroughs have occurred specifically in relation to workplace mediation and conflict coaching and can, conceivably, be transferred into both areas. For instance, Jameson et al. (2010) work on mediator emotional elicitation strategies could not only be used to advance mediation practice, it could also provide important new tools for conflict coaches, particularly in models such as the Comprehensive Conflict Coaching model (Brinkert 2006; Jones and Brinkert 2008) that incorporate an emotional point of view within the coaching conversation.

Ongoing Cautions

As with conflict in general, there are both potential opportunities and potential challenges in the development of workplace mediation and conflict coaching. The relative emphasis on opportunities in relation to the propositions and priority actions (above) provides a rationale for focusing on challenges or cautions here.

Ongoing Caution #1: Exclusivity of approaches to theorizing and researching should be resisted. Particularly in terms of conflict coaching but also somewhat relevant in terms of workplace mediation, emphasis needs to be placed on growing the written conversation with additional contributions by scholars or scholar-practitioners, in particular. Currently, the overall enterprise of conflict coaching remains in an early stage where more participation needs to be encouraged and a broader range of ideas anticipated. In time, as more contributions are made and allied theory and research evolve, there will be an increasing responsibility on specific communities to recognize the relevance of what has come before and to blend it with the unique community frames. As noted above, communities can include proponents of specific models, sites or sectors of application, and specific academic or applied disciplinary groups. It is not that communities should only address their narrow interests. All should be welcomed and, in fact, encouraged to also offer well-developed written perspective on theory, research, and application at the more general level in the way this chapter attempts to do.

It might also be helpful for there to be at least a temporary working assumption that additional research findings will be contextually-situated, even in studies where quantitative methods are applied and claims of statistical significance are made. This is a theory and research caution aimed primarily at scholars but also those practitioners and sponsors involved in such areas. The ADR and executive coaching fields are highly qualitative in nature given the centrality of language and context, including cultural context, to the work and overall dynamics of the interactions. Also, although roles and processes may sometimes appear as neutral and function as impartial and therefore appear to some as non-ideological, ideology is always implicit. These are values-saturated undertakings with different communities, organizations, and individuals implicitly or explicitly choosing to align with different values.

The concern here is on making sure that at least reasonably well-considered attempts at developing theory, research, and practice should be embraced so that a substantial overall body of work is generated. It is already clear that theoreticians and/or practitioners in both the ADR and executive coaching areas of the conflict coaching field can make theoretical and practical claims (as well, in some cases, research claims) for the validity of their work. However, validity of practice in one setting does not presuppose the lack of validity of another practice in another setting or even that same setting.

Ongoing Caution #2: Attempts to heavily enforce the boundaries of conflict coaching and workplace mediation at the applied level should be resisted since there just is not enough theory and research to warrant such action. This is a practice-related caution directed primarily at insiders in the field. It relates to issues of the competency and credentialing of practitioners and the positioning of such in the marketplace, especially when claims of competency are decontextualized and especially when superior competence relative to other approaches is asserted. It is currently impossible to be definitive, at a broad level at least, about there being one best model or one best type of practitioner or one best form of training. Of course, this does not mean that blatantly irresponsible practice, including practice devoid of a theoretical and research foundation, should be overlooked. However, there is a certain face validity in the fact various practitioners with various models have been active over a considerable number of years.

Ongoing Caution #3: The related need for more transparent practice and, in particular, the need for practitioners and sponsoring organizations to be clear about the level of independence of organization-supported ADR and allied processes. This is a practice-related caution intended to protect the basic interests of clients and sponsors as well as would-be clients and sponsors in the field. Recognition that workplace mediators and conflict coaches have a wide range of academic and training backgrounds, acknowledgement that some organization-funded practitioners are heavily aligned with management while others are independent of management, increased integration of processes and roles, and different definitions of workplace mediation and coaching puts a high burden on practitioners and sponsors to be transparent with all those they are working. The diversity of the workplace mediation and conflict coaching areas means that it is going to continue to be challenging for casual observers and would-be parties or clients or sponsors to easily make sense of the offerings. The burden of understanding is not on them but on those offering such services.

Conceptualizing Workplace Mediation and Conflict Coaching in an Even Wider Expanse

It is not inconsistent to at once recognize and encourage diversity within workplace mediation and conflict coaching and, simultaneously, suggest a general unifying framework to make sense of the overall effort, including actions more broadly being carried out in workplace-related ADR and executive coaching. Three helpful elements in this effort are the following: content goals drawn from Appreciative Inquiry (Cooperrider and Whitney 2005); "positive narrative expansion" process language

(Brinkert 2016) based on the nature and function of conflict narratives (Kellett and Dalton 2001); and possible additional positioning of workplace conflict processes within the field of positive organizational studies (Cameron and Dutton 2003).

Content Goals from Appreciative Inquiry

Appreciative Inquiry (AI) is a philosophy and group process (Cooperrider 1986; Cooperrider and Srivastva 1987; Cooperrider et al. 2000) rooted in the social constructionist perspective (Gergen 2015). It emphasizes existing strengths, positive future possibilities, participation of all relevant parties to an issue, and the creation of realities in communication. The AI goals of people, profits, and planet (Cooperrider and Whitney 2005) are the main point of focus for the current proposal here. "People" relates to all those involved with a given issue ideally sharing involvement with exploration, decision-making, and execution around that issue. "Profits" concerns the financial success of organizations and individuals using AI. "Planet" refers to environmental sensitivity and could be understood to belong to a sense of respect for the larger issue of sustainability as part of any AI process.

People, profits, and planet are, arguably, a straightforward, relevant, and forward-looking set of goals for efforts to deepen and broaden workplace mediation and conflict coaching efforts. The future success of these individual areas and future success of the intersection of these areas depends on a high level of consideration for all those involved, especially participants to the processes. The importance on profit-making or, minimally, financial responsibility is a major consideration for most, if not all, organizations, practitioners, and parties involved with these processes. Perhaps it needs to be stated more boldly as a central goal since this could lead to more transparency around whose financial interests are being met and, accordingly, how other issues of control over process involvement and control of information relate to financial interests. For instance, an individual seeking mediation or coaching needs to know whether such service has an organizational agenda attached to it. The point is not whether such an agenda exists so much as whether the agenda is clear to the would-be party(ies). Finally, the threat of climate change is so well-documented and so potentially severe (Mann and Kump 2015) that those involved with workplace mediation and conflict coaching have a responsibility to have their work show at least some degree of sensitivity to this preeminent human problem.

Positive Narrative Expansion Process Language

The notion of "positive narrative expansion" as conflict transformation (Brinkert 2016) is largely based on the function of narratives in driving and changing conflict (Kellett and Dalton 2001) and on the centrality of the themes of identity, emotion, and power in making sense of and more effectively managing conflict situations (Brinkert 2006; Jones and Brinkert 2008) but it can apply beyond conflict. It is well-established that the nature of destructive conflict often involves participants getting stuck in negative and limiting communication patterns where the past, current, and/ or potential positive narratives of the individual parties and the parties in relationship are halted, damaged, or even seemingly destroyed (Cooperrider 1986; Cooperrider and Srivastva 1987; Cooperrider et al. 2000). Ideally, individual parties in a workplace mediation, for example, craft and align positive individual stories that align with their relationship story(ies) and their organization's story(ies). Positive narrative expansion can characterize the goal, means, and outcome for shifting out of a negative conflict situation or even preemptively avoiding one (Brinkert 2016). Conflict theoreticians, researchers, practitioners, sponsors, and parties can conceive of specific tools of positive narrative expansion (e.g., the potential of an apology for transforming a conflict). They can also conceive of entire processes (e.g., workplace mediation or conflict coaching, etc.) or the overall organizational dispute system as an initiative for positive narrative expansion. In the context of this chapter, the concept of positive narrative expansion is chiefly presented as a way for a single organization or even the entire workplace mediation and conflict coaching enterprise to reframe or doubly frame all conflict-related efforts, especially as innovations such as preventative mediation (Bollen and Euwema 2016) and the activist ombuds (Gadlin 2014) take hold. And, as shared immediately below, the concept of positive narrative expansion could be engaged in an even wider sense.

Additional Positioning Within the Field of Positive Organizational Studies

De Dreu's (2008) and Bollen and Euwema's (2016) writing pushes conflict practice beyond the traditional conflict arena. A secondary framing of the field's offerings is worthy of consideration. Scholars, practitioners, and sponsors in the workplace conflict area should consider the potential in connecting their work with the advancing field of positive organizational studies (Cameron and Dutton, 2003) or other similarly named emerging initiatives. Third party processes work (Giebels and Janssen 2005) but their application is complex (Giebels and Yang 2009) and this suggests the need for more flexibility in offering them. One current example of the crossover between the conflict area and the positive organizational area is the conceptualization and research reporting of gratitude communication as conflict management (Brinkert 2016). While it almost certainly makes sense for the workplace conflict field to maintain a unique identity, situating processes like preventative mediation (Bollen and Euwema 2016) at the crossover with positive organizational studies would be beneficial, as would-be participants and would-be sponsors might find such offerings more appealing. It might also help current conflict scholars and practitioners see new possibilities for their existing talents and efforts.

Conclusion

This chapter began by considering the current state of workplace mediation and conflict coaching as distinct areas and also by considering what has been written about the intersection of the two. This material was crystallized into three propositions, three priority actions, and three cautions. The propositions were diversity of current theory and practice, the need for more research, and the need to use extant theory and research to immediately move practice forward. The priority actions were promotion of sharing through writing by insider communities and relative outsiders, use of conflict coaching to develop preventative mediation, and translation of substantiated insight into revisions of current models. The ongoing cautions were resistance to exclusivity of approaches to theorizing and research, resistance to heavy enforcement of limits around conflict coaching and workplace mediation applications, and the need for more transparent practice. The final section involved a proposal, based on innovations such as preventative mediation to newly co-position the workplace conflict area, not only workplace mediation and conflict coaching but other ADR processes and related processes. This was suggested by connecting to Appreciative Inquiry, positive narrative expansion, and positive organizational studies. It is almost certain that workplace mediation and conflict coaching will continue to grow individually and in tandem. To enhance the clarity, appeal, and integrity of these processes and related processes, others are encouraged to join this conversation about avenues of deliberate growth.

References

Bennett, T. (2013). Workplace mediation and the empowerment of disputants: Rhetoric or reality? *Industrial Relations Journal, 44*, 189–209.

Bennett, T. (2014). The role of workplace mediation: A critical assessment. *Personnel Review, 43*, 764–779.

Bingham, L. B., & Pitts, D. W. (2002). Highlights of mediation at work: Studies of the national redress evaluation project. *Negotiation Journal, 18*, 135–146.

Bollen, K., & Euwema, M. (2012). *The effects of reflexive tactics on objective and subjective mediation success in labour conflicts*. Unpublished manuscript, University of Leuven, Leuven.

Bollen, K., & Euwema, M. (2013). Workplace mediation: An underdeveloped research area. *Negotiation Journal, 29*, 329–353.

Bollen, K., & Euwema, M. (2015). Angry at your boss: Who cares? Anger recognition and mediation effectiveness. *European Journal of Work and Organizational Psychology, 24*, 256–266.

Bollen, K., & Euwema, M. (2016). Preventative mediation: Stopping conflict before it starts. In V. Gama (Ed.), *Mediation: A new perspective on justice*. Rio de Janeiro: Ibmec.

Bollen, K., Euwema, M., & Muller, P. (2010). Why are subordinates less satisfied with mediation? The role of uncertainty. *Negotiation Journal, 26*, 417–433.

Bollen, K., Ittner, H., & Euwema, M. C. (2012). Mediating hierarchical labor conflicts: Procedural justice makes a difference – for subordinates. *Group Decision and Negotiation, 21*, 621–636.

Brinkert, R. (2006). Conflict coaching: Advancing the conflict resolution field by developing an individual disputant process. *Conflict Resolution Quarterly, 23*, 517–528.

Brinkert, R. (2009). The roots of the public policy process: Using conflict coaching to initiate and sustain public manager commitment to citizen engagement. *International Journal of Public Participation, 3*, 63–79.

Brinkert, R. (2010a). Conflict coaching and the organizational ombuds field. *Journal of the International Ombudsman Association, 3*, 47–53.

Brinkert, R. (2010b). A literature review of conflict communication causes, costs, benefits and interventions in nursing. *Journal of Nursing Management, 18*, 145–156.

Brinkert, R. (2011). Conflict coaching training for nurse managers: A case study of a two-hospital health system. *Journal of Nursing Management, 19*, 80–91.

Brinkert, R. (2013). The ways of one and many: Exploring the integration of conflict coaching and dialogue-facilitation. *Group Facilitation: A Research and Applications Journal, 12*, 45–52.

Brinkert, R. (2016). Gratitude communication as conflict management: Advancing a strategy and tactic for positive narrative expansion. In P. M. Kellett & T. G. Matyok (Eds.), *Transforming conflict through communication: Personal to working relationships*. Lanham: Lexington.

Brubaker, D., Noble, C., Fincher, R., Park, S. K. Y., & Press, S. (2014). Conflict resolution in the workplace: What will the future bring? *Conflict Resolution Quarterly, 31*, 357–386.

Cameron, K., & Dutton, J. (Eds.). (2003). *Positive organizational scholarship: Foundations of a new discipline*. San Francisco: Berrett-Koehler Publishers.

Carter, C. (2008, November 25). Limited future for workplace mediation. *Personnel Today, 2008*, 9.

Cooperrider, D. L. (1986). *Appreciative inquiry: Toward a methodology for understanding and enhancing organizational innovation*. Unpublished doctoral dissertation, Case Western Reserve University, Cleveland, OH.

Cooperrider, D. L., & Srivastva, S. (1987). Appreciative inquiry in organizational life. In W. Pasmore & R. Woodman (Eds.), *Research in organization change and development* (Vol. 1, pp. 129–169). Greenwich: JAI Press.

Cooperrider, D., & Whitney, D. D. (2005). *Appreciative inquiry: A positive revolution in change*. San Francisco: Berrett-Koehler Publishers.

Cooperrider, D. L., Sorenson, P., Whitney, D., & Yager, T. (2000). *Appreciative inquiry: Rethinking human organization toward a positive theory of change*. Champaign: Stipes Publishing.

Costantino, C. A., & Merchant, C. S. (1996). *Designing conflict management systems: A guide to creating productive and healthy organizations*. San Francisco: Jossey-Bass.

De Dreu, C. K. (2008). The virtue and vice of workplace conflict: Food for (pessimistic) thought. *Journal of Organizational Behavior, 29*, 5–18.

Diochon, P. F., & Nizet, J. (2015). Ethical codes and executive coaches: One size does not fit all. *The Journal of Applied Behavioral Science, 51*, 277–301.

Ducharme, M. J. (2004). The cognitive-behavioral approach to executive coaching. *Consulting Psychology Journal: Practice and Research, 56*, 214.

Freedman, A. M., & Perry, J. A. (2010). Executive consulting under pressure: A case study. *Consulting Psychology Journal: Practice and Research, 62*, 189.

Gadlin, H. (2014). Toward the activist ombudsman: Conclusion. *Conflict Resolution Quarterly, 31*, 477–479.

Gergen, K. (2015). *An invitation to social construction* (3rd ed.). Thousand Oaks: Sage.

Giebels, E., & Janssen, O. (2005). Conflict stress and reduced well-being at work: The buffering effect of third-party help. *European Journal of Work and Organizational Psychology, 14*, 137–155.

Giebels, E., & Yang, H. (2009). Preferences for third-party help in workplace conflict: A cross-cultural comparison of Chinese and Dutch employees. *Negotiation and Conflict Management Research, 2*, 344–362.

Goldberg, S. B., & Shaw, M. L. (2007). The secrets of successful (and unsuccessful) mediators continued: Studies two and three. *Negotiation Journal, 23*, 393–418.

Jameson, J. K., Bodtker, A. M., & Linker, T. (2010). Facilitating conflict transformation: Mediator strategies for eliciting emotional communication in a workplace conflict. *Negotiation Journal, 26*, 25–48.

Jehn, K. A., Rupert, J., Nauta, A., & Van Den Bossche, S. (2010). Crooked conflicts: The effects of conflict asymmetry in mediation. *Negotiation and Conflict Management Research, 3*, 338–357.

Jones, T. S., & Brinkert, R. (2008). *Conflict coaching: Conflict management strategies and skills for the individual.* Thousand Oaks: Sage Publications.

Kellett, P. M., & Dalton, D. G. (2001). *Managing conflict in a negotiated world: A narrative approach to achieving dialogue and change.* Thousand Oaks: Sage.

Kilburg, R. R. (1996). Toward a conceptual understanding and definition of executive coaching. *Consulting Psychology Journal: Practice and Research, 48*, 134–144.

Kilburg, R. R. (2000). *Executive coaching: Developing managerial wisdom in a world of chaos.* Washington, DC: American Psychological Association.

Kilburg, R. R. (2004). When shadows fall: Using psychodynamic approaches in executive coaching. *Consulting Psychology Journal: Practice and Research, 56*, 246–268.

Levine-Finley, S. (2014). Stretching the coaching model. *Conflict Resolution Quarterly, 31*, 435–446.

Lipsky, D. B., Seeber, R. L., & Fincher, R. (2003). *Emerging systems for managing workplace conflict: Lessons from American corporations for managers and dispute resolution professionals.* San Francisco: Jossey-Bass.

Mann, M. E., & Kump, L. R. (2015). *Dire predictions: Understanding climate change* (2nd ed.). New York: DK.

McDermott, E. P. (2012). Discovering the importance of mediator style — An interdisciplinary challenge. *Negotiation and Conflict Management Research, 5*, 340–353.

Nabatchi, T., Bingham, L. B., & Moon, Y. (2010). Evaluating transformative practice in the US Postal Service REDRESS program. *Conflict Resolution Quarterly, 27*, 257–289.

Nesbit, R., Nabatchi, T., & Bingham, L. B. (2012). Employees, supervisors, and workplace mediation: Experiences of justice and settlement. *Review of Public Personnel Administration, 32*, 260–287.

Noble, C. (2011). *Conflict management coaching: The CINERGY™ model.* Toronto: CINERGY Coaching.

Slaikeu, K. A., & Hasson, R. H. (1998). *Controlling the costs of conflict: How to design a system for your organization.* San Francisco: Jossey-Bass.

Stern, L. R. (2004). Executive coaching: A working definition. *Consulting Psychology Journal: Practice and Research, 56*, 154–162.

Stimec, A., & Poitras, J. (2009). Building trust with parties: Are mediators overdoing it? *Conflict Resolution Quarterly, 26*, 317–331.

Tidwell, A. (1997). Problem solving for one. *Mediation Quarterly, 14*, 309–317.

Ury, W. L., Brett, J. M., & Goldberg, S. B. (1988). *Getting disputes resolved: Designing systems to cut the costs of conflict.* San Francisco: Jossey-Bass.

Van Kleef, G. A., De Dreu, C. K., Pietroni, D., & Manstead, A. S. (2006). Power and emotion in negotiation: Power moderates the interpersonal effects of anger and happiness on concession making. *European Journal of Social Psychology, 36*, 557–581.

Wall, J. A., & Dunne, T. C. (2012). Mediation research: A current review. *Negotiation Journal, 28*, 217–244.

Winter, C. (2005). Mediation und coaching — ein vergleich. *Organisationsberatung, Supervision, Coaching, 12*, 205–216.

Chapter 11
Manager as Mediator: Attitude, Technique, and Process in Constructive Conflict Resolution in the Workplace

Thelma Butts

Introduction

Lederach (2003) sets out that conflict resolution practitioners don't manage conflict, they transform it. This perspective speaks to process and objectives, to a purpose that seeks to harness the potential of a constructive model of conflict resolution for the workplace (Deutsch 1973, 2006). De Dreu and Gelfand (2008) set out that conflict itself is also a process, one which begins with the perception of an individual or group that is at odds with another about interests and resources, beliefs, values, or practices that are important to them.

As a process, not an isolated event, conflict can be affected by a variety of factors and changed or transformed, escalating it, or turning it into a catalyst to create a better understanding and a better workplace. Deutsch (1973, 2006) sets out that when a variety of factors create a positive constructive cooperation, or a negative destructive competition, they also create a self-propagating cycle. This chapter offers a case study set forth in three scenarios to demonstrate the positive self-propagating effect of constructive cooperation and constructive conflict resolution in the workplace.

To transform conflict, a manager benefits from several related factors. These include a constructive conflict resolution attitude (Deutsch 2006), skills in applying a variety of techniques that facilitate communication, problem-solving and leadership (Poitras et al. 2015), a sound understanding of power and trust dynamics (Coleman 2006; Lewicki 2006) and information on the effect of process. By process, we mean the effect of distinct roles, including third-party roles, one may adopt when intervening in conflict so as to make a deliberate and optimum choice for how

T. Butts (✉)
Butts Associates, Conflict Management & Dispute Resolution, Butts Institute for Conflict Resources, Tucson, AZ, USA and Madrid, Spain
e-mail: thelma.butts@buttsassociates.com

© Springer International Publishing Switzerland 2016
K. Bollen et al. (eds.), *Advancing Workplace Mediation Through Integration of Theory and Practice*, Industrial Relations & Conflict Management 3,
DOI 10.1007/978-3-319-42842-0_11

to act, because conflict resolution processes are varied and lead to different outcomes (Baruch-Bush and Folger 1994; Karambayya and Brett 1989; Kolb 1986; Kolb and Sheppard 1985; Riskin 1996, 2003).

When conflict manifests, it may be an opportunity to change things for the better. We must seek to harness its potential, its constructive use in the workplace, and decrease its negative impact (Jehn 1995; Rahim 2002; Simons and Peterson 2000). But how can a manager shift bravely from putting out fires of bickering, and from ignoring festering deeper problems, to "embracing" these uncomfortable workplace dynamics?

The answer does not lay in a single magical technique or third-party role, or a single constructive conflict resolution method. Not even, for example, mediation is a panacea, sometimes direct negotiation or some other process may be better. The manager should adopt a flexible model of constructive conflict resolution which incorporates the five components attitude, technique, process (Deutsch 2006), attention to power (Coleman 2006), and attention to trust (Lewicki 2006). Although attitude and attention to power and trust should remain stable components, technique and process may change depending on the particular situation. As can be seen in the scenarios in this chapter, factors which affect the techniques and process the manager uses include whether the manager is a party to the conflict, the characteristics and needs of the parties, the characteristics of the conflict, and the objectives of the manager and the organization.

Proactive, healthy approaches to conflict can be implemented in varying types of entities from hierarchical, vertical enterprises to the most horizontal of self-directed teams (Bradley et al. 2012; Pascale 1990). Policies and strategies can be chosen, learned and implemented to deal with both internal and external clients (Lipsky et al. 2003). But many times, although the manager may agree with the concepts of constructive conflict resolution methods, and be willing to put these in action, it can be a challenge to incorporate and foster healthy conflict management in the workplace. Additionally, if the organizational culture does not support a positive conflict resolution attitude, the manager may find it more difficult to act constructively when managing conflict (Deutsch 2006).

So, it sounds great but how do we do it? Managers may have learned that a dialogue intended to resolve tension will benefit if he or she translates posturing and rigidly held positions to generate a conversation that instead explores the underlying interests, concerns, priorities and possibilities of the disputants (Fisher et al. 1991). But it can be difficult to operationalize these and other conflict resolution concepts. Conflict resolution skills, from active listening to constructive confrontation, take continued reflection and practice, and thoughtful application to the situation of the moment, because the effectiveness of interventions and techniques is context dependent. This chapter sets out that attitude and appropriate choice of third-party role are necessary adjuncts to technique and strategies that otherwise may fall on infertile ground.

Not all conflict resolution methods have a positive impact on the workplace. Nor will all mediation strategies from current conflict resolution practices have a positive, beneficial change on the workplace. This chapter offers concepts that support managers and team leaders in developing healthy conflict resolution habits, to help them choose from a series of techniques and third party roles, noting how subtle differences in a manager's choice of strategies and handling of conflict can have a profound effect on the workplace environment. Just as mediators learn that the orientation, strategies, and techniques they choose potentially affect the outcome of their mediations (Baruch-Bush and Folger 1994; Fisher et al. 1991; Kovac and Love 1998; Love 1997; Riskin 1996, 2003), the manager will understand that how he or she implements conflict resolution strategies can create different environments in the workplace.

This chapter takes three different scenarios that take place over time in a single case, and sets out a brief cost of conflict analysis in each scenario, considering the potential cost of leaving a problem unresolved, or resolving it in an adversarial stance. Then the manager's intervention in the real case, drawn from constructive conflict resolution practice, is recounted, along with the impact of the strategies. In each scenario, the practical examples of technique and strategies help managers make the jump from theory to practice.

Components of Constructive Conflict Resolution Practice

Based on Deutsch's (2006) theory of cooperation and competition, Coleman's (2006) work on power, Lewicki's (2006) concept of trust and distrust as separate and important factors in interpersonal and workplace relationships, and personal practitioner experience, Table 11.1 lists components of constructive conflict resolution practice in three columns (attitude, technique, and process) with attention given to trust and power. Table 11.1 reflects a general constructive conflict resolution *behavior*, which operationalizes Deutsch's theory, and will be explained through the examples set out in the three scenarios. The horizontal rows in Table 11.1 are not meant to be read as directly related. The columns of technique and process speak to the *method* used in the constructive conflict resolution behavior.

We propose that a healthy constructive conflict resolution *behavior* incorporates a constructive conflict resolution attitude (Deutsch 2006), skills in a variety of techniques, knowing how to use conflict resolution processes of different types depending on the situation, and attention to power and trust dynamics. A constructive conflict resolution *method* is one that achieves beneficial results in the particular case, and sometimes it will be talking directly with the other party, sometimes it will take the shape of a direct or a shuttle negotiation, at other times a mediation, arbitration or some other process may be deemed best, including a hybrid of different interventions.

It is no mystery that communication is essential to any interdependent relationship, including relationships between group members in the workplace. Busy companies spend valuable resources training their employees in communication hoping it will help prevent and deal better with conflict. But even if the communication training is interesting for the participants it often isn't effective because it isn't enough. It's not communication that's missing, it's other negotiation or conflict resolution skills they need to resolve their situation constructively.

Table 11.1 Components of a constructive conflict resolution practice: attitude, technique, and process, with attention to power and trust dynamics

Components of Constructive Conflict Resolution Practice

(Power, Trust, Attitude, Technique & Process)

Power & Trust

The manager understands power ant trust dynamics, and knows personal tendencies in superior and inferior power. He or she uses an understanding of power and trust dynamics when choosing techniques, and when choosing and managing process.

Attitude	Technique	Process
Tendency, orientation, especially of the mind, manifests in behavior that engenders trust	Tools and activity that facilitate communication, problem solving, and leadership	Deliberate and optimum choice of intervention, or approach
The Manager has these characteristics:	The Manager knows how to use these tools and engages in these activities when appropriate:	The Manager considers his approach, chooses, and informs the parties appropriately:
Accessible	Before negotiating on own behalf or intervening in others' conflict, plan: Identify own and other's interests, priorities, alternatives to agreement, and strategies	Understands the impact of resolving based on interests, rights, or power
Preference for cooperation	Constructive confrontation	Knows when to resolve based on interests, rights or power
Respectful	Convening and setting the table for dialogue	Before intervening in conflict with others, he plans: considers own objective, chooses 3rd-party role if appropriate, and plans approach
Good listener	Calm parties, acknowledge emotion, build trust	Regardless of role, knows that techniques are most effective couched in a constructive attitude
Has empathy	Give information Gather information	Is clear with parties about what to expect of a 3rd-party role, of limits
Has emotional intelligence	Paraphrasing and summarizing with empathy	Clearly explains that the intervention takes place within the structure of the organizational rules, hierarchical or other
Self-awareness	Reframing	Acts coherently, i.e., doesn't promise impartiality and then judges

(continued)

Table 11.1 (continued)

Clear	Good use of questions and constructive questions	Ensures employee safety
Constance, integrity	Identify positions and needs/interests	Protects confidentiality if appropriate
Honorable	Identifying and framing issues	Acts with fairness
Flexible	Positive spins	Acts with integrity
Curious, inquisitive	Focus on possibilities	Acts with appropriate patience
Appreciates	Brainstorming	Acts in timely fashion
Strong, firm, secure, serene, patient	Negotiation support	Weighs efficiency against effectiveness of the process

The manager needs more than fledgling communication techniques and glib "conflict management tools." A manager needs the right attitude to deploy the techniques effectively, and skills in a variety of conflict resolution techniques, of which good communication is just one (Deutsch 2006). The manager also needs a sound understanding of third-party roles in conflict so as to recognize that the role he or she chooses, especially repeatedly, can have a profound effect in the workplace (Baruch-Bush 1994; Karambayya and Brett 1989; Kolb 1986; Kolb and Sheppard 1985; Riskin 1996, 2003). Additionally, the manager must have a sound understanding of how power and trust can affect the dynamics in conflict resolution (Coleman 2006; Lewicki 2006).

Conflict Case: Mary and Her Team... the Setting

The following three scenarios are based on a real case. In the first scenario, Mary, the manager, faces an angry team that doesn't welcome her as their new team leader. In the second scenario, Mary intervenes in a conflict that has created intra-team discord based on an upper-management decision, putting her "between a rock and a hard place." The third scenario is based on a stewing conflict between two team members that has not yet spread to the rest of the team. In these scenarios, the manager applied constructive conflict resolution skills that had a profound effect on her team and the company, turning the tables to start a process of creating trust and managing distrust (Lewicki et al. 2016). Managers can have an important impact on how employees feel about their jobs and their company (Purcell and Hutchinson 2007). How a manager handles conflict affects employees' perceptions of factors such as satisfaction and fairness of a conflict resolution process (Karambayya and Brett 1989; Karambayya et al. 1992). This is demonstrated in the following three scenarios.

Each scenario is structured in subsections to facilitate discussion of the topics, and so the reader can easily compare and contrast the settings, the cost of conflict if it is left unattended, and the manager's interventions. In each scenario there are four titled sections. First, (1) the context is set and the problem presented. Then, (2) the paths not chosen by the manager are considered. Following, (3) the manager's action is discussed, and finally, (4) we consider whether mediation was a good option.

Mary and Her Team: The Setting

Mary, a small-statured, 42-year-old manager, and her 12-member team work in a company that employs 150 people in the design and manufacture of lamps and lighting fixtures in a country with a moderate power distance, a measure that reflects to what extent the less powerful persons in the workplace accept inequality in power and consider it normal (Hofstede 1980). Mary's non-unionized company, Lucky Lamps, just 1 year ago was several smaller companies which merged into one to survive the financial crisis. Immediately, the rocky road of assimilation and accommodation of several entities into a single organization may come to mind (Smeets et al. 2006).

Scenario I: "The First Day on the Job"

In this first scenario, Mary, a first-time and unwilling new manager, faces an angry team that doesn't welcome her as their new team leader.

The First Day on the Job: The Context

Just a few months ago Mary was not a manager, nor did she have any such aspiration. One day Mary was called in to the head office and told that she had been given a promotion and would be moving to the Blue Section. The words hadn't sunk in yet and she was thinking about how little she knew about the very different work done in Blue Section when she heard the rest of the message… Mary was to manage the team… she couldn't believe her ears! Mary was not a manager! Mary protested, but the decision had been made. They said they had faith in her and saw potential.

Mary recounts that she had about 5 days to prepare. She reached out to a friend who worked in human resources in a different company. She read the books her friend recommended and they talked, planned, and worried together. The first 3 days on the job Mary was trained by Joe, the lame-duck manager, then he left. She felt cold shoulders and disrespectful glances from several of the male team members. Joe had explained that some were angry because they thought one of them would get the supervisory position. They didn't like her because they knew she knew nothing about their job and had no supervisory experience. With Joe gone, the following Monday Mary would face the team alone for the first time.

"The First Day on the Job"/The Paths Not Chosen

Mary had at least three options. In Option 1 Mary would leave the tension unre-solved, just ignore it and hope it goes away on its own. Or, in Option 2, Mary could take an adversarial stance and "get a good grip" on the team and set some clear, firm rules and sanctions, and show the team who the boss is. Or, in Option 3, Mary could try to talk to the team.

What is the cost of conflict in the different options, namely the effect on the workplace? In Options 1 and 2, it is likely that a power struggle will ensue. The workers had already taken a competitive stance. Mary has a hierarchical type of power bestowed by her title, necessary to create structure and authority to run the organization (Barnard 1946). However, several of the angry team members have, apart from the power of association derived from banding together against Mary, the power to disrupt (Coleman 2006). The team members also have more substantive knowledge than Mary, some are older, and some have experience in leadership or quasi-leadership positions in the pre-merger organizations, all also sources of power that Mary does not have.

In Option 1, not recognizing a clear differential in power will not make the prob-lem disappear, it will probably lead to power struggles, which reduces the likelihood of cooperation. Power struggles lead to use of inflexible strategies and loss of effec-tiveness both in Option 1 and 2. If Mary opts for Option 2 and takes an adversarial or forcing stance, the use of coercion, whether the "low power" team members buckle or fight back, blocks collaborative action (Wiseman and Poitras 2002). If Mary had tried to impose stiff rules to make the team members "behave," intense negative feelings would limit the team member's capacities to respond construc-tively, possibly leading to destructive impulses (Deutsch 1973). Once engaged in a power struggle it is not likely that one of parties would make a cooperative gesture (Lulofs and Cahn 2000).

Depending on the situation, leaving conflict unresolved or using a destructive or non-constructive method of conflict resolution can take a toll, both on a personal level, and on an organizational level. Power struggle and the related retaliation and escalation are costs of this conflict if Mary chooses Option 1 or 2. Leaving the ten-sion unresolved would promote rift and increasingly poor communication as no one speaks of the big ugly elephant in the room. Other possible costs for both Option 1 and 2 on a personal level include irritation, stress, low morale, frustration, and dis-traction from work objectives (CPP Global 2008; De Dreu, van Dierendonck, & Dijkstra, 2004). The potential costs of conflict for the organization for Options 1 and 2 ripple, growing, and include not solving the problem, absenteeism, increased turn-over rate, distracted managers and other costs (CPP Global 2008; Medina, Munduate, Dorado, Martínez, & Guerra 2005). Table11.2 contains lists of possible costs based on predictions from Deutsch's (2006) theory, and personal practitioner experience.

Burke (2006) lists "remedies" for managers based on Hogan et al. (1994), which noted that organizational climate studies routinely show that 60–70 % of the

Table 11.2 Possible costs of leaving conflict unresolved, and of destructive or non-constructive conflict resolution practices

Possible costs of leaving conflict unresolved, and of destructive or non-constructive conflict resolution	
Possible effects on a **personal** level:	Possible effects on an **organizational** level:
Anxiety, irritation	Decreased participation
Fear	Poor leadership
Depression	Solving the wrong problem
Difficulty focusing	Not solving the problem
Detachment	Absenteeism
Physical and psychosomatic ailments	Declining revenue
Apathy, burnout	Increased employee turn-over rate
Loss of commitment to job	Increased human resources costs
Loss in interest in job	Costs of training new employees
Loss of commitment to organization	Tension
Increasing frustration	Distracted leaders
Increasingly poorer communication	Absorbs energy
Feelings of isolation	Energy diverted to conflict
Loss of self-esteem	Decreased attention to positive activity
Distraction from work objectives	Decreased creativity
Decrease in personal work performance	Low morale
Decrease in creativity	Power struggles
Decrease in productivity	Decreased trust and increased distrust
Stress	Decreased communication

employees in any organization or occupational group report that the worst or most stressful aspect of their job is their immediate supervisor, and this costs billions of dollars of lost productivity each year. The "personality defects" deemed responsible include extreme ambition, lack of support for subordinates, insensitivity, arrogance, and poor relations with staff (Hogan et al. 1990). The first item on Burke's list is "Provide 'people management' training for supervisors and managers," and the second is that while job knowledge is important for credibility, more important for managers and people in leadership positions are such qualities as conceptual ability, emotional intelligence which includes self-awareness, and a controlled desire to make a difference for reasons associated with organizational goals and not for personal aggrandizement. These qualities listed by Burke have to do with a manager's attitude and we turn to this next.

"The First Day on the Job"/The Manager's Action: Mary's Attitude

How can Mary transform this conflict? She thought about what they must be saying about her. And then she also thought about how the team members must feel. She had made the jump from thinking only about herself to thinking about the other and putting herself in their shoes. This was empathy. She recounts she felt bad for herself and she felt bad for the team members, and she felt bad about the whole unreal situation. She decided to be honest with the team, and make some promises to them she felt she could keep.

Mary's Attitude

On Monday morning Mary met with the team to assign the "quotas" and orders due from her team by the end of the week, just like Joe had trained her. Instead of handing out the orders, she asked the team to sit down for a moment. She remembers she was nervous, and so she remained standing... she said it was to "have some power over them," hoping this would make them listen to her. She started by saying, "If you'll excuse me I'll stand for now until you know me because I'm short and if I sit you probably won't be able to see me." A few people smiled or laughed a little. The light touch of humor had helped lower the tension a bit. Then she said, "Thank you for sitting with me for a moment. I know we have a busy week. I just want to talk with you all together for a minute so that we can have a chance to clear the air" (some team members shifted in their seats and some sighed).

"I would like to hear your thoughts because we are in an awkward situation, and I would like us to talk about it. I feel bad about the situation, and I feel bad for all of you. And I feel bad myself. I know very little about this department. You all are the experts here, especially you two, Max and Jack, and you, Bob. (Mary had made sure to learn everyone's names and she nodded toward the three older, most experienced team members.) I have all the respect in the world for you, I want you to know that. I loved my job, but they plucked me up and put me here to work with you. I will tell you frankly, I still can't believe it, I was happy where I was. I want to do a good job, I have three kids at home to feed so I *have* to do a good job. But not just because of that, but because I want to be a great team leader for you, and I want us to be a great team together. So, I just want to start off by saying I don't know much about the work here, but I look forward to learning from you and working with you, and for you. And I know little about management, but I can promise you two things, you can always come to me for help, and I will work hard to learn how to be a good manager, a good team leader. Let's take a few minutes to talk...we can have a longer meeting later on, but let's start off the week talking just a few minutes... I'd like to know how this is affecting you, how are you doing?"

Mary and some of the team members recount that they went on to talk for a very short while, but a few of the team members, those that were most against Mary reserved their comments. So she didn't win them over immediately. But that first encounter was key to setting the team on the right path.

Mary used several elements from the attitude and technique columns of Table 11.1. When approaching a difficult conversation, it is useful to address emotions first, by acknowledging the feelings of others, expressing one's own feelings, and taking responsibility for one's own contribution to the situation (Bollen and Euwema 2015; Stone et al. 1999). Mary had acknowledged the concerns and needs of the team, a crucial step in constructive conflict resolution, whether done directly or with the help of a mediator. However, the senior team members (and their supporters) felt their position of status had been undermined by Mary's arrival. Augsburger (1992) sets out that recognizing hierarchy, here the team members' age, experience, and subject matter expertise, encourages cooperation. When Mary acknowledged this hierarchy, the power the team had, she increased the likelihood of cooperation. This helped to calm the team, and begin to build trust, critical to both her personal and professional relationship with the team and its members (Lewicki 2006). When receiving training in conflict resolution, managers should be supported in a process that helps them become aware of their tendencies to react in situations in which they have superior or inferior power to others (Coleman 2006).

Mary was a party in this conflict and as such cannot be seen as a third party, she was not mediating the dispute. But she used the techniques and had the attitude necessary for constructive conflict resolution. Mary's approach that Monday morning was a conciliatory gesture which began to create trust and dismantle distrust, for trust and distrust are distinct elements and not opposite ends of a single spectrum of trust. (Lewicki 2006; Lewicki et al. 2016). When Mary revealed information about herself she created affiliation with the team, and when she acknowledged the team members as "experts" more knowledgeable than her she granted them status. These two actions were powerful ways to deal with the team's emotions and promote trust to further negotiations (Fisher and Shapiro 2005; Pruitt 1981).

Mary signaled to the team that she was ready for real problem solving as she forfeited the opportunity to compete, admitted her lack of management skills, and hoped the team would reciprocate (Pruitt 1981). In her new job, Mary had encountered an "armed" team but the disarmament began when Mary gave her side of the story. She gave the team information and context, and in so doing she allowed the team to see her as a human like them. Likewise, a mediator often encourages the parties to tell their side of the story to create opportunities for respect and understanding between the parties.

Mary's approach to the conflict with her team was effective. Her technique was successful because it was couched in the right attitude. If her attitude had been arrogant, her talk with the team would not have had the same effect. Mary had demonstrated in a few words that she is accessible, has a preference for cooperation and collaboration, is respectful and appreciative, has empathy, is self-aware, and is strong and serene (See Table 11.1). Mary's attitude is part of her personality, and Goldberg and Shaw's (2007) research shows that a mediator's personality is important in conflict resolution, even more so than techniques. They found that the most important attributes of successful mediators are not abilities in using techniques but rather those that build the disputant's confidence in the mediator, such as friendliness and empathy, honesty and integrity. Although Mary was not mediating in this situation, her approach started a process of conflict transformation.

Would the team members have been better off using a grievance procedure if the organization had one in place? Are grievance procedures a constructive method of conflict resolution? Mary's organization is a non-union setting. Polster (2011) sets out that over the last 50 years non-union employers have increasingly adopted formal grievance procedures which allow employees to challenge a company decision or policy, and also appeal manager adjudications of the challenge. The intent of the employer is to signal fairness and provide a better process for dispute resolution. However, the way grievance procedures are usually set up escalate, rather than calm, the situation, making the process a destructive, or non-constructive conflict resolution method because employees are encouraged to take a position and defend it, and they do so, including through the appellate process.

Therefore, Polster (2011) recommends that employers use mediation in their grievance programs to avoid escalation and focus instead on finding a workable solution through dialogue, protecting the relationship. This is because the techniques and attitude of a mediator assist negotiations, decrease tensions, and promote joint problem-solving (Moore 2003). Additionally, parties who use grievance mediation learn some of the mediator's dispute resolution techniques and are better able to resolve grievances (Goldberg 2004).

"The First Day on the Job"/Was Mediation a Good Option?

A basic tenet of mediation is that a mediator cannot be not be personally involved as a party in the dispute he or she is called to mediate. A mediator is by definition a third party, that is, someone not a participant in the dispute. This is a key consideration for managers addressing conflict. If a manger decides mediation is a good option, but the manager is a party in the conflict, the manager must bring in a mediator, whether it is an external mediator or someone else from within the organization. Mary was involved in this conflict and could not have served as mediator.

A higher manager could have mediated between Mary and her team. But if the parties can handle the dialogue on their own, a mediator is not needed. Mediation would have been possible but not ideal in this situation. In mediation, the team might have denied giving Mary the cold shoulder and nasty looks, and not accepting her. Mediation at this stage may have started out the relationship on a crutch. Mediation is not a panacea, it is a very good constructive conflict resolution method, but it is a third-party process. Compare a mediator intervening in this case (third-party process) with the effect Mary had talking things out as she did with the team (direct negotiation). This case exemplifies the need for managers to be able to apply constructive conflict resolution methods to disputes in which he or she is involved as a party. Next, in Scenario II, we consider a conflict where Mary again uses constructive conflict resolution techniques, is not involved as a party, and again does not mediate.

Scenario II: "The Promotion"

In this second scenario, Mary intervenes in a conflict that has created intra-team discord based on an upper-management decision.

The Promotion: The Context

Three months later an unfortunate event created conflict in Mary's team. Under her leadership, the team had begun to take on a new cohesiveness and comfortable workplace context it never had under Joe, the previous manager. Good-natured Johnny, a 30 year-old team member, was a team favorite. He always helped out, either working extra or trading shifts to ease tight calendars, helping others with their work, making sure the coffee was on…always with a great attitude and some jokes to brighten the day. Sometimes he skipped part of his breaks to catch up the workload. Johnny had worked with his pre-merger company since he was 18, and never went to college. Jane, 26 and a recent college graduate, had been hired after the merger, about a year before the incident.

One day, news came to the team that upper management had named Jane to receive a promotion which entailed a raise and a title change in her job description. Mary had given her opinion that the promotion should go to Johnny but management had said Johnny didn't have a college degree, to which company policy gave preference. It was an unpleasant surprise that shook the team. The team was angry at what they considered an unfair and disrespectful situation since they felt the obvious and better candidate for the promotion was Johnny. He did the same job as Jane but was much better at it, was a great team member, was older and had seniority. They attributed the upper-management's choice as a slight to the pre-merger workers of Johnny's previous employer. And they took it out on Jane. They gave her the cold shoulder, looked past her, didn't talk to her; generally ignored her. Jane felt terrible. Although she liked Johnny, she felt bad about the way she was being treated, and she began to get angry at the team for not being happy for her and "taking sides" with Johnny. Johnny didn't say much, but he was in low spirits.

"The Promotion"/The Paths Not Chosen

Mary had at least three options. In Option 1 Mary would leave the tension unresolved, just ignore it and hope it goes away on its own. Or, in Option 2, Mary could take an adversarial, or forcing, stance, defend the upper management decision and quash the discord, threatening to "write up" any team member that continued to complain or made Jane feel bad. Or, in Option 3, Mary could try to talk to the team.

What is the cost of conflict in the different options, namely the effect on the workplace?

In Options 1 and 2, it is possible a power struggle will ensue between Johnny and Jane. However, it may only be one-sided (or between the team and Jane) as Jane seeks recognition and respect from the team members, but Johnny just becomes dejected and gloomy, and not wanting problems, doesn't compete with Jane. Although Jane might feel backed by Mary in Option 2, the ensuing effects of Options 1 and 2, especially for the team, are very similar; the conflict would continue. In Option 2, Mary's attempt to suppress the conflict would drive it underground, to fester, because "quashing" the conflict would not resolve it, nor would arguing that Jane had a *right* to the promotion because she fulfilled the company policy of preference for giving promotions to workers with college degrees, and Johnny did not. In this case, like in the previous scenario and in the one that follows, it is often less useful to resolve the conflict based on *rights* or *power*, than on the parties' underlying *interests* and concerns (Ury et al. 1988).

Let's do a quick, interesting exercise. Let's consider the costs of Option 1, leaving the conflict unresolved and just ignoring it, hoping that it will go away. The costs include continuing tension, a possible power struggle between Johnny and Jane, poor communication, gossiping, distraction from work, possible escalation and increased rift, polarization of team members, low morale in the team, decreased self-esteem, performance, and initiative in Johnny, stress for everyone, and possibly isolation for Jane. This is a list of possible costs for Option 1. Notice that the costs of Option 2, resolving with an adversarial stance, imposing a decision, not talking things out... are the same as for Option 1.

The conflict dynamics are similar in Option 1 and Option 2 to the extent that neither option resolves the conflict. A similar result may happen when a party loses a court verdict in an emotional case where the relationship between the disputants is close and must continue after the decision, such as neighbors in a condominium setting, a family-run business, or an inheritance (estate) dispute. The judge renders a decision but the dispute and bad feelings may not be truly resolved. To the extent a constructive conflict resolution method gives voice and participation to parties, it may help address the underlying issues and create solutions that are more englobing and flexible than those a judge can offer. In organizations, the role a third party takes in resolving disputes has implications for the solution as well as the perceptions of procedural and distributive justice (Karambayya and Brett 1989).

Mary has a vested interest in a fair and effective resolution of this conflict in part because she has to live with the results and she needs to maintain good relations with the team. Therefore, according to Karambayya and Brett (1989), it is in Mary's interest to act as problem solver and not as an investigator, judge, or a person who motivates with threats or incentives (Sheppard 1984). However, because of her interest in the resolution, it is possible that instead of a maintaining a third-party role, her intervention may turn into tripartite negotiations (Kolb 1986), between the team members, Jane and herself, or between the team, upper management, and herself.

"The Promotion"/The Manager's Action: Mary's Techniques

A constructive conflict resolution attitude would drive a manager to talk openly with the team, or team members, to speak about the bad feelings so the conflict is addressed directly and doesn't simmer unresolved. Mary decided to talk to the team together at the next morning's shift assignments. She knew it is better to address conflict sooner rather than later but she needed time to reflect (planning and reflection can be important tools in constructive conflict resolution). Mary was concerned about the team morale, the way Jane was being treated, and Johnny's spirit. She also knew that there was no going back on the upper management's decision. It wouldn't be right to do that to Jane, and anyway Johnny was bypassed because he didn't have a college degree, not because he wasn't otherwise a great employee. A manager or mediator is sometimes limited in his or her actions by the organization's decisions, rules, or procedures.

So before talking to the team, Mary took time to think and plan. She thought with empathy about how Jane and Johnny must feel, how the team probably felt, but also about what she hoped to accomplish in the meeting (her needs and the organization's needs). She thought about how she could support all of the team members so they could feel heard and become part of a solution, and stop polarizing the team and making the problem worse. She knew the team was angry with upper management. Some were also angry at her. After all, she was a manager with no management degree. But company policy didn't say managers have to have a management degree, just that preference went to the bearer of a college degree when there was more than one candidate. She wondered if, and how, she had contributed to the situation (Stone et al. 1999), and how Jane and Johnny each contributed to the problem, if at all. Mary also recounted that she didn't feel optimistic anything could be done about the situation and so she didn't feel too creative. She knew this was not good because her pessimism could become a self-fulfilling prophecy. It was unlikely she could change the management decision, but Mary felt it was definitely worth investing time and effort in helping the team talk things out.

When intervening in conflict, a manager needs to be sure not to create false expectations for the parties. The manager's intervention, whatever it is, must fit within the norms and structure of the organization (Wiseman and Poitras 2002). The manager must remember, and remind the parties if appropriate, that the constructive conflict resolution method, whether it be mediation, direct negotiation, or the use of techniques, takes place within the rules and hierarchy of the organization and therefore these must be respected.

Mary recounts that maybe she should have spoken to Jane and Johnny each alone first, and that she had done so, briefly, but mostly just to say congratulations to Jane and that she was sorry to Johnny. Speaking to each alone first may have put them at ease and made them feel more comfortable about approaching the subject together with the team. Additionally, Mary might have learned how Johnny and Jane actually felt, and their needs and concerns, rather than assuming she already had the necessary information. But she wanted to halt the negativity in the team right away if possible. So at shift assignments the following morning she asked the team to sit at the table for a few minutes.

Mary's Techniques

Mary said, "I'd like to talk with you about what happened yesterday to Jane, to Johnny and to us as a team." Mary had thought of turning the floor over to the team to vent at this point, but had decided specifically to not do so until she had said a few things to calm the team and shared a bit of information.

Mary spoke of her contribution to the problem. "I think I could have done a better job of sharing the news with the team and anticipating that you might be surprised. I should have sat down with you and told you that company promotion policy gives preference to employees with a college degree. Johnny is a great team member, and a great guy, but Jane has a college degree and Johnny doesn't and that's what happened." A few team members made comments about how stupid the rules are, and Mary said quickly, "Hey, remember management is management, and rules are rules, we have to be respectful here, we can say we don't agree but hold the insults because the boss would not be cool with that."

"So let's talk about this, you say it isn't fair, but the word "fair" isn't in the rules, you can look in the policy manual, it's no secret, it's diplomas that are rewarded, not only hard work. Jane's got both hard work, a diploma and we love her. Johnny has hard work, almost 12 more years' experience with the company than Jane, and is an amazing person who helps us out a lot... But what can we do?" asked Mary. "I think that Jane would have liked to celebrate but she feels bad for Johnny, and probably even a little angry with the whole situation. Is that right, Jane?" Jane was relieved when Mary verbalized that summary of how she felt because she was afraid if she had said it the team would have ganged up on her... so she was not going to say it, but it was exactly how she felt. But it seemed ok for Mary to say it. And now she felt relieved.

Mediators can paraphrase and summarize things that parties don't explicitly say, asking for confirmation of their understanding. It is a powerful tool that helps create understanding, decrease tension, and move the conversation along. Mary was *facilitating* a conversation rather than *mediating*, she was using constructive conflict resolution techniques in a different process.

The team talked a short while and several of the team members suggested that Mary ask upper management to give Johnny some type of a raise or promotion. Mary said she didn't think it would make a difference but she promised she would take the message as a "team message" to upper management. The team was happy with that. A couple of days later Mary had a message from upper management for the team. Upper management thanked the team for their message and said they wholeheartedly agreed that Johnny is a wonderful worker. And, they added, they hoped Johnny would take advantage of the organization's college tuition program. Nothing changed, but everything changed. The conflict was transformed. Talking

Table 11.3 Possible benefits of constructive conflict resolution practice

Possible benefits of constructive conflict resolution	
Possible benefits on a **personal** level:	Possible benefits on an **organizational** level:
Boosts self-esteem	More cooperation between employees
Boosts confidence	More productive workplace
Increasing sense of connection	More comfortable workplace
Increasing creativity on personal level	More flexible workplace
Leads to more satisfying job	More respectful workplace
More productive workplace	Increasing creativity on team level
Deeper understanding of the problem situation	Less undercover tension
Capacity to learn from past mistakes	Healthier workplace
Stronger mutual respect	Less stress
Sharpened focus	Group cohesion
Enhanced productivity	Better use of energy and attention
Voice and inclusion	

about the conflict together, not leaving it to fester (Option 1), and not prohibiting the team to talk about the problem (Option 2), changed the dynamics. Johnny felt appreciated by the team, and Jane was able to relax and feel part of the group again. The team as well as the organization reaped benefits from the constructive conflict resolution techniques Mary used. Table 11.3 lists some possible benefits of constructive conflict resolution for the individuals involved, and for the organization, many evident in this scenario. This list is based on predictions from Deutsch's (2006) theory, and personal practitioner experience.

"The Promotion"/Was Mediation a Good Option?

In this scenario there is a *root conflict* and a *collateral conflict*. A root conflict is the origin or source of a problem, and a collateral conflict is one that arises as a spillover or secondary problem. Although mediation may be appropriate in both root and collateral conflicts, Mary chose to facilitate a discussion within the team rather than mediate because the team didn't have a dispute with Jane, the *root conflict* was between the team and upper management. A collateral conflict had indeed manifested within the team because of their dissatisfaction with the upper management decision to promote Jane. Even so, the conflict was characterized by general tension and discontent, with no identifiable contraposed parties within the team. If there had been identifiable contraposed parties within the team, Mary could have acted as a third party mediator. If she felt involved in the conflict as well, and there were identifiable contraposed parties, she would not mediate herself, and instead could call in a mediator if permitted.

To have a mediation there must be at least two parties with a dispute and a third party as mediator. Mediating between the team and upper management was not an option (they had made clear to Jane earlier they weren't interested in changing company policy or making an exception), and although Mary did later relay information on behalf of the team, and upper management responded with a message the team accepted, it was not mediation. Likewise, Mary used constructive conflict resolution techniques to *facilitate* a discussion about the team's unhappiness and attitude, but this was also not a mediation. If a party to the conflict refuses to negotiate, there cannot be a mediation. Additionally, if there are not two or more identifiable contraposed parties in a conflict, there cannot be a mediation, by a third party manager or by an external mediator.

In Scenario I, "The First Day on the Job," Mary used a constructive conflict resolution attitude to transform the conflict between herself and the team. In Scenario II, "The Promotion," Mary used a constructive conflict resolution attitude and constructive conflict resolution techniques to transform a team conflict. Next, in Scenario III, Mary uses a constructive conflict resolution attitude and techniques in a constructive conflict resolution process, mediation, to transform a conflict between two team members.

Scenario III: "The Two Rams"

In this scenario two team members have a growing interpersonal dispute which has not yet spread to the rest of the team. The manager notices the increasing tension between the men, at first ignoring it, but when it continues she intervenes, choosing to mediate rather than reprimand the men.

The Two Rams: The Context
Max and Jack, 56 and 58 years old respectively, came from two of the premerger companies. They seemed to Mary to get along fine when she first became team manager. They are the oldest team members, respected by the rest, who sometimes approach one of them for clarification, support, or advice on an order or project.

But Mary noticed increasing tension and spats between Max and Jack. Something new was happening, or something was accumulating, but she didn't know what it was. One day she heard Max and Jack arguing again, and so did other team members.

"The Two Rams"/The Paths Not Chosen

Mary had at least three options. In Option 1 Mary would leave the tension unresolved, just ignore it and hope it goes away on its own. Or, in Option 2, Mary could take an adversarial stance, reprimanding, telling Max and Jack it is insubordinate, disrupting, and unacceptable to fight, even verbally, on the job. Or, in Option 3, Mary could try to talk to Max and Jack, mediating a solution between them.

In the previous two scenarios as well as in this scenario, Mary chooses to talk to resolve the conflict. However, talking or mediating is not the only, or always the best, solution. Depending on the situation, ignoring or using power may also work well. The manager can make this choice considering a variety of possible factors, including the stakes at risk, the gravity and urgency of the situation, the likelihood of agreement by the parties, the need to have the parties get along or have an interest in (buy-in) and comply with the agreement, the need to impose a hierarchical power structure to bring order, and others (Karambayya and Brett 1989, 1994; Kozan et al. 2007; and Kozan et al. 2014). However, the workplace context, like many others in real life, is characterized by imperfect information. To the extent that managers can gather good information through talking they may get a more accurate picture of the situation, make better decisions, and help resolve conflicts better.

What is the cost of conflict in the different options, namely the effect on the workplace? In Options 1 and 2, the conflict between Max and Jack would continue. Additionally, Römer et al. (2012) found that when a leader uses an *avoiding* conflict management style in task conflict, conflict-related stress increases. In Option 2, the conflict would go underground, but would not go away. The costs would be similar for Options 1 and 2. There would be tension, stress would continue, and the rest of the team members may be distracted by the fighting and gossip. Max and Jack may be distracted by planning vengeance, retaliation and generally making life difficult for the other. The team may polarize to support their favorite team member. The work would be disrupted and the conflict may spill over, contaminating other team members or areas. In the next section we see how Mary, a manager not trained in mediation, mediates between the two team members by using constructive conflict resolution techniques.

"The Two Rams"/The Manager's Action: Mary's Mediation

Mary decided she would try to mediate between Max and Jack. When a mediator believes that a poor relationship exists between negotiators, including annoyance or hostility, and the parties trust the mediator, then the mediator has the credibility to attempt to repair the relationship, and rapport building, or trying to create a more harmonious interaction, can be a useful tool (Kressel 1972; Ross and Wieland 1996).

Mary's Mediation

Mary said, "I would like to talk with you both and see what's up, what's happening. I'd like to help if I can. Let's meet in the staff room where we can talk alone together for a little while after lunch, that way you can both have a chance to cool off.

Sitting in the room a few hours later, Mary started the conversation, "I admire you two, and the team does too. We can tell something is going on but we don't know what it is. It's not disruptive to the team yet but we don't want it to get that way. So, I would like us to talk. I'm not going to tell you what to do at this stage, I'm not here to judge this afternoon. I think you two are the ones who know best what's going on, and you two can best decide how to fix it, how to improve your situation. I *am* here, however, as a mediator, as a referee to help keep the conversation useful…and constructive… You don't have to come to any agreement here if you don't want to, we can just gather some information for now and talk again later. But I do want to say we're in a work environment here, guys, so we can't keep this fighting up, ok? Just one thing, it would help me follow your stories if you take turns talking and avoid interrupting each other. Also, just keep in mind that how you say things will affect the other person's ability to listen to you, so can we agree to keep it civil? (Max and Jack nodded.) Sooo… How are you?" Mary got silence in response.

"Ok, let's take turns, Max, you go first," and we'll listen, and then you go, Jack, and we'll listen," said Mary.

Max said, "Jack just needs to respect the work space and keep the radio off. He's here to work, not listen to music!" Mary couldn't believe her ears, this was about the radio?? She didn't think so. (But keep this in mind… it's not good for a mediator to pre-judge.)

Jack shot back quickly, "You're turning into an ol' lady, always ragging!" Mary interrupted and said, "Hang on Jack, this is the part where you and I listen, remember? And remember the "keep it civil" part. Go ahead, Max."

"Jack's work is sloppy, too. You don't put your stuff away, Jack! The materials deliveries pile up! I'm not your maid! That's it, I don't have anything else to say. And don't call me ol' lady again!" said Max.

Jack replied, "Nothing has changed, I'm doing everything the same, only now, Max complains all the time, ALL THE TIME! He nitpicks about everything. Nothing is right for him anymore. Every time I leave the room he turns the radio off, ANNND, he takes it off the station so I have to look for it again. It ticks me off! And I tried to work it out, I went and bought some expensive earphones!"

"Right, and I talk to you and you can't hear me and I have to walk all the way over to you to tell you something, Jack! Like I do with my 13-year-old daughter! And that's when you're there! You leave, and when someone needs something cut, and we can't find you Jack, you're off outside smoking again!"

The men continued and Mary listened.

If Mary had been trained in mediation skills she would have known to summarize their stories with empathy, reframe some of the negative comments taking out the attacks and insults while retaining the information including their emotions, recognize the impact the situation was having on each man, and begin to ask questions looking for Max and Jack's interests (Butts Griggs 2007; Butts Griggs et al. 2005; Munduate et al. 2007).

Jack repeated that nothing had changed in the way he did things except that Max was impossible to work with now. Then Jack said he missed the old Max he used to work with, and when Jack said that, Max became quiet and so did Jack. Mary stayed quiet, too. Silence is a powerful mediator tool. Mary finally asked what had changed. This question is another excellent tool. Max repeated, now in a lower voice, "The radio..." and looked away. And Jack rolled his eyes again and started to speak. But Mary said, "No, wait, Jack, ...Max, tell me more about the radio."

Max then explained that he had never been good in school as a kid, but that now that he was an adult and settled down, he had been interested in going back to school and maybe getting a degree. So about 10 years ago he signed up for some classes at the local community college. Unable to concentrate, and afraid there was something wrong with him, Max went to see a doctor who diagnosed Max as having Attention Deficit Disorder.

Max had never had a problem at work until a few months ago, shortly after Mary arrived. Joe, the previous manager didn't allow the workers to keep radios playing. But Mary did. Jack had gotten a radio and it was absolute torture for Max, who did not want to tell anyone about his disability. When Jack played the radio Max couldn't read, he certainly couldn't order supplies or process orders error-free without checking his work 10 times, and he had a hard time keeping his mind on any task. Many times a day he would walk somewhere and not remember what he was doing, but all this happened only when the radio was on. He had tried earplugs but they didn't work. Jack and Mary were stunned.

Although Jack was bewildered with the change in Max, Max and Jack were friends and had built up trust. They also trusted Mary. Mary's constructive conflict resolution attitude and use of tools over the months since she started as manager had created a context of trust for her team and for healthy conflict resolution. Zand (1972) found high mutual negotiator trust leads to revealing more accurate information in managerial negotiations and discussion groups, and greater influence of highly trusted individuals over the group. Mary had taken on a third-party role as a facilitative, non-evaluative mediator and created a context where Max felt safe enough to reveal his real interest; to be able to work effectively and comfortably. With the additional information Max provided in the mediation, Mary and Jack could work with him to find the best solution. Mary's constructive conflict resolution intervention had again helped to transform a workplace conflict.

"The Two Rams"/Was Mediation a Good Option?

There are a variety of studies that refer to "mediational third-party roles," but it does not seem they are referring always to a facilitative, non-evaluative model of mediation (see Sheppard 1984; Karambayya and Brett 1989). However, in the "mediational" third-party role, from evaluative mediation to facilitative mediation and the transformative model of mediation (Baruch-Bush and Folger 1994), the process always incorporates at least a mediator that does not make the decision, who supports the parties in sharing information and negotiating to find a possible solution. The quantity and quality of input the mediator has on defining the problem, the possible solutions, and the objective of the dialogue is the basis for differentiating the styles or models of mediation; from evaluative, to facilitative, to transformative mediation.

There are different approaches to mediation, and some, like the *transformative* model, have been designed to achieve specific objectives. Transformative mediation explicitly seeks to make the world a better place by empowering people to handle their own conflicts, and improving relationships through recognition (not agreement) of the needs of others (Baruch-Bush and Folger 1994). However, the transformative model of mediation is not analogous to constructive conflict resolution that transforms conflict. The object hoping to be *transformed* in transformative mediation is the individual, not the conflict. In fact, the agreement rate may be lower in transformative mediation as the conflict is often not transformed because the goal of the model is not primarily to reach agreement (Bingham and Nabatchi 2001). When transformative mediation works, the manner the parties express themselves changes from strong emotion to calm, from defensiveness to openness and curiosity, and from speaking about or at the other party to interacting with the other party (Antes et al. 2001).

The way parties express themselves can change in the same way in *facilitative* mediation. However, facilitative mediation differs from transformative mediation in that the primary goal in facilitative mediation is to provide a space for dialogue, negotiation, problem-solving and understanding so that parties can reach agreement if they chose to, in other words, it does not share the altruistic objective of improving the world as primary goal (Baruch-Bush and Folger 1994). The facilitative mediator has the attitude and uses the tools listed in Table 11.1. In comparison, a mediator using the transformative model generally follows the dialogue the parties undertake, intervening only to create or recognize opportunities for empowerment and recognition. A transformative mediator does not do reframing for the parties, does not ask questions to suggest what to consider next in the dialogue, does not focus the conversation on future possibilities, and does not clean up insults or threats or emotions, all constructive conflict resolution tools. These tools are, however, precisely those used by a mediator using a facilitative model, and, potentially, higher agreement rates may be achieved than in transformative mediation (Ardagh 1999), hopefully also truly transforming the conflict.

But can a manager just switch mediator styles? Since *evaluative* and *facilitative* mediation may be plotted on a continuum of mediator styles some argue that they are not necessarily dichotomous (Stulberg 1996), and may be used together in the same mediation. However, Charkoudian et al. (2009) observed mediator interventions and compared the styles mediators actually used to those the mediators self-reported. They found that mediators that were observed to use any directive strategies tend to use mostly directive strategies, and those that were observed to use any elicitive strategies tended to use mostly elicitive strategies throughout the observed mediation case. Additionally, Bingham and Nabatchi (2001) set out that directive or evaluative mediation and other "problem solving" interventions such as facilitative mediation are not compatible with the transformative model of mediation.

Why should mediator style matter to a manager? Evaluative mediators focus on *rights* to give their opinions of how a conflict should settle. In essence it is an autocratic role. Because of this some authors argue that evaluative mediation is not mediation at all (Love 1997; Kovach and Love 1996; 1998). Rights-based conflict resolution often doesn't truly address or solve the conflict and the problem persists (Ury et al. 1988). If Mary had used an evaluative mediation style and focused on rights, she would have promoted Jack's freedom to play the radio, an ineffective "solution" to the problem. Although managers have power to impose decisions, the findings of Karambayya et al. (1992) suggest that supervisory experience influences the use of autocratic role behaviors, and experienced supervisors tend to avoid imposing decisions because they may have learned with time that mediational third-party roles pay off in better-quality outcomes.

The discussion on mediator approaches does not seek to convince the manager to choose one style over the other, rather to set out that the outcomes of the various approaches may be very different, so he or she should choose accordingly. A manager is generally not constrained as are mediators who may have to adhere to the approach and ideology of the program for which they mediate. However, the manager should choose the approach most likely to achieve his or her goals. This is consistent with the notion that constructive conflict resolution behavior chooses a method, composed flexibly of technique and process, to address a conflict in its particular context.

Pinkley, Brittain, Neale & Northcraft's (1995) research found that managers are likely to intervene differently if the goal is efficiency rather than effectiveness. In their study, managers that chose a strategy of "ending as opposed to resolving conflict" focused on efficiency and were not concerned with solving the underlying causes of the dispute (Pinkley et al. 1995). A manager who knows evaluative mediation may not reach the true underlying issue may judge whether the "efficiency" in a faster "resolution" using evaluative mediation is over-shadowed by the potential failure to surface the real problem, as demonstrated in the Two Rams scenario. In some cases, there may be no underlying, unknown issues, or the situation may best be served by a managerial decision, and evaluative mediation may be a better choice.

Poitras et al. (2015) studied managerial mediation competency and found that although the nature of the managers' roles may make it challenging to be neutral, and the voluntariness of the worker's participation is questionable, their studies suggest that the mediation skills typically associated with neutral third parties in general are similar to those employed by managers who mediate conflicts between employees. These skills are tools and activity that facilitate communication and problem solving, and are set out in the Technique (center) column of Table 11.1. Mary used these types of skills in all three scenarios.

So What's a Manager to Do?

We now consider how a manager can decide what process to use in a conflict situation, including when mediation is a good choice, and when it is not. Conflict is a natural element of the daily workplace and a manager may deal usually with tension or disputes through dialogue and direct negotiation, that is, "talking things out." But sometimes, a manager must call a specific process into play. The process may be formal or informal, and depending on the nature of the situation and the actors and issues involved, a given process may be more or less indicated. Pinkley et al. (1995)) found that when choosing strategies for intervening in conflict, managers are influenced both by the nature of the problem and their goals, so that manager's strategies are a unique combination of an individual´s choices and situational factors. Goals include objectives such as efficiency, effectiveness, fairness, and disputant satisfaction (Sheppard 1983).

In situations where general direct dialogue has not resolved a problem, the manager can consider whether the solution is negotiable. Urgent situations, safety issues, the need to enforce policy, or remove barriers to allow proper business function may not be negotiable. These types of problems may need to be resolved by processes different than problems whose solutions are negotiable, or, are not negotiable but talking about the problem is desirable. When there is no perceived benefit in employee participation or the solution is not negotiable, a managerial decision or third-party imposed decision may be necessary or more appropriate. However, the use of power, or *forcing* processes (Blake & Mouton 1964; Pruitt & Rubin 1986) should be weighed because Römer et al. (2012), found that *forcing* increases conflict-related stress in task, process and relationship conflict. Additionally, women may use their problem-solving abilities and be more effective in helping to construct positive outcomes when they have less, rather than more authority over the disputants (Benharda et al. 2010). Peterson and Harvey (2009) suggest that managers can use their power to encourage and manage group processes rather than force outcomes.

In situations where the solution is negotiable, and employee participation is desirable, the manager should determine whether there is an identifiable conflict between two or more identifiable parties. A party can be composed of one or more people. For example, general low morale with sporadic spats is not an identifiable conflict between identifiable parties, so a different process, like facilitation, should be used because mediation requires an identifiable conflict and identifiable parties. Another key consideration in choosing a process, and who is to lead it, is whether the manager is directly involved as a party.

The manager may create a process that fits the needs of the parties and the situation. Employee participation may be beneficial even in cases where the solution is not negotiable. The facilitation Mary conducted to discuss the bad feelings generated by Jane's promotion is an example of this. Although the manager makes the decision in this case, it is constructive conflict resolution, problem-solving, behavior. Römer et al. (2012) found problem-solving behavior by managers had a beneficial effect that lowered conflict-related stress in relationship conflicts.

When Mediation Is a Good Choice and When It Is Not

Mediation may be a good choice when the parties are able to negotiate for themselves, that is, express themselves and defend their interests. This is arguably difficult for some people generally, and in some situations for most people. For example, people that usually use an *avoiding* or *yielding* style (Blake & Mouton 1964; Pruitt & Rubin 1986) may be uncomfortable, and maybe even weak, in a mediation that requires them to sit across from their "adversary." The manager can improve this situation by assuring the needs and interests of these parties are tended to, by creating the opportunity for them to speak by asking shrewd questions, and by carrying out the mediation in separate rooms when necessary, a technique named *caucusing*.

Situations that are difficult for most people include disputes involving their superiors, and others where self-determination is compromised. Organizations may institute norms so that mediation is used only among co-workers at a similar level, and only with great care and safety measures when a superior is involved as a party. When a superior is involved it is very difficult to "balance power," and additionally, the mediation must be carried out within the rules and structure of the institution. Therefore, the question is not, "how should the mediator balance power?" but rather, "how should the mediator ensure self-determination?" Because self-determination, along with voluntariness, are key principals that define the mediation process, situations where these are compromised should be avoided, or handled carefully, for example, parties may choose to mediate assisted by their lawyers.

Mediation may not be appropriate in a variety of other situations or settings as well. Cases of criminal nature should not be hidden in mediation. Serious power imbalance, even between co-workers, that cannot be "corrected," is another preliminary consideration for exclusion. Additionally, the parties must have power to make the type of agreement they are seeking. When setting precedent is important, or an investigation is required, or a party wants a determination of who was "right" or "wrong," mediation is not appropriate. Mediation is usually confidential, works to find mutually acceptable solutions, and does not end with an adjudicated declaration, but rather with a consensual agreement. The quality of the consensual agreement is important. In this vein, Dolder (2004) sets out harsh criticism, cautioning against potential problems in workplace mediation, including mediator manipulation of parties, lack of quality control, and legislators who create disempowering settings for disputing parties.

Conclusion

Mediation is a valuable tool for exploring interests, creating understanding, rebuilding relationships, and creating lasting solutions. It promotes participation in the resolution, and gives voice to the parties in conflict, making it more likely to solve underlying issues. Consensual participation may result in buy-in and more stable agreements, whether it is because the employee helped construct the solution or because it is a question of honor; he gave his word to abide by the voluntary agreement (McEwen and Maiman 1989).

Mediation can be a formal or informal process. A manager can mediate informally by using the constructive conflict resolution techniques of a mediator, many of these are set out in Table 11.1. Mary's talk in the "Two Rams" scenario is an example of using mediation informally to talk out a problem. A manager's use of mediator techniques can be even less structured than the meeting in that scenario and be part of the way he or she carries out daily conversations. Indeed, using constructive conflict resolution techniques naturally and as a normal part of workplace dialogue can be an important part of constructive conflict resolution behavior.

Because there are different mediation approaches, not all mediation is alike. A mediator who does not use basic constructive conflict resolution techniques such as exploring parties' interests, and instead, for example, focuses only rights, may be ineffective to truly resolve a conflict (Peterson and Harvey 2009). A manager that knows how to use constructive conflict resolution techniques may serve as guarantor of mediations by external mediators, and therefore of the quality of conflict resolution in his or her workplace.

This chapter has illustrated that how a manager addresses conflict can have a profound effect on the workplace. A manager can choose different processes depending on the situation, and whether he or she is a direct party in the conflict or the conflict involves others. A general set of constructive conflict resolution techniques and strategies based in cooperation may be used for a variety of ends, creating a context which follows Deutsch's crude law of social relations: cooperation comes from cooperation and elicits cooperative response, and competition comes from and induces competition, therefore creating either positive or negative contexts in which the manager will manage conflict. Key to constructive conflict resolution is the manager's attitude which will couch the techniques and process he or she chooses...creating trust, and a more productive and comfortable workplace.

References

Antes, J. R., Folger, J. P., & Della Noce, D. J. (2001). Transforming conflict interactions in the workplace: Documented effects of the USPS REDRESS™ program. *Hofstra Labor & Employment Law Journal, 18*, 429–467.

Ardagh, A. (1999). Transformative mediation: The opportunity and the challenge. *The ADR Bulletin, 2*(1), 1–3.

Augsburger, D. W. (1992). *Conflict mediation across cultures: Pathways and patterns.* Louisville: Westminster- John Knox.

Barnard, C. I. (1946). Functions and pathology of status systems in formal organizations. In W. F. Whyte (Ed.), *Industry and society* (pp. 46–83). New York: McGraw-Hill.

Baruch-Bush, R. A., & Folger, J. P. (1994). *The promise of mediation.* San Francisco: Jossey-Bass.

Benharda, I., Brett, J., & Lempereur, A. (2010). Gender and role in conflict management: Female and male managers as third parties. *Negotiation and Conflict Management Research, 6*(2), 79–93.

Bingham, L. B., & Nabatchi, T. (2001). Transformative mediation in the USPS REDRESS program: Observations of ADR specialists. *Hofstra Labor & Employment Law Journal, 18*(2), 399–427.

Blake, R., & Mouton, J. S. (1964). *The managerial grid.* Houston: Gulf.

Bollen, K., & Euwema, M. (2015). Angry at your boss: Who cares? Anger recognition and mediation effectiveness. *European Journal of Work and Organizational Psychology, 24*(2), 256–266.

Bradley, B. H., Postlethwaite, B. E., Klotz, A. C., Hamdani, M. R., & Brown, K. G. (2012). Reaping the benefits of task conflict in teams: The critical role of team psychological safety climate. *Journal of Applied Psychology, 97*(1), 151–158.

Burke, W. W. (2006). Conflict in organizations. In M. Deutsch, P. T. Coleman, & E. C. Marcus (Eds.), *The handbook of conflict resolution. Theory and practice* (pp. 781–804). San Francisco: Jossey-Bass.

Butts Griggs, T. (2007). Handling anger in mediation: Concepts and strategies. *Portularia Journal of Social Work, 7*(1–2), 39–59.

Butts Griggs, T., Munduate, L., Barón, M., & Medina, F. J. (2005). Intervenciones de mediación. In L. Munduate & F. J. Medina (Eds.), *Gestión del conflicto, negociación, y mediación* (pp. 265–305). Madrid: Pirámide.

Charkoudian, L., Ritis, C. D., Buck, R., & Wilson, C. L. (2009). Mediation by any other name would smell as sweet—Or would it? The struggle to define mediation and its various approaches. *Conflict Resolution Quarterly, 26*, 293–316. doi:10.1002/crq.234.

Coleman, P. T. (2006). Power and conflict. In M. Deutsch, P. T. Coleman, & E. C. Marcus (Eds.), *The handbook of conflict resolution. Theory and practice* (pp. 120–143). San Francisco: Jossey-Bass.

CPP Global. (2008). *Workplace conflict and how businesses can harness it to thrive.* CPP Global Human Capital Report. Retrieved from: www.cpp.com/pdfs/CPP_Global_Human_Capital_Report_Workplace_Conflict.pdf

De Dreu, C. K. W., & Gelfand, M. J. (2008). Conflict in the workplace: Source, functions, and dynamics across multiple levels of analysis. In C. K. W. De Dreu & M. J. Gelfand (Eds.), *The psychology of conflict and conflict management in organizations* (pp. 3–54). New York: Taylor and Francis.

De Dreu, C. K. W., van Dierendonck, D., & Dijkstra, M. T. M. (2004). Conflict at work and individual well-being. *International Journal of Conflict Management, 15*(1), 6–26.

Deutsch, M. (1973). *The resolution of conflict: Destructive and constructive process.* New Haven: Yale University Press.

Deutsch, M. (2006). Cooperation and competition. In M. Deutsch, P. T. Coleman, & E. C. Marcus (Eds.), *The handbook of conflict resolution. Theory and practice* (pp. 23–42). San Francisco: Jossey-Bass.

Dolder, C. (2004). The contribution of workplace mediation to workplace justice. *Industrial Law Journal, 33*(4), 320–342.

Fisher, R., & Shapiro, D. (2005). *Beyond reason: Using emotions as you negotiate.* New York: Viking.

Fisher, R., Ury, W., & Patton, B. (1991). *Getting to yes: Negotiating agreement without giving in.* New York: Penguin Books.

Goldberg, S. B. (2004). How interest-based, grievance mediation performs over the long term. *Dispute Resolution Journal, 59*(4), 8–15.

Goldberg, S. B., & Shaw, M. L. (2007). The secrets of successful (and unsuccessful) mediators continued: Studies two and three. *Negotiation Journal, 23*(4), 393–418.

Hofstede, G. (1980). *Culture's consequences: International differences in work- related values.* Newbury Park: Sage.

Hogan, R., Raskin, R., & Fazzini, D. (1990). The dark side of charisma. In K. E. Clark & M. B. Clark (Eds.), *Measures of leadership* (pp. 343–354). West Orange: Leadership Library of America.

Hogan, R., Curphy, G. J., & Hogan, J. (1994). What we know about leadership: Effectiveness and personality. *American Psychologist, 49,* 493–504.

Jehn, K. (1995). A multimethod examination of the benefits and detriments of intragroup conflict. *Administrative Science Quarterly, 40*(2), 256–282.

Karambayya, R., & Brett, J. M. (1989). Managers handling disputes: Third party roles and perceptions of fairness. *Academy of Management Journal, 32*(4), 687–704.

Karambayya, R., & Brett, J. (1994). Managerial third parties: Intervention strategies, process and consequences. In J. Folger & T. Jones (Eds.), *New directions in mediation communication research and perspectives* (pp. 175–192). Thousand Oaks: Sage Publications.

Karambayya, R., Brett, J., & Lytle, A. (1992). Effects of formal authority and experience on third-party roles, outcomes, and perceptions of fairness. *Academy of Management Journal, 35*(2), 426–438.

Kolb, D. M. (1986). Who are organizational third parties and what do they do? In M. A. Bazerman, R. A. Lewicki, & B. H. Sheppard (Eds.), *Research on negotiations in organizations* (Vol. 1, pp. 207–278). Greenwich: JAI.

Kolb, D. M., & Sheppard, B. H. (1985). Do managers mediate, or even arbitrate? *Negotiation Journal, 1*(4), 379–388.

Kovac, K., & Love, L. P. (1996). Evaluative mediation is an oxymoron. *Alternatives to High Cost of Litigation., 14*(3), 31–32.

Kovac, K., & Love, L. P. (1998). Mapping mediation: The risk of Riskin's Grid. *Harvard Negotiation Law Review, 3*(71), 72–73.

Kozan, M. K., Ergin, C., & Varoglu, D. (2007). Third party invention strategies of managers in subordinate' conflicts in Turkey. *International Journal of Conflict Management, 18*(2), 128–147.

Kozan, M. K., Ergin, C., & Varoglu, K. (2014). Bases of power and conflict intervention strategy: A study on Turkey's managers. *International Journal of Conflict Management, 25*(1), 38–60.

Kressel, K. (1972). *Labor mediation: An exploratory survey.* Albany: Association of Labor Mediation Agencies.

Lederach, J. P. (2003). *The little book of conflict transformation.* New York: Good Books.

Lewicki, R. J. (2006). Trust, trust development, and trust repair. In M. Deutsch, P. T. Coleman, & E. C. Marcus (Eds.), *The handbook of conflict resolution: Theory and practice* (pp. 92–119). San Francisco: Jossey-Bass.

Lewicki, R., Elgoibar, P., & Euwema, M. (2016). The tree of trust: Building and repairing trust in organizations. In P. Elgoibar, M. Euwema, & L. Munduate (Eds.), *Building trust and constructive conflict management in organizations* (Vol. 2). Dordrecht: Springer International.

Lipsky, D. B., Seeber, R. L., & Fincher, R. D. (2003). *Emerging systems for managing workplace conflict*. San Francisco: Jossey-Bass.

Love, L. P. (1997). The top ten reasons why mediators should not evaluate. *Florida State University Law Review, 24*, 937.

Lulofs, R. S., & Cahn, D. D. (2000). *Conflict: From theory to action* (2nd ed.). Boston: Allyn and Bacon.

McEwen, C. A., & Maiman, R. J. (1989). Mediation in small claims court: Consensual processes and outcomes. In K. Kressel, D. Pruitt, & Associates (Eds.), *Mediation research* (pp. 53–67). San Francisco: Jossey-Bass.

Medina, F. J., Munduate, L., Dorado, M. A., Martínez, I., & Guerra, J. M. (2005). Types of intra-group conflict and affective reactions. *Journal of Managerial Psychology, 20*(3–4), 219–230.

Moore, C. W. (2003). *The mediation process: Practical strategies for resolving conflict* (3rd ed.). San Francisco: Jossey-Bass.

Munduate, L., Butts Griggs, T., Medina, F. J., & Martinez-Pecino, R. (2007). *Manual para la mediación laboral*. Sevilla: Consejo Andaluz de Relaciones Laborales.

Pascale, R. T. (1990). *Managing on the edge: How the smartest companies use conflict to stay ahead*. New York: Simon and Schuster.

Peterson, R. S., & Harvey, S. (2009). Leadership and conflict. Using power to manage in groups for better rather than worse. In D. Tjosvold & B. Wisse (Eds.), *Power and interdependence in organizations* (pp. 281–298). Cambridge: Cambridge University Press.

Pinkley, R. L., Brittain, J., Neale, M. A., & Northcraft, G. B. (1995). Managerial third-party inter-vention: An inductive analysis of intervenor strategy selection. *Journal of Applied Psychology, 80*(3), 386–402.

Poitras, J., Hill, K., Hamel, V., & Pelletier, F. B. (2015). Managerial mediation competency: A mixed-method study. *Negotiation Journal, 31*(2), 105–129.

Polster, J. C. (2011). Workplace grievance procedures: Signaling fairness but escalating commit-ment. *New York University Law Review, 86*, 638–671.

Pruitt, D. G. (1981). *Negotiation behavior*. New York: Academic.

Pruitt, D. G., & Rubin, J. (1986). *Social conflict: Escalation, stalemate, and settlement*. New York: Random House.

Purcell, J., & Hutchinson, S. (2007). Front-line managers as agents in the HRM-performance causal chain: Theory, analysis and evidence. *Human Resource Management Journal, 17*(1), 3–20.

Rahim, M. A. (2002). Toward a theory of managing organizational conflict. *International Journal of Conflict Management, 13*(3), 206–235.

Riskin, L. L. (1996). Understanding mediators' orientations, strategies, and techniques: A grid for the perplexed. *Harvard Negotiation Law Review, 1*(7), 7–51.

Riskin, L. L. (2003). Decision making in mediation: The old grid and the new grid system. *Notre Dame Law Review, 79*(1), 1–53.

Römer, M., Rispens, S., Geibels, E., & Euwema, M. C. (2012). A helping hand? The moderating role of leaders' conflict management behavior on the conflict-stress relationship of employees. *Negotiation Journal, 28*(3), 253–277.

Ross, W. H., & Wieland, C. (1996). The effects of interpersonal trust and time pressure on manage-rial mediation strategy in a simulated organizational dispute. *Journal of Applied Psychology, 81*, 228–248.

Sheppard, B. H. (1983). Managers as inquisitors: Some lessons from the law. In M. Bazerman & R. Lewicki (Eds.), *Negotiating in organizations* (pp. 193–213). Beverly Hills: Sage.

Sheppard, B. H. (1984). Third party conflict interventions. A procedural framework. In B. M. Staw & L. L. Cumings (Eds.), *Research in organizational behaviour* (pp. 141–190). Greenwich: JAI. Vol. 6.

Simons, T., & Peterson, R. (2000). Task conflict and relationship conflict in top management teams: The pivotal role of intragroup trust. *Journal of Applied Psychology, 85*, 102–111.

Smeets, V., Ierulli, K., & Gibbs, M. (2006). *Mergers of equals and unequals* (IZA Discussion Paper No. 2426). Retrieved from http://nbn-resolving.de/urn:nbn:de:101:1-2009030919

Stone, D., Patton, B., & Heen, S. (1999). *Difficult conversations: How to discuss what matters most*. New York: Penguin Books.

Stulberg, J. (1996). Facilitative versus evaluative mediator orientations: Piercing the "grid" lock. *Florida State University Law Review, 24*, 985.

Ury, W. L., Brett, J. M., & Goldberg, S. B. (1988). *Getting disputes resolved*. San Francisco: Jossey-Bass.

Wiseman, V., & Poitras, J. (2002). Mediation within a hierarchical structure: How can it be done successfully? *Conflict Resolution Quarterly, 20*(1), 51–65.

Zand, D. E. (1972). Trust and managerial problem-solving. *Administrative Science Quarterly, 17*(2), 229–239.

Chapter 12
Conflict-Positive Organizations: Applying Mediation and Conflict Management Research

Dean Tjosvold, Paulina Wan, and Moureen Tang

Managers and employees regularly confront conflict with each other as well as with customers and suppliers. They disagree as they propose various ideas to make decisions and as they express their frustrations as they coordinate their work, they use conflicts to reflect upon and update their products and methods. Industrial relations professionals and researchers have emphasized that conflict is inevitable in organizations and that managers, employees, and industrial relations and other human resource professionals should be prepared to manage them openly and fairly (Burgess et al. 2014; Buttigieg et al. 2014; Macneil and and Bray 2014). Employees, for example, inevitably have grievances that should not be ignored but dealt with by established procedures in order to restore relationships and coordination (Kougiannou et al. 2015; Whalen 2008). Managing conflict is thought to be the effective, fair way for owners, managers, and employees to develop resolutions that share the benefits and the burdens of their joint work (Premalatha 2012). Conflicts dealt with constructively help organizations meet the diverse needs for efficiency and profitability while at the same time promoting employee well-being (Boxall 2014; Greer et al. 2013).

Mediation has a long history in conflict management research and practice as it identifies various activities designed to support disputants in resolving their conflicts by developing mutually beneficial solutions (Poitras et al. 2015). Union and company representatives mediate as they handle grievances (Budd and Colvin 2008;

The authors thank WU Xinru Crystal for her valuable assistance in developing this chapter.

D. Tjosvold (✉)
Team and Conflict Management Center, Jiangxi University of Science and Technology, Jiangxi, China
e-mail: tjosvold@ln.edu.hk

P. Wan • M. Tang
Department of Management, Lingnan University, Tuen Mun, Hong Kong SAR, China

© Springer International Publishing Switzerland 2016
K. Bollen et al. (eds.), *Advancing Workplace Mediation Through Integration of Theory and Practice*, Industrial Relations & Conflict Management 3, DOI 10.1007/978-3-319-42842-0_12

Dhiaulhaq et al. 2014; Lounsbery and Cook 2011) and managers and employees mediate as they discuss formal and informal complaints (Elizabeth 2013; Harris et al. 2012; Latreille et al. 2012). The aim of this chapter is to help organizations prepare and empower members so that they can mediate and manage their conflicts constructively even without outside intervention.

Managing conflict constructively is often challenging (Bradley et al. 2013). The most common and available mediation activity is to assist disputants to discuss and deal with their conflicts directly and constructively. This chapter argues that organizations can be developed in such a way that managers and employees understand the value of conflict management and practice the skills of constructive dialogue. It shows how managers, employees, IR and HRM professionals can use theory and research on conflict management and mediation to develop conflict-positive organizations that support constructive conflict management between managers and employees as well as within and between teams, departments and organizations (Poitras et al. 2015; Tjosvold and Wang 2013). Within conflict-positive organizations, managers and employees recognize that conflicts need to be managed directly and fairly and that employees are encouraged to voice their opinions and express their frustrations (Tjosvold 1991). As they expect each other to respond openly, they find initiating as well as resolving conflicts much easier.

Developing these conflict–positive organizations requires considerable investment. Managers and employees should understand the nature of productive discussions and develop open-minded skills; they should also strengthen their relationships because high quality relationships are foundations for constructive discussion (Tjosvold et al. 2014b).

This chapter has five sections. The first one argues that employees need leadership so that they know that they and their colleagues understand and are jointly committed to managing conflict cooperatively. The second part argues that conflict management theory can provide teams and organizations with a common understanding of conflict and the major approaches they have to deal with their conflicts. The third section reviews research documenting that managing conflict cooperatively for mutual benefit very much supports organizations and teams. The fourth section identifies important ways for managers and leaders to develop cooperative goals and open-mindedness discussion for cooperative conflict management. The last part uses a case study of an organization applying theory and research to become more conflict-positive.

Leadership for Motivation

Managers, team members, and employees confront many conflicts, including how to consider and deal with their conflicts (Tjosvold et al. 2014a). They have different opinions about the nature of conflict and how these conflicts should be dealt with. Is it better to forget and to move on to different issues, or should they discuss directly their issues with each other, or should they let their superiors decide or suppress the conflict, or should they involve a neutral third party from outside the company? Differences in understanding the nature of conflict and how to deal with it are often not discussed directly and openly (Argyris and Schon 1996). Differences in understanding frustrate conflict management practice because conflict is something that people do together; if one protagonist is unwilling or unable to discuss conflicts openly and effectively, it's very difficult to manage conflict (Deutsch 1973; Deutsch et al. 2014).

The theory of cooperation and competition can provide a common understanding of conflict and how managers and employees can manage them. Leaders are needed to use this theory to develop a foundation of understanding among employees and managers of constructive conflict management. This common understanding of constructive conflict and also a mutual commitment to making conflicts productive highly contribute to conflict-positive organizations.

Effective leadership has long been thought to require "working with and through others". Similarly, managers have to work with and through disputants if they are going to foster effective mediation. Managers might act as a mediator by asking disputants to engage in direct, face-to-face discussions with each other to develop mutually beneficial resolutions. But for the mediation to be successful, disputants have to express their ideas and feelings directly, work to understand the opposing views, and to develop mutually beneficial solutions (Polster 2011). Disputants must confront their conflicts together and develop resolutions. Managers must work with and through disputants to be effective mediators.

Conflict Theory as a Common Mission and Guide

Theories of conflict management can help organizational members identify their own and each other's approaches to conflict. Theories can also help them reach agreement on how they would like to address disagreements. Since most conflicts require joint resolution, both sides have to agree to a new way of interacting. Imposing resolutions might be appropriate under some conditions, but not as a general approach to conflict management.

This section shows the value of applying the theory of cooperation and competition (Deutsch 1973) to define and manage conflict. The theory does not identify one strategic action suitable for all conflicts, but is a foundation for how managers and employees can decide how to deal with their specific conflicts.

Defining Conflict

Researchers as well as managers have typically considered defining conflict of secondary importance; indeed, they have resolved differences by including several notions into their definition of conflict (Barki and Hartwick 2004). This section proposes that defining conflict as incompatible actions is a much stronger foundation for research than defining conflict as opposing interests.

Deutsch's (1973) theory of cooperation and competition defines conflict as incompatible activities; one person's actions interfere, obstruct or in some way get in the way of another's action (Tjosvold et al. 2014a). Conflicts can be based on opposing goals and interests but also occur when people have common goals. They may for example disagree about the best means to achieve their common goals. Incompatible activities occur in both cooperative and competitive contexts. Whether the protagonists believe their goals are cooperative or competitive very much affects their expectations, interaction, and outcomes as they approach conflict.

Cooperative and Competitive Contexts of Conflict

Deutsch (1973) theorized that how group members believe their goals are related very much affects the nature of relationships and interaction that they develop. Cooperation occurs when individuals perceive that they can reach their goals if and only if the other individuals with whom they are cooperatively linked also reach their goals, that is, there is a mutual positive relationship among goal attainments. In this case, people in a group will promote each other's efforts to achieve their goals. In conflict, emphasizing cooperative goals by demonstrating a commitment to pursue mutual benefit solutions has been shown to create high quality solutions and strengthen relationships (Deutsch et al. 2014).

Competition occurs when individuals perceive that they can obtain their goals if and only if the other individuals with whom they are competitively linked fail to obtain their goals, that is, there is a perceived negative relationships among goal attainments. As one disputant reaches his or her goals, the others cannot reach their goals.

Approaches to Managing Conflict

Understanding goal interdependence (whether it is competition or cooperation) very much affects how people discuss and negotiate their conflicts (Deutsch 1973). With cooperative goals, disputants negotiate for mutual benefit. People take a "we are in it together" attitude and seek solutions that will benefit all. With these positive expectations, they are more likely to discuss issues directly and open-mindedly where they consider and integrate each other's views as they seek to develop mutually beneficial solutions by engaging in mutual problem solving (De Dreu et al. 2001). The interaction induced by cooperative goals is labeled the cooperative approach to conflict management (e.g., Alper et al. 2000; Chen et al. 2005; Tjosvold 2008; Tjosvold et al. 2006).

Disputants may also believe that their goals are competitive. They treat conflict as a win-lose contest and engage in actions as overstating their own position to get their way and demanding that others agree with their position. These disputants expect that others will not reciprocate openness and concessions and may even obstruct efforts; protagonists are often inflexible, resulting in deadlocks or the imposing of a solution by the more powerful ones. The interaction process induced by competitive goals is called the competitive approach to conflict (Alper et al. 2000; Chen et al. 2005; Tjosvold 2008).

Research has also recognized that disputants may avoid conflict by trying to smooth over conflict and minimize direct exchange. They communicate that opposing ideas should be minimized rather than discussed openly (Peng and Tjosvold 2011). Avoiding conflict has proved ineffectual as a general approach to managing conflict (Friedman et al. 2006; Ng and Feldman 2011; Tjosvold and Sun 2002).

Impact of Approaches

To the extent that mediators and disputants develop strong cooperative goals and low levels of competition, they have laid the groundwork for effective mediation and the constructive resolution of conflicts. Mediators often call face-to-face meetings for disputants in order for them to understand each other's ideas and positions and to create mutually beneficial resolutions. Many studies document that a strong cooperative context where disputants believe that their goals are cooperatively related promotes listening and understanding opposing views, integrating these views to create new, mutually beneficial resolutions that disputants accept and implement (Deutsch et al. 2014; Tjosvold et al. 2014b).

Disputants who believe their goals are competitively related are unprepared to engage in mediation activities effectively. Studies indicate that competitors tend to avoid open and direct discussion if they can (Tjosvold et al. 2014a). When they discuss directly with each other, competitive disputants, though they may listen and understand others' views, they often reject and disparage the opposing views. They try to show that their views are superior and should dominate and "win" the discussion by forcing others to accept their resolutions. People who assume that their conflicts are competitive are unlikely to be able to develop constructive ways of managing their conflicts despite opportunities to meet and discuss.

The next section briefly reviews research documenting the value of the cooperative approach to conflict for organizations. The following section outlines how managers and other mediators help disputants develop cooperative conflict management by strengthening cooperative goals and open-minded discussion skills.

Constructive Role of Cooperative Context

Several studies have demonstrated that cooperative management of conflict has both short-term and long-term significant benefits for both organizations and individuals in many situations (Halpert et al. 2010; Somech et al. 2009; Tjosvold et al. 2014a). This section illustrates the value of managing conflict cooperatively by reviewing research on how it contributes to leadership.

Leadership researchers have very much supported that successful leaders develop high quality relationships with employees so that they can coordinate and work with and through individual employees (Graen and Uhl-Bien 1995). Studies also indicate that managing conflict cooperatively with individual employees develops and maintains these quality relationships (Chen and Tjosvold 2006, 2008; Chen et al. 2008).

Recently, researchers have begun to understand that leaders may have their effects not just simply on the individuals but also on how employees relate to each other (DeGroot et al. 2000; Dionne et al. 2004). For example, studies have shown that leaders using a variety of leadership styles are effective to the extent that they help employees manage conflict cooperatively so that they can coordinate and make decisions effectively.

For example, a study conducted in India investigated the impact of leadership values on conflict management among subordinates (Bhatnagar and Tjosvold 2012). Results showed that productivity values encouraged cooperative, open-minded controversy and team effectiveness and productivity. The study's findings suggest that leader productivity values coupled with cooperative conflict management provide a foundation for effective teamwork. Zhang et al. (2011) found that transformational leadership improved team coordination and performance when subordinates employees managed conflict cooperatively. Servant leadership emphasizes service to others, team consensus, and the personal development of individuals (Wong et al. 2015); findings indicate that teams with servant leaders discussed their disagreements, frustrations, and difficulties cooperatively and worked out solutions for the benefit of the team and their customers. Although servant leaders maybe thought of as avoiding conflict, they were found to promote open and constructive conflict management.

These and other recent studies emphasize the value of quality relationships between leaders and employees and among employees. Through these relationships, leaders can motivate employees and help them manage conflict and perform.

Developing Cooperative Conflict Management

Conflict management is something to do as well as to understand. Key ways to develop cooperative conflict management are strengthening cooperative goals and developing open-minded discussion skills (Tjosvold and Tjosvold 2015).

Cooperative Goals

Ideally as they approach a conflict, managers and employees realize that they have a strong cooperative context. They realize that they have a common task in that they should make one set of recommendations, develop and produce a new product, or solve a problem together. Team members are encouraged to integrate their ideas and develop one solution and product.

Understanding that they need to coordinate and use each other's abilities helps convince disputants they have cooperative goals. They recognize that their own personal rewards are based on team performance, they receive more tangible and intangible rewards the stronger the team performance. Disputants who have built a community where they know each other as persons and identify as a team also have cooperative goals. As their goals are cooperative, they realize that their achievement and rewards depend to a great extent on how effective the whole team is. Disputants then are likely to conclude that they "are in this together" and that they "sink or swim together". At this point, they will want to resolve their conflicts cooperatively.

Open-Minded Discussion

With these cooperative goals, disputants must still work out their conflicts. Mediators can help disputants develop open-minded discussion skills that complement cooperative goals (Richter and Tjosvold 1980; Tjosvold and Deemer 1980; Tjosvold and Tjosvold 2015). Employees can be trained to express their own views and prepare to be direct and persuasive. Disagreeing is an opportunity to know opposing positions as well as to develop and express one's own. Listening and understanding opposing views as well as defending one's own makes discussing issues more challenging but also more rewarding.

Disputants recognize that conflict is an opportunity to develop new solutions. They do not assume that only their own and the opposing view exists, they can put together the best ideas from several standpoints to create new alternatives. Conflicts are opportunities to resolve their disputes but they may have to engage in repeated discussions to reach an agreement that is mutually beneficial. They may, for example, be unconvinced that the evidence warrants modifying their original positions. They may have to continue to discuss their opposing views until they develop a mutually beneficial resolution.

Teams and organizations can develop supportive norms and patterns to help team members be open with their ideas, open to other views, and integrate them. Managers and employees understand that they should seek the best reasoned judgment, not winning; they criticize ideas, not people; they listen and learn everyone's position, even if they do not agree with it; they differentiate positions before trying to integrate them; and they change their mind when logically persuaded to do so.

Becoming a Conflict Positive Organization

We (Tjosvold and Tjosvold 2015, 1995) have been experimenting and applying cooperative conflict management in our family business since the mid-1970s. We provide residential services for people with special needs from nursing care, developmental assistance, elderly, and traumatic brain injury. Like other businesses, ours also has conflicts and it is more effective for the clients and employees when they are managed cooperatively. We want employees throughout the company to join us as we use the theory of cooperation and competition and related ideas to understand and strengthen the business.

Workshops

Workshops promote continuous learning and reinforcement for staff of their cooperative interdependence and need to discuss conflicts open-mindedly. Managers and employees get involved through short lectures, structured activities, and reflection to learn more about cooperation and competition and how managing conflict cooperatively can help them strengthen their teamwork and leadership.

These workshops are particularly valuable because managers and employees are learning ideas and practicing their open-minded discussion skills together. They can see that people throughout the organization want to and are developing the skills of cooperative conflict management. Workshops are concrete ways for leaders to develop shared understanding and common commitment to managing conflict cooperatively.

Book Clubs for Leadership and Mediation

Book Clubs are an important way for using theory and research to develop cooperative, open-minded leadership and teamwork throughout the company. Mary, as the CEO of the company, offers managers and supervisors from different units within the company to form a Book Club to read and discuss a teamwork and leadership book, such as one of our own (Tjosvold and Tjosvold 2015). Before a session, they read a chapter and prepare to discuss and criticize the ideas of the chapter. They also reflect on their own experiences by identifying concrete times when they faced a similar problem. During later sessions, they describe specific times when they have used ideas from the book to strengthen their leadership.

For example, after reading a chapter on managing a conflict with an employee, they talk about specific times when they managed a conflict with one of their employees. They brainstorm concrete ways that they can apply the chapter's ideas so that they can manage conflict with employees more effectively. At the next meeting, they discuss their attempts to apply the ideas and get suggestions for how to continue and improve their efforts at dealing with conflicts with employees openly and constructively. This way, managers and supervisors encourage and provide concrete support to improve their conflict management.

Team discussion of ideas, reflecting on experiences, and making commitments on how to improve are powerful ways to learn and become a leader. People throughout the company use the model to have fruitful conversations about their experiences as they develop their teamwork and leadership. The model helps everyone have a common understanding of the kind of conflict management they want to use and the qualities of the organization they want to develop.

Conclusion

This chapter has summarized a theory and team oriented approach to mediation that has been less used than the traditional reliance on outside experts. We are not saying that leaders can easily adopt this team approach and help disputants manage their own conflicts cooperatively and directly. Indeed, managers and employees have to work hard in order to understand the theory of cooperation and competition and develop the teamwork needed to apply it effectively. However, to work in an organization is to be in conflict (Maynes and Podsakoff 2013). To take advantage of joint work requires ongoing conflict management.

Research challenges the common assumption that conflict is harmful and that the less of it and the quicker it is resolved the better. We know that conflict, when managed cooperatively, can solve problems, get things done, strengthen relationships, and enhance individuals. Current research suggests that mediation can highly contribute to the effectiveness of organizations.

References

Alper, S., Tjosvold, D., & Law, K. S. (2000). Conflict management, efficacy, and performance in organizational teams. *Personnel Psychology, 53*(3), 625–642.

Argyris, C., Schon, D. A., & Schon, D. A. (1996). *Organizational learning II: Theory, methods and practice*. Reading: Addison-Wesley.

Barki, H., & Hartwick, J. (2004). Conceptualizing the construct of interpersonal conflict. *International Journal of Conflict Management, 15*(3), 216–244.

Bhatnagar, D., & Tjosvold, D. (2012). Leader values for constructive controversy and team effectiveness in India. *The International Journal of Human Resource Management, 23*(1), 109–125.

Boxall, P. (2014). The future of employment relations from the perspective of human resource management. *Journal of Industrial Relations, 56*(4), 578–593.

Bradley, B. H., Klotz, A. C., Postlethwaite, B. E., & Brown, K. G. (2013). Ready to rumble: How team personality composition and task conflicts interact to improve performance. *Journal of Applied Psychology, 99*, 385–392.

Budd, J. W., & Colvin, A. J. S. (2008). Improved metrics for workplace dispute resolution procedures: Efficiency, equity, and voice. *Industrial Relations, 47*(3), 460–479.

Burgess, J., Cameron, R., & Rainnie, A. I. (2014). Contemporary research on work, workplaces and industrial relations in Australia. *The Economic and Labour Relations Review, 25*(1), 5–9.

Buttigieg, D. M., Deery, S. J., & Iverson, R. D. (2014). Voice within trade unions? A test of the voice and loyalty hypothesis. *Journal of Industrial Relations, 56*(1), 3–23.

Chen, Y. F., & Tjosvold, D. (2006). Participative leadership by American and Chinese managers in China: The role of relationships. *Journal of Management Studies, 43*, 1727–1752.

Chen, Y. F., & Tjosvold, D. (2008). Goal interdependence and leader-member relationships for cross-cultural leadership in foreign ventures in China. *Leadership & Organization Development Journal, 29*, 144–166.

Chen, G., Liu, C. H., & Tjosvold, D. (2005). Conflict management for effective top management teams and innovation in China. *Journal of Management Studies, 42*, 277–300.

Chen, Y. F., Tjosvold, D., & Wu, P. G. (2008). Effects of relationship values and goal interdependence on Guanxi between foreign managers and Chinese employees. *Journal of Applied Social Psychology, 38*, 2440–2486.

De Dreu, C. K., Evers, A., Beersma, B., Kluwer, E. S., & Nauta, A. (2001). A theory-based measure of conflict management strategies in the workplace. *Journal of Organizational Behavior, 22*(6), 645–668.

DeGroot, T., Kiker, D. S., & Cross, T. C. (2000). A meta-analysis to review organizational outcomes related to charismatic leadership. *Canadian Journal of Administrative Sciences/Revue Canadienne des Sciences de l'Administration, 17*(4), 356–372.

Deutsch, M. (1973). *The resolution of conflict*. New haven: Yale University Press.

Deutsch, M., Coleman, P. T., & Marcus, E. C. (2014). *The handbook of conflict resolution: Theory and practice* (3rd ed.). San Francisco: Jossey-Bass Publishers.

Dhiaulhaq, A., Gritten, D., De Bruyn, T., Yasmi, Y., Zazali, A., & Silalahi, M. (2014). Transforming conflict in plantations through mediation: Lessons and experiences from Sumatera, Indonesia. *Forest Policy and Economics, 41*, 22–30.

Dionne, S. D., Yammarino, F. J., Atwater, L. E., & Spangler, W. D. (2004). Transformational leadership and team performance. *Journal of Organizational Change Management, 17*(2), 177–193.

Elizabeth, S. (2013). Overcoming barriers to mediation in intake calls to services: Research-based strategies for mediator. *Negotiation Journal, 29*(3), 289–314.

Friedman, R., Chi, S. C., & Liu, L. A. (2006). An expectancy model of Chinese-American differences in conflict-avoiding. *Journal of International Business Studies, 37*, 76–91.

Graen, G. B., & Uhl-Bien, M. (1995). Relationship-based approach to leadership: Development of leader-member exchange (LMX) theory of leadership over 25 years: Applying a multi-level multi-domain perspective. *Leadership Quarterly, 6*, 219–247.

Greer, I., Schulten, T., & Böhlke, N. (2013). How does market making affect industrial relations? Evidence from eight German hospitals. *British Journal of Industrial Relations, 51*(2), 215–239.

Halpert, J. A., Stuhlmacher, A. F., Crenshaw, J. L., Litcher, C. D., & Bortel, R. (2010). Paths to negotiation success. *Negotiation and Conflict Management Research, 3*, 91–116.

Harris, L., Tuckman, A., & Snook, J. (2012). Supporting workplace dispute resolution in smaller businesses: Policy perspectives and operational realities. *The International Journal of Human Resource Management, 23*(3), 607–623.

Kougiannou, K., Redman, T., & Dietz, G. (2015). The outcomes of works councils: The role of trust, justice and industrial relations climate. *Human Resource Management Journal, 25*(4), 458–477. Early View. http://onlinelibrary.wiley.com/doi/10.1111/1748-8583.12075/pdf.

Latreille, P. L., Buscha, F., & Conte, A. (2012). Are you experienced? SME use of and attitudes towards workplace mediation. *The International Journal of Human Resource Management, 23*(3), 590–606.

Lounsbery, M. O., & Cook, A. H. (2011). Rebellion, mediation, and group change: An empirical investigation of competing hypotheses. *Journal of Peace Research, 48*(1), 73–84.

Macneil, J., & Bray, M. (2014). Third-party facilitators in interest-based negotiation: An Australian case study. *Journal of Industrial Relations, 55*(5), 699–722.

Maynes, T. D., & Podsakoff, P. M. (2013). Speaking more broadly: An examination of the nature, antecedents, and consequences of an expanded set of employee voice behaviors. *Journal of Applied Psychology, 99*, 87–112.

Ng, T. W. H., & Feldman, D. C. (2011). Employee voice behavior: A meta-analytic tests of the conservation of resources framework. *Journal of Organizational Behavior, 33*, 216–234.

Peng, A. C., & Tjosvold, D. (2011). Social face concerns and conflict avoidance of Chinese employees with their Western and Chinese managers. *Human Relations, 64*(8), 1031–1050.

Poitras, J., Hill, K., Hamel, V., & Pelletier, F. B. (2015). Managerial mediation competency: A mixed-method study. *Negotiation Journal, 31*(2), 105–129.

Polster, J. C. (2011). Workplace grievance procedures: Signaling fairness but escalating commitment. *New York University Law Review, 86*, 638–671.

Premalatha, U. M. (2012). Industrial relations: An approach to improve productivity and profitability referring to select units of Mumbai industries development corporation. *International Journal of Marketing and Technology, 2*(7), 95–102.

Richter, F. D., & Tjosvold, D. (1980). Effects of student participation in classroom decision making on attitudes, peer interaction, motivation, and learning. *Journal of Applied Psychology, 65*(1), 74.

Somech, A., Desivilya, H. S., & Lidgoster, H. (2009). Team conflict management and team effectiveness: The effects of task interdependence and team identification. *Journal of Organizational Behavior, 30*, 359–378.

Tjosvold, D. (1991). *The conflict-positive organization: Stimulate diversity and create unity.* Reading: Addison-Wesley.

Tjosvold, D. (2008). The conflict-positive organization: It depends upon us. *Journal of Organizational Behavior, 29*(1), 19–28.

Tjosvold, D., & Deemer, D. K. (1980). Effects of controversy within a cooperative or competitive context on organizational decision making. *Journal of Applied Psychology, 65*(5), 590.

Tjosvold, D., & Sun, H. F. (2002). Understanding conflict avoidance: Relationships, motivations, actions, and consequences. *The International Journal of Conflict Management, 13*(2), 142–164.

Tjosvold, D., & Tjosvold, M. M. (1995). *Psychology for leaders: Using, motivation, conflict and power to manage more effectively.* New York: Wiley.

Tjosvold, D., & Tjosvold, M. M. (2015). *Building the team organization: How to open minds, resolve conflict and ensure cooperation.* Basingstoke: Palgrave MacMillan.

Tjosvold, D., & Wang, L. (2013). Developing a shared understanding of conflict: Foundations for Sino-Western mediation. *China Media Research, 9*(4), 76–84.

Tjosvold, D., Law, K. S., & Sun, H. (2006). Conflict in Chinese teams: Conflict types and conflict management approaches. *Management and Organization Review, 2*, 231–252.

Tjosvold, D., Wong, A., & Chen, N. Y. F. (2014a). Cooperative and competitive conflict management in organizations. In O. B. Ayoko, N. M. Ashkanasy, & K. A. Jehn (Eds.), *Handbook of conflict management research* (pp. 33–50). Cheltenham: Edward Elgar Publishing.

Tjosvold, D., Wong, A. S. H., & Chen, N. Y. F. (2014b). Constructively managing conflicts in organizations. *Annual Review of Organizational Psychology and Organizational Behavior, 1*, 545–568.

Whalen, C. J. (2008). *New directions in the study of work and employment: Revitalizing industrial relations as an academic enterprise.* Cheltenham: Edward Elgar Publishing.

Wong, A. S. H., Liu, Y., & Tjosvold, D. (2015). Service leadership for adaptive selling and effective customer service teams. *Industrial Marketing Management, 46*, 122–131.

Zhang, X. A., Cao, Q., & Tjosvold, D. (2011). Linking transformational leadership and team performance: A conflict management approach. *Journal of Management Studies, 48*, 1586–1611.

Part IV
New Developments

Chapter 13
Looking Back to Leap Forward: The Potential for e-mediation at Work

Jennifer Parlamis, Noam Ebner, and Lorianne D. Mitchell

In this chapter, we provide an overview of the broad field of Online Dispute Resolution (ODR) so that we can set the stage for a more nuanced discussion of how e-mediation might contribute to dispute resolution mechanisms in the workplace. We discuss the context in which e-mediation has developed and grown, and consider non-e-commerce uses for e-mediation such as the use of e-mediation in workplace conflicts. The primary aims of this chapter are (a) providing an overview of the ODR field and (b) provoking new and promising areas of expansion for e-mediation generally, and in the workplace specifically. We propose several research avenues as well as suggestions for the application of e-mediation to online and in-person workplace disputes based on relevant research. It is our hope that this chapter will encourage further exploration and experimentation in the field of e-mediation at work.

A Brief History of Online Dispute Resolution

Alternative Dispute Resolution (ADR) is a spectrum of legal and extra-legal methods for conflict resolution through which parties attempt to come to an agreement short of litigation ("alternative dispute resolution" n.d.). ADR processes have existed for centuries (Rule 2002) and predate formal court systems (McManus and

J. Parlamis (✉)
University of San Francisco, San Francisco, CA, USA
e-mail: jparlamis@usfca.edu

N. Ebner
Creighton University, Omaha, NE, USA

L.D. Mitchell
East Tennessee State University, Johnson City, TN, USA

© Springer International Publishing Switzerland 2016
K. Bollen et al. (eds.), *Advancing Workplace Mediation Through Integration of Theory and Practice*, Industrial Relations & Conflict Management 3,
DOI 10.1007/978-3-319-42842-0_13

Silverstein 2011). Indeed, indigenous populations from around the world have used mediation and reconciliation approaches that are reflected in current ADR practices (for an example, see Wall and Callister's (1995) discussion of Ho'oponopono, a traditional Hawaiian conflict resolution technique). Modern-day ADR, as it is practiced primarily in the US and elsewhere in the global West, involves using a neutral third party to provide assistance of one sort or another to resolve a conflict between two opposed parties (Benyekhlef and Gelinas 2005). The use of mediation – in which an external third party assists disputing parties to reach agreement but has no power to prescribe agreements or outcomes (Kressel and Pruitt 1989; Wall and Dewhurst 2001) – is fast becoming the process with which many ADR professionals identify the field itself (Mayer 2004).

Over the course of the past two decades, technology has swept across the field of dispute resolution, much as it has many other fields (see, generally, Rule 2002; Abdel Wahab et al. 2012). While many professionals originally resisted the notion of engaging technology for resolving conflicts (and some still do), others saw this as an opportunity for evolutionary growth of the field. Early thinkers on the juxtaposition of technology and dispute resolution realized that the significance technology posed for addressing conflict was deep, substantial, and positively disruptive (see Katsh and Rifkin 2001; Rule 2002). Technology can assist conflicting parties, as well as the third party, in ways so significant that it becomes, in essence, a "fourth party". Conceptualizing technology as a fourth party, as suggested by Katsh and Rifkin (2001), allows for envisioning not only ways in which human third parties can avail themselves of technology to get their work done, but also tasks and roles that technology can perform on its own. First and foremost, of course, is facilitating all of the scheduling, document management and communication tasks (such as – providing a chat room or an email system for interparty communication) that the third party traditionally needs to manage. "The 'fourth party' primarily assists the third party providing conveniences and efficiencies…[and] capabilities that allow tasks to be performed more quickly or at a distance" (Katsh 2012, p. 32). However, the fourth party can go beyond providing administrative support, and this is where the more dramatic shifts lie. The fourth party can not only provide new capacities to the parties in conflict and the third party in conducting and supporting their communications, but going even further, the fourth party can provide substantive input to parties themselves. Finally, technology can perform conflict systems roles to such an extent that the fourth party *supplants* the third party, either by performing large parts of the third party's roles on its own or by rendering them unnecessary (Fig. 13.1).

Online dispute resolution (ODR) is a broad term for conflict or dispute resolution that uses technology as the fourth party. Graham Ross, the founder of TheMediationRoom, defines ODR as "the use of information and communications technology that help parties find a resolution to their disputes" (Ross 2014). Developing since the mid 1990s, ODR has experienced significant growth following the advent of e-commerce and the ubiquity of the Internet for personal and professional use (Abernethy 2003; Ebner 2012a; Goodman 2003). ODR originated primarily in North America (Pearlstein et al. 2012), as businesses and consumers

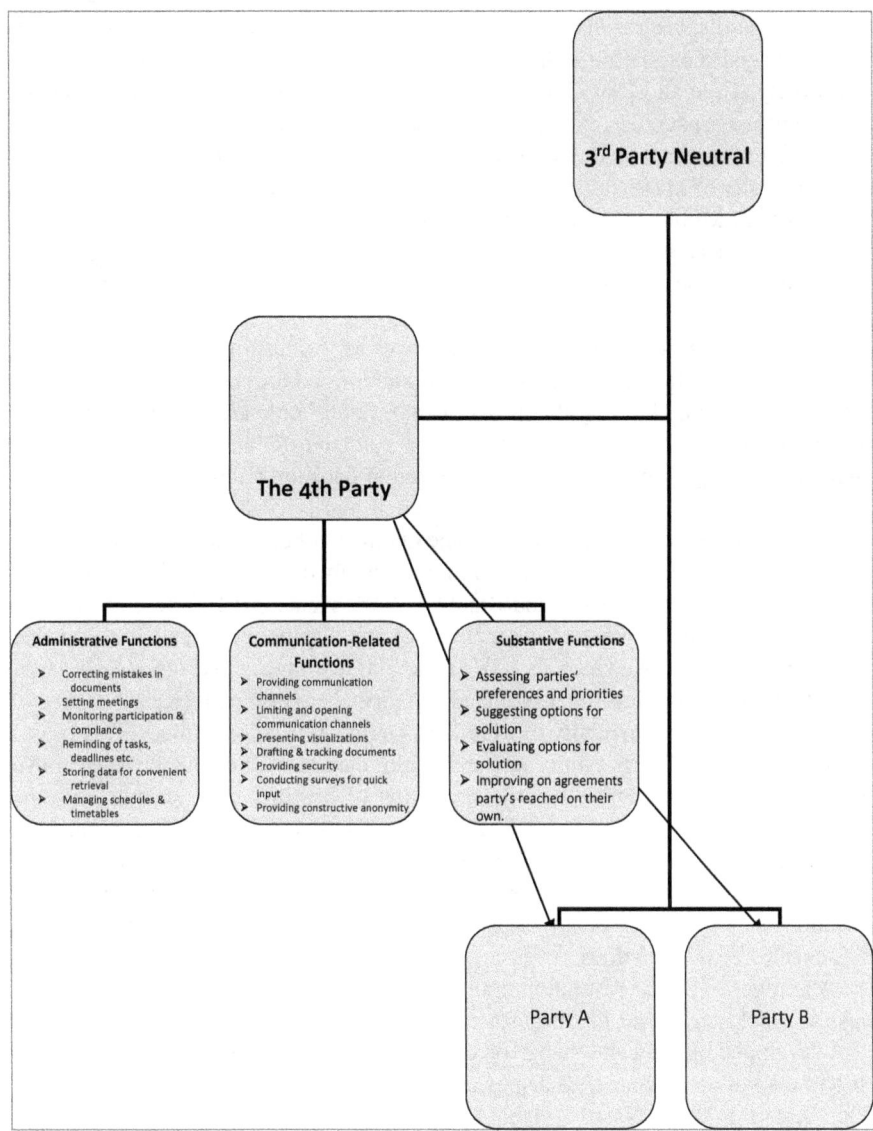

Fig. 13.1 The potential roles and functions of the fourth party

began interacting in cyber-space to buy and sell products. Conflicts and disputes that arose as a result of these interactions had no immediate apparent means for resolution. While conflict resolution service providers were available to deal with conflicts originating in traditional venues and markets, similar capacity was not present in cyberspace (see Rule 2002). E-commerce pioneers (such as eBay and Amazon) established online dispute resolution platforms for disputes arising out of online transactions in their marketplaces. eBay, for example, engaged SquareTrade

as an online dispute resolution provider, for managing processes in which disputants engaged, negotiating either on their own or with the assistance of a neutral
third party (Cole and Blankley 2006). Other ODR initiatives at that time included
conferences sponsored to explore online resolution methods (see www.odr.info) and
ODR endeavors such as the Virtual Magistrate, the Online Ombuds project out of
the University of Massachusetts, and the Cybertribunal project originating out of the
University of Montreal (Benyekhlef and Gelinas 2005; Pearlstein et al. 2012; Katsh
2012) as well as a number of ODR start-ups such as Cyber Settle, WeCanSettle, and
Settlement Online (For a more comprehensive history of ODR see Abdel Wahab
et al. 2012).

These early projects had different objectives as well as different mechanisms of
use. The Virtual Magistrate's goals were to examine disputes arising online, between
users of a system, claiming that posts or information uploaded to that system was
wrong or harmful, and the system's operator – and to offer an inexpensive, efficient
and useful solution in the form of an arbitration decision (Benyekhlef and Gelinas
2005). The arbitration process was conducted primarily via email, and the decisions
were to be posted on a public website. The Online Ombuds office was broader in its
mission and is still active today providing online mediation services for many different types of disputes (Cole and Blankley 2006; Katsh 2012). The Cybertribunal
offered mediation and arbitration services, for any disputes commencing in an electronic environment (Katsh et al. 2001; Rule 2003). Importantly, these early initiatives focused on conflicts that originated in a virtual environment (Katsh 1996) with
one exception: The University of Maryland Online Mediation Project. This project
was designed to address family law and health care-related disputes where conve-
nience, clear and complete records, reduction of hostility and rehearsability and
reprocessability (see Dennis et al. 2008 for discussion of these communication
media characteristics) were explicit goals. This last example is most similar to the
goals and audience for e-mediation in a workplace context where long-term lasting
solutions as well as an eye toward future relationships is critical. We discuss these
issues in more detail below.

A number of online resolution options developed quickly in the 2000s and then,
just as quickly, evolved or disappeared (Pearlstein et al. 2012). For example, one
that developed quickly and then evolved is SquareTrade, originally used by eBay; it
still exists but no longer offers dispute resolution. Others, such as SettlementOnline,
OneAccord and clickNsettle, viable up until the mid-2000s, now no longer exist.
One example of an ODR vendor that has demonstrated staying power was started by
Colin Rule, one of the founders of the systems that e-Bay first used for ODR. Rule
established Modria as an online "resolution center" that uses an automated resolution technique to produce a resolution to a disputant (e.g., a business disgruntled
consumer) by collecting and analyzing information provided by a disputant and
aligning the data with approved procedures and guidelines of the business. In such
a system, the large majority of cases are resolved through the automated system,
and only very few require intervention of a third human party, in addition to the
fourth party.

It is unclear why some ODR platforms stick and others do not. While a thorough discussion of this topic is beyond the scope of this chapter, some brief comments on the topic may be helpful in informing how e-mediation could succeed or remain helpful in a system over the long-term. One possibility is that the e-marketplace changes and evolves at a rapid pace that ODR platforms have difficulty matching. An ODR system deeply embedded into the workings of one particular entity, such as in the case of eBay, can take into account operational changes and can be tweaked anytime the operation is significantly changed. A second, related, idea is that certain types of repeat customer issues and complaints that created the volume of disputes that necessitated certain ODR processes in the first place, no longer existed as issues. As e-businesses adapted and addressed common conflict points, certain primary ODR functions may have become obsolete. Once again, closely matching an ODR system to the larger system it is embedded in, and constantly verifying that the ODR system is delivering what the larger system needs, seems to be key. Finally, those ODR platforms that are the most longstanding or "sticky" seem to be simple, clear, efficient, scalable and adaptable. Taking heed of these points might raise the odds of ensuring a workplace ODR system's efficacy and longevity.

Another important comment to make up front is that, while conducting a wide survey of the many different attempts at initiating and sustaining ODR projects and systems is helpful to give a general sense for ODR's potential to impact conflict, one must be cautious in extrapolating the value of using ODR in any particular context, system or environment such as the workplace-dispute context. Previous ODR projects and initiatives have focused on different types of relationships, that may have more or less pertinence to workplace conflict: some initiatives have intervened in ongoing relationships (e.g., divorce mediation projects) whereas others have attempted to settle one-shot disputes after which there will clearly be no relationship. Further, while some have focused on solving an immediate problem, others have explored changing or transforming relationships. When exploring ODR's application in a particular context, we advise to combine tempering enthusiasm based on ODR's potential in general with a contextual look at its application and success in that particular context.[1]

e-mediation in Context

e-mediation has recently begun to attract attention as an independent subspecialty of ODR. Similar to in-person mediation, e-mediation is a voluntary dispute resolution process assisted by a neutral third party (Ebner 2012a). Different from its

---

[1] In particular, we will note that a lot of the optimism and historic successes underlying the positive narrative of ODR's potential has its roots in ODR's application to resolving specific issues pertaining to buyer/seller transactions on internet marketplaces. This is not to imply that ODR cannot be applied successfully to deeply transforming complex, ongoing, relationships – it is only to provide the type of tempering comment we alluded to in the text.

in-person counterpart, e-mediation is also assisted by a fourth party. e-mediation relies on information technology (synchronous or asynchronous text-based media, audio communication, or video-conferencing) to facilitate the mediation process (Ebner and Thompson 2014; Harmon 2006).

ODR is a rapidly developing field without clear, accepted delineations in terminology, and clear categorizations for processes (see, e.g., Ebner and Zeleznikow 2015). Mediation itself has become a 'fuzzy' term when used as 'e-mediation'. For example, conversely to the third party-conducted process envisioned in the definition above, others have used the term e-mediation to describe processes in which two conflicting parties are given substantive assistance by technology, *without* any involvement by a human third party. e-mediation may be completely automated (with computer-prompted information gathering, auto-decision resolution mechanisms and no human interaction). Some might call this type of fourth party intervention "Assisted Negotiation" or "Automated Negotiation" (e.g., see Smartsettle) rather than e-mediation. The more substantive the fourth party's role is, the more it engages in making tactical recommendations, or calculating optimal outcomes (as opposed to only offering a communication platform or a series of forms parties can fill out and send to one another), the more common it is to find these systems dubbed eNegotiation, Negotiation Support Systems (NSS) and, at times, e-mediation.

We do not aim to settle this issue in this paper. However, in our own discussion in this chapter, we will separate between processes in which human mediators are involved and processes in which technology is intended to preclude the use of human mediators by means of referring to the former as e-mediation and the latter as eNegotiation (following the approach taken by Thiessen et al. 2012). We will mainly focus on e-mediation, but will give some consideration to eNegotiation in order to highlight the potential to create a system that incorporates automated elements together with elements involving human intervention. Both uses of technology might find their place in a workplace e-mediation system, as we will discuss below.[2] This distinction between automated processes and processes with human attention and intervention is necessary, in order to reflect an evolution in the field of ODR itself that will undoubtedly affect the way such processes are developed for workplace mediation.

e-mediation, at this point, has not made significant inroads in 'regular' ADR practice, addressing the cases that a mediator encounters in her day-to-day practice. A variety of reasons may have contributed to this. Party and mediator hesitations about use of technology certainly played a role. Another factor was the high entry

---

[2] Whatever the delineation between e-mediation and eNegotiation might be, the delimitation between e-mediation and eArbitration is crystal clear. As online mediation has developed, so too has online arbitration. In online arbitration processes, the decision might be made by a human arbitrator or generated by a fourth party applying a set of algorithimic rules. Whoever the decision maker is, though, the outcome is clear: parties either abide by the outcome (in binding arbitration, the process which most online arbitration falls under) or one party (or both) rejects it (in nonbinding arbitration); one way or another, the outcome does not reflect a party-negotiated and agreed decision. In mediation, the outcome is always dependent upon party agreement. For more on online arbitration, see Abdel Wahab 2012.

barrier facing an individual mediator wishing to engage in online practice: the need to build a 'platform' on which to host their practice and conduct their processes. At a certain point, this barrier was lowered, as mediators were able to 'rent' use of a platform from larger service providers much as part-time mediators might rent occasional meeting space to conduct mediation sessions in a dispute resolution center (Juripax and TheMediation Room have each offered such services in the past; currently Modria offers something similar). However, more recently, both of these factors are dissolving. Parties and professionals alike are becoming increasingly comfortable with using online communication for many aspects of their lives; carrying this over to dispute resolution is a natural move. Additionally, the barrier of acquiring or building a 'platform' has disappeared, as practitioners realized they could offer to conduct mediation processes over platforms available at low-to-no cost, such as via Skype or Google Hangouts.

As a result, the 'service providers' who dominated the ODR scene for the first decade and a half of the field's development are being joined by a swelling number of ADR practitioners, offering individualized e-mediation services through familiar technologies (Ebner 2012a). This trend is likely to increase interest in developing ODR elements that are not focused on high-volume automation but rather on delivery of personalized, individual, as-close-to-traditional-as-possible, mediation—at a distance.

This shift has implications not only for the mix of professionals offering services but also for the nature of the services themselves and the interparty interaction patterns they involve. Communications theory differentiates between communication patterns and capabilities across different types of media (see Dennis et al. 2008). One basic distinction is between synchronous communication and asynchronous communication. In synchronous communication, parties transmit and receive messages in-real-time, with no time-gap. When communicating asynchronously, a party may receive a message a minute, an hour or a day after it was transmitted, and might respond a minute, and hour or a day after receiving the message, all of which introduces time-gaps into the interaction. Another distinction relates to a medium's capacity to support a variety of contextual cues – the elements of conversation that go beyond the words themselves, such as tone, body language, volume and pace. Changes in communication tools affect the communication they support, and the interactions this gives rise to. Applying this to trends in e-mediation, we suggest that the rise of individualized e-mediation services may contribute to a shift away from the asynchronous, text-based form-based message exchanges that have dominated e-mediation thus far, towards more interactive, synchronous, cue-rich and dynamic interactions. As referred to before, e-mediation used to focus primarily on text-based communication methods; however, nowadays synchronous video seems to be the medium of choice for individual mediators adding an online component to their traditional practice (Ebner 2012a, b). This shift, in turn, may have significant implications for the models of mediation that have hitherto been linked with e-mediation (e.g., these have been more along the directive and problem-solving side of the mediation spectrum rather than on the facilitative or transformative side) (see Hammond 2003). A call for greater focus on e-mediation as a means of transformation in intractable political conflicts has been heard, and is pushing tech-nology and practitioners to stretch e-mediation to adapt for such processes (see Tyler and Raines 2006). This might be of particular importance to workplace e-mediation, given the success of transformative mediation programs in this area (see Nabatchi and Bingham 2001; also see Raines 2005, for discussion of taking a transformative approach in online mediation). All these developments in the field of online mediation, we suggest, highlight the compatibility of such processes for workplace disputes, as we will discuss below.

e-mediation: Not Just for Online Disputes

As mentioned above, historically, ODR generally (and e-mediation more specifi-cally) began as a resolution mechanism for disputes that originated online; however, it quickly evolved to include disputes that have their genesis offline as well. Early on, developments in the field uncovered that e-mediation can be positive for high emotion or high cost issues such as family mediation or workplace conflict (Goodman 2003) as it removes a lot of the contextual cues (such as vocal tone, facial expressions and other non-verbal communication) present in face-to-face mediation that may further escalate existing tension between parties. Of these two counterintuitive contexts (for more on the reasoning for treating these two contexts as related, and for treating them as counterintuitive in terms of ODR-suitability, see Ebner 2012a), the efficacy of e-mediation has been more fully explored and docu-mented in family mediation (Bollen and Euwema 2013; Getz 2010). In the context of workplace mediation, however, there is more conjecture than research.

Importantly, not all workplace disputes are similar, in the context of suitability for e-mediation. Envisioning virtual workplace mediation, involving people in organiza-tions spread out across the globe, or between members of virtual teams working at-a-distance (see, e.g., Ebner 2008; Rule 2003) seems like a reasonable application of the ADR precept of 'fitting the forum to the fuss' (Sander and Goldberg 1994); the suitability of conducting an online process between people who sit together in adjoin-ing cubicles, on the other hand, might require deeper exploration. The one study conducted to date did not involve a full-on online mediation process; rather, it showed that adding an online component to a traditional, face-to-face mediation process, could contribute to its effectiveness; the online component served to eliminate the asymmetry inherent to hierarchal workplace disputes (Bollen and Euwema 2013).

While more research is needed to further explore the reasons why e-mediation might be successfully applied in these contexts, it has been hypothesized that com-plicated ongoing relationships with extensive connections and patterns of dysfunc-tional interpersonal communication might be better served by the structured and controlled e-mediation context (see Syme 2006) – although this is mostly the case in asynchronous applications. In addition, swift resolution and cost reduction have also been put forth as explanations for the growth of e-mediation outside of the e-commerce arena (Lavi 2015).

Implied by some authors (see Tyler and Raines 2006), e-mediation might be appropriate for those who are more "native" to the technology boom. It is suggested that for those born into the technology generation, resolution methods like e-mediation will be considered commonplace and natural. Therefore, e-mediation might be particularly beneficial and appropriate for use with certain generations, regardless of the fact that their geographic location in no way precludes their participation in face-to-face processes. Indeed, it has been argued that e-mediation might expand its traditional repertoire of email, automated processes, telephone and video-conferencing to include virtual reality, holography, mobile phones and internet radio (see Hattotuwa 2006; Syme 2006); doubtlessly all this will occur over time, and new technologies will be incorporated as well. Identifying the most effective communication media for a particular organization—or for particular employees in an organization—will be an important part of designing workplace e-mediation systems.

Research on e-mediation in the Workplace

Research on e-mediation is limited. "Most published studies have focused mainly on descriptions of the phenomenon and discussion of its potential benefits and challenges" (Turel et al. 2007, p. 541). What we provide here is an overview of the limited research along with suggestions for future areas of investigation and implications for e-mediation at work. By e-mediation at work, we mean any dispute or conflict that arises in the context of one's employment, in the same physical space or across the globe. It should be noted that this is not an exhaustive review of this literature or only research on e-mediation in workplace conflicts; rather, it's a selection of research that can provide insight into e-mediation at work and new directions for its development.

Research on Effectiveness of e-mediation

One of the first research projects assessing the effectiveness of e-mediation was conducted by Katsh and colleagues (2000). Researchers collected complaints from individuals using the eBay site. The majority of disputes involved non-delivery, non-payment or reputational issues. A single mediator worked with disputants to resolve the complaint. All communication was managed by the mediator and used text-based communication, e-mail, for all interaction. Out of 225 complaints submitted, 37 had 1 party refuse to participate, 50 were mediated successfully and 58 ended in impasse. The other 80 complaints were not suitable for applying mediation for a number of reasons. For example, some of them were cases in which the complainant notified the project within a day or two that the complaint had been resolved without any intervention by the project. Others were complaints that had nothing to do with the project's specific case-focus of buyer-seller complaints or indeed, had nothing to do with eBay transactions at all. These researchers acknowledged the limitations of the e-mail medium for building trust and facilitating reframing, both critical determinants of success in mediation, and suggested that more sophisticated technology (such as videoconferencing and new software platforms) might lead to greater outcome success.

Druckman et al. (2004) conducted three studies that assessed the impact of technology-facilitated negotiation and mediation on outcomes using comparison groups. This research used a NSS system that performed mediation functions (such as diagnosis and advice) through the use of carefully crafted questions, not a human mediator. They found that technology-facilitated groups that employed a support system to assist in problem identification, analysis and recommendations had significantly more agreement and fewer impasses across seven negotiable issues than those in the "reflection condition" where participants individually reflected on the communications and, in a second experiment, where disputants were given advice only. In addition, satisfaction with the outcome was significantly better for the technology-facilitated group, although process fairness and legitimacy did not differ. In a third study, technology-facilitated mediation (using a NSS) was not shown to differ significantly from live mediation; however, participants indicated a significant preference for a live mediator over technology-facilitated resolution systems. Participants found the live mediator more helpful for overcoming disagreements and resolving issues overall.

More recent research (Bollen and Euwema 2008) conducted jointly with Juripax (a leading European ODR platform based in the Netherlands acquired by Modria in the spring of 2014, see juripax.com/modria), the Dutch Legal Aid Board, University of Tilburg and Catholic University of Leuven, found that roughly 76 % of online mediations resulted in agreement, 8 % in partial agreement and 16 % ended in impasse. Not only did the objective outcomes suggest significant success for e-mediation but also the subjective ratings of well-being, emotions, voice, satisfaction and justice indicated positive outcomes. For example, 75 % of participants indicated that they experienced average to very little or no stress resulting from the online mediation, negative emotions such as anger, frustration and disappointment were only reported to be felt to a "small degree", and roughly 80 % indicated that they would use e-mediation in the future and recommend it to others. This research used human mediators trained in online mediation techniques and Juripax procedures.[3]

Possibly, the most comprehensive study of introducing online mediation into a dispute context unrelated to e-commerce was the Distance Mediation Project (here-

---

[3] We review these findings from a variety of contexts, given the general paucity of research conducted on e-mediation. Of course, one should be cautious in generalizing any set of outcomes and insights across contexts; for example, generalizing from divorce mediation to workplace mediation. Each area has its own particular set of patterns and interests which may not exist, or may not be as salient, in other contexts. We hope to see research and evaluation components attached to e-mediation projects in a variety of areas, providing insights of how each is affected by the online environment.

inafter 'the Project' (see Tait 2013), conducted in British Columbia, Canada between 2007 and 2012. This project stands out not only for its bold approach in implementing online mediation in a structured and professional manner, but also for the in-depth evaluation that accompanied all phases of the project, providing both quantitative and qualitative data and recommendations for best practices. The project focused on family mediation, taking on the challenge of mediating disputes with powerful relational and emotional elements at a distance. After an initial feasibility-probing phase, the next two phases implemented mediation in 23 and 46 mediation cases, respectively. Mediations were conducted over landline telephones, cell phones, videoconferencing and email, usually combing two or more media in any given case. Settlement rates for the Project were equivalent or a little higher than the settlement rates achieved through comparable face-to-face programs. Parties reached full or partial agreement in 70 % of the first run of cases and in 85 % of the second. For those who measure process effectiveness through settlements, these numbers are more than satisfactory. This effectiveness is reinforced by reports of party and mediator satisfaction. Parties were satisfied with the distance mediation process to a very high degree (even in cases where they were less satisfied with the outcome). 78 % of parties who had previously participated in other, face-to-face, mediation processes, thereby having a personal frame of comparison, indicated that their satisfaction the Project mediation compared "favorably" or "very favorably" to their previous experience. When all participants were asked whether they would use online mediation again, should they be faced with another dispute, 73 % responded affirmatively with only 10 % indicating they would prefer a face-to-face interaction. Mediators, too, were very satisfied with working in the online environment. They reported that their assessment of the level of difficulty working with parties online was about the same as working with them in the room, and that both formats produced equally good results. All in all, the Project demonstrated that family mediation can be carried out safely, competently and appropriately through online methods, even when large distances separate between parties and between them and their mediator (all the data and findings for the Project, can be found in Getz 2010; Tait 2013).

The economic impact of ODR was recently explored by Rule (2012). The ODR system used in this research was based on an e-commerce dispute resolution system similar to what might be described as assisted negotiation or eNegotiation. The aim of this research was to go beyond self-reports of satisfaction, which correlate positively with outcome and do not appear to align with consumer behavior. Research showed that users increased activity on the e-commerce website after engaging in its ODR process regardless of the results of this process; they were more active on the site than those who never had a problem to resolve regarding use of the site. While this research did not directly involve e-mediation per se, it does highlight two potential ancillary benefits of ODR that should be part of future research in the e-mediation realm. Both trust (consumer confidence) and loyalty seem to be positively related to engaging in an ODR process. Ebner (2012b) has also suggested that trust generated in an ODR process might spill over to engender other kinds of trust in other related contexts. If this is the case, it is possible that engaging in e-mediation in the workplace, might impact trust and loyalty to particular organizations, units or teams. This could have significant economic impact for organizations by limiting unnecessary turnover and increasing productively, to name only a few outcomes. This is obviously an empirical question to be tested; however, the potential for far reaching positive consequences of e-mediation in the workplace has been implied.

Perceived Usefulness of the Online System

Whether or not disputants will engage in e-mediation is largely dependent on perceptions of usefulness of the online resolution system. Turel and colleagues (2007) found that perceived usefulness of the information system supporting the mediation was a significant predictor of the attitude toward online mediation. Interestingly, the mediator, per se, was not shown to have a significant impact on online mediation attitudes. This suggests that when applying e-mediation in the workplace, employers should be particularly careful to employ an e-mediation platform that is perceived to be useful. This could mean that the online systems are easy to use, allow for organization of the issues, easy review of progress and preparation for the final agreement (all statements in the construct "Perceived Usefulness of the System" in the study by Turel et al. 2007). It should be noted that in e-mediation in the workplace, the disputants might know the mediator personally and the other party very well. This could impact the relationship between perceived usefulness of the mediator and attitudes toward online mediation. As such, we use caution in generalizing from these findings to the workplace. Investigating attitude towards online mediation when the mediator is known would be a possible area for future research.

In a study investigating attitudes toward use of negotiation support systems (NSS), it was found that social acceptance was integral to adoption of a NSS. Researchers found that individuals will ask others' advice and rely heavily on the opinions of referent others when choosing the NSS (Pommeranz et al. 2011). This suggests that organizations implementing an e-mediation system should carefully craft a rollout that creates experiences with the system to build positive word of mouth. In addition, Pommeranz and colleagues (2011) suggest that social networks should be integrated into systems that assist with negotiation, keeping in mind preferences for confidentiality. This research offers a number of other guidelines for NSS that could be applied to e-mediation at work.

Other Variables

Several other variables have begun to gain attention in the e-mediation research literature; these include hierarchy and power, face saving and language use, and gender and justice perceptions. Hierarchical and power differences were investigated in a study assessing "e-supported" mediations where the use of electronic intake procedures with a human mediator was compared with traditional face-to-face intake (Bollen and Euwema 2013). This research found that ratings of satisfaction with the mediation were equivalent for subordinates and supervisors in the e-supported condition but were significantly lower for subordinates in the in-person intake conditions. Thus, the researchers concluded that hierarchical differences were eased when participants utilized an electronic intake process facilitated by a human mediator.

The impact of emotional expression and language use on the likelihood of dispute resolution was investigated using eBay disputes filed for mediation with the SquareTrade resolution website (Brett et al. 2007). They found that negative emotions and commands expressed online in the early stages of the mediation directly back and forth to the disputants decreased the likelihood of resolution while causal accounts increased it. It should be noted that this research involved asynchronous communication before a mediator got involved.

Recent work (Bollen et al. 2014) has investigated the role of gender in asynchronous e-mediation where couples undergoing divorce proceedings exchanged emails with the assistance of a professional e-mediator. Settlement rates were higher than in-person mediation with 84 % of couples reaching agreement. Perceptions of four different types of justice (distributive, procedural, interpersonal and informational) were examined. Procedural and distributive justice were related to agreement for women while informational justice perceptions appeared to be related to men reaching an agreement. These authors suggest that the use of e-mediation procedures might increase women's perceptions of agency and power and advocate for more research in this area.

There is much research yet to be done on e-mediation; "the critical success factors for these services, and specifically the effects of the online environment, are yet to be explored" (Turel et al. 2007, p. 540). Based on our brief review of the literature we see four main areas in which the research can expand. First, e-mediation systems come in many different forms (e.g., technology-automated or assisted by a third party, synchronous or asynchronous) and can use many different technologies (e.g., email, video, phone) as mentioned above. Research should investigate and compare the different technologies and their efficacy. Relatedly, matching technology to context and disputants could be an area of examination. As an example, text-based communication such as email or threaded discussions might be beneficial for technology natives and high emotion disputes, video conferencing or holographic interaction might increase settlement for globally distributed teams with equal power. Second, underlying causal mechanisms for why e-mediation might be successful in some contexts and not others would be very worthwhile. This would allow mediators to adjust techniques to fit particular disputes, personalities or circumstances. Third, variables that might moderate the impact of e-mediation on settlement success should be examined. Currently, very few exogenous variables have been investigated, save a few such as hierarchy and power. The impact of sex, age, status, and culture of the disputants as well as the sex, age, status and culture of the e-mediators should be investigated as they relate to mediation outcomes. Fourth, a greater understanding of e-mediation as practiced across cultures and in different countries would enhance our understanding and application of e-mediation at work.

Suggestions for Workplace e-mediation

Research on e-mediation suggests that it is a low-stress, positive-valence process (Bollen and Euwema 2013) that may increase user trust in the mediation process and outcome (Rule 2012). Building on this foundation, we offer some suggestions to aid in the implementation and administration of workplace e-mediation programs.

First, in order for them to be beneficial to those involved, workplace e-mediation programs must be perceived as useful (Turel et al. 2007). The impartial third party may initiate the process by sharing information supporting the usefulness of e-mediation across several different contexts. Only when trust in the process is established should the third party facilitator/mediator proceed with e-mediation so as not to engage in an exercise in futility.

Second, the mixed results achieved by the studies conducted by Druckman and colleagues (2004) lead us to suggest that technology (the fourth party in the mediation) should be used earlier, rather than later, in the e-mediation process. Specifically, parties in conflict may complete computer-assisted assessments of themselves and the specific issues of the disagreement in order to diagnose the problem and offer initial solutions. This will help make the e-mediation process more efficient in that the 'meeting' (face-to-face or virtual) time with the mediator will be spent on resolving the dispute rather than parties arguing about the details of the related issues.

Third, the e-mediator may initiate joint conversations with the conflicting parties to commence the work of finding a resolution. This will likely prove difficult if the relationship between the conflicting parties is so broken that face-to-face communication is dysfunctional. Given the limitations of email for building trust in mediations (Katsch et al. 2000), we suggest synchronous mediums of communication such as 3-way videoconferencing between the two conflicting parties and the mediator, which would be more effective in low conflict situations than in highly escalated conflicts. Even if the parties are in their offices in the same building, this virtual medium (whether fully or partially synchronous or asynchronous) may remove some of the negative emotions from the situation and de-emphasize possible status differences (Bollen and Euwema 2013) in order for the mediation to proceed. Some excellent examples of e-mediation using Skype conferencing for workplace conflicts can be found at virtualmediationlab.com. These videos show synchronous virtual conferencing with a human mediator. This is very similar to what might be adopted by employers interested in convenient, low cost e-mediation. If asynchronous communication is required, mediators should be well versed in the challenges communication media pose to communication and trust, and the ways to overcome these (see Ebner 2012b).

Fourth, to continue the last point, mediators in an e-mediation project in the workplace must be experts in delivering dispute resolution services at a distance, rather than face-to-face. This may require specialized training in this form of mediation (for an example of training material specifically oriented to this arena, see Ebner and Efron 2012) and a deep understanding of its unique best practices (for an example of best practices developed by and for online family mediation by the Distance Mediation Project, see Jani and Getz 2012). It also requires special mastery of the technological platform being used (Hammond 2003; Getz 2010).

Finally, e-mediation programs should be adaptable so that they will have longevity in the workplace. A point person or committee should periodically review its aims and efficacy as well as its potential for further impact in the workplace. As the root cause of common issues is eradicated, the program should evolve to address other causes of workplace disputes.

To summarize, an effective workplace e-mediation program should be useful, efficient, and adaptable. Of course, each and every one of these elements must be contextualized, in terms of conflict type, parties' typical needs, and the type of technological platform used. Programs may be used to resolve disputes originating either online or in the physical work environment. A second model of workplace e-mediation may consist of a more blended or hybrid format which may be more appropriate for individual organizations that do not have the time, funding, or expertise to develop an ODR platform.

Conclusion

This chapter began by briefly discussing the history and development of ODR. Next, we reviewed e-mediation more specifically, discussed the context in which e-mediation has developed and grown, and considered the non-e-commerce uses for e-mediation. Then, we examined the scant research on e-mediation and offered suggestions for new research streams to expand our knowledge of the e-mediation field. Finally, we explored implications for workplace e-mediation focusing on the necessary conditions required to adopt e-mediation at work. We hope that this chapter encourages efforts to apply e-mediation to disputes that originate at work with co-located colleagues. Seeing e-mediation as not just for dispersed individuals or for e-commerce is a critical paradigm shift.

References

Abdel Wahab, M. S., Katsh, E., & Rainey, D. (Eds.). (2012). *ODR: Theory and practice*. The Hague: Eleven International Publishing.

Abernethy, S. (2003). *Building large-scale online dispute resolution & trustmark systems*. Proceedings of the UNECE Forum on ODR. Retrieved from http://odr.info/unece2003.

Alternative Dispute Resolution. (n.d.). *Cornell University Law School*. Retrieved from www.law. cornell.edu/wex/alternative_dispute_resolution.

Benyekhlef, K., & Gelinas, F. (2005). Online dispute resolution. *LexElectronica, 10*(2). Retrieved from http://ssrn.com/abstract=1336379.

Bollen, K., & Euwema, M. (2008). *Report: Online mediation in divorce cases*. Retrieved from https://www.juripax.com/Publications/Online_mediation_leuven.pdf.

Bollen, K., & Euwema, M. (2013). E-supported mediations: The use of an online intake to balance the influence of hierarchy. *Negotiation and Conflict Management Research, 6*(4), 305–319.

Bollen, K., Verbeke, A. L., & Euwema, M. C. (2014). Computers work for women: Gender differences in e-supported divorce mediation. *Computers in Human Behavior, 30*, 230–237.

Brett, J. M., Olekalns, M., Friedman, R., Goates, N., Anderson, C., & Lisco, C. C. (2007). Sticks and stones: Language, face, and online dispute resolution. *Academy of Management Journal, 50*(1), 85–99.

Cole, S. R., & Blankley, K. M. (2006). Online mediation: Where we have been, where we are now, and where we should be. *The University of Toledo Law Review, 193*, 1–22.

Dennis, A. R., Fuller, R. M., & Valacich, J. S. (2008). Media, tasks, and communication processes: A theory of media synchronicity. *MIS Quarterly, 32*(2), 575–600.

Druckman, D., Druckman, J. N., & Arai, T. (2004). e-Mediation: Evaluating the impact of an electronic mediator on negotiating behavior. *Group Decision and Negotiation, 13*(6), 481–511.

Ebner, N. (2008). Online dispute resolution: Applications for e-HRM. In T. Torres-Coronas & M. Arias-Oliva (Eds.), *Encyclopedia of human resources information systems: Challenges in e-HRM*. Hershey: Idea Group Reference Publishing.

Ebner, N. (2012a). E-mediation. In M. S. Abdel Wahab, E. Katsh, & D. Rainey (Eds.), *ODR: Theory and practice* (pp. 369–398). The Hague: Eleven International Publishing.

Ebner, N. (2012b). ODR and interpersonal trust. In M. S. Abdel Wahab, E. Katsh, & D. Rainey (Eds.), *ODR: Theory and practice* (pp. 214–248). The Hague: Eleven International Publishing.

Ebner, N., & Efron, Y. (2012). Rough day @ work: Resolving conflict through an online simulation. In E. Biech (Ed.), *The 2012 Pfeiffer annual of training* (pp. 67–76). San Francisco: Pfeiffer.

Ebner, N., & Thompson, J. (2014). @Face value? Nonverbal communication and trust development in online video-based mediation. *International Journal of Online Dispute Resolution, 1*(2), 103–124.

Ebner, N., & Zeleznikow, J. (2015). Fairness, trust & security in online dispute resolution. *Hamline Journal of Public Law and Policy, 36*(2), 143–160.

Getz, C. (2010). *Evaluation of the distance mediation project: Report on phase II of the technology-assisted family mediation project*. Retrieved from http://www.mediatebc.com/PDFs/1-2-Mediation-Services/Distance-Mediation-Project---Evaluation-Report.aspx.

Goodman, J. W. (2003). The pros and cons of online dispute resolution: An assessment of cyber-mediation websites. *Duke Law and Technology Review, 2*(1), 1–16.

Hammond, A. M. G. (2003). How do you write 'yes'? A study of the effectiveness of online dispute resolution. *Conflict Resolution Quarterly, 20*(3), 261–286.

Harmon, K. M. J. (2006). The effective mediator. *Journal of Professional Issues in Engineering Education and Practice, 132*(4), 326–333.

Hattotuwa, S. (2006). Transforming landscapes: Forging new ODR systems with a human face. *Conflict Resolution Quarterly, 23*(3), 371–382.

Jani, S., & Getz, C. (2012). *Mediating from a distance: Suggested practice guidelines for family mediators* (2nd ed.). Mediate BC Society: Vancouver. Available at http://www.mediatebc.com/PDFs/1-14-Family-Mediation---FAQs/Guidelines_Mediating-from-a-Distance-(Second-editi. aspx last viewed August 19th 2015.

Katsh, E. (1996). Dispute resolution in cyberspace. *Connecticut Law Review., 28*(4), 953–980.

Katsh, E. (2012). ODR: A look at history. In M. S. Abdel Wahab, E. Katsh, & D. Rainey (Eds.), *Online dispute resolution: Theory and practice* (pp. 21–37). The Hague: Eleven International Publishing.

Katsh, E., Rifkin, J., & Gaitenby, A. (2000). E-commerce, e-disputes, and e-dispute resolution: In the shadow of the "eBay law". *Ohio State Journal of Dispute Resolution, 15*(3), 705–734.

Katsh, M. E., & Rifkin, J. (2001). *Online dispute resolution: Resolving conflicts in cyberspace.* New York: Wiley.

Kressel, K., & Pruitt, D. G. (1989). Conclusion: A research perspective on the mediation of social conflict. In K. Kressel & D. G. Pruitt (Eds.), *Mediation research: The process and efffectiveness of third-party intervention* (pp. 394–435). San Francisco: Jossey Bass.

Lavi, D. (2015). No more click? Click in here: E-mediation in divorce disputes—the reality and the desirable. *Cardozo Journal of Conflict Resolution, 16*(2), 479–541.

Mayer, B. S. (2004). *Beyond neutrality: Confronting the crisis in conflict resolution.* San Francisco: Josey-Bass.

McManus, M., & Silverstein, B. (2011). Brief history of alternative dispute resolution in the USA. *CADMUS, 1*(3), 100–105. Retrieved from http://www.cadmusjournal.org/node/98.

Nabatchi, T., & Bingham, L. B. (2001). Transformative mediation in the USPS redress program: Observations of ADR specialists. *Hofstra Labor and Employment Law Journal, 18*, 399–427.

Pearlstein, A., Hanson, B., & Ebner, N. (2012). ODR in North America. In M. S. Abdel Wahab, E. Katsh, & D. Rainey (Eds.), *Online dispute resolution: Theory and practice* (pp. 443–464). The Hague: Eleven International Publishing.

Pommeranz, A., Wiggers, P., Brinkman, W. P., & Jonker, C. M. (2011). Social acceptance of negotiation support systems: Scenario-based exploration with focus groups and online survey. *Cognition, Technology & Work, 14*(4), 299–317.

Raines, S. S. (2005). Can online mediation be transformative? Tales from the front. *Conflict Resolution Quarterly, 22*(4), 437–451.

Ross, G. (2014). Online dispute resolution. What? Why? When? *Civil Mediation Council, Leeds.* Retrieved from PowerPoint lecture: http://webcache.googleusercontent.com/search?q=cache:PFxa2UpLM_kJ:www.civilmediation.org/downloads-get%3Fid%3D638+&cd=2&hl=en&ct=clnk&gl=us.

Rule, C. (2002). *Online dispute resolution for business: B2B, e-commerce, consumer, employment, insurance, and other commercial conflicts.* San Francisco: Wiley.

Rule, C. (2012). Quantifying the economic benefits of effective redress: Large e-commerce data sets and the cost-benefit case for investing in dispute resolution. *University of Arkansas Little Rock Law Review, 34*, 767–833.

Sander, F. E., & Goldberg, S. B. (1994). Fitting the forum to the fuss: A user-friendly guide to selecting an ADR procedure. *Negotiation Journal, 10*(1), 49–68.

Syme, D. (2006). Keeping pace: On-line technology and ADR services. *Conflict Resolution Quarterly, 23*(3), 343–357.

Tait, C. (2013). *Evaluation of the distance mediation project*: Report on phase III of the technology-assisted family mediation project. Retrieved from http://www.mediatebc.com/PDFs/1-2-Mediation-Services/Distance-Family-Mediation-Evaluation-Report-FINAL.aspx.

Thiessen, E., Miniato, P., & Hiebert, B. (2012). ODR and eNegotiation. In M. S. Abdel Wahab, E. Katsh, & D. Rainey (Eds.), *ODR: Theory and practice* (pp. 341–368). The Hague: Eleven International Publishing.

Turel, O., Yuan, Y., & Rose, J. (2007). Antecedents of attitudes towards online mediation. *Group Decision and Negotiation, 16*(6), 539–552.

Tyler, M. C., & Raines, S. S. (2006). The human face of on-line dispute resolution. *Conflict Resolution Quarterly, 23*(3), 333–342.

Wahab, M. S. A., Katsh, E., & Rainey, D. (2012). *Online dispute resolution: Theory and practice.* The Hague: Eleven International Publishing.

Wall, J. A., & Callister, R. R. (1995). Ho'oponopono: Some lessons from Hawaiian mediation. *Negotiation Journal, 11*(1), 45–54.

Wall, V. D., & Dewhurst, M. L. (1991). Mediator gender: Communication differences in resolved and unresolved mediations. *Mediation Quarterly, 9*(1), 63–85.

Chapter 14
It Takes Three to Tango: The Geometry of Workplace Mediation

Lourdes Munduate, Katalien Bollen, and Martin Euwema

The Changing Context of Workplace Mediation

During recent years, there has been a growing interest in the field of employment relations in the use of mediation as an important way to resolve disputes in the workplace (Bollen and Euwema 2015; Coleman in this volume). In the United States, mediation already has a long tradition in addressing different types of employment disputes, particularly in the public sector (Mareschal 2005) and more recently its use has increased in other sectors (Kressel 2014). In contrast to the United States, Europe has traditionally shown a marked reluctance to use extrajudicial strategies like mediation as a mean of settling disputes in the workplace, partly due to the stronger role of unions and legalization of labor relations (Rodriguez-Piñero et al. 1993). Currently however, labor mediation is more often promoted as a constructive way to limit the high costs of work disputes both at a collective and interpersonal level (De Palo et al. 2011; Sanders 2009). One example of the trend to promote mediation in and among European countries refers to the European Mediation Directive approved by the European Parliament in 2008. The stated objective is 'to facilitate access to dispute resolution and to promote the amicable settlement of disputes by encouraging the use of mediation and by ensuring a balanced relationship between mediation and judicial proceedings' (Art. 1). In line with this, the situation in the UK as described in this volume (see Deakin) reflects

L. Munduate (✉)
Faculty of Psychology, University of Seville, Seville, Spain
e-mail: munduate@us.es

K. Bollen
Department of Educational Research and Development, Maastricht University, Maastricht, The Netherlands

M. Euwema
Department of Psychology, University of Leuven, Leuven, Belgium

© Springer International Publishing Switzerland 2016
K. Bollen et al. (eds.), *Advancing Workplace Mediation Through Integration of Theory and Practice*, Industrial Relations & Conflict Management 3,
DOI 10.1007/978-3-319-42842-0_14

the Government's intention to promote the use of mediation as a way to increase efficiency in employment relations and to reduce 'the burden' on the employment tribunal system. This shift to a more informal and less confrontational method than grievance and disciplinary procedures (Davey and Dix 2011) involves not only the traditional large and public sector organizations or the new cooperatives in the third sector, but also government initiatives to pilot mediation networks within small and medium enterprises (Bennet 2013, 2014; BIS 2012). The same trend in the use of mediation can be observed in other regions such as Australia (Macneil and Bray 2013), Indonesia (Dhiaulhaq et al. 2014) or New Zealand, where mediation has been successfully incorporated into the legal framework by the Labour Reform (Anderson 2001; Corby 1999) and South Africa (see Jordan and De Wulf in this handbook).

The increased interest in mediation also reflects the changing nature of 'the social contract' between employer and employees which focuses more on individualized labor relations, or i-deals (Rousseau 2005). This is in line with the shift from formal dispute resolution to more 'interest-based' conflict management systems in organizations in which primary attention is paid to underlying interests, needs and wishes of parties instead of collective rules.

In this discussion, we address first the developments in the field of workplace mediation and its relation to the changing nature of employment relations and workplace mediation. In doing so, we refer to social exchange theory (Blau 1964; Munduate et al. 2016).

Another important issue to explore is the effectiveness of workplace mediation, and on a broader level the effectiveness of organizational dispute systems. In order to assess the effectiveness of mediation, we build further on the "geometry of workplace mediation" already introduced in the first chapter of this handbook. The geometry resulting from the combination of the three dimensions (regulations, roles and relations) as described by the 3R-model. The three dimensions included in the 'geometry' intend to capture the comparison of different properties within a three-dimensional space (Budd and Colvin 2008). Geometry is used as a metaphor to describe the landscape of conflicts. This has been used in the area of industrial relations, for example Hyman's (2001) 'geometry of trade unionism', Budd's (2004) 'geometry of employment relations' and Budd's and Colvin's (2008) 'geometry of disputes resolution procedures'. With this model, Budd and Colvin argue that an optimal dispute resolution procedure provides a balance between efficiency, equity and voice. The underlying assumption of these geometric models indeed is, that there should be a balance along diverse dimensions. These can be qualitative, such as in Budd and Colvin's model, however with the 3-R model we propose a contingency approach where characteristics of regulations, roles and relations together define the most appropriate design of a mediation system, as well as specifics of the mediation at hand. Criteria of efficiency, equity and voice might gain quite different weight depending on the regulations, roles and relations in a specific society, industry and organization.

The Paradox of Workplace Mediation Practice and Research

Three different though related social and economic factors meet in the field of labor relations to increase the use of mediation as a dispute resolution process, as enshrined in various chapters: ongoing individualization, new roles for employees and managers, and high pressures on judicial procedures.

First, the institutional structures of industrial relations transform by a declining coverage of union representation, alternative forms of employee's representation and new types of relationships between employees and employers (Munduate et al. 2016). This trend concentrates on individualization of employment relations and on developing flexible forms of dispute resolution processes at the level of the workplace such as mediation, next to a formal legal system (Budd and Colvin 2014; Dolder 2004).

Second, traditional forms of work have altered such as an increase in knowledge-intensive business services, self-managing work teams, lean production and human resource management policies that focus on high-involvement work systems. With higher educated workflows and high involvement of employees, conflict management becomes an even more essential skill at all levels. The different forms of third party assistance described in this handbook add to that, empowering the parties in conflict and in their conflict management. The role of the first line supervisor is emphasized as third party and conflict coach, throughout this volume. This however does not imply a reduction of formal mediation. An important message in most contributions in this handbook being, that mediation is of most value in a cooperative organizational culture, investing in constructive conflict management at a variety of levels. This starts with attitude and skills of management and employees in solving conflicts, as well as reducing barriers to involve third parties to assist early in a conflict process. Such informal dispute resolution procedures and collaborative conflict cultures contribute to better business performance and sustainability in employment relations (Boxall 2014; Gelfand et al. 2012).

Third, the collapse and the frequent inefficiency of the judicial system to solve workplace disputes (e.g. costs, delays, excessive formality and imposed solution) have driven policy makers to avoid the often confrontational routes of grievance and discipline in organizations (Bennet 2013). The new employment strategies are more focused on the interests of the parties, and search for the promotion of trust and rebuilding of damaged relationships (Lewicki et al. 2016).

These tendencies have fostered the provision and use of mediation-based services, both public and private. These services provide information, advice, public and in-house training courses, and help in case of employment disputes using independent mediation interventions or institutionalized public services, such as the Advice, Conciliation and Arbitration Service (ACAS) in the UK. As stated by Coleman et al. in this volume, the good news for mediation practitioners is that today there are plenty of different intervention techniques and strategies available for mediators which allow great flexibility when seeking to resolve disputes in the workplace.

Despite the increasing use of workplace mediation (Bollen and Euwema 2013a), there has been little empirical research that focuses in depth on workplace mediation or its effectiveness (Bollen and Euwema 2013a). Only in the beginning of the 1990s (Brett and Goldberg 1983; Conlon and Ross 1993; Karambayya et al. 1992; Kolb 1986; Lewicki and Sheppard 1985; Ury et al. 1993; Shapiro and Brett 1993), there has been some fragmented research on the role of third parties.

Effectiveness of labor mediation is often measured in terms of agreements and costs, compared with court and tribunal procedures. Recently, focus has shifted more towards satisfaction of parties with procedure and outcomes, on short and long term (Bollen et al. 2014; Budd and Colvin 2008; Dolder 2004; Poitras and Le Tareau 2009).

The paradox of mediation is that despite the increasing demands for mediation interventions, the practice of mediation in the employment field remains unsupported by systematic evidence-based research (Bollen and Euwema 2013a; Coleman et al. in this volume; Poitras and Le Tareau 2009). As Dolder (2004: 321) states: 'Somewhat surprisingly, the lack of research into the realities of mediation practice has not deterred policy makers from facilitating the movement away from tribunal-based disputes resolution'. Therefore, human resource managers trying to design effective dispute resolution systems in organizations, union leaders and experts in industrial relations advocating certain systems, or policymakers promoting or restricting various systems, need a common set of standards for evaluating and comparing workplace dispute resolution procedures (Budd and Covin 2008). In the absence of such standards there is a tendency to rely on fragmented research on the topic and anecdotal evidence regarding mediation's success in achieving agreements, and the beneficial impact of mediation in working relations to persuade organizations and individual disputants to accept prescriptive workplace services (Dolder 2004). This paradox of mediation is a concern shared by the authors of this volume, who try to fill this gap with evidence based contributions. In this sense, the different chapters in this handbook serve as a necessary bridge for the integration of both these fields which facilitate a significant development of workplace mediation as well as in a broader sense effective ways of conflict management and dispute resolution.

Social Exchange in Employment Relations and the Use of Workplace Mediation Frameworks

Workplace mediation cannot be examined in isolation from the underlying conflicts and patterns of relations in the workplace. The context of industrial relations and conflict management theories are the cornerstones of this handbook. The increasingly individualized nature of employment relationships and the shift from formal procedures of dispute resolution to more 'interest-based' conflict management systems design in organizations (Bennett 2014; Goldberg 2005), call for research on how contemporary conflict management systems could be implemented best in today's complex organizations. More specifically, which new developments of workplace mediation could be promoted, what are the most effective ways of mediation given certain situations, and how to integrate workplace mediation in a broader system of conflict management and resolution? Before we come back to this, we focus on analyzing the fit between ways of alternative conflict resolution and the new 'social contract' in employment relations.

A good starting point to understand the core social processes involved in the changing relationship between employers and employees and the role of workplace mediation in this framework, is social exchange theory, as first outlined by Blau (1964) and widely applied to current employment relations (see Guest 2004, 2016; Munduate et al. 2016). A central theme in this theory is that employees and employers may develop exchanges for social or economic reasons (e.g., pay and benefits) (Garcia et al. 2016). Traditionally, exchange is perceived in terms of economic value. That is, economic outcomes that address financial needs, are typically contractual and tend to be tangible such as wages or working conditions. However, exchanges can stand for something beyond plain material needs (e.g., being taken care of by the organization) and address parties' social needs and tend to be symbolic, such as justice, dignity or experience of recognition. These social outcomes send the message that the other party is valued and/or treated with dignity (Cropanzano et al. 2005; Shore et al. 2006). Both aspects of exchange are core to industrial relations and it is precisely these relational aspects – operationalized through indicators such as trust, commitment, empowerment and organizational support-, which gain relevance in today's workplace (Munduate et al. 2012). Consequently, the quality of the social aspect in employment relationships has been more and more embraced by contemporary scholars in analyzing the new industrial relations field (see Coyle-Shapiro and Conway 2004). It is clear that the use of workplace mediation fits very well with this interest for social relations (Goldberg 2005). Workplace mediation can be motivated both from economic and social exchange, reducing costs of conflict, and improving relations (Bennett 2013).

Workplace mediation seeks to avoid the often confrontational route of traditional procedures. Rather than attributing blame between disputants, mediation looks to promote trust and rebuild damaged relationships for the future (Bennet 2013; Lewicki et al. 2016).

The long-term perspective, highly promoted by mediation strategies, is also embedded in social exchange theory (Shore et al. 2006), predicting a positive return when one party does another a favor. This may explain the findings of Goldberg (2005) and Bennett (2013, 2014) showing the potential of mediation of rebuilding damaged relationships for the future. Social exchange theory offers a theoretical base as well as specific rules for the repair and development of constructive relations in the workplace and mediation is well situated in this framework.

The 3-R -Model and the Geometry of Workplace Mediation

The individualization of employment relations promotes the provision of private (or public) mediation services that 'may symbolize a movement towards facilitating the freedom of workers to negotiate their individual arrangements. This assumes that the parties are equal in the employment relationship and capable of participating in the production of individual solutions' (Dolder 2004: 322).

At the same time however, often a disparity of power is observed between the disputants on a subjective level (perception of power) or on a formal level (occupation of a certain hierarchical position). The pertinent question in workplace mediation therefore is: Are disputants sufficiently capable of negotiating with each other as equals, or will this merely reinforce the existing power imbalance? (Bollen and Euwema 2013b, 2015; Dolder 2004; Sanders 2009).

This topic of power imbalance is especially accentuated by the criticism of workplace mediation's appropriateness in cases of bullying and harassment (Branch et al. 2009; Keashly and Nowell 2011). This criticism argues that mediation could be seen as a shift towards silencing social criticism by hiding the process of conflict resolution from the public scrutiny (Ridley-Duff and Bennett 2011). Furthermore, in the extent that mediation focuses on the future and reconciliation, it has no mechanism to address or 'punish' past behavior, where in case of clearly defined victims and offenders such might be desirable (Keashly and Nowell 2011).

In order to assess the suitability and appropriate forms of mediation, it is needed to assess the qualities and effectiveness of employment relations (Munduate et al. 2016). Budd and Covin (2008) refer in this context to the geometry of the employment relations in order to evaluate dispute resolution alternatives.

Efficiency is the effective use of scarce resources and captures concerns with productivity, competitiveness, and economic prosperity. Equity entails fairness in both the distribution of economic rewards (such as equality in wages and benefits), the administration of employment policies (such as non-discriminatory selection and promotion processes), and the provision of employee security (such as safety standards and unemployment insurance). Voice is the ability to have meaningful employee input into workplace decisions both individually and collectively. While efficiency is a standard of economic or business participation; equity is a standard of treatment. Budd and Covin (2008) state that applying this framework to dispute resolution procedures provides a rich analytical framework in which researchers, practitioners, and policy-makers can analyze dispute resolution systems along the dimensions of efficiency, equity and voice. How does this relate to the 3-R model of workplace mediation?

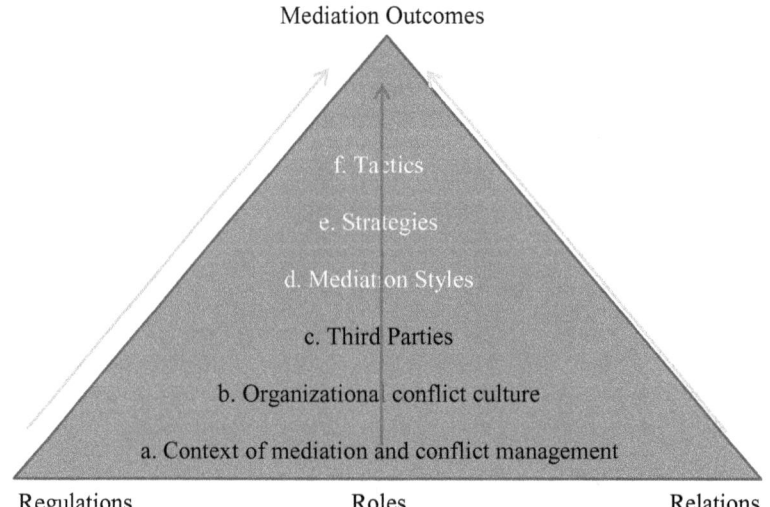

Mediation Outcomes

f. Tactics

e. Strategies

d. Mediation Styles

c. Third Parties

b. Organizational conflict culture

a. Context of mediation and conflict management

Regulations   Roles   Relations

Throughout this volume we have searched to understand and promote mediation effectiveness at two levels: case and system. The 3-R model of regulations, roles and relations can be applied at both, case and system level. The three criteria of Budd and Covin (2008) primarily help to evaluate mediation outcomes at system level. Such systems can be societal, sectoral and organizational. However, we believe these criteria can also offer a framework to evaluate the effectiveness of mediation cases. Through this, the 3-R model offers a multi-level approach to analyze mediation effectiveness. Outcomes and effectiveness of mediation cases are determined to a large extend by the surrounding system, as is symbolized in the 3-R model. We explore here both the mediation system and case level shortly.

Regulations and Roles Promoting Efficiency

The efficiency of the mediation system has been traditionally evaluated in terms of the optimization of limited resources, especially time and money (Bingham 2004). The findings of Golberg's (2005) research in the US, with a resolution rate of 86 %, indicate that this alternative can help resolve cases quicker and reduce the number of cases that move to litigation, therefore saving time, money and distress of the participants. In the same direction, the findings of Bennett (2014) on mediation in higher education in the UK, show the potential of mediation to reduce costs in terms of time and the emotional distress of the disputants going through the formal process, which in the worst case could lead to a costly employment tribunal hearing. The inclusion of emotional distress as a non-financial cost is considered a good indicator of efficiency by Budd and Covin (2008) as disputants may suffer psychological costs and disrupt social relations, which, in turn, negatively affect organizational efficiency and individual careers. Finally, the extent to which the system fosters productive employment is proposed as another indicator of efficiency (Budd and Covin 2008). Supporting this dimension, the study of Bennet (2014) reported that the implementation of mediation systems at universities in the UK coincides with a drive for performance management for all staff and especially for academic staff. These outcomes therefore strongly encourage to implement accessible workplace mediation services.

Proposition 1 Regulations and Roles should promote access and use of high quality mediation services.

Efficiency also is an important criteria for evaluation of mediation cases. Investment of time and money, and particularly timeliness of procedures, contribute a lot to the quality of mediation. In this sense also new technology can contribute to efficiency (see Parlamis in this handbook). Furthermore, the use of external and internal mediators can contribute substantially to access and efficiency of mediation (Jordaan and DeWulf this handbook).

Proposition 2 Regulations of mediation and roles of mediators should promote efficiency in the mediation process, thereby reducing different costs of all parties involved.

3-Rs Promoting Equality in Relations

The equality criteria of the mediation process can be markedly improved. This brings our focus on the relational dimension of the 3-R model. Equality has been traditionally evaluated in terms of 'fairness' and the underlying judgements of procedural justice by participants (Goldberg 2005; Goldman et al. 2008; Shapiro and Brett 1993; Kals et al. this handbook). This aspect of the equality of the mediation process, in comparison to other alternative dispute resolution systems, is the base of the model proposed by Ridley-Duff and Bennett (2011). Their theoretical framework for understanding different dispute resolution alternatives distinguishes between authority driven alternatives based on standards of evaluation of facts and arguments (such as litigation and arbitration) where law is the highest authority, and experience driven alternatives based on standards of legitimation of perspectives (such as conciliation and mediation) where the disputants are the highest authority. The authority driven alternatives look for the 'best practice' as defined by law, while other alternatives look for the 'discovery of appropriate practice' in the process. Taking into account these differences, mediation strategies begin to challenge the social power base of managers (authority) that was used in traditional discipline and grievances processes. As Ridley-Duff and Bennett (2011:116) point out: 'There is a difference between equal treatment that maintains a commitment to a framework of pre-agreed standards (…) and equality in a dispute resolution process that does not prejudge what the process or potential outcomes will be'. In this sense, from the different dispute resolution alternatives included in the model by Ridley-Duff and Bennett (2011), mediation is the best situated as it promotes equality standards. Supporting this claim, it is important to mention a key finding from Bennett's (2014) research in the higher education sector which showed that the strength of the mediation process was its ability to address 'power imbalance' between disputants. These results also support the proposed model assertion that mediation is a shift towards genuine power distribution (Ridley-Duff and Bennett 2011). Nevertheless, the relational qualities in terms of power distribution in societies, sectors of industry, and organizations, will determine to what extend and in what form mediation contributes to structural power balance between different parties in workplace conflict. In contexts with temporary jobs and workers with very limited rights, who are almost disposable, mediation is unlikely to flourish. Though even in such conditions, mediation might be beneficial for those workers (see Jordaan and DeWulf on the experiences in South Africa). To promote equality, all stakeholders should be involved in designing and implanting this system.

Proposition 3 Promoting equality through mediation in workplace conflict, requires active participation of all stakeholders in the design and implementation of such system.

When analyzing relational qualities, and particularly equality between contestants, at case level two issues should certainly be taken into account in mediation: is the relation to be continued, and is the relation hierarchical? Firstly, will this relation continue or is the mediation part of a process of ending the contract of one of the conflicting parties? Like divorce mediation, such exit mediation can provide some benefits also for the party leaving the organization. However, structural power differences should be taken into account here. Labor laws provide a regulating framework to balance power feed the use of mediation. A potential risk of mandatory mediation is to further diminish the power position of the relative weak party (see Sulches et al. this handbook).

Secondly, in case of hierarchical relations, the premise should not be equality between parties (Bollen et al. 2010). Some argue that structural power relations are such, that even an open dialogue through mediation is unlikely to happen, and other agents (e.g. employee representatives or lawyers) should best act on behalf of the party. The structural inequalities between parties therefore determine if and what form of mediation will be beneficial for both, and particularly for the weaker party (Bollen et al. 2013b). Other roles should be taken into account here, both internal and external, to determine if and how mediation can contribute to equality.

Proposition 4 Mediators should analyze and respect inequalities between conflicting parties in workplace conflicts, adapting their strategies to promote power balance and achieve optional outcomes.

3-Rs Promoting Voice

The voice dimension of mediation captures the extent to which this alternative offers a more 'democratic' route to dispute resolution. Participation is intrinsically important in the mediation process and it supports the need for disputants to have more ownership over the overall process (Constantino 1996; Constantino and Merchant 1996). With this approach 'a mediator can guide individuals towards identifying their common interests while leaving them to negotiate potential solutions' (Ridley-Duff and Bennett 2011: 111).

This implies that in designing systems, procedures, roles and relations all should promote voice for participants. This is for workplace mediation certainly not evident, particularly not with structural power differences between the parties, societal and organizational cultures in which it is customary to listen and obey authorities, it is not evident parties will experience they gain voice. Also the structuring of the mediation, with limited time available and focusing only on the 'business' issue at hand, might limit essentially voice for parties. Building a trusting relation between mediator and parties, defining roles which contribute to that, and regulations providing sufficient time and resources, will contribute to the experience of voice by parties. This might be an important argument to use internal mediators, and even informal internal mediators, in workplace conflicts. As these typically have already developed a trusted relation with parties, have deeper understanding of the context, and have more time available to work with both parties. Therefore, designing the dispute system requires the analysis of the organizational culture and structure.

Proposition 5 Procedures, roles and relations within a mediation system should recognize the structural difficulties to give voice to all parties in workplace conflict, and adapt to the societal and organizational cultures to optimize such voice.

Giving voice to parties in workplace mediation is essential, and contributes highly to perceived effectiveness and satisfaction. This is particularly true for low power parties in the conflict (Bollen et al. 2010, 2014). Making sure these parties have voice, and are heard, if only by the mediator, helps in achieving positive outcomes. Creating voice might require specific interventions by the mediator, such as bringing in other colleagues or experts, caucusing, or online tools promoting reflecting and information sharing at a moment and place parties feel safe to act. The 3-Rs all can be beneficial here. Regulations offering flexibility to work, Roles in terms of good alignment between the different parties involved, adequate alignment, and communication between these, including referral to the mediator and follow up, will help to set the stage. The different relations between primary parties and the different third parties will contribute to establishing trust. Not only in the mediator, however also in the process, where other involved actors have to play a role, being senior management, HR or internal conflict coaches. Such alignment helps to build up trust, promoting voice not only in the mediation, however also in the follow up. Thus contributing to long term effectiveness of mediation.

Proposition 6 To promote voice to all parties in mediation, the mediation should be aligned with regular organizational procedures, roles and relations, relevant for the conflicting parties. The mediator not only addresses the relation between the primary parties, however works systemic.

Conclusion

The major strength of workplace mediation is its potential to promote trust and rebuild damaged relationships through interest-based techniques. This is in line with the social exchange theory emphasizing that interdependent transactions have the potential to generate high-quality relationships. However, mediation is not a panacea for all types of workplace disputes. Especially when punishment or a sense of justice for being wronged is required, then an alternative method of dispute resolution may be required to achieve that result.

One of the key aspects of the paradox of mediation refers to the lack of critical dimensions to evaluate dispute resolution systems beyond speed, satisfaction and acceptance of possible solutions by disputants. The objectives of efficiency, equity and voice provide rich standards for evaluating mediation effectiveness. We explored the contributions of the 3-R model of workplace mediation to both the effectiveness of the mediation system and the effectiveness of specific mediation cases under the prism of these standards. The combination of the dimensions of regulations, roles and relations enshrined in the 'geometry of workplace mediation' provide a contingent approach to the design of optimal and effective workplace mediation systems depending on the specific society, industry and organization. We have seen that the 3-R model of workplace mediation is well situated as a conflict management and resolution system for the promotion of efficiency, equity and voice standards. This model can also be used to focus the orientation of scholars, practitioners and governments in looking for new developments in the design of workplace mediation. In this sense, future research could explore specific combinations of these dimensions that best fit specific sectors, organizations or cases of workplace mediation. Overall, it takes three to tango. This not only refers to the interplay of conflicting parties and the mediator. Also the developments around the 'geometry of workplace mediation' with regard to the notions of regulations, roles and relations involve an intricate dance in terms of their contribution to the objectives of efficiency, equity and voice.

References

Anderson, G. (2001). *Labour's labour law: Labour law reform in New Zealand under a labour government*. London: Institute of Employment Rights.

Bennett, T. (2013). Workplace mediation and the empowerment of disputants: Rhetoric or reality? *Industrial Relations Journal, 44*(2), 189–209.

Bennett, T. (2014). The role of workplace mediation: A critical assessment. *Personnel Review, 43*(5), 764–779.

Bingham, L. (2004). Employment dispute resolution: The case for mediation. *Conflict Resolution Quarterly, 22*(1–2), 145–174.

BIS. (2012). *Regional-mediation-pilot-schemes-up-and-running*. London: Department for Business Innovation and Skills. Available at: http://news.bis.gov.uk/Press-Releases/Regional-Mediation-Pilot-Schemes-up-and-running-67b90.aspx.

Blau, P. M. (1964). *Exchange and power in social life*. Piscataway: Transaction Publishers.

Bollen, K., & Euwema, M. (2013a). Workplace mediation: An underdeveloped research area. *Negotiation Journal, 29*(3), 329–353.

Bollen, K., & Euwema, M. (2013b). The role of hierarchy in face-to-face and e-supported mediations: The use of an online intake to balance hierarchy. *Negotiation and Conflict Management Research, 6*(4), 305–319.

Bollen, K., & Euwema, M. (2015). Angry at your boss: Who cares? Anger recognition and mediation effectiveness. *European Journal of Work and Organizational Psychology, 24*(2), 256–266.

Bollen, K., Euwema, M., & Müller, P. (2010). Why are subordinates less satisfied with mediation? The role of uncertainty. *Negotiation Journal, 26*(4), 417–433.

Bollen, K. N., Verbeke, A. L., & Euwema, M. C. (2014). Computers work for women: Gender differences in supported divorce mediation. *Computers in Human Behavior, 30*, 230–237.

Boxall, P. (2014). The future of employment relations from the perspective of human resource management. *Journal of Industrial Relations, 56*(4), 578–593.

Branch, S., Ramsay, S., & Barker, M. (2009). Workplace bullying. In T. Redman & A. Wilkinson (Eds.), *Contemporary human resource management* (3rd ed., pp. 517–541). Harlow: FT Prentice Hall.

Brett, J., & Goldberg, S. (1983). Grievance mediation in the coal industry: A field experiment. *Industrial and Labor Relations Review, 37*(1), 49–69.

Budd, J. W. (2004). *Employment with a human face: Balancing efficiency, equity, and voice*. New York: Cornell University Press.

Budd, J., & Colvin, A. (2008). Improved metrics for workplace dispute resolution procedures: Efficiency, equity, and voice. *Industrial Relations, 47*(3), 460–479.

Budd, J. W., & Colvin, A. J. (2014). The goals and assumptions of conflict management in organizations. In *The Oxford handbook of conflict management in organizations*, 12.

Conlon, D. E., & Ross, W. H. (1993). The effects of partisan third parties on negotiator behavior and outcome perceptions. *Journal of Applied Psychology, 78*, 280–290.

Corby, S. (1999). *Resolving employment rights through mediation: The New Zealand experience*. London: Institute of Employment Rights.

Costantino, C. (1996). Using interest-based techniques to design conflict management systems. *Negotiation Journal, 12*(3), 207–215.

Costantino, C., & Strickles Merchant, C. (1996). How to design conflict management systems. *CPR Institute for Dispute Resolution, 14*(4), 48–49.

Coyle-Shapiro, J. A. M., & Conway, N. (2004). The employment relationship through the lens of social exchange. In J. Coyle-Shapiro, L. M. Shore, S. Taylor, & L. Tetrick (Eds.), *The employment relationship: Examining psychological and conceptual perspectives* (pp. 5–28). Oxford: Oxford University Press.

Cropanzano, R., Goldman, B., & Folger, R. (2005). Self-interest: Defining and understanding a human motive. *Journal of Organizational Behavior, 26*, 985–991.

Davey, B., & Dix, G. (2011). *The dispute resolution regulations two years on: The ACAS experience* (ACAS paper no. 7/11). London: ACAS Publication.

De Palo, G., Feasley, A., & Orecchini, F. (2011). *Quantifying the cost of not using mediation – a data analysis*. Brussels: European Parliament, Directorate General For Internal Policies.

Dhiaulhaq, A., Gritten, D., De Bruyn, T., Yasmi, Y., Zazali, A., & Silalahi, M. (2014). Transforming conflicts in plantations through mediation: Lessons and experiences from Sumatra, Indonesia. *Forest Policy and Economics, 41*, 22–30.

Dolder, C. (2004). The contribution of mediation to workplace justice. *Industrial Law Journal, 33*(4), 320–342.

Garcia, A., Pender, E., & Elgoibar, P. (2016). The state of art: Trust and conflict management in organizational industrial relations. In P. Elgoibar, M. Euwema, & L. Munduate (Eds.), *Building trust and constructive conflict management in organizations*. Dordrecht: Springer Verlag.

Gelfand, M. J., Leslie, L. M., Keller, K., & de Dreu, C. (2012). Conflict cultures in organizations: How leaders shape conflict cultures and their organizational-level consequences. *Journal of Applied Psychology, 97*(6), 1131–1147.

Goldberg, S. (2005). How interest based grievance mediation performs in the long term. *Dispute Resolution Journal, 60*(4), 8–15.

Goldman, B. M., Cropanzano, R., Stein, J. H., Shapiro, D. L., Thatcher, S., & Ko, J. (2008). The role of ideology in mediated disputes at work: A justice perspective. *International Journal of Conflict Management, 19*(3), 210–233.

Guest, D. E. (2004). The psychology of the employment relationship: An analysis based on the psychological contract. *Applied Psychology: An International Review, 53*, 541–555.

Guest, D. (2016). Trust and the role of the psychological contract in contemporary employment relations. In P. Elgoibar, M. Euwema, & L. Munduate (Eds.), *Building trust and constructive conflict management in organizations*. Dordrecht: Springer Verlag.

Hyman, R. (2001). *Understanding European Trade Unionism: Between market, class and society*. London: Sage.

Karambayya, R., Brett, J., & Lytle, J. (1992). Effects of formal authority and experience on third-party roles, outcomes, and perceptions of fairness. *Academy of Management Journal, 35*(2), 426–438.

Keashly, L., & Nowell, B. (2011). Conflict, conflict resolution and bullying. In S. Einarsen, H. Hoel, D. Zapf, & C. Cooper (Eds.), *Bullying and harassment in the workplace: Development in theory, research and practice* (2nd ed., pp. 423–445). Bora Raton: CRC Press, Taylor and Francis Group.

Kolb, D. M. (1986). Who are organizational third parties and what do they do? In R. J. Latreille, P. L. (2010). Mediating workplace conflict of success, failure and fragility. ACAS Research Paper, 13/11.

Kressel, K. (2014). The mediation of conflict: Context, cognition, and practice. In M. Deutsch, P. T. Coleman, & E. Marcus (Eds.), *The handbook of conflict resolution: Theory and practice* (3rd ed., pp. 817–848). San Francisco: Josey-Bass.

Lewicki, R. J., & Sheppard, B. H. (1985). Choosing how to intervene: Factors affecting the use of process and outcome control in third-party resolution. *Journal of Occupational Behavior, 6,* 49–64.

Lewicki, R., Elgoibar, P., & Euwema, M. (2016). The tree of trust: Building and repairing trust in organizations. In P. Elgoibar, M. Euwema, & L. Munduate (Eds.), *Building trust and constructive conflict management in organizations*. Dordrecht: Springer Verlag.

Macneil, J., & Bray, M. (2013). Third-party facilitators in interest-based negotiation: An Australian case study. *Journal of Industrial Relations, 35,* 699–722.

Mareschal, P. M. (2005). What makes mediation work? Mediators' perspectives on resolving disputes. *Industrial Relations: A Journal of Economy and Society, 44*(3), 509–517.

Munduate, L., Euwema, M., & Elgoibar, P. (Eds.). (2012). *Ten steps for empowering employee representatives in the New European industrial relations: New European industrial relations NEIRE handbook*. Aravaca: McGraw Hill.

Munduate, L., Euwema, M., & Elgoibar, P. (2016). Constructive conflict management in organizations: Taking stock and looking forward. In P. Elgoibar, M. Euwema, & L. Munduate (Eds.), *Building trust and constructive conflict management in organizations*. Dordrecht: Springer Verlag.

Poitras, J., & Le Tareau, A. (2009). Quantifying the quality of mediation agreements. *Negotiation and Conflict Management Research, 2*(4), 363–380.

Ridley-Duff, R., & Bennett, A. (2011). Towards mediation: Developing a theoretical framework to understand alternative dispute resolution. *Industrial Relations Journal, 42*(2), 106–123.

Rodríguez-Piñero, M., Del Rey, S., & Munduate, L. (1993). The intervention of third parties in the solution of labour conflicts. *European Work and Organizational Psychologist, 3*(4), 271–283.

Rousseau, D. M. (2005). *I-deals, Ideosyncratic deals employees bargain for themselves*. New York: M.E. Sharpe.

Sanders, A. (2009). Part one of the Employment Act 2008: 'better' dispute resolution? *Industrial Law Journal, 38*(1), 30–49.

Shapiro, D. L., & Brett, J. M. (1993). Comparing three processes underlying judgments of procedural justice: A field study of mediation and arbitration. *Journal of Personality and Social Psychology, 65,* 1167–1177.

Shore, L. M., Tetrix, L. E., Lynch, P., & Barksdale, K. (2006). Social and economic exchange: Construct development and validation. *Journal of Applied Social Psychology, 36*(4), 837–867.

Ury, W. L., Brett, J. M., & Goldberg, S. B. (1993). *Getting disputes resolved*. San Francisco: Jossey-Bass.